Gretchen Bering

THE VEGETARIAN GOURMET COOKBOOK

THE VEGETARIAN GOURMET COOKBOOK

Paul Southey

VNR VAN NOSTRAND REINHOLD COMPANY
NEW YORK CINCINNATI TORONTO LONDON MELBOURNE

Photographs by Roger Phillips
Design and Art Direction by
Mike Rose
Color illustrations by
Anne Winterbottom and Lucy Su
Monochrome illustrations by
Vana Haggerty
Step-by-step drawings by Rob Shone

Nutrition Consultants:
Jacqui Badcock, B.Sc., S.R.D., Ph.D.
and Inger Meinertzhagen, B.Sc.

Library of Congress Catalog Card
Number 79-27053

ISBN 0-442-23851-7

Printed in Great Britain.

Published in 1980 by Van Nostrand Reinhold Company
A division of Litton Educational Publishing, Inc.
135 West 50th Street, New York, NY 10020, U.S.A.

16 15 14 13 12 11 10 9 8 7 6 5 4 3 2 1

Library of Congress Cataloging in Publication Data
Southey, Paul
Vegetarian gourmet cookbook.

Bibliography: p.
Includes index.
1. Vegetarian cookery. 2. Nutrition.
3. Canning and preserving. 4. Food, Frozen.
I. Title.
TX837.S685 641.5'14 79-27053
ISBN 0-442-23851-7

Contents

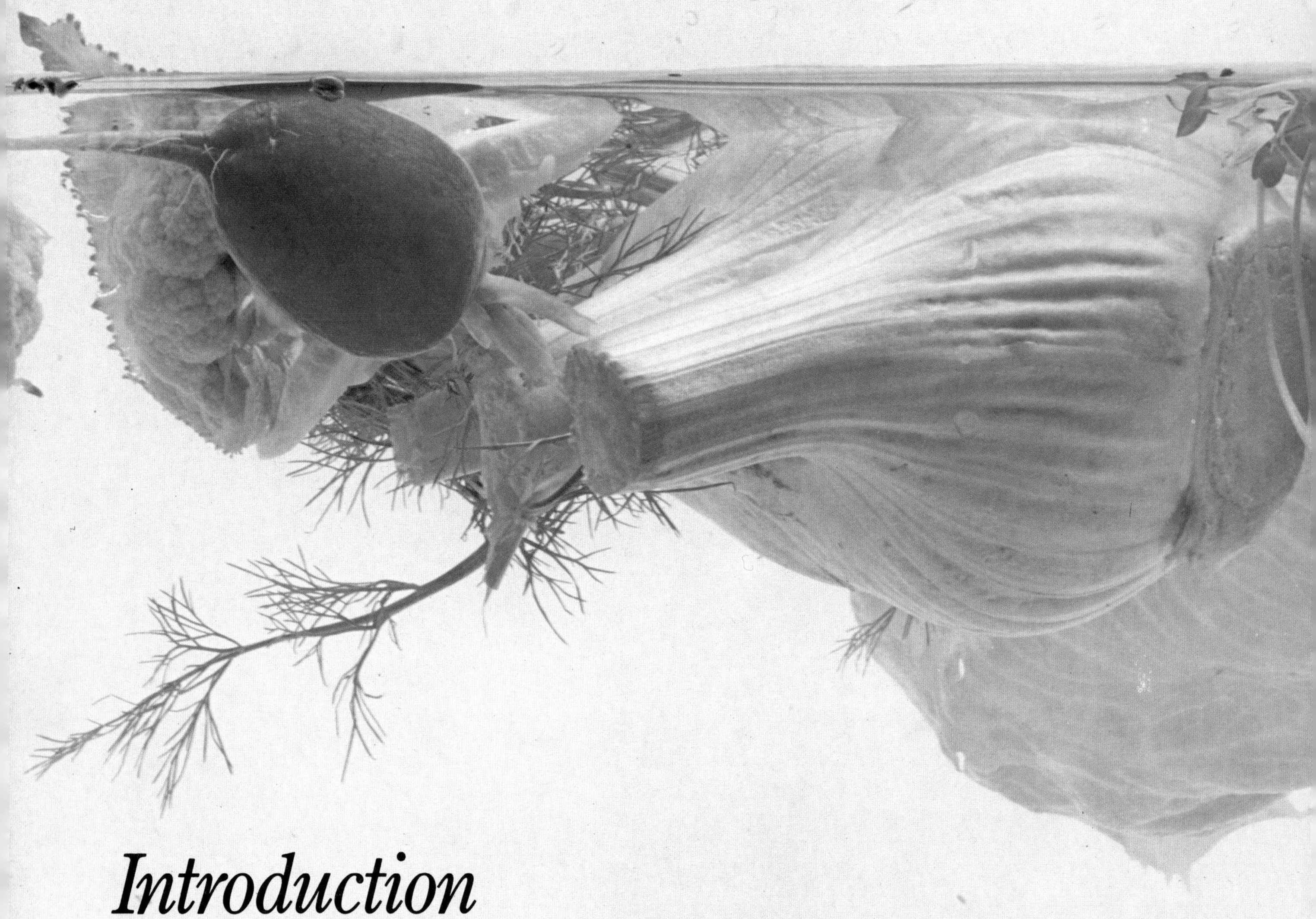

Introduction

What is vegetarianism? It is a belief in following a diet that includes no meat of any kind and therefore does not rely on the slaughter of animals for the provision of food. Vegetarianism is not a new discovery, nor is it a 'fad' or trend. At various times throughout our recorded history, people in many countries have successfully followed a vegetarian regimen for economic, religious, cultural or ethical reasons. Philosophers down the ages have expounded its virtues; writers and artists have followed its precepts; those who abhor cruelty to animals in any form have been converted to its principles and those to whom it represents a healthier way of life in stressful times have taken up its practice.

More and more, people seem to be looking toward vegetarianism as a partial solution to the approaching world food crisis – as the population increases. Medical authorities have some reason for believing that protein gained from natural food sources such as plants may be more easily assimilated in the body than that gained from animal sources, and is better for our general health.

The aim of this book is to present a collection of recipes for vegetarians who include eggs, milk and milk products in their diet (it is not primarily intended for vegans, who eat no animal produce of any kind). I wanted to show that a vegetarian cuisine ranks among the best in the world and can be as varied and appetizing as the more 'conventional' meat-oriented *haute cuisine*. The vegetarian need not rely solely on the produce of the kitchen garden; a whole variety of exciting foods – exotic fruits, vegetables, nuts, seeds, legumes, cereals from all over the world – is at his disposal to enrich his daily diet; and all the proteins, vitamins, minerals and trace elements necessary for a healthy, active, enjoyable life can be gained from these, as well as from eggs, milk, cream and a whole variety of cheeses.

Herbs and spices play their part in gourmet cooking

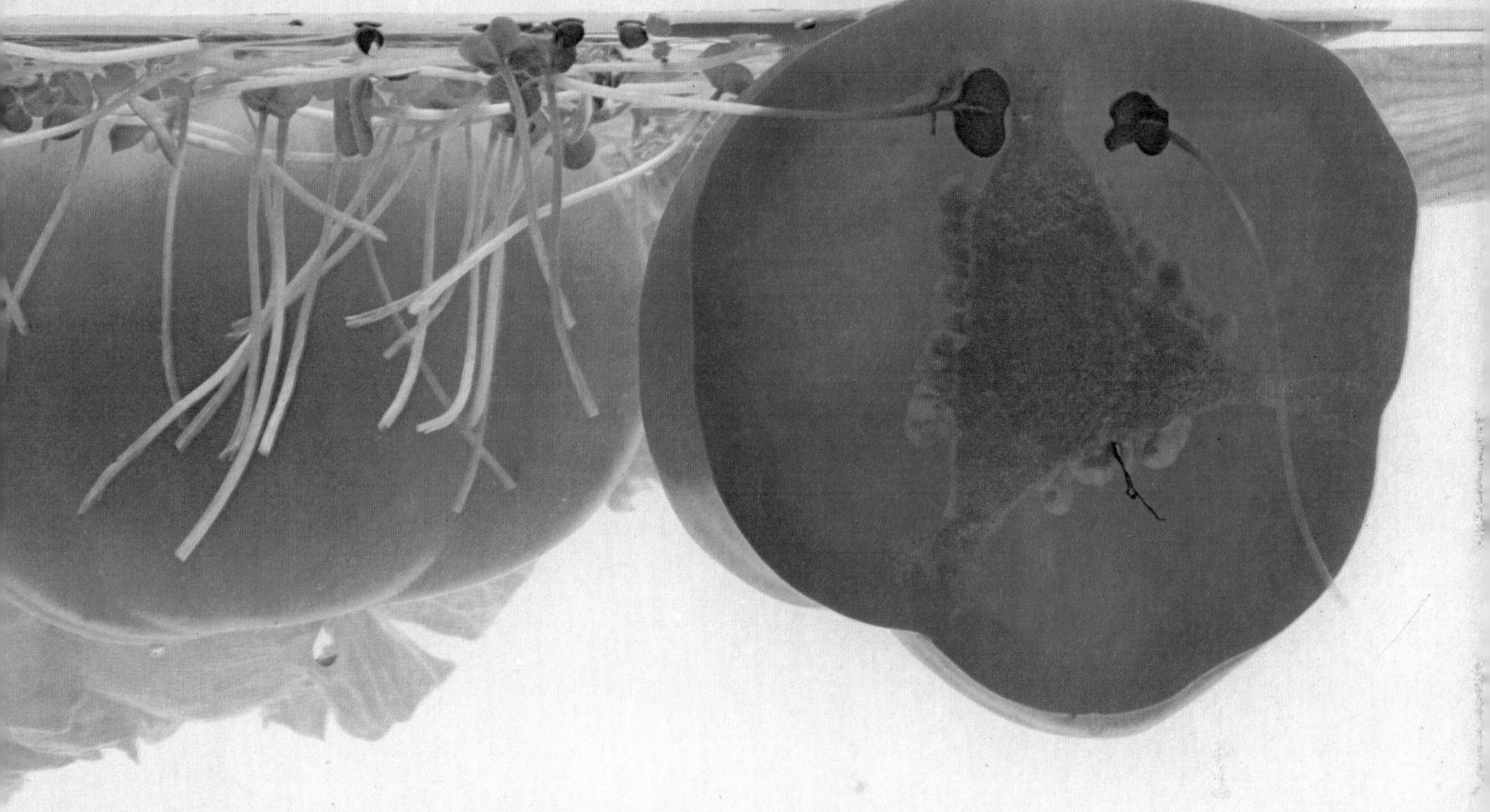

and a little judicious tasting will soon tell you how much or how little – and in what combination – best suits your palate. The very best cooks learn the art of experimentation early in life and treat recipes as a guide and not as a set of inflexible rules . . .

I am fond of wine, love entertaining, and enjoy the classic, four-course meal with the appropriate wines and side dishes. When I became a vegetarian, I saw no reason for giving up one of life's greatest pleasures. I have therefore worked out, tested, amended and created a number of recipes for the enterprising cook. Some of these can be used singly, or with a salad, as a simple supper or 'one-pot' meal; others can be combined into elaborate dinner party menus. The conscientious dieter may find my use of eggs, cream, butter and olive oil excessive, but I am not suggesting that you overindulge in rich food, or eat a five-course gourmet dinner every day!

When using my recipes for entertaining, I would suggest that you read through the complete recipe *before* beginning to cook. Check through the ingredients and measure them carefully before you start; by planning your cooking, you will accomplish more with less effort.

One of my main preoccupations on becoming a vegetarian was to calculate my daily intake of protein and to make sure I was eating enough. Accordingly, we have given – as accurately as is possible – the protein and the Calorie content of each dish, in portions where this seemed sensible, to help you calculate your own menu without effort. A Table showing the recommended daily intake is given on page 208, and we have included further Tables, giving the protein and Calorie content of many of the main foods in 100 gram and 1 ounce quantities to help you when compiling recipes.

Eat well, and enjoy your food, for as Talleyrand, that great French statesman, said: 'Show me another pleasure like dinner, which comes every day and lasts an hour.'

The Ingredients

No one can begin to cook without the basic ingredients and on the following pages we present a visual glossary of many of the raw ingredients available to the vegetarian cook. It cannot pretend to be fully comprehensive; such an undertaking would be outside the scope of this book, but we have gathered together as many as possible over a considerable period of time and most of them are to be found in the recipes.

It is a fact of commercial practice that, as the supply of fruits and vegetables becomes more highly organized and efficient, our choice is becoming more and more limited to those varieties which are high-yielding, travel well and are convenient to use. The best way to enjoy greater variety is, of course, to grow your own. If this is not possible, do not be afraid to ask your supplier if you

need a particular type – a cooking apple that will not fall into pulp, or a waxy potato for use in salads; it is surprising what a little detective work will produce. I always make a point of asking for a particular variety and often do succeed in finding it or, if it is not available, the reason why.

Familiarize yourself with the infinite variety of vegetables, fruits, seeds, nuts, cereals and legumes, and the oils and fats that come from them. Choose cheeses with care; use honey for sweetening wherever possible and raw brown sugar instead of the highly refined white; learn to appreciate and work with all the available flours; make wholewheat pastry and rye breads. For the good cook, the joy lies in the choosing and preparation of the raw ingredients – as well as in the cooking and serving of a nutritionally balanced and visually exciting meal.

ROOTS AND TUBERS

1 TURNIP
Early ones available in fall.
Main crop available in fall and winter.
The staple food of northern and central Europe until the introduction of the potato in the sixteenth century, contain sugar and starches. Early ones are best in taste and texture. Purée old roots.

2 RUTABAGA
Available from fall to spring.
Known as 'Swedish turnips' outside the United States, rutabaga is larger and sweeter than turnip, with orange-yellow flesh. Like most root vegetables, rutabagas store well.

3 SCORZONERA
4 SALSIFY or OYSTERPLANT
Available mid-fall.
These two different roots are similar in taste and the cooking method needed. Scozonera has a nearly black skin: both have white flesh which discolors quickly, so cook them in water with added lemon juice. Serve in a Bechamel or Tomato sauce.

5 GIANT RADISH
Available autumn and winter.
Often sold under the name 'mooli', this radish can be grated for salad or cooked like turnip. (not shown)

6 HORSERADISH
Available from fall to early spring.
Native to Europe, this peppery pungent root is grated raw for flavoring sauces.

7 CARROT
Early ones available from midsummer.
Main crop available all year round.
Carrots are particularly rich in vitamin A. The tiny, early ones are most delicious; scrape or peel the coarser maincrop carrots and use for soups and casseroles. Both are good to eat raw.

8 KOHLRABI
Available from late summer through winter.
Botanically related to the cabbage, kohlrabi is the enormously swollen base of the stem. It has a mild, sweet and rather nutty flavor. Cook small young kohlrabi unpeeled.

9 PARSNIP
Available in fall and throughout winter.
Parsnips are rich in sugar and starch. Avoid roots with brown markings or woody tops. Remove very hard cores, if necessary, before cooking.

10 BEET
Available all year round; at its best in late summer.
Long-rooted beets are grown, but round ones are more tender and tasty. The smaller the root, the sweeter the flavor. Buy uncooked beets if possible, without bruises or broken skin, as these bleed when cooked. The tops of young beets can be used like spinach.

11 CELERY ROOT or CELERIAC
Available from late fall through winter.
This rough-skinned root has creamy-white flesh with a pronounced celery flavor. Shred it raw and eat, tossed in a Vinaigrette dressing or Mayonnaise.

12 JERUSALEM ARTICHOKE
Available late fall and winter.
A relative of the sunflower and native to North America, this knobbly tuber has a lightly smoky flavor. It contains inulin, a sugar substitute used by diabetics. Cook in acidulated water to prevent discoloration.

POTATO
Varieties available all year round.
Once a luxury for the rich, the potato is now the staple diet of millions. As an important food crop, however, it is a relative newcomer, and has only been widely cultivated in Europe since the eighteenth century. There are a vast number of varieties, differing widely in flavor and texture. Larger, maincrop potatoes can be either waxy – good for slicing when cooked and for use in salads – or floury – best for purèeing, baking or roasting. Sadly, the choice of potatoes available is limited to a few, high cropping varieties.

13 MAINCROP POTATOES
Available from late summer onward.
These are known as 'whites'; they store better than the tiny new potatoes, but should be kept in a cool, airy place. Avoid buying potatoes with green patches on the skin – these contain poisonous alkaloids. Reject potatoes with fungus marks. Smaller red-skinned potatoes are Red Pontiacs (14).

15 NEW POTATOES
Available in late spring and early summer.
Freshly-dug new potatoes have an incomparable sweet, earthy taste and a crisp, juicy texture which diminishes with storage.

16 SWEET POTATO
Available throughout the winter.
Either red, white or purple skins enclose white or yellow, sweet-tasting flesh. Cook as ordinary potatoes, but boil in the skins.

17 YAM (not shown)
Available in winter.
The name 'yam' is loosely applied to any tropical root crop and, in America, to sweet potatoes. A true yam is one of the cultivated species of the Dioscera family.

20 WHITE SKINNED ONIONS
21 PICKLING ONIONS
Available from midsummer to fall.
Known also as pearl or button onions, this variety is lifted before it is full size.

22 GARLIC
Available all year round.
Strongest and most pungent member of the onion family, garlic is primarily used as a seasoning, in small amounts. It contains the antibiotic allicin. Garlic keeps well when stored in a dry place.

THE ONION FAMILY
Varieties available all year round.
One of the earliest cultivated foods, with many shapes; generally, the warmer the climate the larger and milder the onion.

18 SPANISH ONION
The largest and mildest in flavor – excellent and juicy for use in salads.

19 RED SKINNED SHALLOTS
Available fall and early winter.
Small and delicately-flavored, use them in subtle sauces.

23 LEEK
Available from late summer to spring.
A long established, hardy winter vegetable, cook the white stems of leeks and use the green tops for soup. Now cultivated for salads.

24 SCALLION
Available from spring onward.
Originally the thinnings from the onion bed, spring onions are now cultivated for salads.

BRASSICAS AND LEAVES

1 CABBAGE

Varieties available all year round

Cabbages contain valuable amounts of vitamin C and minerals, but their nutritional value can be greatly lessened by overcooking. It is better to steam them or cook in a very little boiling water and use any that may be left for stocks or soups. With all varieties, when choosing cabbage, look for firm hearted ones. See that the base of the stalk is not dry or withered, check that the outer leaves are not yellowed or limp and that there are no loose, curling leaves on the outside.

2 WINTER CABBAGE

Remember that it will not respond to overcooking. Despite its tough texture when raw and its thick crinkled leaves, it has a relatively mild flavor.

PURPLE SPROUTING BROCCOLI (not shown)

Available late winter and spring

One of the more hardy types of broccoli, less fine in flavor than calabrese, but both this and the white sprouting variety are milder, sweeter and richer than the cauliflower.

4 LARGE-HEADED BROCCOLI

Available late winter and spring

The single purple head of Cape broccoli is shown, but the white-headed type is commoner. Choose heads with tight curds and fresh leaves, as for all types of broccoli. Broccoli goes well with cheese. Try it steamed or boiled.

6 SPRING CABBAGE or SPRING or COLLARD GREENS

Available in early spring

These are young cabbages picked early in the season before the heart has a chance to develop. Choose greens with thick, firm leaves and cook them on the day you buy them as they wilt very quickly.

3 CALABRESE

Available in summer

The Italian sprouting broccoli, or calabrese, is a feathery palish green. These fronds grow after the first, tightly-packed head has been cut and are thought by many to be superior in flavor. Much sought-after during the summer months, it is not as easy to grow as the white or purple-sprouting types. Choose broccoli with firm, straight juicy stems and tightly packed curds. It is delicious served on its own with a Butter sauce.

5 CAULIFLOWER

Available from late fall to summer

After the pea, this is one of the most consistently popular vegetables. Winter cauliflowers have green leaves that curl tightly around the flower heads, or curds. Summer cauliflowers have leaves that are more spread out. If the leaves are limp, it is a sign that the vegetable has been too long out of the ground. Choose cauliflowers with firm, close-textured heads and no brown specks.

7 WHITE CABBAGE

Available late fall and winter

Deliciously mild in flavor and good to eat either cooked, or shredded raw in salads such as coleslaw. The white cabbage is distinguished by its color and very tightly packed leaves. Reject any with outward curling leaves or brown patches and do not be tempted to overcook or it will be limp and tasteless.

8 RED CABBAGE
Available fall and early winter
This variety has a characteristic, slightly sour flavor. It takes much longer to cook than other varieties and is therefore especially suitable for braising, marinating and pickling. Try it sliced thinly in salads.

10 CHINESE CABBAGE
Another mild-tasting but non-hearting cabbage that is excellent when lightly cooked or, preferably, stir-fried. It looks rather like a paler variety of Romaine lettuce and its crisp texture is much appreciated in salads.

12 GREENS
The leaves of many other plants, such as turnip (as shown here), beet, mustard greens and even dandelion are all good sources of vitamin C and minerals. Choose fresh-looking, tender young leaves and once again – do not overcook them.

9 BRUSSELS SPROUTS
Available in fall and winter
Brussels sprouts look exactly like miniature cabbages and have a delicate, nutty flavor all their own. The smaller they are, the better they taste; large ones become coarse-textured. Choose firm, green, close-wrapped heads without any yellowing leaves or other obvious signs of wilting. Some say the flavor is improved by a touch of frost.

11 KALE (not shown)
Available in winter
Kale is a variety of non-hearting cabbage that has no solid head. Its broad curly leaves grow alternately from a thick central stalk and vary in color from dark green to purple. The stalk and leaf ribs may have to be discarded if they prove too tough.

13 SPINACH
Available all year round
The popular name of this plant is sometimes used to describe the leaves of Swiss chard as well as the true spinach. Summer spinach has round leaves, while the winter variety has leaves that are more spiky in shape. When buying, look for fresh, crisp leaves and handle them with extreme care as they bruise very easily. Do not wash them unless you are going to use them right away, otherwise they will go limp. Spinach shrinks amazingly during cooking – it should be cooked with just water left from rinsing clinging to the leaves – so buy twice as much as you think you will need. Spinach stalks make a welcome addition to the stock pot.

PODS AND SEEDS

1/2 GREEN BEANS
Available all year round
The pods of these are eaten before the bean itself is fully developed. If the pod is young and tender, it should break cleanly when snapped in half; green beans are sometimes called 'snap beans' for this reason. All varieties are now stringless.

3 CORN
Available summer and fall
Freshly picked corn is best to eat; a milky fluid should run from a kernel when its skin is punctured. The husks should be stiff, pale green and silky. Delicious boiled or steamed and simply served with melted butter.

4 OKRA
Available midwinter to early summer
Originally a native of the West Indies, usually eaten while still slightly underripe. It is glutinous in texture and therefore good for thickening casseroles. Choose pods that are less than 6 inches long. Also known as ladies' fingers.

5 SNOW or SUGAR PEAS or MANGETOUT
Available in spring
Called *mangetout* because these sweet-tasting young pods are eaten whole, snow peas should be crisp and juicy. Delicious stir-fried.

6 PEAS
Available in spring and summer
At their very best in early summer, peas were the first vegetables ever to be canned or frozen; now much of the early crop goes to the frozen food industry. Early varieties are smooth-skinned; later ones are wrinkled. Both should have bright green, juicy pods without blemishes.

7 FAVA BEANS (not shown)
Available spring through to fall
Fava beans are a good source of protein and can be served in their pods if very young and small. Large ones are sold shelled and should be skinned after cooking. Look for bright green juicy pods and serve skinned beans with a herb butter.

STALKS AND SHOOTS

8 ASPARAGUS
Available in early summer
A member of the lily family, the asparagus has been popular since Roman times. An immature shoot which is cut off early in the season, it quickly loses flavor once cut. Avoid asparagus with thin or woody stems.

9 FLORENCE FENNEL
Available all year round
Also known by its Italian name, *finocchio*, this swollen stem base has a refreshing flavor halfway between celery and aniseed. Good to eat braised, or chopped raw in salads; choose fennel that is pale in color, with a bulb that feels heavy for its size.

10 CELERY
Available all year round; better in winter.
One of the oldest-known 'medicinal' plants, its crisp stalks are white or green and the leaves of young shoots can be used to flavor casseroles, or eaten raw in salads. When buying, choose stalks that are fleshy and crisp.

11 GLOBE ARTICHOKE
Available all year round
The most suitable varieties for eating are those with slightly rounder tops to the leaves, making them less prickly to handle. It is the fleshy part at the base of each leaf that is scraped off and eaten, the choicest part being the heart (see page 111).

12 BELGIAN ENDIVE
Available fall and winter
A slightly bitter-tasting, succulent salad vegetable with broad, tightly packed silvery leaves. If the leaves are more green than white, it is likely to be very bitter. Good for braising, choose endive that are plump and well-shaped.

13 WATERCRESS
Available all year round
At its best from March to early summer, this small-leaved, peppery-tasting dark green leaved plant adds piquancy to salads and is often used as a garnish. The leaves should be a good, dark green, not yellowing.

14 MUSTARD AND GARDEN CRESS
Available all year round
One of the easiest, most satisfying seeds to sprout (see page 203), mustard and cress adds a tang to any salad. Can be grown indoors.

15 BEAN SPROUTS (Mung beans or Alfalfa)
Available all year round
Try growing these indoors yourself (see page 203) to add crunchy-textured protein to your salads. A classic ingredient in Chinese cooking; low in calories so useful for dieters – unless stir-fried, one of the nicest ways to cook them.

16 RADISH
Available all year round
A peppery-tasting root vegetable popular in salads. This is the red type which adds a pleasing contrast in color as well as texture. Also try the oval-shaped white radish, which should be sliced and salted before use.

LETTUCE
Available all year round, best in summer
The basic ingredient of most green salads; though soft-hearted hothouse varieties are available during winter they are so limp you should choose a more seasonal vegetable, such as chicory or endive. Watch, too, for Chinese cabbage (see page 39). Choose lettuce with crisp, fresh leaves, firm hearts – where appropriate

17 ROMAINE
Easily recognizable by its long, spear-shaped leaves – a crisp and succulent type.

18 ICEBERG
Pale green, tight leaved, crisp-hearted cabbage type – crunchy textured and popular.

19 BOSTON
A soft-leaved, round cabbage-type available in summer; early maturing and small in size.

20 CHICORY
Available late fall and winter
Chicory has a very curly, rather tough leaf with a pleasant, slightly bitter taste. It is paler in color than lettuce, especially in the center of the head.

FUNGI

MUSHROOMS

The best ones to find are the large, wild, field-grown mushrooms, but care must be taken if you are gathering them yourself. Some fungi are deadly poisonous. Either buy a definitive, illustrated book on the subject (see bibliography), or take an experienced picker with you.

1 FIELD MUSHROOMS

Available late summer and early fall

Field mushrooms are the largest and coarsest in texture, but have the best and strongest flavor. They can be white or brown and, when fully opened, are flat-topped. Pick mushrooms with unwrinkled skins and stalks that are moist at the base and show no signs of withering. Fry or broil them on the day they have been picked – or bought.

2 MOREL

Available in spring.

One of the best-flavored of all edible fungi, the morel makes a superb garnish to most savory dishes. It is not often seen in markets outside Europe, but if you are lucky enough to find this distinct, dark crinkly mushroom, you would be wise to keep the location to yourself . . .

3 ENOK or OYSTER MUSHROOM

Available in winter

Another variety of edible mushroom it is similar in flavor to the field mushroom, is paler in color with a distinctive curling cap.

4 BUTTON MUSHROOM

Available all year round

The commercially grown white variety, which is sold as button mushrooms when unopened, cap mushrooms when half-open and 'flats' when fully opened. Use them sliced raw in salads, marinated in French dressing, or cooked in dishes where the black spores of field mushrooms would spoil the appearance of the finished dish.

5 TRUFFLE

Something of a rarity and therefore very expensive, the truffle grows completely underground and has to be hunted out by specially trained dogs. The black truffle from Périgord is considered the finest; Italian truffles are beautiful pale fawn inside. Both are used in sauces and for garnishing dishes.

THE VEGETABLE FRUITS

Back row from left to right:

6 PUMPKIN

Available late summer and fall

A large winter squash with characteristic, bright orange flesh. Pumpkins can grow up to 100 lb in weight. They are often sold in sections because of their size and weight. Look for dense, non-fibrous flesh and firm outer skin. Pumpkin can be boiled, steamed, baked or roasted – or served in a traditional spiced dessert pie.

7 EGGPLANT

Available all year round

This beautiful, exotic vegetable fruit has a tough, dark purple skin – occasionally you find white skinned ones – and yellow, mealy flesh. It should be sliced and sprinkled with salt to drain out any bitter juices before cooking. Eggplants can be baked, stuffed, fried, or dipped in batter and deep-fried. Choose vegetables with smooth, shiny skins that feel heavy for their size.

8 AVOCADO
Available all year round
A rich-tasting vegetable fruit, the avocado contains vitamins of the B complex and a high proportion of fat. The rather knobbly dark green or purplish skin encloses soft, smooth, pale green or yellow flesh surrounding a large seed. Best served on its own with a Vinaigrette dressing as an appetizer, or to contrast with sharper flavors in a salad. Test for ripeness by gently pressing the rounded end to see if it is soft. Reject avocados with dark patches or wrinkled skins.

9 PEPPER
Available all year round
A bright, tropical vegetable fruit full of vitamin C; the ripe ones are a glorious red or yellow, the unripe a rich and vibrant green. The pepper seems designed for holding a savory stuffing. Ripe red peppers have a milder, sweeter flavor than the green ones and are good to use in salads. The crunchy, more pungent green ones give flavor to cooked dishes; if used raw, some people find them difficult to digest. Look for bright, firm, shiny fruits with no trace of dullness and no wrinkled patches on the skin.

10 TOMATO
Available all year round
Originally grown as a decorative plant, the tomato has now become a favorite salad vegetable. Home growers should try the yellow tomatoes, which have a particularly good flavor. Use the small green ones for pickling. Choose firm, unbruised tomatoes for salads; softer, riper ones will do for soups and purées.

11/12 SUMMER SQUASH
These are harvested when young and tender; they vary greatly in shape and color – from pale green to bright orange, yellow and cream, and have descriptive names such as golden, patty pan or crookneck. The seeds of some can be eaten as well as the flesh. Choose firm ones with tender skins and bake, boil or steam them.

WINTER SQUASH (not shown)
Fully mature, these squashes have hard skins and are heavy for their size. Some seem designed to hold a variety of savory stuffings and be served with a richly flavored sauce.

13 ZUCCHINI
Available all year round
A type of squash, specially bred and usually picked before it grows to 6 inches in length. The smaller they are, the better the flavor. Some varieties need to be sliced and salted, like the eggplant, to drain away bitter juices before cooking. To test for this, cut off a slice and if it tastes bitter, give it the salt treatment.

14 CUCUMBER
Available all year round
There are two basic types of cucumber: the type with a knobbly skin, which is grown outdoors and usually considered to have a better flavor than the greenhouse cucumber, which is the one known as the European cucumber in the markets. Modern varieties have had the more indigestible qualities bred out of them. The small gherkin cucumber is used for pickling. Choose firm, straight, bright-skinned cucumbers not more than about 2 inches in diameter.

HERBS

1 CHIVES
A member of the onion family, but now considered a culinary herb. Its thin, grass-like, mild-flavored leaves go well with many delicate egg dishes, cottage cheese and on salads. Use scissors for snipping over food.

2 ROSEMARY
Spikes of rosemary give a most appetizing fragrance to casseroles, soups and many vegetable dishes. If using fresh, make sure the spikes are very finely chopped, or tie in a cheesecloth bag. Add rosemary when making scones or pastry.

3 DILL
The feathery leaves of dill, with their subtle flavor of caraway, can be used in salads, sauces and dishes where the stronger, more pungent dill seed (page 20) is not required.

4 OREGANO
This is related to marjoram, but much more powerful in flavor. Used in Italian dishes – add it to Tomato sauce for pasta, casseroles and the filling for Ravioli.

5 LEMON BALM
A perennial herb with a piercing aroma, used in tisanes and marinades. Try a leaf or two in your usual brew of tea.

6 BAY
An essential component of any *bouquet garni*, the bay leaf combines well with and complements many other flavors. Add bay leaves when cooking cabbage.

7 BERGAMOT
This herb has attractive red flowers, the petals of which can be sprinkled on salads. Add the leaves to iced drinks or fruit cups. It is not to be confused with the Bergamot orange from which an aromatic oil is obtained.

8 APPLE MINT
One of the most fragrant members of the mint family; others worth investigating are eau-de-Cologne mint, peppermint, and spearmint (see right). Use with discretion in sauces, salads and vegetable dishes.

9 MARJORAM
Marjoram and thyme are two of the best-known herbs and the one can be substituted for the other. Marjoram has the more delicate flavor, however, and goes well with egg dishes.

10 BORAGE
A herb with a distinct, cucumber flavor, now only used in drinks. Its attractive blue flowers can be candied to decorate cakes.

11 ANGELICA
Often used to flavor liqueurs and fruit syrups; add angelica leaves when stewing apples or pears. The stems are candied and used to decorate cakes.

12 SAGE
The broad, flat, crinkled leaves of sage impart their unmistakable flavor to any dish. Include sage in your stuffing mixtures, but try some in yeast dough too.

13 SAVORY
The spiky leaves of winter savory taste of rosemary and sage – with a dash of pepper; summer savory has a similar but milder flavor. Both go well with bean dishes; I use them in my herb butters.

14 PARSLEY and FRENCH PARSLEY
Two types of our most familiar herb, used to garnish so many dishes and rich in vitamin C. An essential ingredient of Tabbouleh (page 133) and a perennial favorite.

15 TARRAGON
A welcome addition to most cream sauces and Mayonnaise or Béarnaise sauce – one cannot describe the aroma without going into the realms of fantasy! French tarragon has the best flavor.

16 THYME
Another very familiar herb, much partnered by sage in flavorings, but similar itself to marjoram. Add it when cooking eggplants, mushrooms or carrots, or to a scone mixture.

17 SPEARMINT
The most commonly grown variety of mint; use as for Apple mint.

18 LOVAGE
An uncommon herb which deserves to be better known. It has a celery-like flavor with a distinct spiciness – use in *bouquets garnis* or chopped and sprinkled over salads.

19 CHERVIL
The flavor of these little leaves is fresh and spicy – use with watercress and parsley for an Omelette fines herbes. It goes well with egg dishes and in salads.

20 BASIL
Sweet basil (as shown) has larger leaves than bush basil and its *rapport* with the tomato is well known. A basic ingredient of Pesto (page 75), try its sweet, pungent, aromatic flavor with other vegetables.

NOTE: If dried herbs are used, halve the quantity you would use for fresh herbs. Dried herbs have a much stronger flavor.

SPICES

1 MUSTARD SEED
Also found in a red or dark brown form. Whole mustard seed is not as pungent as when ground; try mixing red and yellow in varying proportions.

2 MACE
This is the lacy coating of the NUTMEG (shown left), both of which come from the same tropical tree, mace being fuller, stronger and sweeter than the nutmeg it encases.

3 CLOVES
These are dried flower buds, pungent and spicy, used in mulled wine, stewed fruit – especially apples – and with caution in vegetable dishes.

4 CARAWAY SEEDS
The oil from this is used to make the German liquer Kümmel (the German name for caraway); use the seeds in sponge cakes and to subtly flavor vegetable dishes and sauces.

5 CARDAMOMS
One of the basic spices used in Indian cooking, and also popular in Scandinavia, the seeds are contained inside the fibrous shell.

6 CHILI PEPPERS
A variety of red, green and dried Mexican chili peppers, all from the *capsicum* family; used in curry powders, the seeds and fruit are also ground cayenne

7 FENNEL
Both the dried stalks (shown) and the seeds are used in European and Far Eastern cooking. They have a celery-like, aniseed flavour.

8 DILL SEED
The name comes from the Norse word 'to lull', and it is used to make dill water – good for the digestion. The seeds are used in making dill pickles; try them with potato salad, scrambled eggs or sautéed cabbage.

9 CURRY POWDER
Indian cooks always blend their own, varying the proportions of the spices to suit the dish (see Garam masala, page 200).

10 CUMIN
The powder ground from the seeds, with fenugreek (right) gives commerical curry powder its flavor. Use with legumes.

11 PAPRIKA
A sweet, warm-tasting aromatic red pepper, it loses its flavor if stored for too long. Use it in salad dressings and beaten into cottage cheese for filling baked potatoes.

12 CAYENNE PEPPER
A very hot pepper, to be used with extreme caution, made from a blend of dried chili peppers Use sparingly.

13 CINNAMON
It comes from the bark of a tree of the laurel family; available in powdered or stick form. It does not keep its aroma long. Try it with apples, or to flavor your coffee.

14 GINGER
A powder made from the dried root – use a little in casseroles and composite dishes – and for flavoring cakes.

15 TURMERIC
A bright yellow powder ground from the root, used in rice dishes or to give an exotic touch to simple vegetable dishes.

16 SAFFRON
This comes from the organge stigmas of a mauve crocus – buy the filaments to be more sure of getting the genuine article.

17 CORIANDER
Seeds and leaves are both used in Middle Eastern cooking and Indian dishes.

18 ALLSPICE
Also known as Jamaica pepper, allspice tastes like a blend of clove, cinnamon and nutmeg.

19 FENUGREEK
One of the ingredients used in commerical curry powders. Use very sparingly – the flavor is 'raw' and unsubtle.

20 WHITE PEPPERCORNS
These are black peppercorns (see right) with the wrinkled outer layer removed. White pepper is sharper than black; use in dishes where black pepper would spoil the appearance

21 JUNIPER BERRIES
A basic flavoring of gin, crushed juniper blends well with other spices.

22 BLACK PEPPERCORNS
I always specify 'freshly ground pepper', as ready-ground pepper loses its flavor quickly, like most other spices.

23 STAR ANISEED
Much used in Chinese cooking and to flavor alcoholic drinks.

24 POPPY SEEDS
Delicious when sprinkled on bread, cakes and rolls when baking.

25 VANILLA BEANS
Store in a jar of sugar; use to infuse in milk for making custards, crushing the beans for a stronger flavor.

LEGUMES AND PULSES

Legumes and pulses – dried peas, beans and lentils – play an important part in the vegetarian diet. An excellent source of protein, they are worth exploring in their amazing variety, from the soy bean – high in protein but so delicately flavored that added herbs and spices are needed – to the distinctively flavored red kidney bean, with an 'earthy' taste all its own. Pulses are relatively simple to prepare but, unless you have a pressure cooker, take quite a long time – varying from 2-3 hours to overnight – to soak and cook. A great deal depends on the type of bean, when it was harvested and how long it has been stored. Further details are given on page 123. It is best to adjust the seasoning toward the end of the cooking time, as protracted cooking tends to extract or lessen the added flavors. Some beans are delicious served cold in salads and make a vital contribution in this respect to summer dishes.

4 MUNG BEANS
Good for sprouting (page 201), extensively cultivated in Africa, China and the United States.

5 GREEN LENTILS
The basis of many spicy Indian dishes, try them with butter and chopped parsley. Turn brown when cooked.

6 HARICOT or NAVY BEANS
Use these with other beans in salads, soups or cooked with rosemary and garlic.

The eighteen varieties illustrated are:

1 BLACK BEANS
Extensively used in Caribbean dishes and in Chinese cooking – try them spiced with ginger or cumin; garlic and Tomato sauce.

2 WHOLE GREEN PEAS
Serve green peas accompanied by other vegetables; cook them with onions, garlic or shallots.

3 SPLIT GREEN PEAS
These make good, thick soups and purées swirled with mint and cream.

7 ADZUKI BEANS
Rather high in carbohydrate, these taste sweeter than other beans; good for sprouting as well as for cooking as a vegetable.

8 FAVA BEANS
These can be either white or brown and the skins must be removed after cooking as they are very tough – unless you buy them ready-skinned. Serve them puréed, hot or cold; if cold, season well and dress with lemon juice.

9 RED KIDNEY BEANS
These have an earthy 'country' quality I find very satisfying. Serve them with rice and a Tomato sauce; hot in casseroles, or cold in salads.

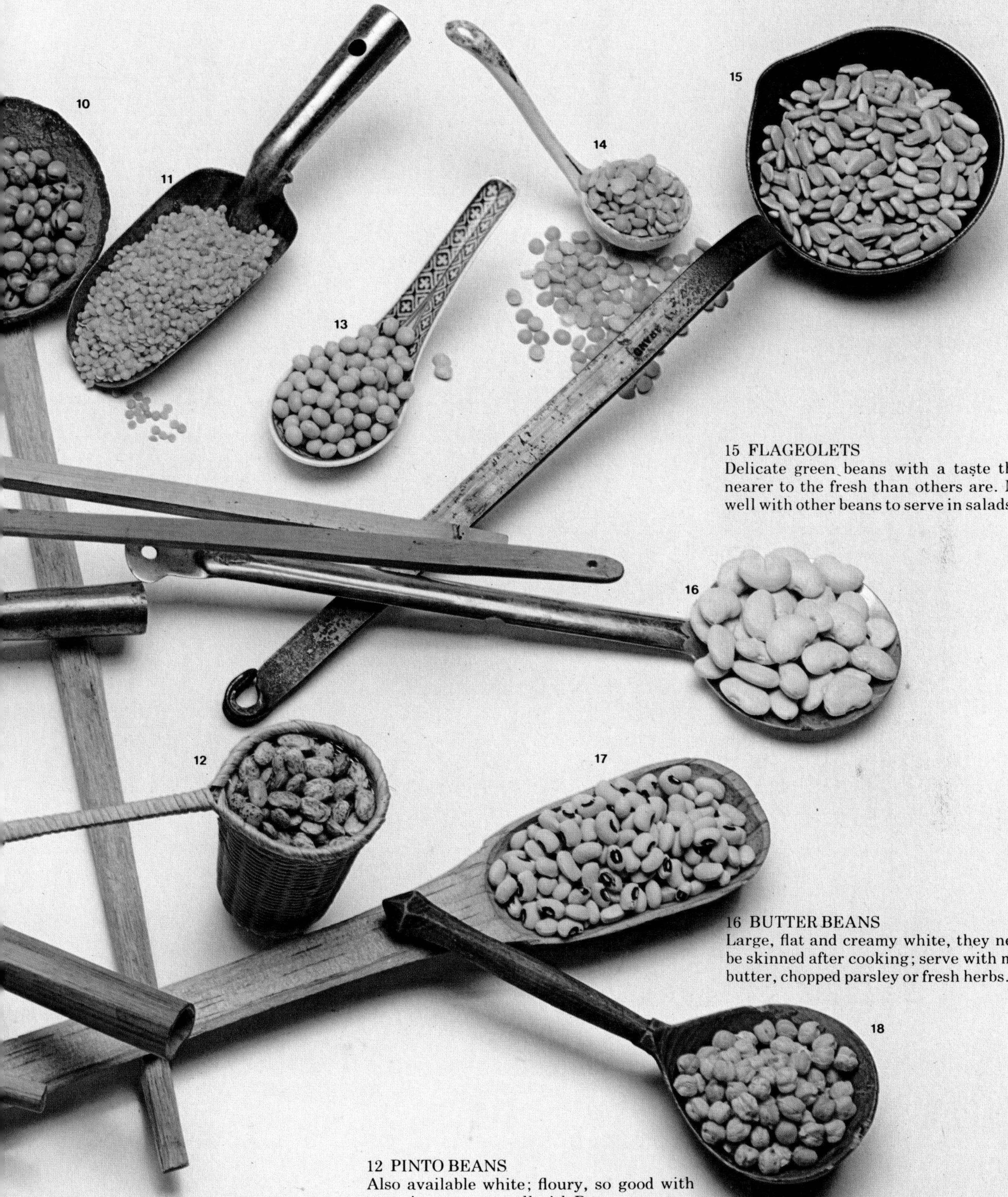

15 FLAGEOLETS
Delicate green beans with a taste that is nearer to the fresh than others are. Mixes well with other beans to serve in salads.

16 BUTTER BEANS
Large, flat and creamy white, they need to be skinned after cooking; serve with melted butter, chopped parsley or fresh herbs.

12 PINTO BEANS
Also available white; floury, so good with pasta in soups, go well with Parmesan.

10 EGYPTIAN BROWN BEANS
The *ful medames* of Egypt; try them with lemon juice, oil, garlic.

11 RED LENTILS
Good for thickening soups, making dhal to accompany curries. Mild-flavored, they purée quickly.

13 SOY BEANS
The high-protein food – mild-flavored so use lots of spices. Coarse-crushed soy grits take much less time to cook.

14 SPLIT YELLOW PEAS
Also make good thickenings for soups; they can also be cooked, spiced and deep-fried as small cakes or patties.

17 BLACK-EYED PEAS
A 'soul food' when cooked and served with onions and rice.

18 CHICK PEAS
Need the longest soaking and cooking of all the beans; eat them hot or cold, or make Hummus (page 64).

PASTA

Pasta – as its name implies – is made from a basic flour and water paste, sometimes with egg added to lighten the texture, add richness and, of course, protein. The best quality pasta is made from the hard durum wheat semolina flour, which itself contains a high proportion of protein and produces a firm pasta which does not break down in cooking. Wholewheat flour makes a thicker-textured but very tasty pasta, especially if made at home (see page 74). Pasta can be 'plain' or flavored with spinach (pasta verde) and it comes in an amazing variety of shapes, a selection of which are illustrated here.

1 Durum wheat (semolina flour) spaghetti
2 Wholewheat spaghetti
3 Egg noodles
4 Nidi (nests) of plain tagliatelle and tagliatelle verdi
5 Cannelloni
6 Wholewheat macaroni
7 Rigatoni
8 Tortiglioni
9 Farfalle (the smaller ones are called farfalletti)
10 Conchiglie (shells) and conchiglietti
11 Wholewheat anelli
12 Lasagne verdi and wholewheat lasagne
13 Ravioli

CEREALS AND FLOURS

Top row from left to right:

WHOLEWHEAT or GRAHAM FLOUR
Fine-ground, for making cakes and pastry. I sift out the coarser bran and make up the quantity with extra sifted flour when making fine-textured cakes.

WHOLE GRAIN
The highly nutritious whole seed of the wheat itself. Rich in protein, vitamins and oils it needs long slow cooking.

UNBLEACHED WHITE FLOUR
I use this in preference to bleached white flour when making flavored cakes (eg. coffee), as it masks the flavor less than wholewheat flour.

STONE GROUND WHOLEWHEAT FLOUR
I use this flour when making bread and for other yeast cookery.

REFINED WHITE ALL-PURPOSE FLOUR
I prefer not to use this bleached flour.

CORNMEAL
Either yellow or white, depending on the color of the kernel from which it was ground. Use it to make Corn bread rolls (page 152).

Second row from left to right:

COARSELY GROUND CORNMEAL
The kind you use for making Polenta (page 124) and dumplings for vegetable casseroles.

BUCKWHEAT or KASHA
Used extensively in Russia, where it is still eaten from the hand – it is very nutritious.

BUCKWHEAT FLOUR
Make Blinis (page 60) with this; much used in Russian cooking.

ROLLED OATS
The coarsest quality available, used for breakfast cereals; rolled oats make delicious sweet oatcakes (page 164). Sprinkle them on the tops of loaves before baking.

OATMEAL
Comes in varying grades – use this one for bread, scones and griddle cakes.

RYE FLOUR
This is light; the darker the color, the stronger the taste of rye. I suggest mixing them when making bread as dark rye dough is sticky to handle.

Third row from left to right:

SOY GRITS
Ground from the protein-rich soybean (page 23), they take much less time to cook.

BULGUR
Made by part-cooking wholewheat until the grains are about to burst, then dried and ground. Make sure you are not given cracked wheat instead, as this takes much longer to prepare. Use bulgur for Tabbouleh (page 133).

COUSCOUS
Coarse-ground semolina made from wheat, it can also be made from millet. Much used in North Africa and Eastern Europe, it is steamed over a casserole.

BARLEY MEAL
Add a little to the mixed flours when making bread to give it a distinctive flavor.

SEMOLINA
Taken from the endosperm at the heart of the wheat, it is ground to varying grades; used fine for puddings, coarse for couscous.

MILLET
Usually thought of as bird seed, it can be ground and used in cooking. It is highly nutritious and has a nutty flavor.

Bottom row from left to right:

LONG GRAIN BROWN RICE
Use this unpolished rice whenever possible as it still has valuable vitamins, minerals and protein left. Long-grain is best for Indian, Chinese and Middle Eastern dishes, SHORT GRAIN BROWN RICE for puddings.

SHORT GRAIN WHITE RICE
White, polished rice has the outer layers removed by milling. Used for puddings.

LONG GRAIN WHITE RICE
The rice I favor for savory dishes when the brown version is not available.

RICE FLOUR
Gluten-free, used by professional bakers to control the stickiness of their dough. Can be used for thickening soups, and for cookies.

WILD RICE
Very expensive, but well worth it. Not a true rice, it is the seed of a grass of another kind.

OILS AND FATS

Edible oils are the liquid form of fats which, in the vegetarian diet, are taken mainly from vegetables, cereals, nuts and seeds. Medical opinion is not in complete agreement about the possible connection between the consumption of fatty acids and the onset of cardiovascular disease; as a general rule, nutritionists recommend that you watch your total intake of fats and edible oils. Those obtained from vegetable sources, containing polyunsaturated fatty acids, may be preferable to the saturated fatty acids from animal sources. The Basic Nutrition chapter, beginning on page 208 discusses this question in more detail.

Since it is impossible to avoid using fats and edible oils in cooking, here are some of the ones I usually use:

Above, from left to right:

1 WALNUT OIL
A delicious, highly flavored oil, used in the south of France interchangeably with olive oil. Try it on your salads.

2 SUNFLOWER SEED OIL
This is often used in place of olive oil though it has, of course, a much blander flavor. Try soaking olives in it, so that it will acquire a slight olive flavor.

3 PEANUT OIL
A similar oil to sunflower seed oil, but with a more pronounced flavor – unless it is deodorized in the processing.

4 SESAME SEED OIL
A beautifully-flavored oil pressed from sesame seeds and greatly used in Oriental and Middle Eastern cooking.

5 TAHINI PASTE
This is made from sesame seeds and oil, and a basic ingredient in the classic Hummus (page 64), found throughout the Middle East.

6 OLIVE OIL
This is the oil most often used in French and Italian cooking; I would use it for preference in most of my dishes – it has an incomparable flavor. The first pressing, known as '*huile vierge*' is the strongest in flavor – and difficult to find!

7 ALMOND OIL
Mainly used in making confectionery, try a little for frying salted almonds.

8 SOYBEAN OIL
An almost tasteless, refined oil pressed from the soybean. It can be used both for cooking and for dressing salads.

9 SAFFLOWER SEED OIL
This, too, has very little flavor once it is refined. It is low in fatty acids.

10 CORN OIL
For me, this oil has a rather unpalatable flavor; many people prefer to use it for deep fat frying.

IMPORTANT:
Never heat the oil used for deep fat frying to above 375°F, or it will spontaneously ignite. The danger signal is a blue haze over the pan. Sunflower seed oil should not be heated to above 360°F. A cube of dry bread should brown in 60 seconds at this temperature.

11 SHORTENING
A creamy, white cooking fat made from vegetable oils and designed to be used in close-textured cakes,

12 MARGARINE
A solid fat of varying degrees of firmness which can be used instead of butter, although the flavor of the finished dish will not be the same. Choose a margarine made from vegetable oils; some brands have added vitamins.

NUTS AND SEEDS

The term *nut* is used to describe a number of seeds, kernels or plants and fruits which, botanically speaking, are not all nuts. However, nuts can be divided for convenience into categories based on similarity of flavor. First we have the Brazils, hazelnuts, pecans and walnuts, all of which have a rich, oily flavor and firm texture. Then there are the pistachios and pine nuts, both of which have a slightly resinous taste. Almonds, cashews and chestnuts are sweeter; chestnuts go floury after cooking.

Coconuts are in a class of their own, in flavor somewhere between Brazils and almonds but

the nut is hollow and contains a sweet, vegetable milk.

Serve nuts whole, coarsely chopped or ground; add them to cooked dishes, sprinkle them over vegetables or salads as a garnish and you will be adding extra protein and nourishment to your diet; nuts generally have a high food value. Almonds are at the top of the league, followed by Brazils, walnuts and hazelnuts. Chestnuts come last, but are very popular, especially roasted.

If you can, beg *fresh* nuts from friends who have them growing in the garden. Many store-bought nuts are kiln dried or roasted, and this alters their flavor – especially walnuts which can taste quite acrid if kiln-dried.

13 SUNFLOWER SEEDS
Best eaten raw – a good source of protein and vitamins; sprinkle over salads or cereals.

14 SESAME SEEDS
A valuable source of vitamins and minerals, e.g. magnesium, calcium and phosphorus.

15 CASHEW NUTS unsalted and salted
Sprinkle these sweet, crescent-shaped nuts over salads, or bake in a nut loaf (page 106).

16 WALNUTS
Pickle these in midsummer, before the shell has matured and hardened.

17 SHREDDED COCONUT
The dried, shredded meat of the COCONUT (*extreme right*), used in curries and sweet dishes and as a flavoring for cakes.

18 CHESTNUTS
These very popular nuts can be baked, boiled, mashed, made into flour, puréed, or served as a vegetable.

19 PISTACHIOS
A very sweet, rich-tasting nut which, when peeled is a characteristic pale green.

20 PECANS
A relative of the walnut, it has a smooth shell and a milder flavor.

21 HAZELNUTS
Sometimes confused with the larger cob nut, hazelnuts are used in cakes; good toasted.

22 ALMONDS whole, shelled and green
Toast and salt them to eat as snacks; grind or shred and add to cakes.

23 PINE KERNELS
The aromatic nuts of certain pine trees, these are always sold shelled.

24 PEANUTS or GROUNDNUTS
Rich in fat content and protein, this nut is made into oil, butter or flour; serve as a vegetable, or ground in loaves.

25 WATER CHESTNUTS
Not strictly speaking, a nut, but with a crisp texture. Used in Chinese cooking.

26 BRAZIL NUTS
A large, meaty nut with a very hard shell.

EGGS
Apart from familiar white and brown HENS EGGS (*front right*), the eggs of some other birds can be eaten. A blue-tinged DUCK EGG (*far left*) should only be used in recipes in which it will be thoroughly cooked; a tiny spotted QUAIL'S EGG and a larger dark-shelled GULL'S EGG (*behind*) are both rich-tasting and considered delicacies. A GOOSE EGG (*behind right*) is strongly flavored and very large!
Vegans, who eat no animal produce, will certainly not eat eggs, though they are high in protein and very nourishing. Put an egg into a bowl of water. If it is fresh, it will lie flat; if aging, it will have a tendency to float as the bubble of air under the shell at the broad end enlarges.
Never place eggs straight from the refrigerator into boiling water, or the shell will almost certainly crack. The older the egg, the more likely the shell is to crack in any case. Store eggs pointed-end downward, as they keep longer if the yolk is resting on the white and not on the bubble of air.

MILK
Milk makes a very valuable contribution to the diet, being rich in protein, vitamins, calcium and other minerals. It is, in fact, the most complete single food we know. Vegans do not drink milk, using instead the 'milk' that comes from nuts. The quality of any milk depends on the time of the year – summer pasture milk being traditionally the best – the breed of the animal and the type of fodder provided. Commercially available milk goes through varying processes to produce different 'grades' and to destroy harmful bacteria.

CREAM
This contains varying amounts of butterfat which is separated off the milk by centrifugal force. The higher the concentration of fat, the thicker the cream

When whipping thick cream, have the bowl and utensils chilled; when whipping very fresh cream, add a little lemon juice. If you overwhip cream, however, you are left with butter and buttermilk. Buttermilk is a very good source of protein and has a sour, slightly cheesy taste. Sour cream is available commercially – delicious with fresh or cooked fruit, or in casseroles.

DRIED MILK
Skimmed powdered milk has had all the cream removed and therefore keeps longer than milk in its liquid form. Low in calories and good for anyone on a weight-reducing diet. 'Instant' dried milk has been processed to make it more soluble in beverages such as tea and coffee.

YOGURT
This is made from milk, cows' or goats', which has been purposely soured by bacteria. Make sure, when buying yogurt, that it has a fresh culture in it; some commercially available yogurt has been sterilized. It is easy to make your own (page 200) – then you know it will be fresh!

CHEESE
Cheese poses a particular problem for the vegetarian as most contain animal rennet, which is used to curdle the milk or cream. Rennet-free Cheddar and Cheshire cheeses are available from many health food stores, and there is a movement to use a vegetable-based enzyme instead. Hard cheeses are highest in protein and generally lowest in calories, except for cottage cheese. Here is a selection of the cheeses containing rennet:

1 PARMESAN
Strong-flavored, hard Italian cheese that is matured for two years. Buy it by the piece and grate it as you need it.

2 RICOTTA
A very soft Italian cream cheese with a mild and pleasant flavor. Use for cooking.

BEL PAESE (not shown)
A popular Italian soft cheese with a mild, sweet flavor; goes well with fresh soft fruit at the end of a meal.

3 GORGONZOLA
Italy's most famous blue-veined cheese, ripe and sharp and very crumbly in texture.

4 CAMEMBERT and 5 BRIE
Two of France's best known soft cheeses, similar in flavor, Brie being slightly milder. At their best in early spring.

6 SWISS GRUYERE
The genuine article, with very small holes, unlike French Gruyère which closely resembles 7 SWISS EMMENTHAL a very similar cheese. Use any of these for making Fondue.

8 EDAM and 9 GOUDA
The two most familiar Dutch hard cheeses, the Edam being saltier, the Gouda having its characteristic red, waxy skin. Both these are excellent toasted.

10 DERBY SAGE and 11 RED WINDSOR CHEESE
Just two of a number of British specialities worth trying if you can. Green-veined Derby is flavored with fresh sage, red with annatto berries.

12 CHEDDAR CHEESE
A most popular, rich-tasting cheese, made the world over under its original name. Its flavor deepens as it matures.

13 ROQUEFORT
The famous French blue-veined cheese, made from ewe's milk; the curds are mixed with breadcrumbs to give its characteristic veining. Use to flavor salad dressings.

14 BLUE STILTON
This has been called the 'King' of English cheeses. There is a white Stilton, too, which is younger, chalk-white and very crumbly. It naturally tastes milder than the blue.

15 GOATS' CHEESE
To represent the many varying 'members' of the Chèvre family of cheeses: this one is soft, chalky and sharp; yellower, smoother types tend to be sweeter in flavor.

16 MOZZARELLA
Originally made from buffalo milk, now from cow's milk! Mild-flavored and good for cooking as it does not go stringy when heated.

17 COTTAGE CHEESE
Knobbly-textured, mild-flavored and made from skimmed milk, therefore good for a weight-reducing diet.

18 CURD CHEESE
Made from curdled milk – make your own by adding lemon juice and straining the soured milk through clean muslin. See page 200 for the Indian Chhana and Panir.

19 CREAM CHEESE
Full-fat, soft and creamy; try flavoring it with fresh herbs or garlic. It can also be sweetened. With a little cream added it makes a delightful accompaniment to fresh summer berries.

20 FETA
Goat's cheese from Greece, feta is white, firm and sharp-tasting. It is delicious sprinkled over salads.

A SELECTION OF FRUIT

1 APPLES
Just three examples of the abundance of varieties that are available for dessert use and for cooking. Cooking apples can be divided into two types: those which fall rapidly to a pulp and those which hold their shape. Use tiny, sour crab apples for making jelly.

9 PEACH
Yellow-skinned varieties may be freestone, with juicy soft flesh, or of the clingstone type, with flesh that does cling firmly to its pit. Wash the velvety skins thoroughly, or peel them.

10 NECTARINE
A variety of smooth-skinned peach with a flavor best described as somewhere between a peach and a plum.

14 GRAPES
Both white and black grapes should have a bloom on them – choose large branches for preference, bearing juicy but not overripe fruit.

2 PEAR
Again, many varieties are available, each with a slightly different flavor. Buy dessert pears when slightly underripe and allow them to ripen fully indoors to lessen the risk of bruising.

3 CHERRIES
Both black and white (red-skinned) cherries make good dessert fruit. I use the slightly bitter Morellos for cooking and making jam.

4 PLUMS
All dessert plums, whether red-, golden- or dark purple-skinned, should have a bloom on them. Types include the small, tart-tasting damson and the bright green-skinned gage; both are good for jam.

5 CRANBERRIES
Their sharp, distinctive flavor makes delicious sweet or savory jelly 'sauces'; traditionally served with turkey.

6 RASPBERRIES
The least juicy of soft fruits and slightly sharper in taste than the strawberry, raspberries are usually served with sugar and cream; they make superb sherbets, creamy ices and jam. Use fresh fruit on the day you buy.

7 LOGANBERRIES
A native of the United States, a cross between a raspberry and a blackberry, these are larger, softer and juicer than raspberries.

8 BLACKBERRIES
'Blackberrying' in the fall and blackberry and apple pies soften thoughts of the onset of winter for me! Cultivated blackberries are larger than wild ones; both deteriorate quickly so take care not to bruise them. Blackberries make excellent jams and sherbets.

11 GOOSEBERRIES
These characteristically sharp-tasting green or pink-tinged berries make particularly good jams or pie fillings.

12 BLACK and RED CURRANTS
Delicious in jams and jellies, ice creams or sherbets; cooked together, they make a delicious compôte – use less black currants as the flavor is much stronger.

13 APRICOTS
Picked fresh, they have an incomparable flavor. Add a piece of vanilla bean when poaching the fruit and use the almond-flavored kernel when making jam – add about 6 for each 1lb of fruit.

15 STRAWBERRIES
The cultivated berries are large and well-flavored, but for the gourmet there is nothing to touch the tiny, wild *fraises de bois*. A strawberry purée freezes well.

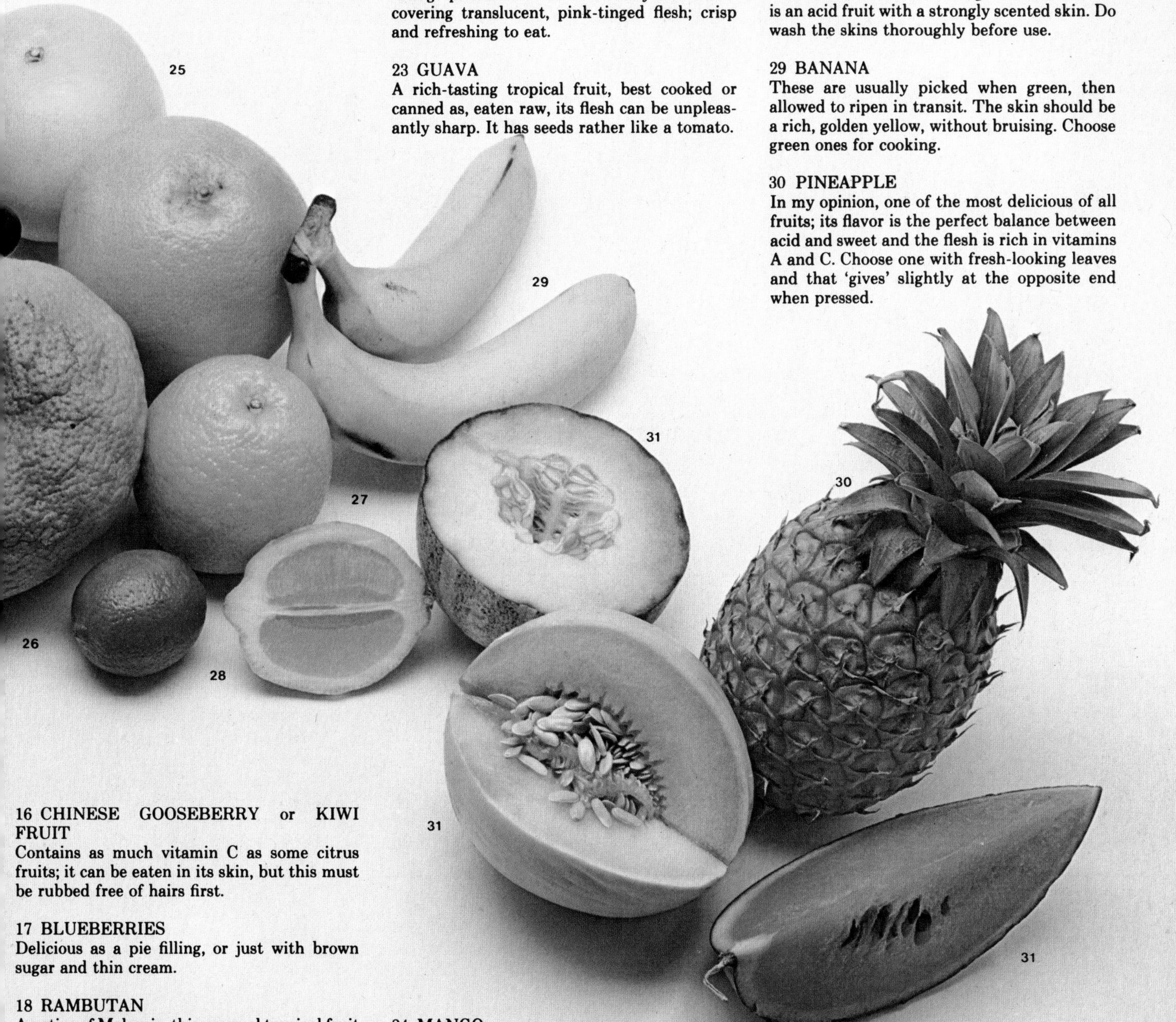

16 CHINESE GOOSEBERRY or KIWI FRUIT
Contains as much vitamin C as some citrus fruits; it can be eaten in its skin, but this must be rubbed free of hairs first.

17 BLUEBERRIES
Delicious as a pie filling, or just with brown sugar and thin cream.

18 RAMBUTAN
A native of Malaysia, this unusual tropical fruit has white flesh with a refreshing, sweet-sour taste. Can be eaten raw or cooked.

19 PASSION FRUIT
Its tough, wrinkled skin is a sign of ripeness! A juicy fruit full of seeds, which can be eaten – or strained off and the juice used to flavor molded creams.

20 MANGOSTEEN
Another unusual tropical fruit from Malaysia, its white, segmented flesh tastes rich and syrupy. Best eaten fresh.

21 DATES
These fresh dates are moist and plump; as they dry, the sugar content becomes more concentrated and the flavor strengthens. Buy unpitted dates, if buying dried ones.

22 LYCHEE
A large-pitted fruit with a curiously brittle skin covering translucent, pink-tinged flesh; crisp and refreshing to eat.

23 GUAVA
A rich-tasting tropical fruit, best cooked or canned as, eaten raw, its flesh can be unpleasantly sharp. It has seeds rather like a tomato.

24 MANGO
Large, yellow-skinned, red-tinged tropical fruits. Their skin has a faint aroma of turpentine and the fruit is fragrant and spicy. Choose fruit that is heavy with no brown spots.

25 GRAPEFRUIT
Two fine examples here – the more familiar yellow-skinned variety and the pink-tinged grapefruit.

26 UGLI
A cross between a grapefruit and a tangerine, combining the best of both.

27 ORANGE
This is a cultivated variety with few seeds. Use the smaller, bitter Seville oranges for making marmalade. Blood oranges taste sweetest and have red-flecked flesh.

28 LEMON and LIME
The lemon, like the smaller, green-skinned lime is an acid fruit with a strongly scented skin. Do wash the skins thoroughly before use.

29 BANANA
These are usually picked when green, then allowed to ripen in transit. The skin should be a rich, golden yellow, without bruising. Choose green ones for cooking.

30 PINEAPPLE
In my opinion, one of the most delicious of all fruits; its flavor is the perfect balance between acid and sweet and the flesh is rich in vitamins A and C. Choose one with fresh-looking leaves and that 'gives' slightly at the opposite end when pressed.

31 MELONS
These belong to the same family as the cucumbers and squashes. Their flesh is fragrant, contains 94% water and about 5% sugar. Three varieties are shown: the round, ridged, green-tinged cantaloupe, the oval, golden-skinned honeydew and the unmistakable, seed-embedded red flesh of the watermelon. Tap lightly with the knuckles – a melon should sound hollow and resonant.

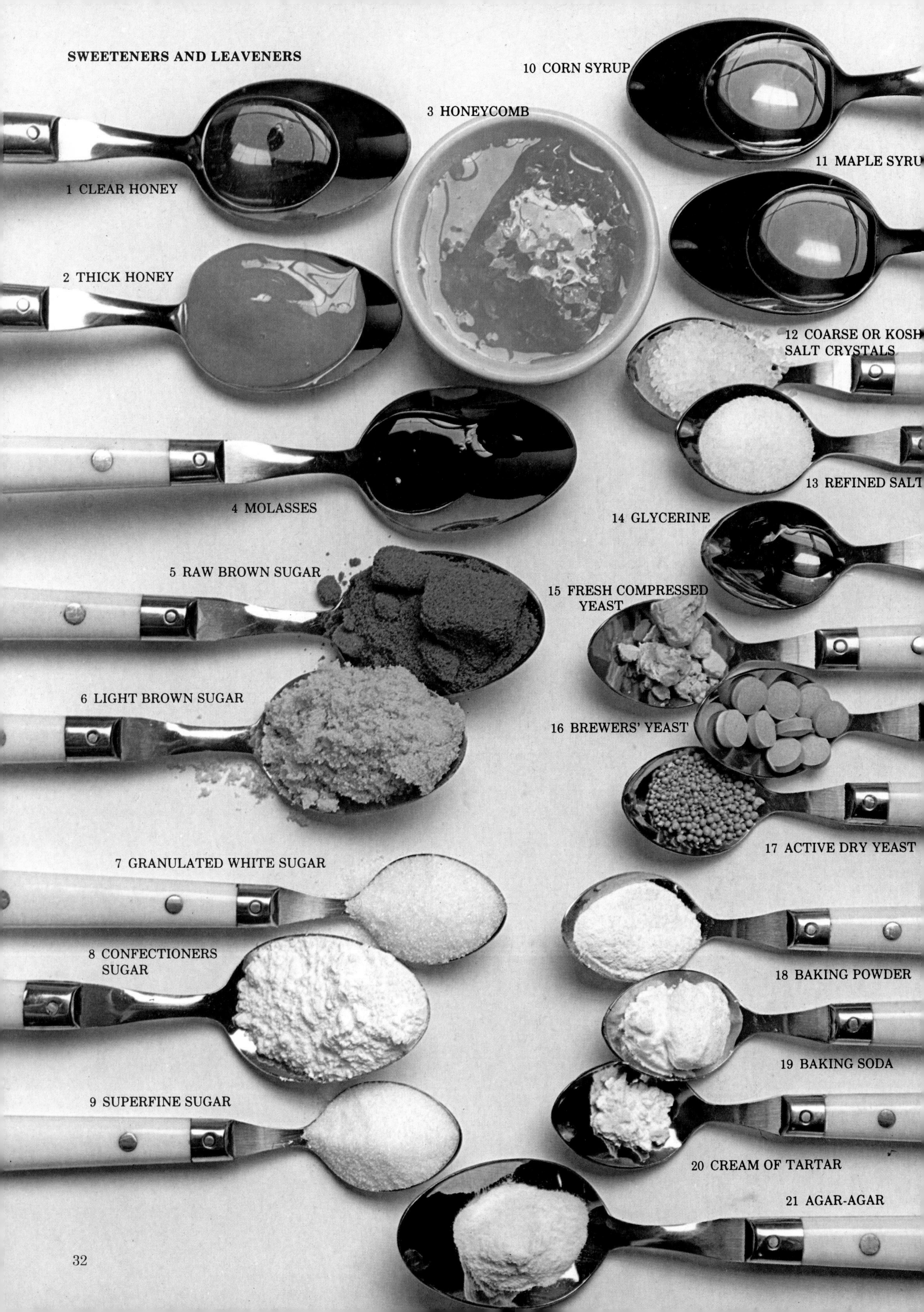
SWEETENERS AND LEAVENERS
1 CLEAR HONEY
2 THICK HONEY
3 HONEYCOMB
4 MOLASSES
5 RAW BROWN SUGAR
6 LIGHT BROWN SUGAR
7 GRANULATED WHITE SUGAR
8 CONFECTIONERS SUGAR
9 SUPERFINE SUGAR
10 CORN SYRUP
11 MAPLE SYRU
12 COARSE OR KOSH SALT CRYSTALS
13 REFINED SALT
14 GLYCERINE
15 FRESH COMPRESSED YEAST
16 BREWERS' YEAST
17 ACTIVE DRY YEAST
18 BAKING POWDER
19 BAKING SODA
20 CREAM OF TARTAR
21 AGAR-AGAR

Soups

A good soup makes one of the best introductions to any meal, whether it is a well-flavored clear consommé, a smooth-textured creamy soup, a warm, welcoming vegetable broth or a sophisticated chilled soup for a summer's evening.

Recipes for all of these are to be found in the following chapter. If substantial, such as a Minestrone or a Scotch broth, and served with freshly baked wholewheat bread, a soup can be a meal in itself.

With a blender, food mill or strainer, it is a simple matter to make any number of nourishing soups using a selection of the best vegetables on hand, a good, rich vegetable stock and a little imagination. Try combining onion with beet and orange, or cabbage with apple and lemon . . .

Most cream and puréed soups are good served cold, but remember that chilled soups need to be a little more highly flavored than if served hot. Triangles of thin toast spread with a Herb butter make a delicious accompaniment to vegetable soups: crisp Almond or Hazelnut cookies are best with fruit soups.

Making Stocks

As a good vegetable stock is used as the basis of many of the soups in this chapter, here are two recipes to enable you to make your own.

Homemade stock does, of course, take time and effort to prepare, but the consequent improvement in taste does a great deal to enhance the quality of the finished soup.

Stocks are divided into two types: brown and white. Brown stock is richly colored because the ingredients are lightly fried to color them well before liquid is added, while in white stocks the vegetables are fried, but not allowed to brown and are more delicate in color and flavor.

When making stock. I tend to avoid using too many brassicas as I find their flavor too pronounced. However, the water in which they have been cooked can be used as part of the liquid.

It is important to remember that vegetable stock does not keep well beyond 24 hours and should, therefore, be made freshly for each soup, or made in advance and frozen. In this case, make four times the given quantity and freeze in convenient portions.

Of course, for emergencies, vegetarian bouillon cubes are available, but, if you *are* using these, check the seasoning carefully as they tend to be salty.

Brown vegetable stock

CALORIES PER PORTION: 120 (502 kJ)
PROTEIN CONTENT PER PORTION: 5 grams
PREPARATION AND COOKING TIME: 2 hours

2 tablespoons olive or sunflower oil
2 cups finely chopped onions
2 cups thinly sliced carrots
½ lb tomatoes, cut in halves crosswise
1 lb mixed green leaves (lettuce, cabbage, root tops, spinach), any wilting leaves removed
2 pints water
1-2 teaspoons brewers' yeast

Heat the oil in a deep thick-based pan over gentle heat. Add the onions and carrots and cook them gently for about 30 minutes, or until they are golden brown.

Meanwhile, broil the tomatoes until they are a good brown, then add them to the onions and carrots with the greens. Stir in the water, bring it to a boil, then lower the heat and simmer the stock gently for 1½ hours. Stir in the brewers' yeast. Measure the stock in a jug and add enough water to make it up to 2 pints. Strain back into the pan, pressing the vegetables against the sides of the strainer to extract all the juices. The stock is now ready to use as directed

This recipe makes 2 pints, enough for a first course of soup for four.

Clear stock

If the recipe specifies a clear stock, leave it until cold, then beat in 2 egg whites and bring slowly to a boil. When the egg coagulates and floats to the surface, turn down the heat and simmer for 1 minute, then strain the clarified stock through a piece of fine, clean cheesecloth.

White vegetable stock

CALORIES PER PORTION: 150 (615 kJ)
PROTEIN CONTENT PER PORTION: 2.5 grams
PREPARATION & COOKING TIME: 2 hours

2 tablespoons olive or sunflower oil
2 cups finely chopped onions
1⅓ cups diced potatoes
½ cup finely chopped celery
⅔ cup thinly sliced parsnip, quartered first if large
1 cup thinly sliced carrot, quartered first if large
1 cup thinly sliced turnip, quartered first if large
2 bay leaves
2 pints water

Heat the oil in a deep, thick-based pan, add the onions, potatoes and celery and cook over moderate heat for 10 minutes. Take care not to let the vegetables color *at all*, and turn them over from time to time so that they cook evenly.

Add the remaining vegetables, the bay leaves and the water and stir well. Bring to a boil, lower the heat and simmer gently for 1 hour.

Measure the stock in a jug and make it up to 2 pints with water. Strain twice, pressing the vegetables against the sides of the strainer to extract as much flavor and goodness as possible, without actually rubbing the vegetables through. Discard the vegetables; the stock is now ready for use and is enough to make soup for four.

Consommé Basquaise

This classic consommé is also good served chilled.

Serves 4
CALORIES PER PORTION: 195 (820 kJ)
PROTEIN CONTENT PER PORTION: 6 grams
PREPARATION & COOKING TIME: 30 minutes

1 tablespoon butter
1 cup finely diced red pepper
2 pints clear brown vegetable stock
¼ cup boiled rice
salt
freshly ground pepper
4 teaspoons chopped chervil

Melt the butter in a pan over gentle heat, add the diced pepper and cook gently for 15 minutes, taking care that it does not burn. Meanwhile, pour the stock into a pan and bring to a boil.

Stir the hot stock into the cooked pepper, then add the rice and simmer for 5 minutes. Adjust the seasoning, pour into warmed soup bowls, sprinkle the chervil over and serve.

Consommé Brancas

Serves 4
CALORIES PER PORTION: 125 (515 kJ)
PROTEIN CONTENT PER PORTION: 5 grams
PREPARATION & COOKING TIME: 30 minutes

2 pints clear brown vegetable stock, with at least ¼ lb fresh sorrel leaves included in the making
1 cup finely shredded sorrel leaves
1 cup finely chopped lettuce leaves
salt
freshly ground pepper

Pour the stock into a pan and bring to a boil. Add the sorrel leaves, the lettuce and salt and pepper to taste, then lower the heat and simmer for 15 minutes. Adjust the seasoning if necessary, pour into warmed soup bowls and serve hot with thin slices of freshly made wholewheat toast.

If sorrel is not easily obtainable, try this recipe using spinach instead.

Consommé Colbert

Serves 4
CALORIES PER PORTION: 205 (845 kJ)
PROTEIN CONTENT PER PORTION: 12 grams
PREPARATION & COOKING TIME: 15 minutes

2 pints clear brown vegetable stock
salt
4 eggs
4 teaspoons finely chopped chervil

Pour the stock into a pan, bring it to a boil, then keep it hot. Fill a separate shallow pan with water and bring it to a boil, then lower the heat to keep it just simmering. Add a little salt, then break the eggs carefully into the water one at a time, so that the yolks do not run.

After about 3-4 minutes, when the egg whites are set but the yolks are still soft, remove each egg with a slotted spoon, trim neatly and place in the bottom of a warmed, shallow soup bowl. Pour in the hot stock slowly so as not to disturb the eggs, then sprinkle with chervil. Serve hot, with very thin slices of freshly made toast.

Consommé Crecy

Serves 4
CALORIES PER PORTION: 150 (632 kJ)
PROTEIN CONTENT PER PORTION: 5 grams
PREPARATION AND COOKING TIME: 40 minutes

1 tablespoon butter
1 cup diced carrot
2 pints clear brown vegetable stock
salt
freshly ground pepper

Melt the butter over gentle heat, add the carrot and cook it over moderate heat for about 20 minutes, taking care not to burn or brown it. Bring the stock to a boil in a large saucepan (if not already prepared make the stock now).

When the carrot is tender, add it with its juices to the hot stock and simmer for a further 5 minutes. Adjust the seasoning, pour the consommé into warmed soup bowls and serve.

Okra consommé

Be sure to use freshly bought fennel seeds, otherwise the flavor of the soup will be impaired.

Serves 4
CALORIES PER PORTION: 170 (712 kJ)
PROTEIN CONTENT PER PORTION: 8 grams
PREPARATION & COOKING TIME (INCLUDING MAKING THE STOCK) 2 hours

2 pints clear brown vegetable stock with 3 cups coarsely chopped okra and ½ teaspoon crushed fennel seeds in the making
salt
freshly ground pepper
1 cup thinly sliced okra
¼ cup boiled rice
pinch of cayenne pepper

Strain the stock into a pan and season it well with salt and pepper. Add the okra and rice, stir well and bring the stock to a boil. Lower the heat and allow the soup to simmer for 10 minutes, stirring occasionally to prevent the vegetables sticking and burning. Add the cayenne pepper before adjusting the seasoning, then pour into warmed soup bowls.

Mushroom soup

Serves 4
CALORIES PER PORTION: 420 (1765 kJ)
PROTEIN CONTENT PER PORTION: 7 grams
PREPARATION & COOKING TIME: 1 hour

12 tablespoons butter
1 cup finely chopped onion
4 cups finely chopped mushrooms
1 tablespoon wholewheat flour
2 pints brown vegetable stock
½ cup dry red wine
1 teaspoon prepared French mustard
2 teaspoons brewer's yeast
salt
freshly ground pepper

Melt 6 tablespoons of the butter in a pan, add the onion and cook until golden brown. Add the mushrooms and continue cooking until the juices run and the mushrooms are dark and shiny. Work the remaining butter into the flour on a plate with a fork until it forms a smooth paste (kneaded butter or beurre manié). Add the stock to the mushrooms and bring to a boil, then lower the heat and add the kneaded butter, wine and mustard. Stir vigorously until the kneaded butter has dissolved, then continue cooking for a further 20 minutes, stirring occasionally.

Add the brewer's yeast, stir well and adjust the seasoning. Pour the soup into warmed bowls and serve garnished with croûtons.

Scotch broth

This is a thick, substantial soup and this recipe should be enough for 8.

CALORIES PER PORTION: 130 (538 kJ)
PROTEIN CONTENT PER PORTION: 3 grams
PREPARATION & COOKING TIME: 2 hours

¼ cup olive or sunflower oil
2 cups finely chopped onion
2 cups thinly sliced carrots, quartered first if large
2 cups diced turnips
2 cups diced parsnips
⅓ cup pearl barley
1½ quarts water
½ teaspoon dried thyme
1 teaspoon salt
freshly ground pepper
2 teaspoons brewer's yeast
2 bay leaves
2 cups halved and thinly sliced leeks

Heat the oil and fry the onion and carrots over moderate heat until the edges are just beginning to brown, then add the rest of the ingredients except the leeks. Bring the soup to a boil, lower the heat and simmer very gently for 1 hour before adding the leeks. Simmer the soup for a further 30 minutes, adding a little more water if necessary.

Discard the bay leaves, adjust the seasoning if necessary, and serve with chunks of Wholewheat bread (page 151).

Three winter-warming soups – serve them all with chunks of freshly-made wholewheat bread. Top: Consommé Basquaise with rice, red peppers and fresh chervil; Center: a delicious Minestrone. Below: Mushroom soup is richly flavored with onions and red wine

Brown lentil soup

Serves 4
CALORIES PER PORTION: 150 (627 kJ)
PROTEIN CONTENT PER PORTION: 6.5 grams
PREPARATION & COOKING TIME: 1½ hours

2 tablespoons olive or sunflower oil
2 medium onions, thinly sliced
⅔ cup brown lentils
2½ cups water
1 bay leaf
2 inch stick of cinnamon
4 cloves, coarsely ground
2 cloves of garlic, peeled and finely chopped
salt
freshly ground pepper

Heat the oil in a pan and fry the onions over moderate heat until golden brown, stirring from time to time to prevent them sticking. Add the lentils with the water, the bay leaf, cinnamon stick, cloves and garlic. Increase the heat and let the soup simmer for 45 minutes, or until the lentils are tender and beginning to soften.

Remove the cinnamon stick and bay leaf, and work the lentils with their cooking liquid through a blender or food mill, then rub through a strainer until they are puréed. Alternatively, rub them twice through a strainer.

Return the purée to a clean pan, make up the quantity to 2 pints with extra water, if necessary, then adjust the seasoning and bring the soup to a boil. Serve with chunks of fresh Wholewheat bread (page 151).

Note: If you prefer a rough-textured soup, omit the straining and puréeing and serve the soup as soon as the lentils are soft.

Minestrone

Serves 6
CALORIES PER PORTION: 200 (830 kJ)
PROTEIN CONTENT PER PORTION: 8 grams
PREPARATION & COOKING TIME: 1 hour

2 tablespoons olive or sunflower oil
2 cups finely chopped onions
1 cup thinly sliced carrots, quartered first if large
1 cup sliced celery
1 cup diced potatoes
1 cup skinned and chopped tomatoes
2 cups coarsely chopped green or white cabbage
1 cup shelled fresh or frozen peas
1 cup chopped green beans
1 cup cooked soybeans
1 cup dry red wine
2 quarts hot water
2 teaspoons brewer's yeast
4 cloves of garlic, peeled and finely chopped
¼ lb stellette, or spaghetti broken into very short pieces
salt
freshly ground pepper
1 cup freshly grated Parmesan cheese

Heat the oil in a large pan and fry the onions, carrots and celery until the vegetables are golden brown, stirring well so that they cook evenly. Add the rest of the ingredients except the salt, pepper and Parmesan and bring the soup to a boil. Lower the heat and let it simmer for 20-30 minutes, adding a little extra water if necessary, then season with salt and pepper. Serve with chunks of freshly made Wholewheat bread (page 151) and hand a bowl of Parmesan separately.

For a change, serve with Pesto (page 75) also handed separately.

Avgolemono (Greek lemon soup)

Serves 4
CALORIES PER PORTION: 220 (920 kJ)
PROTEIN CONTENT PER PORTION: 7 grams
PREPARATION & COOKING TIME: 20 minutes

2 pints white vegetable stock
¾ cup boiled long-grain rice
salt
2 eggs
grated rind of ½ lemon
juice of 1-2 lemons, depending on size
freshly ground pepper

Bring the stock to a boil, add the cooked rice to the pan and bring the stock back to a boil before seasoning with salt. Lower the heat and simmer gently for 5 minutes. Break the eggs into a bowl and beat thoroughly with the lemon rind and juice, then add a little of the hot stock. Stir well, then pour this slowly back into the stock in the pan. Remove the pan immediately from the heat, or the eggs may curdle instead of blending into the soup. Stir until the mixture is well mixed and smooth. Adjust the seasoning, pour into warmed soup bowls and serve with slices of Poppy seed braid (page 154).

Carrot and orange soup

Serves 4
CALORIES PER PORTION: 310 (1302 kJ)
PROTEIN CONTENT PER PORTION: 5 grams
PREPARATION & COOKING TIME: 50 minutes

6 tablespoons butter
4 cups coarsely shredded carrots
½ cup finely chopped onion
2½ cups water
1 tablespoon wholewheat flour
1¼ cups milk
finely grated rind of 1 orange
¼ cup orange juice
salt
freshly ground pepper

Melt two thirds of the butter in a pan over gentle heat, add the carrots and onion and cook them for about 5 minutes. Stir in the water, bring it to a boil, then cover the pan and let the soup simmer for 20 minutes.

Meanwhile, melt the remaining butter in a separate pan over gentle heat, sprinkle in the flour and cook for 1-2 minutes, stirring continuously. Take the pan off the heat and gradually stir in the milk. Return the pan to the heat and bring the sauce to a boil, stirring all the time until it thickens. Transfer the sauce to a double boiler to keep hot.

Rub the carrots, onion and their cooking liquid through a strainer, or work first in a blender and then rub through a strainer, so you have a completely smooth purée. Return this to a large, clean pan, add the orange rind and juice and bring the soup to a boil. Remove the pan from the heat, stir in the hot sauce, season with salt and pepper and serve — if you like — with a swirl of cream in each bowl.

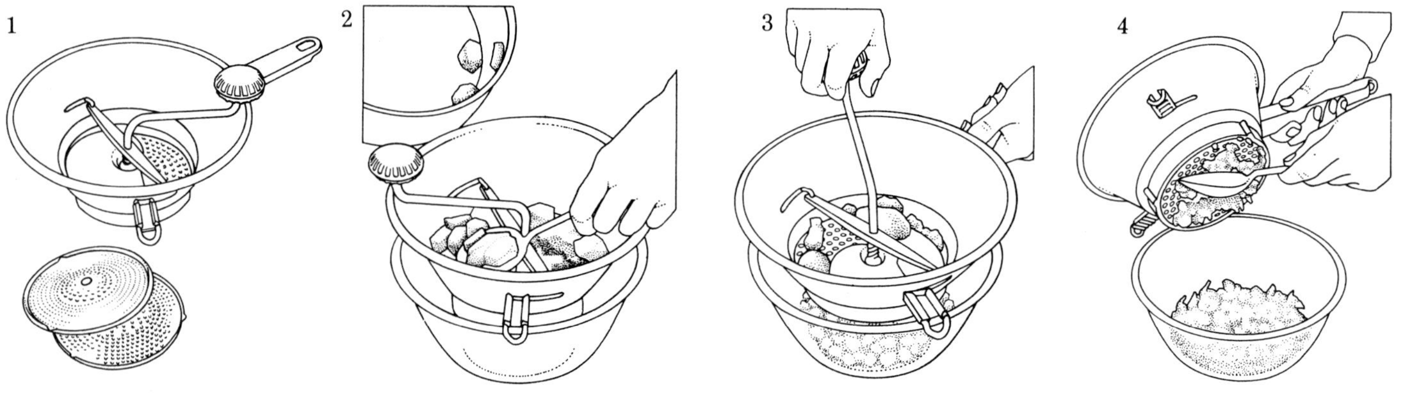

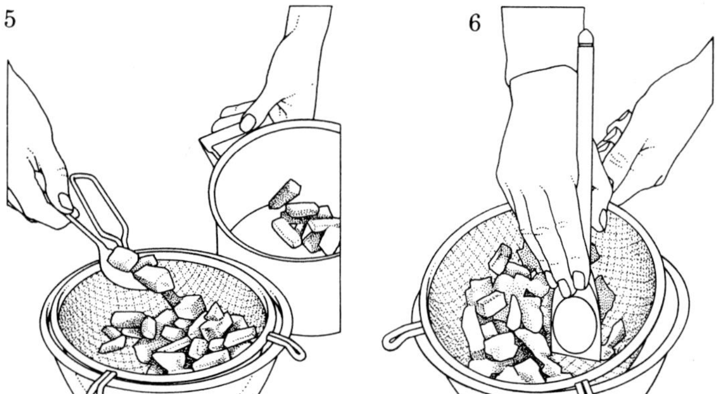

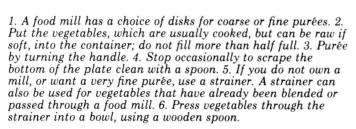

1. A food mill has a choice of disks for coarse or fine purées. 2. Put the vegetables, which are usually cooked, but can be raw if soft, into the container; do not fill more than half full. 3. Purée by turning the handle. 4. Stop occasionally to scrape the bottom of the plate clean with a spoon. 5. If you do not own a mill, or want a very fine purée, use a strainer. A strainer can also be used for vegetables that have already been blended or passed through a food mill. 6. Press vegetables through the strainer into a bowl, using a wooden spoon.

Chinese cabbage, corn and mushroom soup

This soup is basically a clear consommé with a cabbage, corn and mushroom garnish. It is important that the cabbage should still be slightly crisp when the soup is ready.

Serves 4
CALORIES PER PORTION: 155 (640 kJ)
PROTEIN CONTENT PER PORTION: 7 grams
PREPARATION & COOKING TIME: 2¼ hours

2½ tablespoons olive or sunflower oil
2 cups finely chopped onions
1⅓ cups finely chopped turnips
½ cup roughly chopped tomatoes
2 pints water
¼ teaspoon star aniseed
2 teaspoons brewer's yeast
salt
freshly ground pepper
2 eggs, separated
¼ cup thinly sliced mushrooms
3 tablespoons corn kernels
1-2 Chinese cabbage (pak choy) leaves, finely shredded

Heat 2 tablespoons of the oil in a pan over gentle heat, add the onions and turnips and cook over gentle heat for about 15 minutes, stirring well, until the vegetables are just about to turn color. Add the tomatoes and stir until reduced to a pulp. Pour in the water, add the aniseed and brewer's yeast and season with salt and pepper. Bring the soup to a boil, then lower the heat and simmer gently for about 1 hour.

Measure the stock and make it up to 2 pints with extra water. Strain it, pressing the vegetables against the sides of the strainer to extract as much flavor and goodness as possible, without actually rubbing the vegetables through. Leave the soup until slightly cooled, then clarify with the egg whites (see the instructions for this under Clear stock on page 34).

Meanwhile, heat the remaining oil in a separate pan, add the mushrooms and cook them until soft and shiny. Drain on paper towels. Add the corn to the soup, bring it to a boil, then lower the heat and simmer for 5 minutes before adding the mushrooms and cabbage. Beat the egg yolks to a smooth cream and stir them very slowly into the soup. Simmer it for a few moments until the egg yolks have set into fine strings. Adjust the seasoning, pour into warmed soup bowls and serve.

Corn, Chinese cabbage, mushroom and trailing egg soup

Serves 4
CALORIES PER PORTION: 865 (3620 kJ)
PROTEIN CONTENT PER PORTION: 30 grams
PREPARATION & COOKING TIME: 20 minutes

2½ cups Brown vegetable stock
¾ cup cooked corn kernels
1 cup thinly sliced button mushrooms
1 tablespoon soy sauce
1 teaspoon lemon juice
¼ teaspoon monosodium glutamate — MSG — (optional)
2 eggs, well beaten
1 cup finely shredded Chinese cabbage (pak choy)
salt

Bring the stock to a boil, add the corn and mushrooms and simmer for 4 minutes. Stir in the soy sauce, lemon juice and MSG (if using), then dribble the eggs very slowly into the boiling liquid, stirring continuously, so that they form thin shreds.

Add the Chinese cabbage and cook for a further 2 minutes or until the cabbage is thoroughly hot and the soup has returned to a boil. Add a little salt, if necessary, and serve immediately.

Leek, tomato and potato soup with saffron

Serves 4
CALORIES PER PORTION: 205 (865 kJ)
PROTEIN CONTENT PER PORTION: 7 grams
PREPARATION & COOKING TIME: 45 minutes

3 tablespoons butter
1 cup diced potatoes
4 cups halved and thinly sliced leeks
2 tablespoons wholewheat flour
1¼ cups milk
1¼ cups water
2 generous pinches of saffron strands soaked in a little water for 10 minutes to soften
1 cup coarsely chopped ripe tomatoes
salt
freshly ground pepper

Melt the butter in a saucepan over gentle heat, then put in the potatoes and cook for 5 minutes without allowing them to brown. Add the leeks and continue cooking for 10 minutes without allowing them to color. Stir the vegetables from time to time — they should be gently 'stewed' in the butter rather than fried. Now sprinkle in the flour and stir well, then pour on the milk and the water. Bring the soup to a boil, stirring it frequently. Add the saffron in its soaking water, lower the heat and let the soup simmer for about 15 minutes.

Meanwhile, cook the tomatoes down to a pulp over low heat, adding a little water, if necessary. Strain the pulp to remove the skin and seeds and keep the purée hot until the soup is ready to serve. Season the soup with salt and pepper, pour it into warmed soup bowls, swirl a little tomato purée into each bowl and serve.

Cream of asparagus soup

Use as much fresh asparagus in this recipe as you can — according to availability and price; ½ lb is about the minimum.

Serves 4
CALORIES PER PORTION: 350 (1457 kJ)
PROTEIN CONTENT PER PORTION: 10 grams
PREPARATION & COOKING TIME: 45 minutes

2 tablespoons butter
3 tablespoons all-purpose flour
2½ cups milk
1 lb trimmed asparagus
salt
freshly ground pepper
⅔ cup heavy cream (optional)

Melt the butter over gentle heat, then sprinkle in the flour. Cook for about 1 minute, stirring continuously, but do not allow it to brown. Remove the pan from the heat and gradually add the milk, stirring well between each addition. Return the pan to the heat, increase the heat and bring to a boil, stirring all the time until the sauce thickens. Transfer the soup to a double boiler. Cover the surface with a sheet of buttered wax paper and cook over a gentle heat for about 20 minutes to let the soup mature.

Meanwhile, cook the asparagus in enough boiling, salted water to come halfway up the stalks for 10-15 minutes, or until very tender. Drain off and measure the cooking water; make this up to ⅔ cup with a little extra water, then stir this into the sauce in the pan.

Cut the tips off the eight best asparagus spears and reserve them before stirring the rest of the asparagus into the sauce. Work the soup through a blender, then rub it through a strainer to make it really smooth. If you do not have a blender, mash the asparagus well with a fork before rubbing it through the strainer.

Return the soup to a clean pan to reheat, then season with salt and pepper and serve with two of the reserved asparagus tips in each bowl. Add a swirl of cream to each bowl before adding the asparagus tips, if desired.

Tomato and orange soup

Serves 4
CALORIES PER PORTION: 145 (602 kJ)
PROTEIN CONTENT PER PORTION: 2.5 grams
PREPARATION & COOKING TIME: 45 minutes

4 tablespoons butter
1 cup finely chopped onion
2 lb ripe tomatoes, quartered
thinly pared rind of ¼ orange
¼ cup orange juice
1 small bay leaf
1 teaspoon raw brown sugar (optional)
salt
freshly ground pepper

Melt the butter in a pan over gentle heat, add the onion and cook until transparent but not browned. Add the tomatoes, orange rind and juice, and the bay leaf. Bring the soup to a boil, lower the heat and simmer for 15 minutes, or until the tomatoes have turned into a pulp. Rub through a strainer and return the purée to a clean pan. Bring to a boil, add the sugar, if using, then season the soup with salt and pepper. Serve hot with freshly made wholewheat toast.

Note: If the tomatoes do not make quite enough pulp and juice, or if the purée is too thick, add enough water to make it up to 2 pints before bringing the soup back to a boil.

Pumpkin soup

Serves 6
CALORIES PER PORTION: 45 (190 kJ)
PROTEIN CONTENT PER PORTION: 1 gram
PREPARATION & COOKING TIME: 1 hour

2 tablespoons butter, or olive or sunflower oil
3 cups peeled and diced pumpkin
1 cup finely chopped onion
¼ teaspoon ground cinnamon
grated rind of ¼ orange
2 pints water
salt
freshly ground pepper

Melt the butter in a pan over gentle heat and add the pumpkin and onion. Cook the vegetables for about 10 minutes, stirring occasionally, until they are just beginning to brown, then sprinkle in the cinnamon. Add the orange rind and continue cooking for a few more minutes. Stir in the water and bring it to a boil, then lower the heat and let the soup simmer for 20-30 minutes, or until the pieces of pumpkin are soft and tender. Pour the soup into a blender and work it until smooth, then rub the purée through a strainer to remove any strings — or just rub the soup through a strainer.

Return the soup to a clean pan, season with salt and pepper and bring back to a boil. Serve with slices of dark Rye bread.

Four deliciously creamy, filling soups. From the left: Tomato and orange soup, garnished with fresh basil leaves; Cream of asparagus, also good served chilled; Pumpkin soup flavored with cinnamon and Front: Corn chowder – be sure to use freshly-bought fennel seeds or the taste will be very bland

Corn chowder

Serves 4
CALORIES PER PORTION: 410 (1715 kJ)
PROTEIN CONTENT PER PORTION: 18 grams
PREPARATION & COOKING TIME: 35 minutes

4 tablespoons butter
½ onion, thinly sliced
1⅓ cups diced potatoes
½ teaspoon fennel seeds
salt
freshly ground pepper
2 pints milk
½ cup dried skimmed milk
¾ cup corn kernels
½ cup grated Cheddar cheese

Melt the butter in a pan over gentle heat and cook the onion and potatoes for 5 minutes without letting them color. Stir them occasionally to prevent them sticking. Add the fennel seeds and season with salt and pepper, then stir in the milk. Lower the heat and let the soup simmer for 20 minutes, stirring it occasionally. Put the soup through a blender and work until smooth. Add the dried milk and blend for a few moments longer until dissolved; otherwise, rub the soup through a strainer, then stir in the dried milk.

Return the purée to a clean pan, add the corn kernels and bring it slowly back to a boil. Take the pan off the heat, sprinkle in the cheese and stir until it has melted. Serve in warmed soup bowls with wholewheat croûtons.

Cream of pea soup

Serves 4
CALORIES PER PORTION: 365 (1522 kJ)
PROTEIN CONTENT PER PORTION: 12 grams
PREPARATION & COOKING TIME: 30 minutes if using frozen peas; 1 hour if using fresh peas

8 tablespoons butter
4 cups shelled fresh or frozen peas
1 cup finely chopped onion
⅔ cup water
2½ cups milk
salt
freshly ground pepper

Melt the butter in a pan over gentle heat and add the peas, onion and water. Cook over moderate heat until the peas are just tender; the exact time will depend on whether fresh or frozen peas are used — fresh peas will take at least 25 minutes. Stir in the milk, salt and pepper, increase the heat and bring the soup to a boil, stirring all the time.

Pour the soup into a blender and work it to a smooth purée, or rub it through a strainer. Return the soup to a clean pan and bring to a boil again. Thin it down with a little extra hot milk if necessary to make it up to 2 pints. Adjust the seasoning and serve with wholewheat croûtons. Do not overcook this soup or the flavor will be spoiled.

Cream of leek soup

Serves 4
CALORIES PER PORTION: 385 (1615 kJ)
PROTEIN CONTENT PER PORTION: 10.5 grams
PREPARATION & COOKING TIME: 55 minutes

8 tablespoons butter
1 lb leeks, washed, cut in half lengthwise, then sliced
2 tablespoons wholewheat flour
2 pints milk
salt
freshly ground pepper

Melt the butter over low heat, add the leeks and cook them very gently for about 15 minutes until they are just tender. Take care that they do not brown or this will spoil the flavor of the finished soup. Sprinkle in the flour and stir until the leeks are evenly coated.

Remove the pan from the heat and gradually add the milk, stirring well between each addition. Return the pan to the heat and bring the soup to a boil, stirring all the time until it thickens.

Pour the soup into a blender, and work until smooth, then rub it through a strainer to remove any remaining fibers, or mash the cooked leeks thoroughly with a fork or the back of a spoon before rubbing them through the strainer. Return the soup to a double boiler and bring it back to a boil. Cover the surface with a sheet of buttered wax paper and allow it to stand for about 10 minutes to mature before seasoning with salt and pepper. Serve with wholewheat croûtons.

Artichoke soup

Serves 4
CALORIES PER PORTION: 125 (522 kJ)
PROTEIN CONTENT PER PORTION: 4 grams
PREPARATION & COOKING TIME: 45 minutes

2 tablespoons butter
1 cup finely chopped onion
1 lb Jerusalem artichokes, thinly sliced
1 pint water
1 pint milk
salt
freshly ground pepper

Melt the butter over low heat, and cook the onion in it until transparent, taking care that it does not color. Add the artichokes and cook them gently for about 5 minutes, then pour on the water, bring it to a boil, lower the heat and simmer the vegetables for 15 minutes. Pour the soup into a blender and work to a smooth purée or rub the cooked vegetables through a strainer. Return the purée to a clean pan, add the milk and bring the soup back to a boil. Season with salt and pepper and serve with wholewheat croûtons.

Cream of cauliflower soup

Serves 6
CALORIES PER PORTION: 260 (1075 kJ)
PROTEIN CONTENT PER PORTION: 8 grams
PREPARATION & COOKING TIME: 45 minutes

1 ¼ lb head cauliflower, broken into florets, but including the chopped stem and some of the leaves
8 tablespoons butter
¼ cup finely chopped onion
2 pints milk
2 egg yolks
salt
freshly ground pepper

Cook the cauliflower over gentle heat in about ¾ inch water for about 15 minutes, or until just tender, adding a very little extra water if necessary. While it is cooking, melt the butter in a separate pan over gentle heat and fry the onion until transparent. Do not allow it to color. Drain the cauliflower, reserving 2 tablespoons of the cooking water. Add this to the onion with the cooked cauliflower, stir well, then pour the vegetables into a blender.

Add the milk and egg yolks and work until quite smooth; season with salt and pepper, then rub the soup through a strainer to remove any remaining fibers. If you do not have a blender, rub the vegetables through a food mill or twice through a strainer.

Return the soup to a clean pan and reheat, stirring continuously, but do not allow it to boil or the egg yolks will curdle. As soon as the soup thickens, pour it into a warmed tureen or bowls and serve garnished with croûtons.

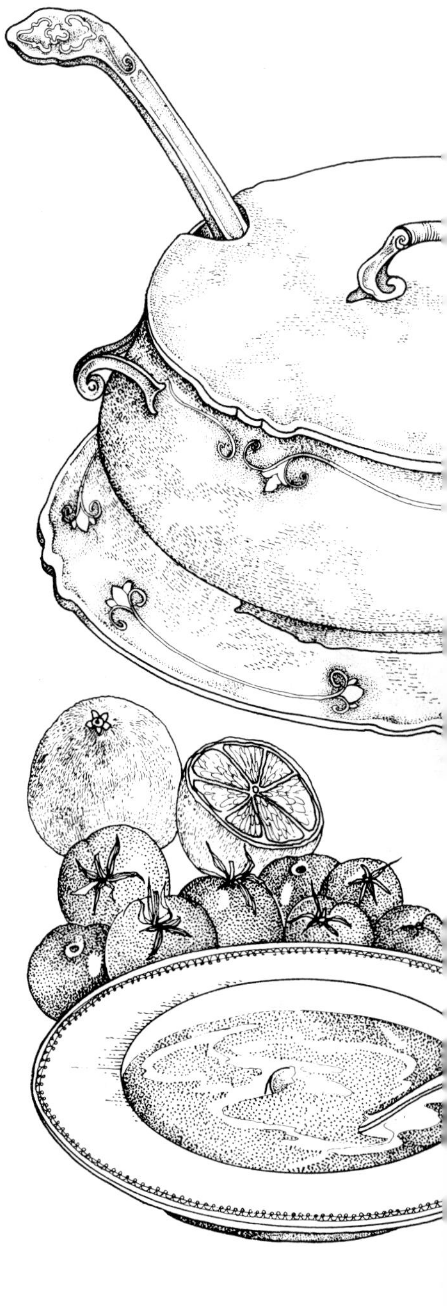

Chestnut soup

Serves 4
CALORIES PER PORTION: 435 (1815 kJ)
PROTEIN CONTENT PER PORTION: 5 grams
PREPARATION & COOKING TIME: 2 hours

1 lb whole chestnuts
2 tablespoons butter
½ cup finely chopped onion
2 pints white vegetable stock
salt
freshly ground pepper
⅔ cup sour cream
a little freshly grated nutmeg

Slit the chestnuts down one side and bake them in a 400°F oven for 10-15 minutes until the skins are crisp. Carefully remove the skins and the membranes covering the nuts, holding the nuts in a dish towel to protect your hands.

Melt the butter in a pan over gentle heat and cook the onion until just golden brown before pouring on the stock. Stir well, add the skinned nuts and simmer for 20-30 minutes, or until the nuts are tender. Rub them, with their cooking liquid, through a strainer or food mill, or work to a purée in a blender. Rub this again through a strainer until it is really smooth, then season it with salt and pepper.

Reheat the soup a little and pour into warmed soup bowls. Swirl a little sour cream in the center of each and sprinkle with grated nutmeg just before serving.

Walnut soup

Serves 4
CALORIES PER PORTION: 350 (1455 kJ)
PROTEIN CONTENT PER PORTION: 6 grams
PREPARATION & COOKING TIME: 1 ¼ hours

1 cup shelled fresh walnuts
2 tablespoons butter
½ cup finely chopped onion
2 tablespoons wholewheat flour
2 pints white vegetable stock
1 bay leaf
1 small strip of lemon rind
salt
freshly ground pepper
2 walnuts, halved

Put the walnuts in a pan, add enough water to cover, and bring it to a boil. Lower the heat and simmer the nuts for 5 minutes, then remove the pan from the heat. While they are still hot, carefully remove any traces of outer skin from the nut kernels, using a sharp-pointed knife. If the nuts are still hot the skin is much easier to remove, so take them out of the pan one by one with a slotted spoon as you peel them. Work the peeled nuts in a blender or nutmill until they are very finely ground.

Melt the butter over gentle heat, add the onion and cook until transparent, taking care that it does not color. Sprinkle in the flour and continue cooking for 1-2 minutes, stirring continuously. Remove the pan from the heat and gradually add the stock, stirring well between each addition. Return the pan to the heat and bring the soup to a boil, stirring all the time until it thickens. Add the bay leaf and lemon rind, then lower the heat and simmer for about 10 minutes, removing the lemon rind if its flavor becomes too pronounced.

Add the walnuts and simmer for 10 minutes more, then rub the soup through a medium-meshed strainer. Season it with salt and pepper and serve; garnish each portion with a halved walnut, or croûtons.

To emphasize the walnut flavor, fry the croûtons in a mixture of walnut oil and butter. You need a blender or nutmill to make this soup.

Cheese and onion soup

Serves 4
CALORIES PER PORTION: 465 (1937 kJ)
PROTEIN CONTENT PER PORTION: 16 grams
PREPARATION & COOKING TIME: 40 minutes

2 pints white vegetable stock
4 tablespoons butter
1 cup finely chopped onion
7 tablespoons wholewheat flour
1 ½ cups crumbled or coarsely grated Cheddar or Stilton cheese
1 bay leaf
salt
freshly ground pepper

Pour the stock into a pan and heat to just below boiling point. Melt the butter in a separate pan over gentle heat, add the onion and cook it until it is transparent. Sprinkle in the flour and stir until the onion is well coated, then cook for a further 1-2 minutes, stirring all the time. Add the cheese, stir until melted and well absorbed into the mixture, then gradually add the hot stock and continue stirring until the soup thickens.

Add the bay leaf, season with salt and pepper, then transfer the soup to a double boiler. Cover the surface with a sheet of buttered wax paper, then heat the soup gently for about 20 minutes so that it matures. Discard the bay leaf, adjust the seasoning and serve with fresh wholewheat biscuits or crisp toast.

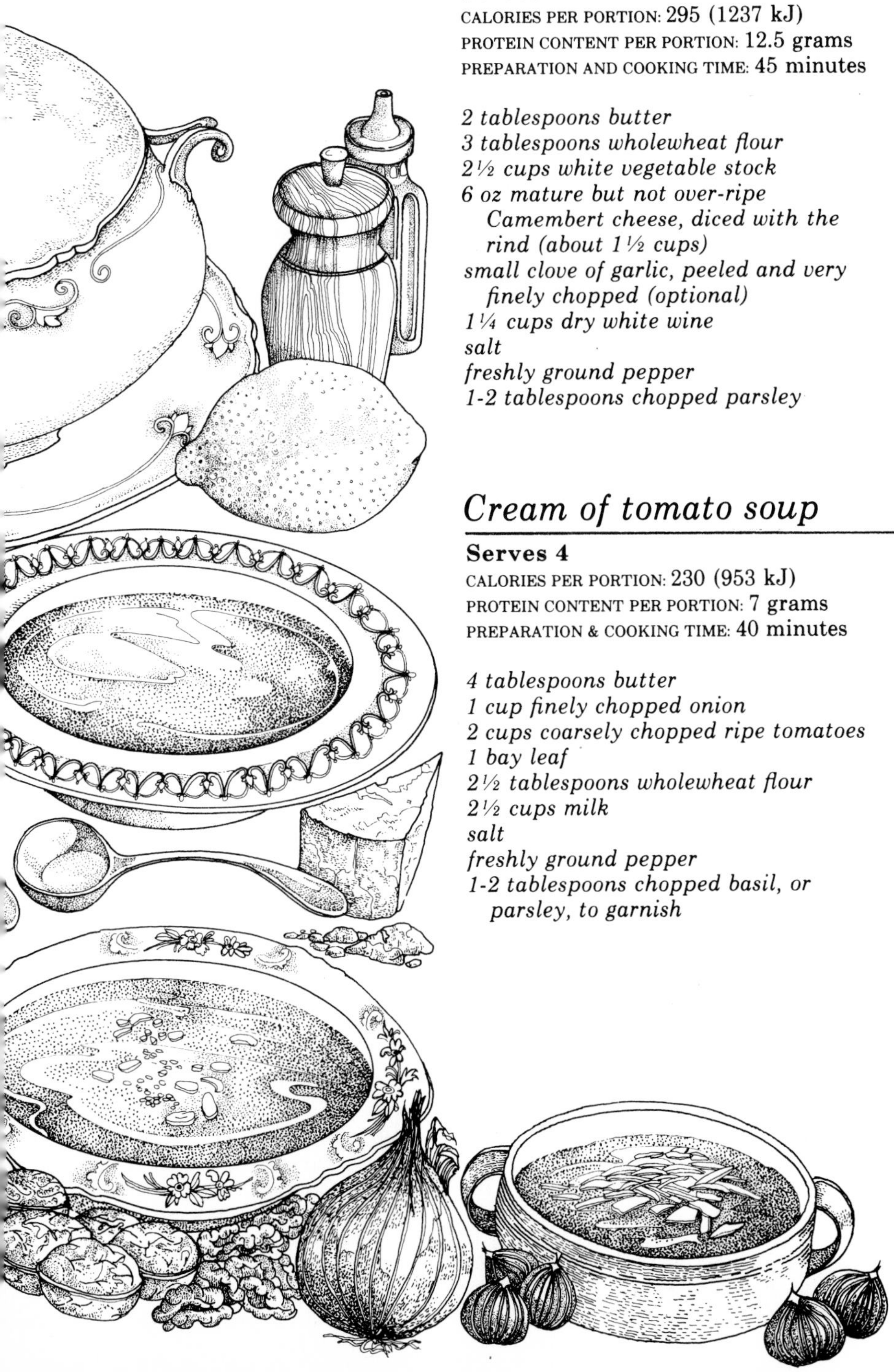

Camembert soup

Serves 4
CALORIES PER PORTION: 295 (1237 kJ)
PROTEIN CONTENT PER PORTION: 12.5 grams
PREPARATION AND COOKING TIME: 45 minutes

2 tablespoons butter
3 tablespoons wholewheat flour
2 ½ cups white vegetable stock
6 oz mature but not over-ripe Camembert cheese, diced with the rind (about 1 ½ cups)
small clove of garlic, peeled and very finely chopped (optional)
1 ¼ cups dry white wine
salt
freshly ground pepper
1-2 tablespoons chopped parsley

Melt the butter in a pan over gentle heat, then sprinkle in the flour. Cook for 1-2 minutes, stirring continuously, then remove the pan from the heat and gradually add the stock, stirring well between each addition. Return the pan to the heat and bring to a boil, stirring all the time until the sauce thickens.

Lower the heat, add the cheese with the garlic, if used, and stir briskly until the cheese has melted. Add the wine and simmer for about 10 minutes until the alcohol has evaporated and only the flavor of the wine is left. Season with salt and pepper, then strain the soup into a large bowl. Skim off any excess fat, pour the soup into warmed bowls, sprinkle with parsley and serve hot with wholewheat biscuits.

Cream of tomato soup

Serves 4
CALORIES PER PORTION: 230 (953 kJ)
PROTEIN CONTENT PER PORTION: 7 grams
PREPARATION & COOKING TIME: 40 minutes

4 tablespoons butter
1 cup finely chopped onion
2 cups coarsely chopped ripe tomatoes
1 bay leaf
2 ½ tablespoons wholewheat flour
2 ½ cups milk
salt
freshly ground pepper
1-2 tablespoons chopped basil, or parsley, to garnish

Melt half the butter in a pan over gentle heat, add the onion and cook until transparent, taking care not to let it color. Add the tomatoes and bay leaf and cook down into a pulp.

Meanwhile, melt the rest of the butter in a separate pan, sprinkle in the flour and cook for 1-2 minutes, stirring continuously. Remove the pan from the heat and gradually stir in the milk, then return the pan to the heat, season, and bring to a boil, stirring all the time until the mixture thickens. Transfer the soup to a double boiler and cook gently for about 20 minutes.

Remove the pan containing the tomatoes from the heat, discard the bay leaf and work the pulp in a blender, or rub it through a strainer. Return the purée to a clean pan and bring it to a boil, then stir the bubbling purée into the gently simmering soup. Adjust the seasoning, sprinkle with basil or parsley and serve at once.

Note: Do not allow this soup to stand for long before serving or it will separate and the acid in the tomatoes will curdle the milk. If it does, work it in a blender, or rub through a strainer until smooth, then reheat.

Cream of celery soup

Serves 4
CALORIES PER PORTION: 265 (1103 kJ)
PROTEIN CONTENT PER PORTION: 9 grams
PREPARATION & COOKING TIME: 1 hour

4 tablespoons butter
4 cups chopped celery
1 cup finely chopped onion
1 tablespoon wholewheat flour
2 pints milk
½ teaspoon salt
freshly ground pepper
⅔ cup heavy cream
a sprinkling of paprika

Melt the butter over gentle heat, add the celery and onion and cook for 20 minutes, stirring occasionally to make sure the vegetables cook evenly without browning. This should concentrate the flavors, rather than actually fry the vegetables. Sprinkle in the flour and cook for 1-2 minutes, stirring continuously until the vegetables are well coated.

Remove the pan from the heat and gradually add the milk, stirring well between each addition. Return the pan to the heat and bring to a boil, stirring all the time until the mixture thickens. Season with salt and pepper.

Transfer the soup to a double boiler. Cover the surface with a sheet of buttered wax paper and cook very gently for at least 20 minutes to let the soup mature.

Pour the soup into a blender and work it until smooth, or mash the celery with a fork, then rub the soup through a strainer. Return the soup to the pan, adjust the seasoning and bring to a boil before serving with a swirl of cream and a sprinkling of paprika on each bowl.

Cream of onion soup

Serves 4
CALORIES PER PORTION: 270 (1120 kJ)
PROTEIN CONTENT PER PORTION: 9 grams
PREPARATION & COOKING TIME: 1 hour 10 minutes

4 tablespoons butter
2 medium onions, thinly sliced
2½ tablespoons wholewheat flour
2 pints milk
1 bay leaf
pinch of freshly grated nutmeg
salt
freshly ground pepper

Melt the butter over gentle heat, add the onions and cook them until transparent, taking care that they do not brown. Sprinkle in the flour and cook for 1-2 minutes, stirring all the time until the onions are well coated. Remove the pan from the heat and gradually add the milk, stirring well between each addition. Return the pan to the heat, increase the heat and bring the soup to a boil, stirring all the time until it thickens. Lower the heat and cook the soup for about 5 minutes before pouring it into a blender and working it to a smooth purée, or rubbing through a strainer.

Return the soup to a double boiler and add the bay leaf, nutmeg and salt and pepper. Cover the surface with a sheet of buttered wax paper and cook over gentle heat for 20 minutes longer to allow the soup to mature. Discard the bay leaf, adjust the seasoning, pour into warmed soup bowls and serve with croûtons.

Jellied consommé

Serves 4
CALORIES PER PORTION: 150 (622 kJ)
PROTEIN CONTENT PER PORTION: 5 grams
PREPARATION & CHILLING TIME: 4¼ hours

2 pints clear brown vegetable stock (page 34), including 1 cup mushrooms in the making
salt
freshly ground black pepper
1 tablespoon agar-agar
¼ cup sherry (optional)
1-2 tablespoons chopped parsley
4 lemon wedges

Make up the stock, adjust the seasoning and allow it to cool, then sprinkle on the agar-agar. Bring the stock back to a boil, stirring briskly all the time, then lower the heat and allow the stock to simmer for 5 minutes. Put it aside to cool. Add the sherry, then chill the consommé until jellied. Chop it up or scoop out small chunks of jellied consommé and pile it into four individual glass bowls. Sprinkle with parsley and serve with lemon wedges and thin brown toast.

Chilled avocado soup

Serves 4
CALORIES PER PORTION: 580 (2422 kJ)
PROTEIN CONTENT PER PORTION: 15 grams
PREPARATION & CHILLING TIME: 1½ hours

4 large avocados, weighing about 1¾ lb altogether
juice of 1 lemon
1 pint white vegetable stock
1 pint plain yogurt, or cold Béchamel sauce (page 196)
salt
freshly ground pepper

Peel the avocados, cut them into chunks and mix them with the lemon juice. Put them, with the stock and the yogurt or Béchamel sauce, into a blender and work to a smooth purée, or rub through a food mill or nylon strainer. Season with salt and pepper and chill thoroughly before serving with thin slices of wholewheat bread and butter, or thin brown toast.

Note: The avocados will cause this soup to discolor slightly if it is left to chill for more than 2 hours, so don't be tempted to make this soup the night before. If the surface does discolor, stir well before serving.

Perfect for a summer's eve, chilled soups that are subtle and refreshing. Top: an Orange and lemon soup, served with thin Almond cookies. Right: chilled Avocado soup – this can be made with a base of either yogurt or Béchamel sauce. Below: Jellied consommé made from a rich Brown vegetable stock, garnished with lemon

Chilled orange and lemon soup

Serves 4
CALORIES PER PORTION: 60 (252 kJ)
PROTEIN CONTENT PER PORTION: 0.5 grams
PREPARATION & CHILLING TIME: 3 hours

½ lb cooking apples
½ lb pears
2 pints plus ¼ cup water
2 inch strip of lemon rind
2 inch strip of orange rind
2 tablespoons wholewheat flour
½ teaspoon grated orange rind
2 tablespoons lemon juice
¼ cup orange juice
a little sugar
4 thin orange slices

Peel the apples and pears and cut them into chunks. Put these with the cores in a pan with 2 pints of water. Bring to a boil, add the strips of lemon and orange rind, then lower the heat and simmer the soup for 20 minutes or until the fruit is tender and pulpy. Remove the pieces of rind and rub the soup through a strainer or a food mill. Mix the flour with the remaining cold water to make a thin cream and stir it into the purée. Return it to a clean pan, bring back to a boil, then lower the heat and simmer the soup for a further 5 minutes.

Allow it to cool slightly, then add the grated orange rind, the lemon and orange juice and a little sugar to taste. Leave to chill before refrigerating. Float a thin slice of orange on each bowl and serve with thin Almond cookies.

Gazpacho

Serves 4
CALORIES PER PORTION: 185 (775 kJ)
PROTEIN CONTENT PER PORTION: 7 grams
PREPARATION & CHILLING TIME: 2½ hours

1 lb tomatoes
1¼ cups cold water
2 cloves of garlic, peeled and finely chopped
2 tablespoons olive or sunflower oil
2 tablespoons lemon juice
a little iced water (see method)
salt
freshly ground pepper

Accompaniments
1 cup finely chopped Bermuda onion
1 cup finely chopped red pepper
2 hard-cooked eggs, finely chopped
4 slices of wholewheat bread, crusts removed and cut into slices

Put the tomatoes into a blender with the cold water, garlic, oil and lemon juice and work until smooth. Pour the soup into a bowl, cover it and chill for 2 hours, or until required. Put the onion, pepper, chopped eggs and bread cubes into separate bowls. Make up the chilled soup to 2 pints with a little iced water just before serving, mix well and season with salt and pepper. Float a few crushed ice cubes on top, if liked, and hand the accompaniments separately, so that each guest can make his own choice.

Gazpacho has been photographed, with its accompaniments, as part of a summer buffet party on page 182.

Chilled apple soup

Serves 6
CALORIES PER PORTION: 160 (670 kJ)
PROTEIN CONTENT PER PORTION: 1 gram
PREPARATION & CHILLING TIME: 3 hours

1 lb cooking apples
2 pints plus 1-2 tablespoons water
3 inch strip of lemon rind
½ cup sugar
2 inch stick of cinnamon
2 tablespoons wholewheat flour

Peel and dice the apples and put them, with their cores, into a pan with the 2 pints water, the lemon rind, sugar and cinnamon stick. Bring to a boil. Lower the heat and allow the soup to simmer for 20-30 minutes, or until the apples have cooked down into a pulp. Rub them through a strainer or food mill and return the purée to the rinsed out pan.

Mix together the flour and the remaining 1-2 tablespoons of water in a bowl to make a thin cream and stir it into the purée. Bring the soup to a boil, lower the heat and let it simmer gently for 5 minutes. Strain the soup through a strainer and let it cool before chilling.

Serve the soup thoroughly chilled with Almond or Hazelnut cookies.

Chilled pear soup

Serves 4
CALORIES PER PORTION: 65 (272 kJ)
PROTEIN CONTENT PER PORTION: 1 gram
PREPARATION & CHILLING TIME: 3 hours

1 lb unripe pears
2 pints plus 2 tablespoons water
1 vanilla bean, broken into pieces
2 tablespoons wholewheat flour
a little sugar

Peel and cut the pears into chunks and put them, with their cores, in a pan with the 2 pints of water and the pieces of vanilla bean. Bring to a boil, then lower the heat and simmer the soup for about 30 minutes, or until the pears are tender and pulpy. Remove the pieces of vanilla bean during the cooking if the flavor becomes too pronounced.

Rub the pulp through a strainer or food mill, take out any remaining vanilla bean and return the purée to the pan. Bring the soup back to a boil.

In a bowl, stir the flour into the remaining water to make a thin cream, then add a little of the boiling liquid from the pan. Stir well and pour it back into the pear soup, then lower the heat and let the soup simmer for a further 5 minutes. Sweeten with a little sugar to taste, then allow to get cold before chilling. Serve with Almond or Hazelnut cookies (page 164).

Chilled almond soup

For this soup, you need a blender for crushing the nuts.

Serves 4
CALORIES PER PORTION: 370 (1537 kJ)
PROTEIN CONTENT PER PORTION: 11 grams
PREPARATION & CHILLING TIME: 3 hours

2 cups blanched and skinned almonds
2 pints cold water
½ lb potatoes, boiled in their skins, then peeled
salt
a few drops of rose water

Put the almonds into a blender with the water and work at high speed until the almonds have turned into a smooth purée. Strain this through a medium-fine strainer, pressing the purée against the sides to extract as much of the milk as possible, then strain it again through a very fine strainer so that the milk is completely smooth and not at all gritty. There should be about 2½ cups of almond milk by this time, so make it up to 2 pints with extra water. Put the milk into the blender with the still warm potatoes and work until smooth.

Strain the soup again through a very fine strainer and season it lightly with salt. Add a few drops of rose water — not enough to mask the flavor of the almonds — and serve the soup well chilled with thin Almond or Hazelnut cookies (page 164).

Cucumber and yogurt soup

Serves 4
CALORIES PER PORTION: 70 (295 kJ)
PROTEIN CONTENT PER PORTION: 6 grams
PREPARATION & CHILLING TIME: 3 hours

1 lb cucumber, peeled and thinly sliced
salt
1 pint plain yogurt
2 teaspoons finely chopped fresh mint
½ teaspoon grated lemon rind
1-2 tablespoons lemon juice
1 pint iced water
freshly ground pepper

Spread out the sliced cucumber and sprinkle it with salt. Leave it for 30 minutes to get rid of any bitter juices, then rinse the cucumber slices under running water and pat them dry. Put the cucumber with the yogurt, mint, lemon rind and juice and water into a blender and work until smooth. Season with salt and pepper and chill for about 2 hours. Serve it with warm wholewheat Pitta bread (page 154), as the contrast between the warm bread and the chilled soup is particularly satisfying.

Note: If you do not have a blender, you can chop the drained, sliced cucumber almost to a pulp before mixing it into the rest of the ingredients. It still makes a good soup.

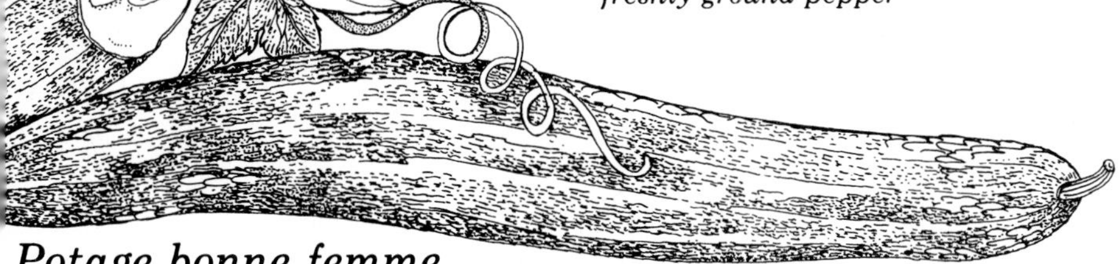

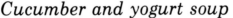

Potage bonne femme

This soup is equally good served hot.

Serves 4
CALORIES PER PORTION: 270 (1122 kJ)
PROTEIN CONTENT PER PORTION: 6.5 grams
PREPARATION & CHILLING TIME: 2 hours

2 to 4 tablespoons butter, depending on the absorbency of the potatoes
¾ lb potatoes, thinly sliced
1 cup finely chopped onion
1 cup halved and sliced leeks
2 cups thinly sliced carrots
2 pints water, or half water and half milk
salt
freshly ground pepper

Melt the butter over gentle heat, add the potatoes and onion and cook for 5 minutes, stirring from time to time to prevent them sticking and burning. Add the leeks, half the carrots and the water, or water and milk; bring to a boil, lower the heat and simmer the soup for 20 minutes, stirring occasionally. Meanwhile, simmer the remaining carrots in a little salted water in a separate pan until tender.

When the main vegetables are cooked, put them with their cooking liquid into a blender and work until smooth, then rub the purée through a strainer; or rub the vegetables and liquid twice through a strainer.

Thin down the purée with a little extra cold water if the soup is too thick, then season well with salt and pepper. Allow to cool before chilling. Pour into individual soup bowls and float the separately cooked, drained carrot slices on the top. Serve with thin slices of wholewheat toast.

Hungarian goulash soup

This is a substantial soup, making enough for 6 large helpings.

CALORIES PER PORTION: 120 (490 kJ)
PROTEIN CONTENT PER PORTION: 4 grams
PREPARATION & COOKING TIME: 1½ hours

2 tablespoons olive or sunflower oil
2 cups finely chopped onions
2 cups thinly sliced carrots, quartered if large
2 cups shredded white or green cabbage
1 cup diced green pepper
2 cloves of garlic, peeled and thinly sliced
2-3 tablespoons paprika
1 tablespoon wholewheat flour
2 pints water
2 teaspoons brewer's yeast
salt
½ lb potatoes, thickly sliced
a little sugar (optional)

Heat the oil in a large pan and fry the onions and carrots until the onions are golden brown and the carrots are just beginning to brown, then add the cabbage, pepper and garlic. Sprinkle in the paprika, then add the flour and mix thoroughly before adding the water. Increase the heat and bring the soup to a boil, stirring all the time. Now add the brewer's yeast and season to taste with salt. Lower the heat and let the soup simmer for about 30 minutes.

Add the potatoes, bring the soup back to a boil and simmer for a further 30 minutes, stirring it from time to time.

Drain the vegetables, reserve the liquid and make it up to 2 pints with water. Return the vegetables to the pan and add the cooking liquid and a little sugar, if liked, to counteract the bitterness of the paprika. Bring the goulash soup back to a boil once more before serving with thick slices of dark Rye bread (page 151).

Note: If you like, you can omit the potatoes from the soup itself, boil them separately, peel them and add one to each serving. Choose a medium-sized potato for each guest.

Borscht

This recipe should make enough for 8 servings.

CALORIES PER PORTION: 185 (771 kJ)
PROTEIN CONTENT PER PORTION: 3 grams
PREPARATION & COOKING TIME: 1½ hours

3 tablespoons olive or sunflower oil
2 cups finely chopped onions
1 cup diced celery
1 cup finely diced carrots
1 lb beets, peeled and cut into thin strips
1 cup diced parsnips
1 cup shredded white cabbage
2 cloves of garlic, peeled and finely chopped
1½ quarts water
2 tablespoons wine vinegar
salt
freshly ground pepper
1 cup finely shredded potatoes
1¼ cups sour cream

Heat the oil in a pan and fry the onions, celery and carrots until golden brown. Add the rest of the ingredients except the potatoes and sour cream and bring the soup to a boil. Put in the shredded potatoes and simmer for 30-40 minutes until the vegetables are tender and the potatoes have broken down and thickened the soup. Adjust the seasoning, if necessary, before serving the soup with a little sour cream swirled into each portion, accompanied by the traditional Pirozhki.

Pirozhki

Makes 12
TOTAL CALORIES: 2100 (8780 kJ)
TOTAL PROTEIN CONTENT: 69 grams
PREPARATION & COOKING TIME: 3 hours

1¾ cups wholewheat flour
1 cake compressed yeast
½ teaspoon raw brown sugar
3 tablespoons warm milk
2 eggs, well beaten
4 tablespoons butter
1 teaspoon salt

The filling
½ cup strained cottage cheese
1 tablespoon finely chopped onion
¾ cup boiled long-grain rice
1 hard-cooked egg, finely chopped
salt
freshly ground pepper
1 egg, well beaten

Put the flour to warm. Mix the yeast with the sugar and milk and keep it in a warm place until it is frothy, then add the beaten eggs. Melt the butter and gently stir it in. Sift the warmed flour with the salt, make a well in the center and pour in the yeast and egg mixture. Knead it well until a smooth dough is formed, adding a little more flour if the dough is too moist. Leave it in a warm place for 20-30 minutes to rise.

Meanwhile, make the filling. Mix together the cottage cheese, onion, rice and hard-cooked egg to make a paste; season this well with salt and pepper.

When the dough has risen to about double its volume, punch it down and turn it out onto a floured board. Roll it out very thinly — to about ¼ inch thickness — and cut out twelve rounds about 3 inches in diameter.

Put a spoonful of the filling in the center of each round and brush the edges with a little beaten egg. Fold over and gently seal each Pirozhki, stretching the dough a little, if necessary. Leave them in a warm place for 10 minutes to prove. Preheat the oven to 350°F and bake on a well buttered baking sheet for about 20 minutes. Alternatively, they can be deep fried in oil and drained on paper towels.

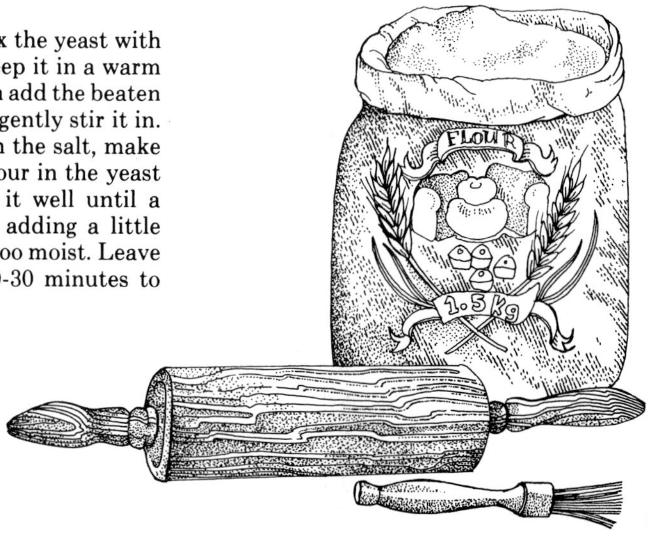

Appetizers

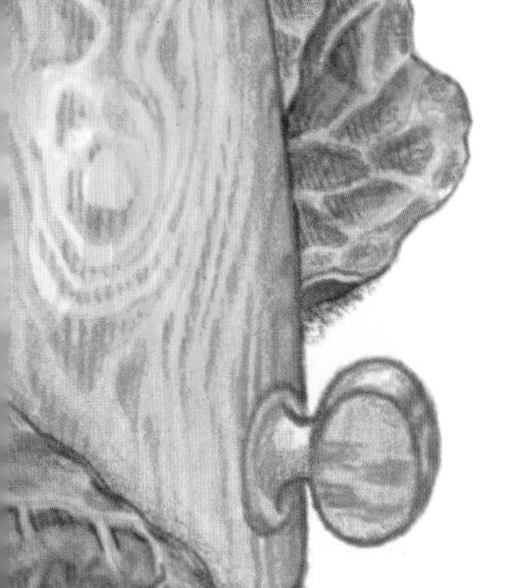

However much skill, inspiration and effort has gone into the main course, it is still the appetizer that creates for your guests the first impression of the meal to come. Whether you choose a soup from the preceding chapter, a simple salad, a soufflé perhaps, or one of the ideas on the following pages, your appetizer sets the scene. It is the prelude or overture to what is in store and must complement and not overshadow the rest of the meal.

In my opinion, an appetizer should be simple. For some people, a bowl of Ratatouille served hot or cold, a bowl of black or green olives or juicy cherry tomatoes, and a crusty loaf still warm from the oven, would be the perfect appetizer . . . If you prefer something a little more elaborate, serve the Salad platter on page 57.

In this chapter, you will find recipes for cold appetizers, followed by hot appetizers and lastly, a selection of savory dips to serve with Crudités.

Stuffed grapefruit

Serves 4
CALORIES PER PORTION: 120 (485 kJ)
PROTEIN CONTENT PER PORTION: 4 grams
PREPARATION & CHILLING TIME: about 1½ hours

2 grapefruit
½ cup shelled walnuts, preferably freshly picked
2 tablespoons finely diced red pepper
2 tablespoons thinly sliced preserved ginger
4 teaspoons Kirsch

Cut each grapefruit in half, and with a grapefruit knife or a similar sharp-pointed knife, carefully cut out the flesh. Remove all the skin and pith from the flesh, divide it into segments and put them into a bowl.

Simmer the walnuts in a little water for 4-5 minutes, take them out of the hot water one at a time with a slotted spoon and remove the skins with a sharp-pointed knife. (It is easier to do this while the nuts are still hot.) Slice the nuts and mix them with the grapefruit segments, red pepper and ginger.

Trim the rim of each grapefruit shell into a zig-zag pattern and fill with the grapefruit mixture. Chill for about 1 hour.

Sprinkle each grapefruit half with a teaspoon of Kirsch before serving.

Melon salad

Serves 4
CALORIES PER PORTION: 265 (1105 kJ)
PROTEIN CONTENT PER PORTION: 9 grams
PREPARATION & CHILLING TIME: 1½ hours

1 lb honeydew melon, peeled, seeded and diced
1 cup finely shredded carrot
1 cup diced Edam cheese
½ cup skinned and chopped tomatoes
⅓ cup finely chopped preserved ginger

The dressing
1 tablespoon lemon juice
3 tablespoons olive or sunflower oil
1 tablespoon finely chopped watercress
1 tablespoon finely chopped parsley
1 teaspoon finely chopped mint
salt
freshly ground pepper
a pinch of cayenne

Mix together the melon, carrot, cheese, tomatoes and ginger. Make the dressing by beating the lemon juice, oil, watercress and herbs together, then season to taste with salt, pepper and cayenne. Pour the dressing over the salad and mix thoroughly. Pile the salad into individual glass bowls and chill for 45 minutes before serving.

Note: This will go well with a Herb or Garlic loaf (page 132), and makes a good light lunch dish.

Stuffed potatoes

Serves 4
CALORIES PER PORTION: 445 (1860 kJ)
PROTEIN CONTENT PER PORTION: 4 grams
PREPARATION & COOKING TIME: 1¼ hours

2 large potatoes, weighing about ½ lb each
⅓ cup thinly sliced pitted or stuffed black or green olives
⅓ cup thinly sliced pickles
1 teaspoon curry powder
8-9 tablespoons Mayonnaise (page 126)
4 lettuce leaves, to garnish

Wrap each potato in foil and bake in a 400°F oven for about 1 hour, or until the potato feels soft when pierced with a fork or thin skewer. Unwrap the potatoes and leave them to cool. Cut each one in half and scoop out the middle, leaving only a thin shell about ¼ inch thick. Roughly chop the cooked potato and mix it with the olives and pickles, reserving a few olive slices for a garnish.

Mix the curry powder into the mayonnaise, then combine this with the potato, olive and pickle mixture. Pile this in the potato skins and garnish with olive slices. Place each potato half on a plate covered with a crisp lettuce leaf for serving.

Vegetables à la grecque

Serves 4
CALORIES PER PORTION: 95 (392 kJ)
PROTEIN CONTENT PER PORTION: 2.5 grams
PREPARATION & COOKING TIME: 45 minutes
CHILLING TIME: 1-2 hours

8 pearl onions, tops and bottoms off
2 tablespoons olive or sunflower oil
1 cup finely chopped onion
2 cups skinned and roughly chopped tomatoes
1 clove of garlic, peeled and finely chopped
1 cup dry white wine
1 tablespoon lemon juice
salt
freshly ground pepper
½ lb head cauliflower, broken into small florets
8 button mushrooms

Drop the pearl onions into boiling water and leave them for 5 minutes, then drain, cool and peel.

Heat the oil and fry the chopped onion over moderate heat until transparent. Add the tomatoes, garlic, wine, lemon juice and a little salt and pepper to taste. Lower the heat and cook gently until the tomatoes make a thick sauce, then add the cauliflower and pearl onions. Simmer the vegetables gently in the sauce for about 10 minutes, or until the cauliflower florets are cooked but still firm. Wipe the button mushrooms and add them for the last 5 minutes. Take out all the vegetables and arrange them in a serving dish.

Boil the sauce to reduce it to about 1 cup, stirring briskly all the time, then adjust the seasoning before pouring it over the vegetables.

Chill well and serve with thinly sliced wholewheat bread spread with a Herb butter (page 198).

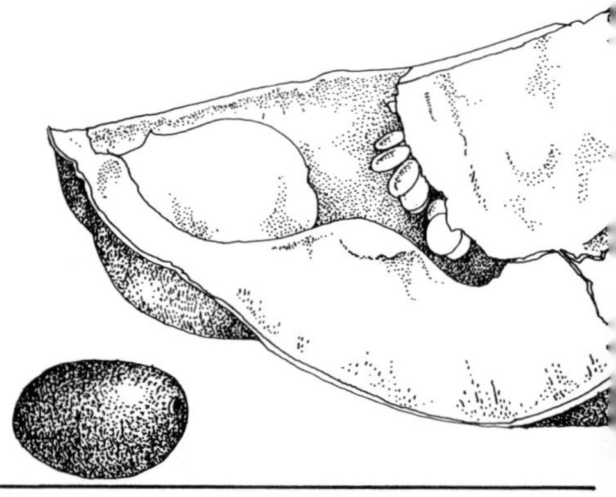

Stuffed avocado

Serves 4
CALORIES PER PORTION: 345 (1400 kJ)
PROTEIN CONTENT PER PORTION: 6 grams
PREPARATION & CHILLING TIME: 1¼-2 hours

2 medium-sized avocados

The filling
1 red pepper, cut into thin strips
½ cup strained cottage cheese
grated rind and juice of 1 lemon
salt
freshly ground pepper
1 small clove of garlic, peeled and very finely chopped
1 egg white

To prepare the filling: pour boiling water over the strips of red pepper and leave them for 5 minutes. Drain, then refresh them by plunging into cold water. Mash the cottage cheese in a bowl with the grated lemon rind, a little salt, pepper and the garlic. Beat the egg white until very stiff, then fold it gently into the cheese mixture.

Drain the red pepper strips, dry well on paper towels, then chop them into small cubes, reserving a few for the garnish. Gently fold them into the cheese mixture. Chill for 1-2 hours. Before using the filling, drain off any clear liquid that has come to the surface.

Just before serving, cut the avocados in half, remove the seeds and brush the insides with lemon juice to stop the flesh turning brown. Pile the cheese mixture in them and garnish each with the reserved diced red peppers.

Lebanese avocado salad

Serves 4
CALORIES PER PORTION: 280 (1170 kJ)
PROTEIN CONTENT PER PORTION: 8.5 grams
PREPARATION & CHILLING TIME: 1¼ hours

1-2 cloves of garlic, peeled and crushed
1¼ cups plain yogurt
2 large avocados, peeled and cut into chunks
2 cups finely diced red peppers

Mix the garlic into the yogurt and gently fold in the avocado chunks. Pile the mixture into a serving dish, sprinkle the red peppers over the top, cover and chill for 1 hour. Serve with warm Pitta bread (page 154).

Asparagus with tarragon mayonnaise

Serves 4
CALORIES PER PORTION: 1000 (4190 kJ)
PROTEIN CONTENT PER PORTION: 32 grams
PREPARATION & COOKING TIME: 30 minutes
CHILLING TIME: 1 hour

2 lb trimmed fresh asparagus
salt
1 pint Mayonnaise (page 126) made with tarragon vinegar
2 tablespoons finely chopped tarragon

Try this as an alternative to serving asparagus with melted butter, or Hollandaise sauce.

Tie the asparagus in bundles, stand them upright in a tall, deep pan and cook them in a little boiling salted water — with the asparagus heads in the steam — for 15-20 minutes, or until the stalks are tender. Drain, cool, untie the asparagus and chill well. Meanwhile, prepare the mayonnaise, using tarragon vinegar instead of wine vinegar, and mix in the chopped tarragon about 1 hour before serving. Serve the asparagus with the mayonnaise handed separately. (You will need finger bowls and napkins.)

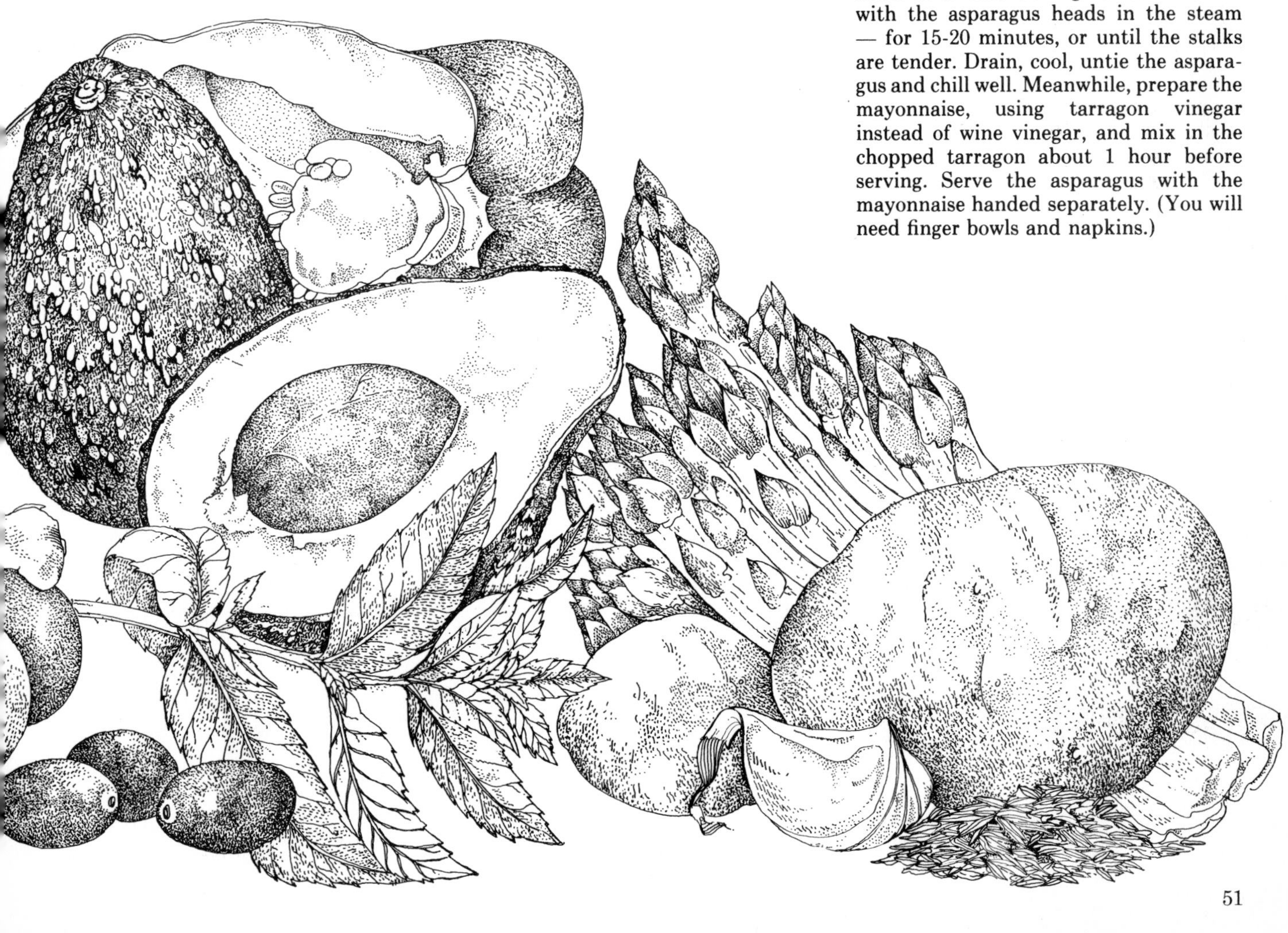

Cauliflower mayonnaise

Serves 4
CALORIES PER PORTION: 970 (4062 kJ)
PROTEIN CONTENT PER PORTION: 4.5 grams
PREPARATION & COOKING TIME: 30 minutes
CHILLING TIME: 20 minutes

1 lb head cauliflower, broken into small florets
1 pint Mayonnaise (page 126)
1-2 tablespoons finely chopped parsley

Cook the cauliflower in a very little boiling salted water until just tender; it should take no more than 10 minutes, as the cauliflower should still be fairly firm. Drain well and allow it to cool.

Dip each floret in the mayonnaise until well coated, then arrange the florets in a mound on a serving dish. Sprinkle with chopped parsley and chill for 15-20 minutes before serving.

Tomato gelatin mold

Serves 4
CALORIES PER PORTION: 105 (427 kJ)
PROTEIN CONTENT PER PORTION: 3 grams
PREPARATION & COOKING TIME: 30 minutes
SETTING TIME: 3 hours

2 tablespoons olive or sunflower oil
1 cup finely chopped onion
salt
freshly ground black pepper
2 lb ripe tomatoes, roughly chopped
1 bay leaf
1 large clove of garlic, peeled and finely chopped
2 teaspoons agar-agar
2 tablespoons cold water
1 teaspoon wine or cider vinegar
grated rind and juice of ½ lemon
bunch of watercress, to garnish

Heat the oil and cook the onion gently until transparent, adding salt and pepper and taking care the onion does not brown. Add the tomatoes, bay leaf and garlic and cook to a pulp over gentle heat — about 15 minutes.

Rub the pulp through a nylon strainer or a food mill, return it to a clean pan, bring to a boil and continue boiling briskly, stirring all the time, until it is reduced to a little less than 2½ cups.

Mix the agar-agar to a smooth cream with the cold water, then slowly pour on the boiling tomato pulp, stirring constantly. Return this to the pan, stir in the vinegar and lemon rind, bring to a boil again and continue boiling for a further 2 minutes. Strain in the lemon juice, then pour into a 2½ cup capacity ring mold. Allow to cool, then place in the refrigerator and chill for at least 3 hours, or until set.

Turn the gelatin out of the mold, fill the center with watercress and serve with freshly made wholewheat toast.

Note: Canned tomatoes may also be used for this recipe. Drain well before heating the tomatoes.

A selection of cold appetizers. Left: Tomato jelly mold, garnished with watercress. Center: Eggs, coated with a tangy Green mayonnaise. Right: Jellied asparagus – serve this with helpings of thick Green mayonnaise and thin slices of wholewheat toast

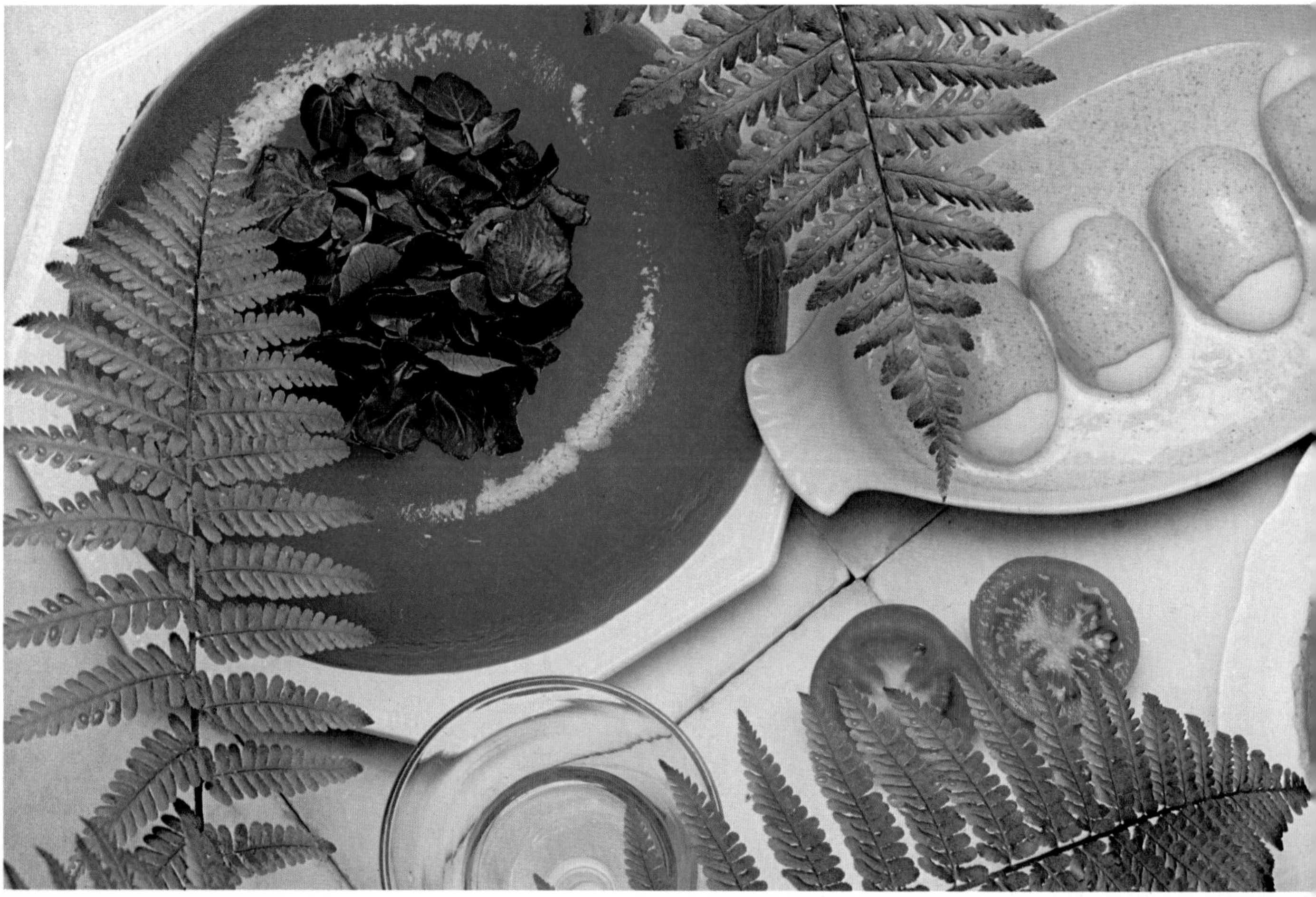

Jellied asparagus

Serves 4
CALORIES PER PORTION: 80 (345 kJ)
PROTEIN CONTENT PER PORTION: 6 grams
PREPARATION & COOKING TIME: 50 minutes
SETTING TIME: 2 hours

¾ lb trimmed fresh asparagus
salt
2½ cups well-flavored clear Brown vegetable stock
2 teaspoons agar-agar
a little green food coloring (optional)

Tie the asparagus in bundles, stand them upright in a tall, deep pan and cook them in a little boiling salted water — with the heads of the asparagus in the steam — for 15-20 minutes, or until tender. Drain off any cooking liquid and make it up to 2½ cups with stock. Pour all but 3 tablespoons of this into a pan and bring to a boil. Mix the agar-agar in a bowl to a smooth cream with the reserved cold stock, then gradually pour the boiling stock onto it, stirring briskly as you do so. Return the stock to the pan and cook it for 2 more minutes.

Place 16 of the asparagus spears on the bottom of a 2½ pint capacity mold, cutting them to fit as necessary and arranging them to radiate from the center. Chop the remaining asparagus into pieces about ¾ inch long, and add these to the stock with just enough green food coloring (if used) to make it an attractive color.

Allow the stock to cool slightly, then carefully ladle into the mold just enough liquid to cover the asparagus spears. Put into the refrigerator to set and, when it has, slowly pour the rest of the stock into the mold and leave it to cool.

When it is completely cold, chill the gelatin in the refrigerator for 2 hours. Turn it out and serve with a Green mayonnaise (page 126).

Note: Canned asparagus may also be used, in which case use the liquid from the can to make up to 2½ cups with stock. Frozen asparagus is also suitable, and should be cooked according to the directions on the package.

Eggs in tarragon gelatin

Serves 4
CALORIES PER PORTION: 200 (845 kJ)
PROTEIN CONTENT PER PORTION: 8 grams
PREPARATION & CHILLING TIME: 2 hours

4 small Oeufs mollets (page 72) or hard-cooked eggs
2 pints clear Brown vegetable stock (page 34)
1 tablespoon dried tarragon
2 teaspoons agar-agar
salt
freshly ground pepper
4 sprigs of tarragon, to garnish

Prepare the Oeufs mollets, if you are using them, and keep them warm in a pan of hot water. Meanwhile, put the stock and dried tarragon into a pan and boil until the liquid is reduced to 2½ cups. Sprinkle in the agar-agar, stir well, then simmer for 5 minutes before seasoning to taste with salt and pepper. Place each egg in a ramekin or cocotte dish, fill each one with strained stock and float a sprig of tarragon on top. Leave to cool, then chill well before serving. Serve with slices of lightly buttered, freshly made wholewheat toast.

Eggs with green mayonnaise

Serves 4
CALORIES PER PORTION: 910 (3805 kJ)
PROTEIN CONTENT PER PORTION: 20 grams
PREPARATION & CHILLING TIME: 1 hour

4 hard-cooked eggs, cut in half lengthwise
4 thin slices of wholewheat bread, halved, crusts removed and lightly buttered
1½ cups chilled Green mayonnaise (page 126)
sprigs of watercress, to garnish

Arrange the halved eggs, cut side down, on the slices of bread, spoon the green mayonnaise over the eggs, then chill for no longer than 40 minutes before serving, garnished with watercress.

Eggs with curry mayonnaise

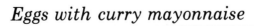

Serves 4
CALORIES PER PORTION: 910 (3805 kJ)
PROTEIN CONTENT PER PORTION: 20 grams
PREPARATION & CHILLING TIME: 1 hour

Follow the above recipe for Eggs with green mayonnaise, but substitute 1½ cups curry mayonnaise (page 127) for the Green mayonnaise.

Spinach ramekins

Serves 4
CALORIES PER PORTION: 250 (1047 kJ)
PROTEIN PER PORTION: 6 grams
PREPARATION & COOKING TIME: 45 minutes
CHILLING TIME: about 1 hour

¼ cup olive or sunflower oil
1 lb spinach, very carefully washed
6 tablespoons heavy cream
2-3 tablespoons lemon juice
1 small clove of garlic, peeled and finely chopped
salt
freshly ground pepper
1 cup finely chopped onion

Pour half the oil into a thick-based pan and add the spinach. Cover the pan and cook the spinach over moderate heat for about 7-8 minutes, or until it is almost tender, shaking the pan frequently to stop the spinach from sticking. Remove the lid, lower the heat and continue cooking until any remaining liquid evaporates and the spinach is tender.

Put the spinach in a blender with the cream, lemon juice, garlic, salt and pepper, and work to a smooth purée. Pour this into four ramekins or small individual dishes and chill well.

Fry the onion in the remaining oil until crisp and golden brown. Drain well on paper towels and allow to cool. Just before serving, garnish each ramekin with a sprinkling of onion and serve with crisp, freshly made wholewheat toast.

Note: If using frozen leaf spinach, cook it according to the directions on the package, then drain it well before blending with the other ingredients.

Leeks vinaigrette

Serves 4
CALORIES PER PORTION: 250 (1040 kJ)
PROTEIN CONTENT PER PORTION: 2 grams
PREPARATION & COOKING TIME: 20 minutes
CHILLING TIME: about 1 hour

1½ lb leeks, trimmed

The dressing
1 tablespoon white wine or cider vinegar
1 tablespoon white wine or lemon juice
6-8 tablespoons olive or sunflower oil
½-1 teaspoon coarsely crushed coriander seeds
1 small clove of garlic, peeled and finely chopped
salt
freshly ground pepper

Cut the trimmed leeks in half lengthwise and lay them in a shallow pan with the white tops all pointing in the same direction. Add boiling salted water partly to cover, place the pan over a moderate heat, cover it and simmer the leeks for 10-15 minutes, or until tender.

Meanwhile, make the vinaigrette dressing. Mix together the vinegar, wine or lemon juice, oil, coriander and garlic and beat until the dressing is cloudy and well mixed. Season it with salt and pepper. Drain the leeks well, pour the dressing over them and chill.

Serve with thin slices of wholewheat bread and butter.

Egg mayonnaise tomatoes

Serves 4
CALORIES PER PORTION: 805 (3367 kJ)
PROTEIN CONTENT PER PORTION: 12 grams
PREPARATION & CHILLING TIME: 1 hour

4 large tomatoes, weighing about ½ lb each, or 8 smaller ones
2 tablespoons finely chopped basil
1½ cups thick Mayonnaise (page 126)
salt
freshly ground pepper
4 hard-cooked eggs, coarsely chopped
4 slices of wholewheat bread, crusts removed and lightly buttered

Cut the tops off the tomatoes at the stem end and scoop out the centres. Turn the tomatoes upside down to drain. Discard the juice and seeds and mash the flesh. Mix the basil into the mayonnaise, then add a little of the tomato flesh, but not enough to make the mayonnaise too thin.

Sprinkle the inside of each tomato shell with salt and pepper, mix the chopped eggs with half the mayonnaise and fill the tomato cases. Stand a tomato on each slice of bread and swirl the remaining mayonnaise over the tops. Chill well before serving.

1. Dip each tomato into boiling water for up to 1 minute.

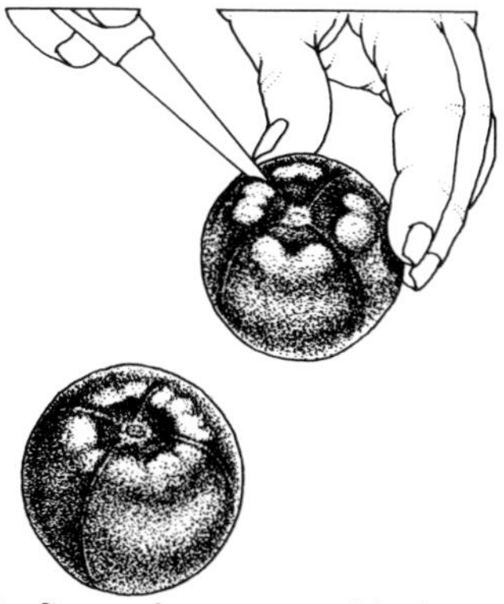

2. Score the tomato skin in quarters, from the top.

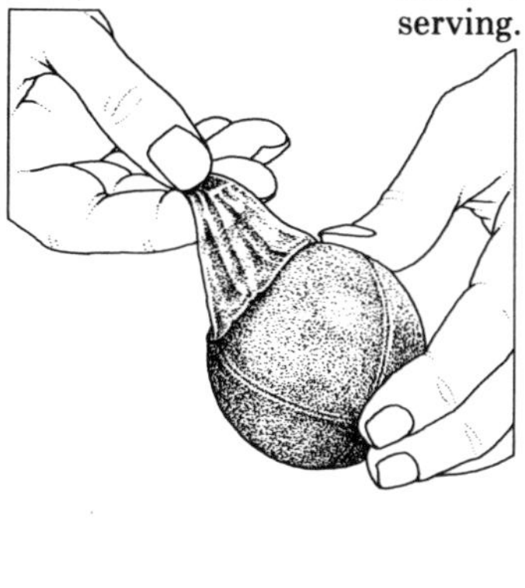

3. Peel off all the tomato skin and discard it.

4. Cut open the tomato and remove all juice and seeds

Tomato sorbet

Serves 4
CALORIES PER PORTION: 100 (417 kJ)
PROTEIN CONTENT PER PORTION: 2.5 grams
PREPARATION & FREEZING TIME: 4½ hours

450 g (1 lb) skinned tomatoes, roughly chopped
25 g (1 oz) finely chopped onion
2 egg yolks
2 tablespoons olive or sunflower oil
salt
1 tablespoon brandy
sprigs of mint or parsley, to garnish

Place all the ingredients, except the parsley, in a blender and work to a smooth purée. Adjust the seasoning, remembering that the flavours will become slightly blander during freezing. Pour the mixture into a suitable china or plastic container, cover tightly and leave in the freezer or freezing compartment of a refrigerator until the edges are set but the centre is still mushy — about 1 hour. Remove from the freezer and stir the mixture well, drawing the sides into the middle, then return it to the freezer and leave it until the edges are set again. Remove and stir the mixture once more, then leave it until frozen hard.

Break the sorbet into small pieces and pile it into individual glasses. Garnish with sprigs of mint or parsley before serving.

Note: If the sorbet has set very hard, remove it from the freezer and leave it in the refrigerator for about 30 minutes to soften before serving.

Curried cheese mousse

Serves 4
CALORIES PER PORTION: 335 (1390 kJ)
PROTEIN CONTENT PER PORTION: 2 grams
PREPARATION & COOKING TIME: 40 minutes
CHILLING TIME: 1½-2 hours

1 tablespoon olive or sunflower oil
1 cup finely chopped onion
2 teaspoons agar-agar
1¼ cups dry white wine
1 cup strained cottage cheese
½ cup boiling water
½ teaspoon curry powder
1 small clove of garlic, peeled and finely chopped
salt
freshly ground pepper
sprigs of watercress, to garnish

Heat the oil and cook the onion over a moderate heat until transparent. Blend the agar-agar with 2 tablespoons of cold water to make a smooth cream, then stir the wine into this and mix thoroughly. Pour this mixture onto the onion and bring to a boil. Lower the heat, simmer for 2 minutes, then pour it into a bowl and place in the refrigerator to set.

Place the set mixture in a blender with the cottage cheese; add the boiling water, curry powder and garlic and work until smooth. Adjust the seasoning. Pour into 4 small dishes, allow to cool, then chill well. Garnish with watercress.

To make onion juice, cut an onion in half across the rings and rotate the halved onion on a glass lemon or orange squeezer. Do not use a wooden one or the flavor will linger.

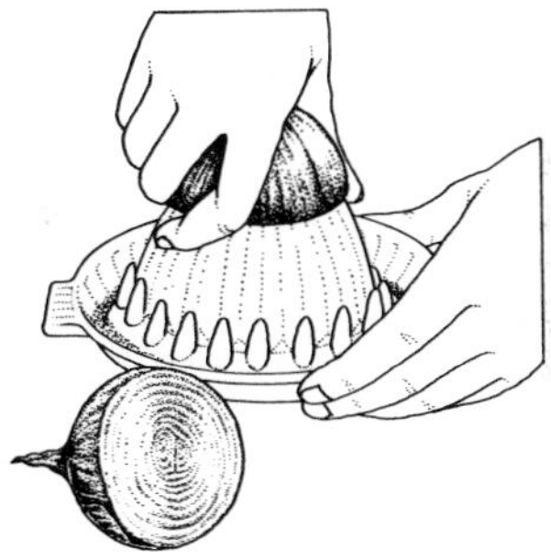

Cheese and tomato mousse

Serves 4
CALORIES PER PORTION: 195 (810 kJ)
PROTEIN CONTENT PER PORTION: 11 grams
PREPARATION & COOKING TIME: 30 minutes
CHILLING TIME: 1 hour

1 lb tomatoes, skinned and cut into eighths
1 cup coarsely grated Cheddar cheese
1 teaspoon finely chopped tarragon
1 teaspoon finely chopped basil
1 cup very finely chopped onion
salt
freshly ground pepper
1¼ cups cold Brown vegetable stock (page 34)
1 tablespoon agar-agar
1 tablespoon wine vinegar
1 teaspoon French-style mustard

Mix together the tomatoes, cheese, herbs and onion and season well with salt and pepper. Stir 6 tablespoons of the stock into the agar-agar to make it into a thin cream, then stir it into the rest of the cold stock. Add the vinegar and mustard and bring it to a boil over a moderate heat, stirring constantly until it thickens. Add the tomato mixture in four helpings, stirring vigorously after each addition to prevent the mousse mixture from setting too soon. When it is thoroughly combined, pour it into a 1-quart capacity soufflé dish and stand it in a shallow bowl of iced water for about 1 hour, until it is cold and firmly set.

Loosen the sides with a knife and carefully ease the mousse free. Unmold it and serve with thin slices of freshly made toast.

Note: Served with a potato salad and a large mixed salad, this makes a very good main course. If preferred, the mousse can be served straight from the bowl.

Egg mayonnaise mousse

Serves 4
CALORIES PER PORTION: 760 (3190 kJ)
PROTEIN CONTENT PER PORTION: 12 grams
PREPARATION & CHILLING TIME: 1 hour

6 hard-cooked eggs
1 teaspoon agar-agar
¼ cup water
1½ cups Mayonnaise (page 126)
1 tablespoon onion juice and pulp (see right)
salt
freshly ground pepper

Chill the eggs in the refrigerator while you mix the agar-agar with the water to a thin cream. Bring this to a boil in a small pan, stirring briskly. Pour half the mayonnaise into a blender, then gradually pour in the dissolved agar-agar as you blend. When the mixture is completely smooth, add it to the rest of the mayonnaise. Stir in the onion juice and pulp and season with salt and pepper. Gently fold the eggs into the mixture and pour it into a 2 pint capacity soufflé dish. Chill well before serving, garnished with watercress, with thin slices of wholewheat toast.

Salad platter

The salad platter consists of seven dishes, all with contrasting flavors and textures. Served together, the dishes combine to make an impressive appetizer to a dinner party for 8. Alternatively, serve it as an appetizer for a summer lunch for 4-6, depending on appetite.

Stuffed tomatoes

TOTAL CALORIES: 345 (1440 kJ)
TOTAL PROTEIN CONTENT: 16 grams
PREPARATION & CHILLING TIME: 2½ hours

8 firm tomatoes, weighing about 1 lb altogether
6 basil leaves, finely chopped
2 tablespoons plain yogurt
½ teaspoon lemon juice
¾ cup fresh wholewheat breadcrumbs
salt
freshly ground pepper
basil leaves, to garnish

Cut off the top of each tomato and scoop out the pulp, discarding the seeds and fibrous cores. Cut a very thin slice from the base of each tomato so that it will stand firmly, taking care not to make a hole through which the filling can run out. Turn the tomatoes upside down to drain.

Mix together the tomato pulp, basil, yogurt, lemon juice and enough breadcrumbs to make a soft purée. Season this with salt and pepper, then fill the prepared tomato cases. Replace the tops as 'lids' and chill well. Garnish each one with fresh basil leaves just before serving.

Oeufs à l'indienne

TOTAL CALORIES: 1240 (5170 kJ)
TOTAL PROTEIN CONTENT: 34 grams
PREPARATION TIME: 40 minutes

4 hard-cooked eggs, cut in half lengthwise
3-4 tablespoons thick Mayonnaise (page 126)
1 teaspoon finely ground cumin seeds
1 small clove of garlic, peeled and crushed
a little lemon juice — see recipe
½ cup long grain rice
1 teaspoon ground turmeric (optional)
sprigs of watercress, to garnish

Remove the yolks from the halved eggs and mash them with enough mayonnaise, cumin and garlic to make a smooth, fairly firm paste. Add a little lemon juice to taste, but not enough to make the mixture too thin.

Cook the rice in plenty of boiling salted water with the turmeric added, if used. Drain the rice well, rinse under running cold water, then drain it again and leave to cool.

Using a pastry bag fitted with a rose nozzle, pipe the yolk mixture into the halved egg whites, or spoon in the mixture with a teaspoon.

Serve the eggs arranged on a bed of rice and garnished with sprigs of watercress.

Marinated mushrooms

TOTAL CALORIES: 1050 (4400 kJ)
TOTAL PROTEIN CONTENT: 2 grams
PREPARATION & CHILLING TIME: 40 minutes

1 cup thinly sliced button mushrooms
2 tablespoons white wine or cider vinegar
¼ cup olive or sunflower oil
2 teaspoons paprika
¼-½ teaspoon chili powder
1 tablespoon lemon juice
1 tablespoon chopped parsley

Put the mushrooms into a serving bowl and prepare the marinade by mixing together the vinegar, oil, paprika, chili powder and lemon juice. Pour the marinade over the mushrooms and mix gently until they are well coated, then chill for 30 minutes.

Sprinkle with a little chopped parsley just before serving and spoon a little of the marinade over each helping.

Five dishes from the Salad platter – a contrast in textures and flavors: Oeufs à l'Indienne; Stuffed tomatoes; Shredded celery root; Stuffed cucumber rings and tasty Marinated mushrooms

Caviare d'aubergines

TOTAL CALORIES: 615 (2560 kJ)
TOTAL PROTEIN CONTENT: 6 grams
PREPARATION & COOKING TIME: 1½ hours
CHILLING TIME: about 1 hour

1 lb eggplants
¼ cup olive or sunflower oil
1 cup finely chopped onion
½ cup finely chopped green pepper
1 cup skinned and coarsely chopped tomatoes
2 tablespoons dry white wine
1 clove of garlic, peeled and finely chopped
salt
freshly ground pepper
1 tablespoon lemon juice
1 tablespoon finely chopped parsley

Preheat the oven to 350°F. Prick the eggplants with a stainless steel fork or skewer, then bake them in the preheated oven for 1 hour, or until the skins are black and the flesh is soft. Take them out of the oven and set aside to cool.

Heat the oil in a pan and fry the onion and green pepper until the onion is golden brown, then lower the heat, add the tomatoes and continue cooking gently until the tomatoes are reduced to a pulp.

Cut the eggplants in half and scoop out the flesh with a teaspoon. Add this to the tomato mixture in the pan, then add the wine and garlic; season with salt and pepper and cook until the mixture is reduced to a thick purée. Remove the pan from the heat and allow the mixture to cool. Transfer to a serving dish, stir in the lemon juice, adjust the seasoning, sprinkle with parsley and chill well.

Serve with slices of crisp wholewheat toast.

Salt eegplant rings to remove bitter juice. Leave ½ hour, then rinse and dry.

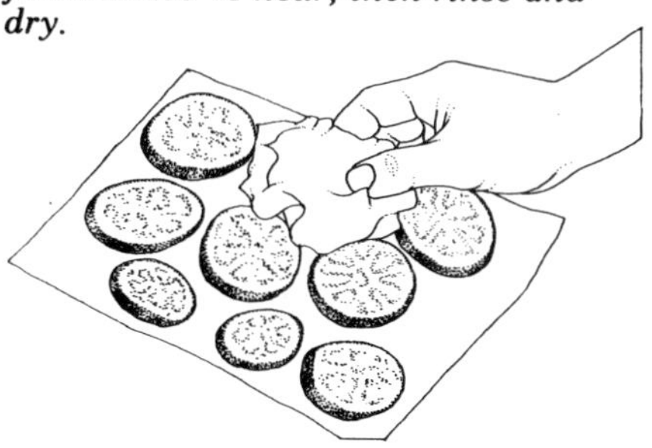

Shredded celery root

TOTAL CALORIES: 1305 (5470 kJ)
TOTAL PROTEIN CONTENT: 7 grams
PREPARATION TIME: 20 minutes

¾ lb celery root, peeled
¼-½ cup well-flavored Mayonnaise (page 126)
sprigs of parsley or watercress, to garnish

Shred the celery root into matchstick-sized julienne strips and blanch these by cooking in a pan of boiling water for about 2 minutes. Drain, rinse under cold running water, drain again and dry the strips well on paper towels. Mix them with just enough mayonnaise to make a thin, even coating. Pile the celery root into a serving bowl and garnish with parsley or watercress.

Stuffed cucumber rings

TOTAL CALORIES: 430 (1810 kJ)
TOTAL PROTEIN CONTENT: 6 grams
PREPARATION TIME: 50 minutes

¾ lb cucumber, cut into eight 2 inch slices
salt
¼ cup cottage cheese
1 clove of garlic, peeled and crushed
1-2 tablespoons milk
freshly ground pepper
¾ lb red or green dessert apples
8 thin slices of cucumber, to garnish

Carefully remove the flesh from inside the cucumber slices, leaving a thin ring of cucumber skin. Chop the flesh into tiny dice about ¼ inch square. Put these into a colander and sprinkle them with a little salt. Leave to stand for about 20 minutes, then rinse under cold running water before draining and drying them well on paper towels.

Mix together the cottage cheese and garlic, then add just enough milk to make a thick, creamy consistency. Season with salt and pepper.

Peel, core and chop the apples into tiny dice to match the cucumber in size, then mix into the cottage cheese.

Arrange the cucumber rings around the edge of a serving plate and fill them with the cucumber and apple mixture. Pile any extra mixture in the center of the plate. Garnish each one with a cucumber slice, cut into a twist, just before serving.

Shredded carrots

TOTAL CALORIES: 560 (2340 kJ)
TOTAL PROTEIN CONTENT: 2 grams
PREPARATION TIME: 15 minutes

2 cups shredded carrots
6 scallions, thinly sliced

The dressing
1 tablespoon lemon juice
1 tablespoon dry white wine
¼ cup olive or sunflower oil
salt
freshly ground pepper

Mix the carrots with most of the scallions, reserving a few of the greener scallion slices for a garnish. Make the dressing by beating together the lemon juice, white wine and oil and pour this over the carrot and onion. Season with salt and pepper, then toss the mixture well and pile it into a small serving bowl. Garnish with the reserved green scallion slices just before serving.

For cucumber rings, cut into 2 inch slices, then scoop out all the seeds.

Imam Bayeldi

This dish is also very good served cold, without the cheese topping.

Serves 4
CALORIES PER PORTION: 135 (570 kJ)
PROTEIN CONTENT PER PORTION: 1 gram
PREPARATION & COOKING TIME: 2 hours

2 eggplants, weighing about ½ lb each
salt
3-4 tablespoons olive or sunflower oil
¼ teaspoon ground cumin
½ teaspoon ground coriander
a sprinkling of freshly ground pepper
½ cup coarsely chopped onion
½ cup skinned and coarsely chopped tomatoes
3 tablespoons seedless white raisins
1 clove of garlic, peeled and finely chopped
¼ cup tomato paste (optional)
1 cup grated Cheddar cheese (optional)

Cut the stems from the eggplants and then slice the eggplants in half lengthwise. Using a teaspoon, carefully scoop out the flesh to leave a shell about ¼ inch thick. Sprinkle salt over the shells and the flesh and place in a colander to drain for 30 minutes. Rinse and dry well.

Preheat the oven to 400°F. Heat the oil, add the cumin, coriander and pepper and cook for about 1 minute, then add the onion and fry it gently until transparent. Cut the eggplant flesh into small chunks, add these to the onion and fry until they are almost soft. Put in the tomatoes, raisins, garlic and tomato paste, if used, and continue cooking until the tomatoes have almost broken down into a purée. If the mixture seems too dry, add up to ¼ cup of water.

Fill the eggplant shells, sprinkle the grated cheese over the tops, if using, and place them in a baking dish.

Bake the eggplants in the preheated oven for about 40 minutes.

Note: Crumpled foil arranged in the baking dish will prevent the eggplants from tilting sideways while they are cooking.

Asparagus au gratin

Serves 4
CALORIES PER PORTION: 190 (795 kJ)
PROTEIN CONTENT PER PORTION: 10 grams
PREPARATION & COOKING TIME: 25-30 minutes

¾ lb trimmed fresh asparagus
2 tablespoons butter
2½ tablespoons wholewheat flour
1¼ cups milk
½ cup grated Cheddar cheese
salt
freshly ground pepper
¼ teaspoon grated lemon rind
about 2 tablespoons finely crumbled fresh wholewheat breadcrumbs

Tie the asparagus in bundles, stand them upright in a tall, deep pan and cook them in a little boiling, salted water, with the asparagus tips in the steam, for 15-20 minutes, or until the stalks are tender. While the asparagus is cooking, make the sauce.

Melt the butter in a small pan over moderate heat, stir in the flour and continue stirring until it thickens. Remove the pan from the heat and add the milk gradually, stirring well between each addition. Return the pan to the heat and bring to a boil, stirring continuously until the sauce thickens. Now beat in most of the cheese, season with salt and pepper and add the lemon rind.

Divide the asparagus between 4 individual flameproof gratin dishes and pour a little of the sauce over each, leaving part of the stalks uncoated. Sprinkle with the breadcrumbs and the remaining cheese and place under the broiler until the top is golden brown and bubbling. Serve immediately.

Note: Frozen or canned asparagus may also be used in this recipe, which also makes a good vegetable dish to accompany a main course.

1. Remove any woody stem bases. These cannot be eaten but can be used to flavor stock. Trim the asparagus to a uniform length to fit the pan.

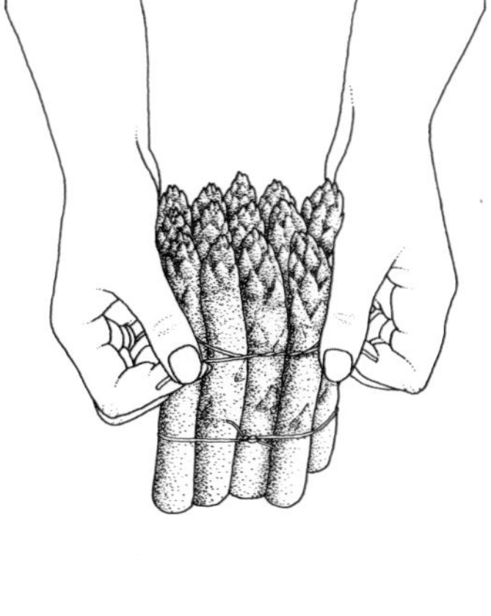

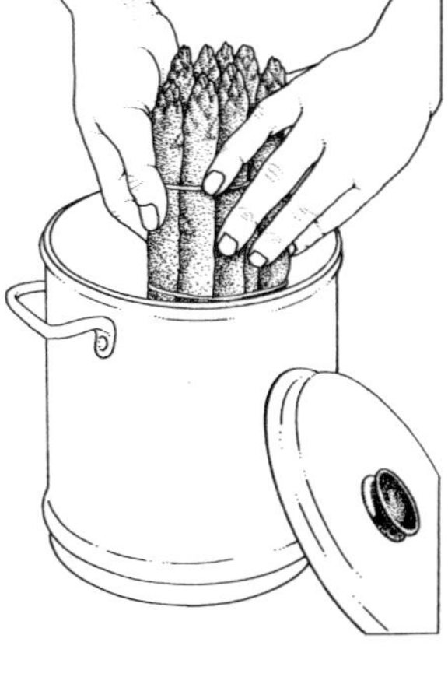

2. Tie the asparagus at top and bottom with thin string.
3. Stand upright in a tall pan, making sure the lid fits comfortably over the tips.

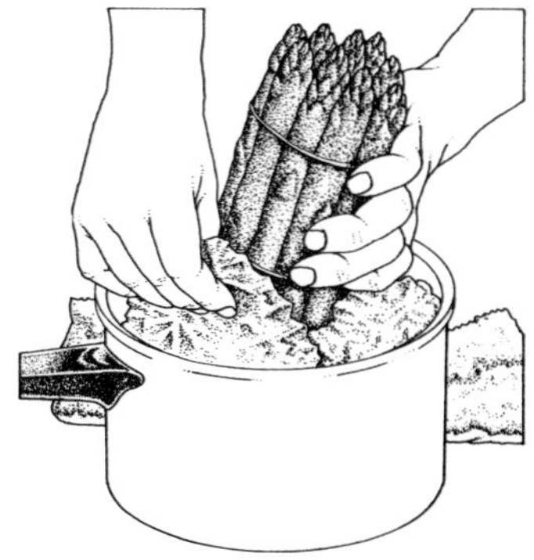

4. If you do not own a suitable tall pan, use foil balls to stand the stems upright, then make a huge foil dome over the whole pan and tie it with string.

Asparagus crêpes

Serves 4
CALORIES PER PORTION: 600 (2525 kJ)
PROTEIN CONTENT PER PORTION: 26 grams
PREPARATION & COOKING TIME: 45 minutes

16 fresh or canned asparagus spears
3 tablespoons butter
3 tablespoons wholewheat flour
1 pint milk
1 ½ cups grated Cheddar cheese
salt
freshly ground pepper
½ teaspoon English mustard powder
8 crêpes made from the Basic recipe (page 82)

Tie the asparagus in two bundles, stand them upright in a tall, deep pan and cook them in a little boiling salted water with the tips in the steam for 15-20 minutes, or until the stalks are tender. While the asparagus is cooking, make the sauce.

Melt the butter in a pan over moderate heat. Stir in the flour and continue stirring until it thickens. Remove the pan from the heat and gradually add the milk, stirring well between each addition. Return the pan to the heat and bring to a boil, stirring continuously until the sauce thickens. Beat in half the cheese, season well with salt and pepper and add the mustard. Lower the heat and simmer the sauce for 2 minutes, stirring all the time.

Place two drained asparagus spears on each crêpe and pour over 2 tablespoons of the cheese sauce. Roll up the crêpes and arrange them, side by side, in a baking dish. Sprinkle the reserved grated cheese over the top and place under the broiler until the cheese on the top is golden brown and bubbling. Serve at once.

Artichokes with rosemary sauce

Serves 4
CALORIES PER PORTION: 285 (1192 kJ)
PROTEIN CONTENT PER PORTION: 4 grams
PREPARATION & COOKING TIME: 1 ½ hours

4 globe artichokes, well washed
salt
4 cloves of garlic, peeled and coarsely chopped
3-4 sprigs of rosemary
1 ¼ cups Béarnaise sauce (page 195), with 2 teaspoons finely chopped rosemary added to the onion and vinegar at the beginning and ½ teaspoon at the end, after straining the sauce

Break off the stems of the artichokes and trim the points of the leaves. Place the artichokes in a pan just large enough to hold them and add water to come almost halfway up their sides. Add salt, garlic and sprigs of rosemary and bring the water to a boil. (There should be enough rosemary to flavor the water strongly.) Cover the pan, lower the heat and simmer for 30-40 minutes, or until an artichoke leaf will pull out easily. Meanwhile, make the sauce, following the recipe given on page 195.

Turn the artichokes upside-down and leave for 5 minutes to drain. Right them and carefully remove the spiky leaves from the center, then scoop out and discard the hairy choke. Arrange each artichoke on a serving dish and fill the center with rosemary-flavored Béarnaise sauce. Hand the rest of the sauce separately.

Favorite hot appetizers – Back: Artichoke with rosemary sauce, adapted from a classic Italian recipe. Front: Imam Bayeldi, a variation on the famous Turkish stuffed eggplant. Right: Russian-style Blinis, served with egg, onion and sour cream

Blinis with egg, onion and sour cream

Serves 4
CALORIES PER PORTION: 285 (1185 kJ)
PROTEIN CONTENT PER PORTION: 10.5 grams
PREPARATION & COOKING TIME: 1 ½ hours

½ cup buckwheat flour
½ cup all-purpose flour, sifted
¼ teaspoon salt
½ cake compressed yeast
¾ cup lukewarm milk and water, mixed
1 egg, separated
1 tablespoon melted butter
1 tablespoon oil or clarified butter

The accompaniments
2 hard-cooked eggs, peeled, chopped and chilled well
10-12 scallions, chopped and chilled well
⅔ cup sour cream, chilled well

Mix the flours together in a bowl and add the salt. Mix the yeast to a cream with a little of the lukewarm milk and water before adding the remainder of the liquid. Stir the yeast liquid into the flours to make a smooth batter and set aside in a warm place for about 30 minutes, or until it has turned frothy and risen to about twice its original volume. (The eggs can be hard cooked and the scallions chopped and put to chill while the batter rises.)

When the batter is ready, 'punch down' the dough and lightly beat in the egg yolk mixed with the melted butter. Beat the egg white until stiff and then fold in.

Heat a griddle or thick-based skillet over a low-to-moderate heat. Brush the griddle or pan with the oil or clarified butter — if using butter, do not allow it to burn. Spoon the batter onto the hot surface, about 2 tablespoons at a time, to make blinis of about 4 inches in size. When the mixture sets and the surface is covered with broken bubbles, turn them over and cook on the other side until this is lightly browned. Repeat until all the batter has been used up, keeping the cooked blinis warm. Serve the chilled chopped eggs, scallions and sour cream as accompaniments in separate bowls.

Each guest helps himself to a hot blini, covers it with egg, scallion and sour cream, then places another blini on top.

Oeufs mollets on artichoke hearts

Serves 4
CALORIES PER PORTION: 380 (1592 kJ)
PROTEIN CONTENT PER PORTION: 17 grams
PREPARATION & COOKING TIME: 65 minutes

4 globe artichokes, well washed
salt
1¼ cups thick Cheese sauce (page 196)
4 Oeufs mollets (page 72)
freshly ground pepper
4 slices of wholewheat bread, crusts removed and fried in butter (croûtes)
1 tablespoon finely chopped parsley

Break off the stems and put the artichokes in a pan just large enough to hold them, adding water to come almost halfway up their sides. Bring to a boil, add salt, turn down the heat and simmer the artichokes gently for about 30-40 minutes, or until a leaf pulls out easily. Make the Cheese sauce while the artichokes are cooking; cover with buttered parchment paper and keep warm in a double boiler.

Prepare the Oeufs mollets and keep them warm in a bowl of hot water. Drain the artichokes well, then scrape off the soft portion at the base of each leaf and rub this through a strainer. Stir the artichoke purée into the Cheese sauce, season to taste and keep hot.

Discard the hairy chokes from the artichokes and set aside the hearts, making sure they sit level by cutting off any bumps or pieces of stem from the base with a sharp knife.

Put the four bread croûtes on warmed serving plates, place an artichoke heart on each, then pour over a little of the hot sauce. Place an egg on top, then coat it with the remaining sauce. Sprinkle with a little parsley before serving.

Sambusak

Serves 4
CALORIES PER PORTION: 645 (2692 kJ)
PROTEIN CONTENT PER PORTION: 16 grams
PREPARATION AND COOKING TIME: 1½ hours

The filling
1 tablespoon olive or sunflower oil
1 cup finely chopped onion
1 teaspoon ground cumin, or to taste
3 cups cooked fresh or frozen peas
salt
freshly ground pepper

The pastry
2¼ cups wholewheat or 2½ cups sifted all-purpose flour
½ teaspoon salt
⅔ cup olive or sunflower oil
¾ cup water
1 egg, lightly beaten
oil for deep frying

To make the filling, heat the oil and fry the onion and cumin in it until the onion is lightly browned. Add the peas, salt and a very little water. Cook, stirring frequently, until the peas are soft, then mash them into a thick, coarse-textured purée. Adjust seasoning; set aside until cold.

For the pastry, put the flour into a bowl and add the salt. Mix the oil with about two-thirds of the water and pour this into the flour. Mix to a firm dough, adding a little more of the water if necessary. Knead lightly and then roll out as thinly as possible.

Using a 3 inch diameter cookie cutter, cut into rounds. Put a teaspoon of filling in the center of each and brush the edges with the beaten egg. Seal the edges together firmly and deep fry in hot oil at 350°F until crisp and golden brown. Drain well and serve hot.

Ratatouille

Serves 4
CALORIES PER PORTION: 165 (695 kJ)
PROTEIN CONTENT PER PORTION: 2 grams
PREPARATION & COOKING TIME: 2¼ hours (including salting the zucchini and eggplant)

2 large zucchini, sliced
1 eggplant, about ½ lb, quartered and sliced
salt
1 medium onion, thinly sliced
¼ cup olive or sunflower oil
1½ cups skinned and coarsely chopped tomatoes
2 large green peppers, thinly sliced
1 large clove of garlic, peeled and finely chopped
freshly ground black pepper

Sprinkle the zucchini and eggplant with salt and leave for about 1 hour, then rinse and pat dry with paper towels. Cook the onion in half the oil until transparent, then add the zucchini and fry them, without browning, for about 10 minutes.

Meanwhile, fry the eggplant in the remaining oil in a separate pan, turning the slices over from time to time until they are just beginning to color. Add the tomatoes to the onion and zucchini and, when the tomatoes have cooked down to a pulp, add the green peppers, cooked eggplant and the garlic. Season to taste. Simmer gently for about 1 hour, until the Ratatouille has become a thick, pulpy mass. This is delicious served hot or cold, and makes a good accompanying vegetable.

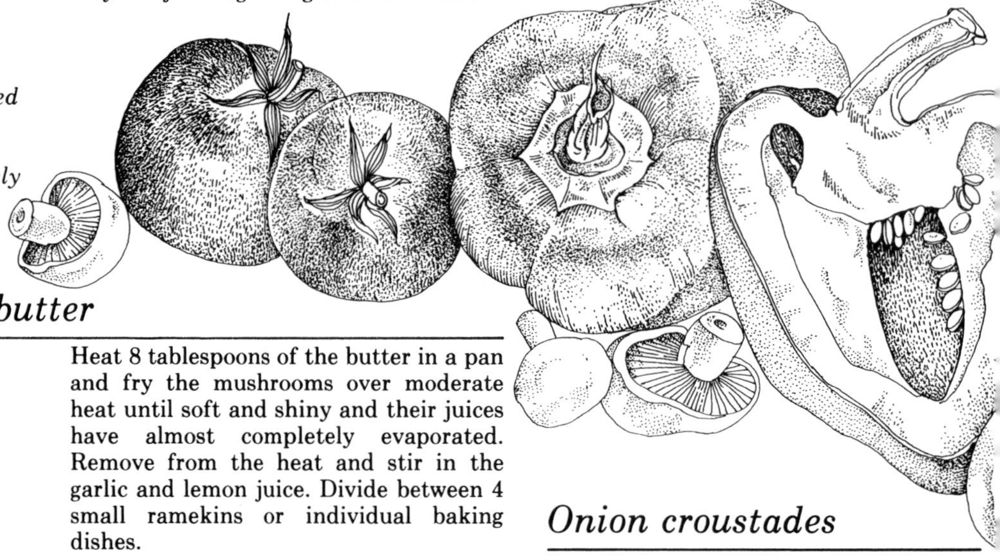

Mushrooms with garlic butter

Serves 4
CALORIES PER PORTION: 255 (1055 kJ)
PROTEIN CONTENT PER PORTION: 2 grams
PREPARATION & COOKING TIME: 30 minutes

10 tablespoons butter
3 cups coarsely chopped mushrooms
1-2 cloves of garlic, peeled and finely chopped
2 tablespoons lemon juice
1 cup fresh wholewheat breadcrumbs
1 tablespoon chopped parsley

Heat 8 tablespoons of the butter in a pan and fry the mushrooms over moderate heat until soft and shiny and their juices have almost completely evaporated. Remove from the heat and stir in the garlic and lemon juice. Divide between 4 small ramekins or individual baking dishes.

Preheat the oven to 400°F. Fry the breadcrumbs in the remaining butter, in a thick-based pan, until crisp and golden brown. Stir frequently to stop the crumbs from sticking and burning. Add the parsley, mix well and sprinkle the mixture over the mushrooms. Press down lightly with a fork and bake in the preheated oven for 10 minutes before serving.

Stuffed onions with oriental rice

Serves 4
CALORIES PER PORTION: 230 (1222 kJ)
PROTEIN CONTENT PER PORTION: 9 grams
PREPARATION & COOKING TIME: 45 minutes

4 onions, weighing about ¼ lb each
salt
½ teaspoon ground turmeric
2 teaspoons olive or sunflower oil
1 tablespoon butter
2 eggs, well beaten
1 teaspoon lemon juice
1 cup plain yogurt

The rice
4 cardamoms
½-1 teaspoon ground turmeric
½-1 teaspoon ground cumin
1 tablespoon olive or sunflower oil
2½ cups boiled brown rice

Cook the peeled onions in boiling salted water for 5 minutes, then drain and cool. Cut each in half across the rings and remove the centers, leaving the two outer layers as a shell. Chop the onion centers finely.

Split the cardamoms, remove the seeds and crush them with the turmeric and cumin, then heat them with the oil for about 1 minute. Add the cooked rice and mix very thoroughly until it is really heated through. Keep it hot until ready to serve.

Heat the turmeric in the 2 teaspoons of oil and the butter and fry the chopped onion in it until it is golden brown. Add the eggs and lemon juice and scramble them quickly. Spoon this spiced egg mixture into the onion shells.

Arrange the rice on a warmed serving plate and place the stuffed onions on top. Serve at once with plain yogurt as a sauce.

Onion croustades

Serves 4
CALORIES PER PORTION: 350 (1465 kJ)
PROTEIN CONTENT PER PORTION: 20 grams
PREPARATION & COOKING TIME: 40 minutes

12 pearl onions
salt
4 large thick slices of wholewheat bread, crusts removed
4-6 tablespoons clarified butter (page 198)
1¼ cups Béchamel sauce (page 196)
1 teaspoon Meaux or other French-style mustard
a few drops of Tabasco sauce
freshly ground pepper
½ lb Edam or Emmenthal cheese, cubed

Peel the pearl onions, drop them into a pan of boiling salted water and cook them for 10-12 minutes, or until soft. Using a 3 inch diameter pastry cutter, cut a circle out of the center of each slice of bread. Heat the clarified butter in a pan and fry the bread circles and the off-cuts until crisp and golden brown. Drain well and keep them hot on a serving plate. Heat up the Béchamel sauce and add the mustard and Tabasco; season with salt and pepper. Put in the cheese cubes and the cooked onions and mix gently into the sauce.

Spoon some of the mixture into the center of each of the fried bread slices and top with the fried bread circles. Serve immediately.

Individual cheese custards

Serves 4
CALORIES PER PORTION: 360 (1505 kJ)
PROTEIN CONTENT PER PORTION: 15 grams
PREPARATION & COOKING TIME: about 1½ hours

1 teaspoon butter
1 teaspoon finely chopped onion
1 teaspoon wholewheat flour
½ cup light cream
½ cup grated strong cheese
2 eggs
2 egg yolks
1¼ cups milk
1¼ cups Béchamel sauce (page 196)
a sprinkling of paprika
sprigs of parsley, to garnish

Melt the butter in a small pan over moderate heat and fry the onion until transparent. Sprinkle in the flour and stir until the onion is well coated, then remove the pan from the heat and gradually stir in the cream. Return the pan to the heat and bring the sauce to a boil, stirring until it thickens. Add the cheese and stir until thoroughly melted. Remove the pan from the heat and let the mixture cool slightly.

Beat together the eggs, egg yolks and milk in a bowl. Stir this into the cheese mixture, then pour it all through a strainer into 4 well-buttered ramekins or small baking dishes. Place these in a pan and pour in enough boiling water to come about one-third of the way up the dishes. Cover the pan with a tight-fitting lid and place over moderate heat. Cook the custards for about 15 minutes, or until they are set, then remove the dishes from the pan and allow the custards to cool.

Preheat the oven to 400°F and heat up the Béchamel sauce. Carefully turn the custards out of their dishes onto an ovenproof platter and coat each with hot Béchamel sauce. Bake in the preheated oven for 10-15 minutes until the custards are lightly browned on top and the sauce is sizzling.

Sprinkle with a little paprika, garnish with parsley sprigs and serve.

Cheese beignets

Serves 8
CALORIES PER PORTION: 253 (1058 kJ)
PROTEIN CONTENT PER PORTION: 10 grams
PREPARATION & COOKING TIME: 1¼ hours

2 tablespoons butter
1 cup finely chopped onion
2½ cups milk
1 teaspoon salt
1 bay leaf
10 tablespoons polenta or corn meal
1 cup grated Cheddar cheese
1 egg, well beaten
⅔-1¼ cups Coating batter (page 194)
oil for deep frying

Melt the butter in a pan over gentle heat, add the onion and fry until golden brown. Add the milk, salt and bay leaf and bring to a boil. Pour in the polenta or corn meal, lower the heat and let it simmer for 5 minutes, stirring all the time. Remove the pan from the heat and gradually stir in the cheese, then beat in the egg.

Pour the mixture onto an oiled work surface, spreading the paste out to a little over ½ inch thick and neatening the edges. Leave until cold.

Cut the paste into 2 inch squares and coat each with the batter. Heat the oil to 350°F, add the squares a few at a time and deep fry until golden brown. Remove them from the pan with a slotted spoon and drain well on paper towels. Keep them hot while frying the remainder. Serve as soon as possible after cooking.

Eggs soubise

Serves 4
CALORIES PER PORTION: 255 (1072 kJ)
PROTEIN CONTENT PER PORTION: 11 grams
PREPARATION & COOKING TIME: 40-45 minutes

4 tablespoons butter
2 cups finely chopped onions
3 tablespoons wholewheat flour
1¼ cups milk
a pinch of freshly grated nutmeg
salt
freshly ground pepper
4 Oeufs mollets (page 72)
4 slices of wholewheat bread, crusts removed and fried in a little extra butter (croûtes)
1 cup thinly sliced button mushrooms
¼ cup grated Cheddar cheese

Melt half of the butter over gentle heat, add the onions and fry until golden brown, stirring frequently so they do not stick. Sprinkle in the flour and cook for 1-2 minutes, stirring all the time. Remove the pan from the heat and gradually pour in the milk, stirring well between each addition. Return the pan to the heat, increase the heat and bring the sauce to a boil, stirring all the time until it thickens.

Pour the sauce into a blender and work at high speed until it is completely smooth. Now return the sauce to the rinsed-out pan, add the nutmeg and season well with salt and pepper. Stand the pan in a larger pan almost full of boiling water or transfer the sauce to a double boiler. Cover the surface of the sauce with a sheet of parchment paper to prevent a skin forming and leave to stand for about 20 minutes to allow the sauce to mature.

Meanwhile, prepare the Oeufs mollets and keep them warm in a bowl of very hot water. Make the bread croûtes, if not already prepared. Melt the remaining butter in a small pan over gentle heat. Add the mushrooms and cook them for 1-2 minutes, stirring them frequently. Keep them hot while you place the bread croûtes on a warmed heatproof plate, put a drained egg on each slice and coat with the onion (soubise) sauce.

Sprinkle the cheese on top, then put the plate under the broiler to melt the cheese slightly. Garnish with the mushrooms before serving.

Crudités with savory dips

Serve a platter of diced or sliced raw vegetables (crudités) as well as the more usual cubes or strips of bread or toast, potato chips or crackers, with hot or cold party dips. For 4 servings, choose about 1 lb of mixed vegetables from the following list; double the amount for 8 people.

As an alternative, these fresh Crudités are delicious served with a bowl of thick Mayonnaise or Aioli sauce (page 126).

Hummus

Serves up to 8
TOTAL CALORIES: 2290 (9570 kJ)
TOTAL PROTEIN CONTENT: 27 grams
PREPARATION TIME: 30 minutes

1 ½ cups cooked chick peas
⅔ cup tahini paste
¾ cup plus 1 tablespoon olive or sunflower oil
1 ¼ cups water
1-2 cloves of garlic, peeled and chopped
6-8 tablespoons lemon juice
1 tablespoon chopped mint or parsley
1 teaspoon paprika

Put the chick peas in a blender with the tahini paste, ⅔ cup each of the oil and water, the garlic, lemon juice and mint or parsley. Work to a thick purée, adding a little more water by degrees. Hummus should be of a thick coating consistency.

Alternatively, pound the chick peas and garlic to a paste in a mortar with a pestle before slowly mixing in the other ingredients, lastly adding the water by degrees, to reach the correct consistency.

Spoon the Hummus into a shallow round dish. Mix the paprika into the remaining 3 tablespoons of oil and pour this over the Hummus. Stir the top into a spiral pattern. Serve with Pitta bread.

Horseradish and nut dip

Serves up to 8
TOTAL CALORIES: 800 (3355 kJ)
TOTAL PROTEIN CONTENT:
PREPARATION TIME: 5-10 minutes

¾ cup salted peanuts
2 tablespoons grated horseradish, or 2-3 tablespoons horseradish cream
⅔ cup heavy cream

Place the peanuts in a blender and work until they are finely chopped. Add the horseradish and heavy cream, and work until you have a thick, fairly smooth dip. Serve with potato chips and celery sticks.

Avocado dip

Serves up to 8
TOTAL CALORIES: 930 (3890 kJ)
TOTAL PROTEIN CONTENT: 19 grams
PREPARATION & CHILLING TIME: 1 ½ hours

2 avocados
1-2 tablespoons onion juice (see page 55)
3 tablespoons lemon juice
salt
freshly ground pepper
1 tablespoon chopped parsley

Peel and seed the avocados and mash them with a stainless steel fork. Stir in the onion juice and 2 tablespoons of the lemon juice and season to taste. Work the mixture in a blender until very smooth, or rub it through a strainer to a purée.

Pile the dip into a serving bowl. Pour a little extra lemon juice over the top to prevent discoloration and chill well. Garnish with chopped parsley.

Cottage cheese dip

Serves up to 8
TOTAL CALORIES: 270 (1300 kJ)
TOTAL PROTEIN CONTENT: 32 grams
PREPARATION TIME: 10-15 minutes

1 cup cottage cheese
1-2 teaspoons curry powder, or to taste
1-2 tablespoons onion juice (see page 55)
1 tablespoon pineapple juice
2 tablespoons crushed pineapple
1 clove of garlic, peeled and crushed
1-2 tablespoons milk
salt
a sprinkling of cayenne

Thoroughly mix all the ingredients except the cayenne, adding just enough milk to make a thick coating consistency. Adjust the seasoning and sprinkle with cayenne

Spicy pineapple dip

Serves 4-6
CALORIES PER PORTION: 100 (417 kJ)
PROTEIN CONTENT PER PORTION: 1 gram
PREPARATION TIME: 20-30 minutes

1 cup chopped fresh/canned pineapple
2 cups finely chopped onions
2 tablespoons olive or sunflower oil
1 teaspoon ground cinnamon
½ teaspoon salt
¼-½ teaspoon chili powder, or to taste
1 tablespoon wine or cider vinegar

Fry the pineapple and onions in the oil until golden brown. Drain off any excess oil and work the pineapple and onion in a blender with the cinnamon, salt, chili powder and vinegar, to a smooth purée.

Masur dhal

Serves 6-8
TOTAL CALORIES: 425 (1785 kJ)
TOTAL PROTEIN CONTENT: 11 grams
PREPARATION AND COOKING TIME: 1 hour

1 teaspoon ground cumin
½ teaspoon ground turmeric
½ teaspoon finely ground fenugreek
½ teaspoon mustard seeds
2 tablespoons olive or sunflower oil
2 cups finely chopped onions
1 cup lentils
1 pint water
½ teaspoon salt
⅛-¼ teaspoon chili powder (optional)
2-4 green chili peppers, seeded and finely chopped

Heat the spices in the oil until they give off a strong aroma. Add the onions and fry over moderate heat until they are soft and golden brown. Add the lentils, water and salt and cook, stirring occasionally, until they are soft and have formed a thick purée. It will take about 30 minutes.

Adjust the seasoning and, if you want a 'hotter' dhal, stir in a little chili powder mixed with a little more oil. Serve hot, with the chopped green chili peppers sprinkled over.

Savory tomato dip

Serves 6
CALORIES PER PORTION: 220 (930 kJ)
PROTEIN CONTENT PER PORTION: 11 grams
PREPARATION TIME: 45-60 minutes

2 ¼ lb ripe tomatoes, coarsely chopped
2 medium onions, thinly sliced
2 cloves of garlic, peeled and finely chopped
6 cardamoms
½-1 teaspoon ground cumin
1 bay leaf
salt
freshly ground pepper
1 tablespoon wine vinegar
1 teaspoon raw brown sugar
a few drops Worcestershire sauce
a little chili powder, to taste

Place the tomatoes and onions in a thick-based pan over gentle heat. Add the garlic, the seeds from the cardamoms, the cumin, bay leaf and salt and pepper to taste. Cook gently for 25-30 minutes until the mixture forms a thick purée, stirring occasionally.

Rub the purée through a strainer into a clean pan and add the vinegar, brown sugar, Worcestershire sauce and chili powder. Bring the mixture to a boil, adjust the seasoning and reduce the mixture if necessary by boiling a little longer. Pour into a serving bowl and serve hot.

Eggs and Cheese

From the ubiquitous bread-and-cheese and the simple breakfast egg to the culinary pinnacle of a superbly risen cheese soufflé, golden-crusted on the outside, irresistibly creamy on the inside – each is a part of the great tradition created by these two basic and protein-rich foods.

So many of the world's most famous dishes have eggs and cheese as their starting point.

When you have tried the following recipes – and they make excellent luncheon dishes, light suppers or, in the case of a soufflé or quiche, delicious dinner party appetizers – follow the example of the Swiss and hold a winter 'raclette' party. Place a large wedge of cheese, preferably Gruyère, close to an open fire; as it softens, cut off slices of melted cheese and serve with hot potatoes boiled in their skins, accompanied by pickles. A speciality of Valais; a perfect meal . . .

Omelets

Many people think that some mysterious talent is required to make a good omelet, or that some secret recipe exists which will ensure success every time. This is not true. The basic ingredients for a plain omelet are simply eggs, butter, salt and pepper. There is no mystery or secret recipe, but a few simple rules should be followed.

Always use a thick-based, smooth-surfaced iron skillet so that the omelet will cook evenly and will not stick. Do not overbeat the eggs until they are frothy — beat them only enough to break the whites and thoroughly mix them into the yolks. Use plenty of the best unsalted butter to oil the pan before cooking the omelet, but pour away any excess before actually beginning to cook. A perfect omelet should be golden brown and almost crisp on the outside, yet still just liquid on the inside so that it provides its own sauce.

Any evenly diced, cooked vegetables — potatoes, peas, carrots, even nuts — may be added with a sprinkling of herbs as a filling, before folding the omelet over to serve it. It is important to see that the vegetables are evenly diced, as it makes such a difference to the finished dish.

Plain omelet

Serves 1
CALORIES: 275 (1150 kJ)
PROTEIN CONTENT: 14 grams
PREPARATION & COOKING TIME: 5 minutes

2 eggs
salt
freshly ground pepper
1 tablespoon clarified or unsalted butter

Put the eggs in a bowl, add salt and pepper to taste and beat the eggs lightly just to mix them.

Melt the butter quickly in a 6 inch thick-based skillet over a moderate to high heat until it is on the point of turning brown. Pour in the eggs and let them cook for a few moments, then tilt the pan and lift the omelet at one edge with a spatula to allow the uncooked mixture to run underneath. Repeat this two or three more times until most of the uncooked mixture has disappeared.

When the surface of the omelet is beginning to set, but still looks a little liquid, tilt the pan and fold the omelet in half with the spatula. Slide it onto a warmed serving plate and serve immediately. Never keep an omelet waiting!

Note: With practice, and enough utensils, it is possible to make 4 omelets at the same time. Beat the eggs and salt and pepper in four separate bowls. Heat the pans on the stove, making sure you have equal heat under all 4 pans. Add a little butter to each pan and allow it to melt. Pour the eggs into each pan in the same order, then cook as for individual plain omelet in turn.

Cheese omelet

Serves 1
CALORIES: 375 (1580 kJ)
PROTEIN CONTENT: 20 grams
PREPARATION & COOKING TIME: 5 minutes

Follow the basic method for Plain omelet, sprinkling on ¼ cup grated Cheddar cheese just before folding the omelet in half. Serve immediately, or the cheese will become stringy.

A tablespoon of chopped fresh herbs may also be added.

Corn omelet

Serves 1
CALORIES: 425 (1770 kJ)
PROTEIN CONTENT: 15 grams
PREPARATION & COOKING TIME: 10 minutes

2 tablespoons clarified or unsalted butter
⅓ cup cooked fresh, frozen or canned corn kernels

Melt the butter in a pan over gentle heat, add the corn and cook gently for 4-5 minutes until tender. The buttery flavor of the corn should be perfect on its own, without extra seasoning.

Make a Plain omelet. Sprinkle the corn over just before folding the omelet in half. Serve immediately.

Scallion omelet

Serves 1
CALORIES: 465 (1940 kJ)
PROTEIN CONTENT: 14 grams
PREPARATION & COOKING TIME: 15 minutes

2 tablespoons clarified or unsalted butter
½ cup finely chopped scallions
1 tablespoon heavy cream
½ teaspoon finely chopped thyme

Melt the butter over gentle heat, add the scallions and cook until tender, without letting them turn color. Pour on the cream, add the thyme and continue cooking until thick and well blended. Remove the pan from the heat and keep hot.

Make a Plain omelet, and spread the scallion mixture down the center just before folding the omelet in half.

Pipérade

Serves 4
CALORIES PER PORTION: 365 (1520 kJ)
PROTEIN CONTENT PER PORTION: 11.5 grams
PREPARATION & COOKING TIME: 20 minutes

¼ cup olive or sunflower oil
4 cups diced red peppers
2 cups skinned and quartered tomatoes
salt
freshly ground pepper
6 eggs
4 slices of wholewheat bread, crusts removed, cut across into triangles and fried in a little butter (croûtes)

Gently heat the oil in a pan, add the peppers and fry them for 5 minutes. Add the tomatoes and continue cooking until the juices have almost boiled away and it has cooked down to a purée. Season with salt and pepper.

Put the eggs in a bowl, add salt and pepper to taste and beat them well. Pour this onto the purée and continue cooking, stirring continuously until the eggs have scrambled into the pepper and tomato mixture. Transfer the pipérade to a warmed serving dish, arrange the fried bread croûtes around the edge and serve immediately.

Omelette paysanne

Serves 4
CALORIES PER PORTION: 360 (1507 kJ)
PROTEIN CONTENT PER PORTION: 16 grams
PREPARATION & COOKING TIME: 30 minutes

4 tablespoons clarified or unsalted butter
3 cups finely diced potatoes
1 cup finely chopped onion
salt
freshly ground pepper
8 eggs

Melt the butter in an 8 inch diameter thick-based skillet over gentle heat, add the potatoes and fry for about 15 minutes until they are nearly cooked through. Cover the pan for the first half of the cooking time, but stir and turn the potatoes occasionally to prevent them sticking. Add the onion and continue cooking for about 5 minutes. By this time the potatoes should be quite tender and the onion transparent. Sprinkle liberally with salt and pepper.

Put the eggs in a bowl with plenty of salt and pepper. Beat them lightly to mix, then pour them over the potatoes. Stir, as though making scrambled eggs, until most of the liquid has set. Place a large, warmed serving plate over the top of the skillet and carefully turn the pan upside down so that the omelet lands on the plate. Serve at once.

Omelet in tomato sauce

Serves 4
CALORIES PER PORTION: 270 (1135 kJ)
PROTEIN CONTENT PER PORTION: 15.5 grams
PREPARATION & COOKING TIME: 30 minutes

3 tablespoons clarified or unsalted butter
1 cup finely chopped onion
1 clove of garlic, peeled and crushed
1½ tablespoons wholewheat flour
salt
freshly ground pepper
2 cups coarsely chopped tomatoes
1 cup red wine
8 eggs
1 tablespoon finely chopped fennel or basil (optional)

Melt 2 tablespoons of the butter in a skillet over gentle heat, add the onion and garlic and cook until transparent but not browned. Add the flour, season with salt and pepper and stir continuously until all the butter has been absorbed. Now add the tomatoes and cook them for 1-2 minutes, stirring to prevent them sticking and burning. Pour in the wine, stir well and bring to a boil, then lower the heat and let the mixture simmer until the sauce thickens. Continue cooking, stirring occasionally for 15-20 minutes.

Meanwhile, make a firm Plain omelet with the rest of the butter and the eggs. Season with salt and pepper. (Cook this in two stages if necessary.)

When the omelet is cooked, cut it into thick slices and place them side by side in a warmed serving dish. Strain on the sauce, turning the omelet slices over so that they are really well coated. Sprinkle with the fennel or basil and serve immediately with cooked brown rice or plainly boiled new potatoes and a salad.

Omelette aux fines herbes

Serves 1

Serve with a small pat of Herb butter (page 198), or sprinkling of grated cheese.

CALORIES: 275 (1150 kJ)
PROTEIN CONTENT: 14 grams
PREPARATION & COOKING TIME: 10 minutes

2 eggs
1 tablespoon clarified or unsalted butter
1 tablespoon finely chopped mixed fresh herbs, (parsley, chervil, watercress, tarragon)

Make a Plain omelet following the basic method, but adding half the herbs to the uncooked egg mixture. Sprinkle the remaining herbs over the cooked omelet just before folding it in half and serving.

Basic cheese soufflé

Serves 4
CALORIES PER PORTION: 275 (1162 kJ)
PROTEIN CONTENT PER PORTION: 17.5 grams
PREPARATION & COOKING TIME: 35-40 minutes

3 tablespoons butter
3 tablespoons wholewheat flour
1 cup milk
1 cup grated Cheddar cheese
salt
freshly ground black pepper
a pinch of freshly grated nutmeg (optional)
4 egg yolks
5 egg whites

Melt 2 tablespoons of the butter in a pan over gentle heat, then sprinkle in the flour. Cook for 1-2 minutes, stirring continuously until it thickens, then remove the pan from the heat and gradually add the milk, stirring well between each addition. Return the pan to the heat, increase the heat and bring it to a boil, stirring all the time until the sauce thickens.

Remove the pan from the heat, beat in the cheese and add salt and pepper to taste, and a pinch of nutmeg, if liked. Leave this to cool slightly before adding the egg yolks and stirring them well into the mixture. Preheat the oven to 400°F and put a 1½ quart capacity soufflé dish to warm.

Beat the egg whites until they stand in stiff peaks. Pour half the cheese sauce on top of the egg whites, then fold in from the bottom to the top until thoroughly combined. Fold in the remaining cheese sauce in the same way.

Melt the remaining butter and quickly brush the inside of the soufflé dish before pouring in the soufflé mixture. Draw a circle in the top of the mixture about halfway from the edge, using a knife brushed with a little extra melted butter — this will produce the raised 'top hat' effect when the soufflé is cooked.

Bake in the preheated oven for about 20 minutes if you like the center of the soufflé to be semiliquid, or for 25 minutes if a drier soufflé is preferred. Serve immediately.

Spinach soufflé

Serves 4
CALORIES PER PORTION: 470 (1232 kJ)
PROTEIN CONTENT PER PORTION: 20.5 grams
PREPARATION & COOKING TIME: 40 minutes

1⅓ cups chopped cooked spinach, well drained

Follow the basic recipe for Cheese soufflé, adding the spinach to the sauce just before the cheese.

Note: If a smooth-textured soufflé is preferred, purée the spinach after draining.

Zucchini soufflé

Serves 4
CALORIES PER PORTION: 335 (1392 kJ)
PROTEIN CONTENT PER PORTION: 18 grams
PREPARATION & COOKING TIME: 35-40 minutes

2 tablespoons butter
2 cups thinly sliced zucchini

Melt the butter in a pan over gentle heat, add the zucchini and cook until they are soft and most of the juices have evaporated. Remove the zucchini from the pan and mash them to a purée.

Follow the basic recipe for Cheese soufflé, adding the mashed zucchini to the sauce just before the cheese.

Corn soufflé

Serves 4
CALORIES PER PORTION: 320 (1340 kJ)
PROTEIN CONTENT PER PORTION: 19 grams
PREPARATION & COOKING TIME: 35-40 minutes

1½ cups corn kernels

Follow the basic recipe for Cheese soufflé, adding the corn to the 2 tablespoons melted butter in the pan before sprinkling in the flour. Cook until the corn is tender before adding the milk.

Scrambled egg with asparagus

Serves 4
CALORIES PER PORTION: 405 (1695 kJ)
PROTEIN CONTENT PER PORTION: 13 grams
PREPARATION & COOKING TIME: 30 minutes

2 medium onions, cut into rings
2 tablespoons olive or sunflower oil
salt
1 lb trimmed fresh asparagus
4 eggs
freshly ground pepper
6 tablespoons butter
4 slices of wholewheat bread, toasted and crusts removed

Fry the onion rings in the oil until crisp; the slower this is done, the better the result — it should take about 20 minutes. Add salt about halfway through, and keep stirring and turning the onions over so that they cook evenly.

Meanwhile, tie the asparagus in bundles and cook in a steamer for 15-25 minutes. (If using frozen or canned asparagus, follow the cooking directions on the package or can.) Beat the eggs and season with salt and pepper. Melt two-thirds of the butter in a pan over gentle heat and pour in the beaten eggs. Cook, stirring constantly, until they just thicken; don't stir them too much or the texture will be too smooth; on the other hand, they mustn't be allowed to burn. When they are ready they should still be moist. Butter the toast and divide the scrambled eggs between the 4 slices. Arrange the asparagus spears on top. Drain the onion rings on paper towels, arrange them over the asparagus and serve hot.

Left: Gougère, a choux pastry ring made with eggs and flavored with cheese, served with a rich Tomato sauce. Right: a superb, light-textured soufflé to melt in the mouth, flavored with cheese and spinach. Serve it for lunch, or as a dinner party appetizer

Gougère

Serves 4

CALORIES PER PORTION: 353 (1480 kJ)
PROTEIN CONTENT PER PORTION: 13.5 grams
PREPARATION & COOKING TIME: 1¼ hours

4 tablespoons butter
⅔ cup water
¾ cup all-purpose flour, sifted
3 eggs
¼ lb strong hard cheese, cut into ¼ inch cubes
about 1¼ cups Tomato or Piquant sauce for serving (page 196)

Preheat the oven to 300°F. Place the butter and water in a medium-sized pan and bring to a boil over moderate heat. Remove the pan from the heat as soon as boiling point is reached and pour in all the flour at once. Beat vigorously with a wooden spoon until all the flour has been absorbed and the mixture 'follows the spoon' and comes away from the side of the pan to form a firm, smooth ball. Cool very slightly and add the eggs one at a time, beating very thoroughly between each addition so that the mixture becomes smooth and shiny. It may be necessary to use only part of the last egg, as the mixture must be firm enough to hold its shape. Fold in two-thirds of the cheese.

Pipe or spoon the mixture into a 10 inch circle on a well-oiled baking sheet. Dot with the remaining cheese cubes and pin a double band of non-stick parchment paper around the outside to hold it in shape so that it rises neatly.

Place the Gougère in the preheated oven and increase the heat to 400°F; choux pastry bakes best on a rising temperature. Bake it for 40 minutes, then turn off the heat, open the oven door slightly and leave the Gougère in the oven for 5-10 minutes to cool while you make or heat up the chosen sauce. Transfer the Gougère to a hot serving platter and serve with the sauce handed separately.

Spinach roulade

Serves 4
CALORIES PER PORTION: 775 (3245 kJ)
PROTEIN CONTENT PER PORTION: 20 grams
PREPARATION & COOKING TIME: 1 hour

The roulade
2 tablespoons butter
1⅓ cups chopped cooked spinach, well drained
salt
freshly ground pepper
5 tablespoons wholewheat flour
⅔ cup milk
3 eggs, separated

The filling
3 tablespoons olive or sunflower oil
5 slices of wholewheat bread, crusts removed and cut into ½ inch cubes
2 cups chopped onions
large pinch of cayenne
1 cup strained cottage cheese

Melt the butter in a pan over gentle heat, add the spinach and cook until any remaining liquid has evaporated. Add salt and pepper to taste, then sprinkle in the flour and cook for 1-2 minutes, stirring continuously. Remove the pan from the heat and gradually add the milk, stirring well between each addition. Return the pan to the heat, increase the heat and bring to a boil, stirring all the time until the sauce thickens.

Remove the pan from the heat and allow the sauce to cool slightly. Preheat the oven to 400°F. Beat the egg yolks, then add them to the spinach sauce and stir until thoroughly mixed. Beat the egg whites until stiff, then fold these into the sauce.

Pour the mixture into a jelly roll pan lined with oiled parchment or wax paper and bake in the preheated oven for 30 minutes.

To make the filling: heat 2 tablespoons of the oil in a pan over gentle heat, add the bread cubes and fry until crisp and lightly browned. Remove from the pan with a slotted spoon and drain well on paper towels. Heat the remaining oil in the pan, add the onions and fry until golden. Remove from the pan with a slotted spoon and drain well.

A few minutes before the roulade is cooked, add the fried bread cubes to the onions with a little cayenne and season with salt and pepper. Add the cottage cheese and melt it over gentle heat, taking great care that it does not boil, or it will go stringy. Continue cooking until the cheese is melted and really hot.

Remove the roulade from the oven and take it out of the pan. Spread thickly with the filling. Roll it up by picking up one end of the paper and gently easing the roulade over the filling into a roll. Serve immediately.

Cheese roulade

Serves 4
CALORIES PER PORTION: 815 (2145 kJ)
PROTEIN CONTENT PER PORTION: 22 grams
PREPARATION & COOKING TIME: 1 hour

1 cup grated Cheddar cheese
3 tablespoons wholewheat flour
½ teaspoon finely chopped thyme or marjoram
salt
freshly ground pepper
a pinch of cayenne
4 eggs
6 tablespoons finely chopped parsley

The filling
2 cups finely chopped onions
2-3 tablespoons olive or sunflower oil, or butter
3 tablespoons wholewheat flour
1¼ cups milk
¾ cup chopped walnuts
½ teaspoon grated nutmeg
salt
freshly ground pepper

First make the filling: fry the onions in the oil or melted butter over moderate heat until they are golden brown, stirring occasionally to prevent them sticking. When they are ready — it should take about 30 minutes — drain off any excess oil or butter, sprinkle in the flour and mix it well in before removing the pan from the heat. Gradually pour on the milk, stirring well after each addition. Return the pan to the heat and bring the sauce to a boil, stirring constantly until it thickens.

Add the walnuts and nutmeg and season well with salt and pepper. Cover the top of the sauce with a piece of buttered parchment paper and stand the pan in a larger pan half full of boiling water, or transfer the sauce to a double boiler over gentle heat and keep warm while you make the roulade.

Line a well-buttered jelly roll pan, 12 × 8 inches, with non-stick parchment paper. Brush this with melted butter and preheat the oven to 400°F.

Mix together the cheese, flour and thyme or marjoram and season to taste with salt, pepper and a pinch of cayenne. Beat the eggs until they are thick and mousse-like. Using a knife, fold the dry flour and cheese mixture into the eggs, pour this into the prepared pan and bake in the preheated oven for 10 minutes. Remove the roulade from the oven, take it out of the pan and spread about half the filling over the top. Roll it up by picking up one end of the paper and gently easing the roulade over the filling, removing the paper as you do so. Place the roulade on a warmed serving platter and spread the rest of the sauce over the top. Sprinkle with parsley and serve with a Polonaise sauce (page 196). Serve with Peperonata or Zucchini provençal.

1. Line the pan with well-buttered paper then quickly pour in the roulade batter, spreading it well into the corners.

2. After baking, spread half the filling over, leaving a slight border. Roll up using the paper to help.

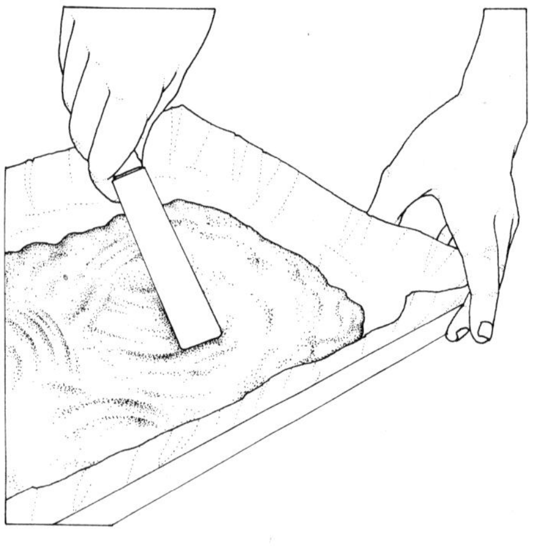

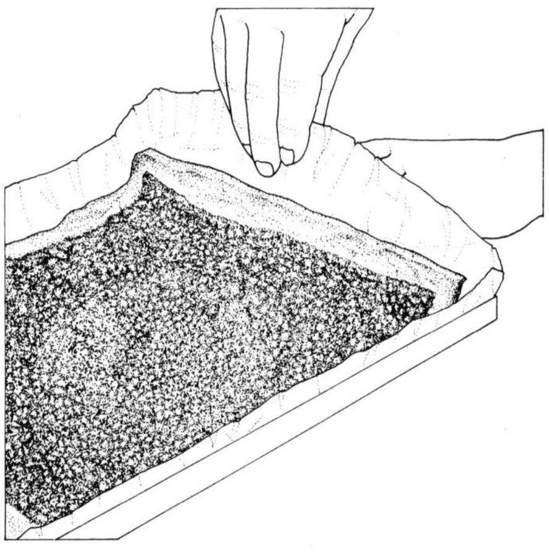

Basic cheese quiche

Serves 4
CALORIES PER PORTION: 365 (1515 kJ)
PROTEIN CONTENT PER PORTION: 12 grams
PREPARATION AND COOKING TIME: 1½ hours

The pastry
1 cup all-purpose flour
¼ teaspoon salt
4 tablespoons unsalted butter
a little iced water

The filling
2 tablespoons butter
½ cup finely chopped onion
3 eggs, beaten
1¼ cups milk
¼ cup grated Cheddar cheese
salt
freshly ground pepper

Sift the flour and salt into a bowl, then cut the butter into the flour, using a knife or a plain pastry cutter. Crumble the mixture with the fingers until it resembles fine breadcrumbs, then stir in just enough water to mix it to a soft but not sticky dough. Wrap the dough in foil and leave to chill in the refrigerator for 30 minutes.

Roll out the chilled dough very thinly on a lightly floured surface, then use it to line an 8 inch diameter pie pan, preferably one with a removable base — quiches are easier to serve from these. Cover the dough with a layer of foil and chill it again while you are making the filling.

Preheat the oven to 400°F. Melt the butter in a thick-based pan over gentle heat, add the onion and fry until it is golden brown. Put the eggs in a bowl, add the milk and cheese, season with salt and pepper and beat until well mixed. Remove the onion from the pan with a slotted spoon and stir it into the egg mixture.

Remove the foil from the pie shell, pour in the filling and bake in the pre-heated oven for 20 minutes, then lower the heat to 350°F and bake for a further 10 minutes. Open the oven door slightly and leave the quiche to settle for a few minutes before taking it out. Remove it from the pie pan and serve warm or cold with a salad.

Note: The chopped onion can be blanched for a few minutes in a little boiling water instead of frying it, if you prefer.

Cauliflower quiche

Serves 4
CALORIES PER PORTION: 370 (1537 kJ)
PROTEIN CONTENT PER PORTION: 12.5 grams
PREPARATION & COOKING TIME: 1½ hours

1 medium head cauliflower, cooked and puréed or broken into small florets

Follow the basic recipe for Cheese quiche, adding the cauliflower to the filling with the cheese. Serve, if liked, with a Spiced apricot sauce (page 197).

Spinach quiche

Serves 4
CALORIES PER PORTION: 380 (1857 kJ)
PROTEIN CONTENT PER PORTION: 15 grams
PREPARATION & COOKING TIME: 1½ hours

1 cup cooked puréed spinach

Follow the basic recipe for Cheese quiche, adding the spinach to the filling mixture with the cheese.

Leek and cheese quiche

Serves 4
CALORIES PER PORTION: 410 (1705 kJ)
PROTEIN CONTENT PER PORTION: 13 grams
PREPARATION & COOKING TIME: 1½ hours

½ lb leeks, very thinly sliced and simmered in a little butter until tender, then well drained

Follow the basic recipe for Cheese quiche, adding the leeks to the filling with the cheese.

Curried eggs

Serves 4
CALORIES PER PORTION: 290 (1215 kJ)
PROTEIN CONTENT PER PORTION: 17 grams
PREPARATION & COOKING TIME: 10-15 minutes

2 tablespoons olive or sunflower oil
1 cup finely chopped onion
1-2 tablespoons finely chopped ginger root
4 teaspoons curry powder, or to taste
1 small clove of garlic, peeled and crushed
½ teaspoon finely grated lemon rind
1½ tablespoons wholewheat flour
1¼ cups strong White vegetable stock (page 34)
1-2 teaspoons lemon juice
4 hard-cooked eggs, cut in half lengthwise
1¼ cups cooked long-grain rice, flavored with turmeric
1-2 tablespoons shredded coconut

Heat the oil, add the onion and ginger root and fry until golden brown, stirring occasionally to prevent them sticking and burning. Add the curry powder, garlic and lemon rind and stir until well mixed. Sprinkle in the flour and cook for 1-2 minutes, stirring continuously. Remove the pan from the heat and gradually add the stock and lemon juice, stirring well between each addition. Return the pan to the heat, increase the heat and bring the sauce to a boil, stirring constantly until it thickens. Add a little extra stock or water if the sauce is too thick.

Lower the halved eggs carefully into the boiling sauce, then turn down the heat and cook them for at least 5 minutes, while you warm up the rice.

Arrange the eggs on a bed of rice, then coat with some of the curry sauce. Sprinkle over the coconut and serve with the rest of the sauce handed separately.

Welsh rarebit

Serves 4
CALORIES PER PORTION: 230 (957 kJ)
PROTEIN CONTENT PER PORTION: 9 grams
PREPARATION & COOKING TIME: 10 minutes

2 tablespoons butter
3 tablespoons wholewheat flour
1 cup grated dry Cheddar cheese
½ cup dark beer
4 slices of warm wholewheat toast

Heat the broiler. Melt the butter in a pan over gentle heat, stir in the flour, then the cheese. Cook until the cheese begins to melt, then pour in the beer and stir the mixture well until all the cheese has melted and it is completely smooth. Pour over the slices of toast and put them under the hot broiler until the tops bubble and turn golden brown. Serve with slices of dill pickle.

Oeufs mollets

Oeufs mollets are, in fact, well-cooked soft-cooked eggs. It should be possible to remove their shells with ease, but the yolks should still be runny. They make very good appetizers for a dinner party, so I have included one or two recipes in the preceding chapter. They also come in handy for a tasty light lunch or supper dish, as the basic Oeufs mollets can be served in a variety of ways.

To cook them: bring the eggs to room temperature, then lower them into a pan of boiling water, using a blanching basket if you are cooking more than one at a time. Do not allow the water to go off the boil for more than a second or two while they are being cooked. Large eggs will take about 6 minutes — allow a little less for smaller eggs — then remove them from the water in the blanching basket and plunge it immediately into a bowl of cold water to prevent the eggs cooking further. Leave for a minute or two.

To peel them tap them gently to crack the shells and then, holding the egg in the palm of your hand, carefully lift up part of the shell, taking the underlying membrane with it. Roll the egg in the hand as you peel off the shell, being careful not to let it break in half. Hold the egg under running water to remove any stubborn bits of shell, then keep in a bowl of cold water in the refrigerator until required.

To reheat them: put the eggs in a bowl of hot, but not boiling, water and leave them for 5 minutes.

In addition to the following recipes, try them on a bed of diced, cooked mushrooms with Madeira sauce; with a mixture of diced, cooked spring vegetables and a rich Béchamel sauce; with lentils and a Provençal sauce; or serve them on a fried bread croûte with a Béarnaise or Maltese sauce (page 127).

The other sauces can be found in the chapter of Basic recipes.

Oeufs mollets Crécy

Serves 4
CALORIES PER PORTION: 460 (1917 kJ)
PROTEIN CONTENT PER PORTION: 13 grams
PREPARATION & COOKING TIME: 35 minutes

4 tablespoons clarified butter, or olive or sunflower oil
1 lb carrots, thinly sliced
4 Oeufs mollets
1¼ cups thick Béchamel sauce (page 196)
4 slices of wholewheat bread, crusts removed and fried in butter (croûtes)
salt
freshly ground pepper

Heat the butter or oil in a thick-based pan over gentle heat. Add the carrots, cover the pan and cook for 20-30 minutes until the carrots are tender and golden brown, turning them over so they do not burn.

Meanwhile, make the Oeufs mollets, or reheat them in a bowl of hot water for 5 minutes. Gently heat up the sauce, and fry the bread croûtes.

Remove the cooked carrots from the heat, sprinkle with salt and pepper and divide them equally between the slices of fried bread, reserving a few slices of carrot for the garnish.

Place an egg on the bed of carrot in the center of each croûte and coat with the hot Béchamel sauce. Adjust the seasoning, garnish with the reserved carrots and serve immediately.

Oeufs mollets in potato nests

Serves 4
CALORIES PER PORTION: 435 (1825 kJ)
PROTEIN CONTENT PER PORTION: 22 grams
PREPARATION & COOKING TIME: 1 hour

½ lb potatoes
2 eggs, well beaten
1 cup grated sharp Cheddar cheese
salt
freshly ground pepper
4 Oeufs mollets
1¼ cups thick Mushroom or Béchamel sauce (page 196)

Cook the potatoes in boiling salted water for 7-10 minutes, or until tender. Drain them, then work through a potato ricer. Add the beaten eggs, reserving a little for brushing the potato nests. Add the cheese, season with salt and pepper and beat well. Preheat the oven to 400°F.

Put the cheese and potato purée into a pastry bag fitted with a large rose nozzle and pipe four circular 'nests' on a well-oiled baking sheet. Bake in the preheated oven for 5 minutes, then brush with the reserved beaten egg. Return to the oven and bake for a further 15 minutes.

Meanwhile, prepare the Oeufs mollets or reheat them in a bowl of hot water for 5 minutes, if necessary.

Gently heat up the Mushroom or Béchamel sauce.

Transfer the cooked potato nests to a warmed serving plate and pour a little hot sauce into the center of each. Place the eggs carefully on top, then coat with the remaining sauce. Serve immediately.

Scotch eggs

Serves 4
CALORIES PER PORTION: 395 (1662 kJ)
PROTEIN CONTENT PER PORTION: 25 grams
PREPARATION & COOKING TIME: 1 hour

2 cups cooked soybeans
1 cup finely chopped onion
½ teaspoon dried thyme
1 teaspoon dried sage
salt
freshly ground pepper
2 eggs, well beaten
4 hard-cooked eggs
¼ cup wholewheat flour
¼ cup fine dried wholewheat breadcrumbs
oil for deep frying

Mince or blend the soybeans with the onion and herbs and season well with salt and pepper. Add half the beaten eggs and bind the mixture together thoroughly. Divide it into 4 portions; pat 1 portion out into a round, put a hard-cooked egg in the center and wrap the soy mixture evenly around it.

Roll each Scotch egg in flour, dip it in the remaining beaten egg, then coat thickly with breadcrumbs.

Heat the oil to 350°F in a deep-fat fryer. Lower the Scotch eggs carefully into the oil and deep fry them for 2-3 minutes, or until they are golden brown. Remove them with a slotted spoon and drain well on paper towels. Leave to cool, then serve cold with a salad.

Pasta

One of the great surprises of Italian cooking, for the uninitiated, is the enormous variety of pasta shapes. It is easy to imagine that, since the basic ingredients are the same, the flavor of each dish must be the same. The shape of the pasta – long, short, hollow, flat or curved – determines how much of the accompanying sauce is taken in with each forkful, and you will be surprised at the difference in taste the shape of the pasta seems to make.

Experiment first with the different types served with the same sauce, then with different sauces and the same pasta shape and you will be amazed at the subtle variations in flavor. Your scope for experimentation is widened by the filled pastas – cannelloni and ravioli – the variations are endless; we have room, alas, for but a few . . . Easy to make, easy to store and very satisfying if you are really hungry, pasta must be the ultimate 'convenience food'. Once you have made your own, using wholewheat flour, you will be reluctant to return to the commercial type. Travel in Italy with a notebook, and you will fill it with yet more recipes to savor.

Basic pasta dough

Wholewheat flour produces a coarser pasta dough than white flour and it cannot be rolled out as thinly, but it nevertheless makes delicious pasta.

Serves 4
CALORIES PER PORTION: 410 (1712 kJ)
PROTEIN CONTENT PER PORTION: 19 grams
PREPARATION & COOKING TIME: 1 hour

3½ cups wholewheat flour, or 4 cups white bread flour, sifted
2-3 eggs
1 teaspoon salt
1-2 tablespoons water

Put the flour in a large bowl, or in a mound on a work surface, and make a well in the center. Beat 2 eggs with the salt and work them lightly into the flour with your fingertips until evenly distributed — the mixture should then resemble fresh breadcrumbs. If necessary, add part of or all the remaining egg to achieve the correct consistency.

Work the mixture to a firm dough on your work surface, adding the water a little at a time until the dough holds together. The exact amount of water used depends on the absorbency of the flour and the size of the eggs. Knead the dough thoroughly for 5-10 minutes until it feels elastic, keeping the hands, dough and work surface well floured.

To make Lasagne verdi

1 Make the pasta dough as directed, adding ½ cup cooked spinach purée, thoroughly drained, after the eggs. Stir the spinach into the flour and egg mixture until evenly distributed, then add just enough water to make a firm dough.
2 Proceed as for Tagliatelle, up to and including stage 4.
3 Cut the dough into 3 inch squares and put in a single layer on a floured baking sheet to dry.

To make Tagliatelle

1 Cut the dough into two equal pieces. Roll one of these into a long 'sausage' with well-floured hands, then sprinkle the work surface, dough and rolling pin lightly with more flour.
2 Starting at one end of the 'sausage', roll a small section of the dough out lengthwise, using fairly gentle pressure. Roll from the center to the left, and from the center to the right, stretching the dough gently as you roll and trying to keep an even thickness.
3 Continue rolling out the dough in this way a section at a time until the end of the 'sausage' is reached, then work back the other way. Roll and stretch the dough until it is about 18 inches long and *almost* thin enough to see through, using more flour as necessary. Keep the ends of the dough square and the sides straight by pushing inwards with the rolling pin from time to time as you work.
4 Repeat this rolling and stretching process with the second piece of dough, remembering that the working the dough receives by repeated rolling is part of the process.
5 Roll up each sheet of dough loosely, then cut across the dough at about ¼ inch intervals with a sharp, thin-bladed knife. Use a sawing action and do not press too hard or the layers will stick together.
6 Unroll the dough ribbons and spread them out on a clean cloth.

1
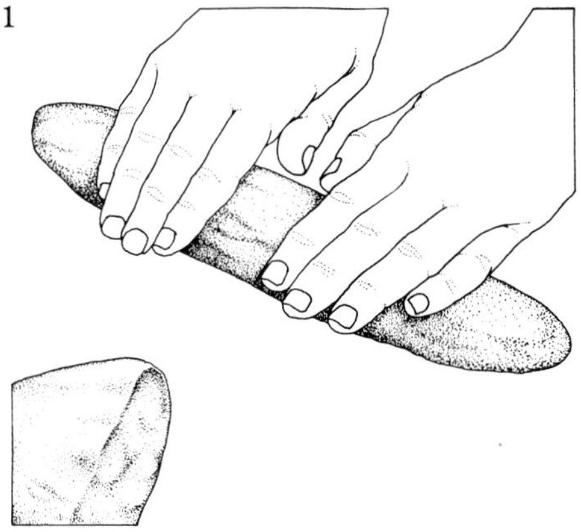

2
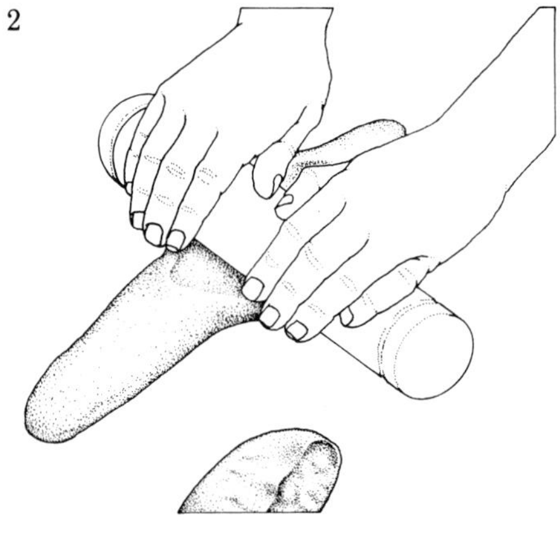

3
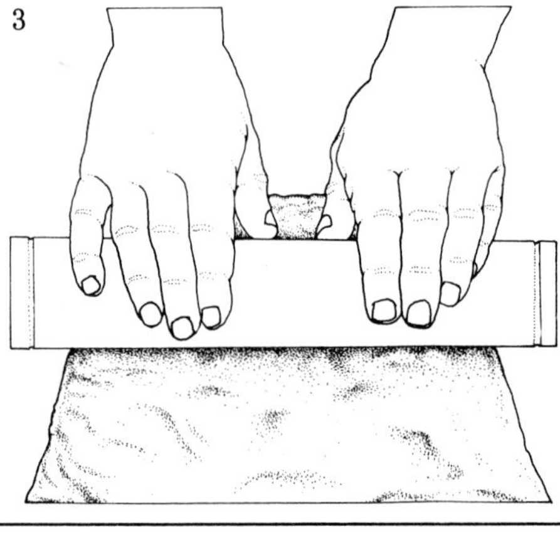

4
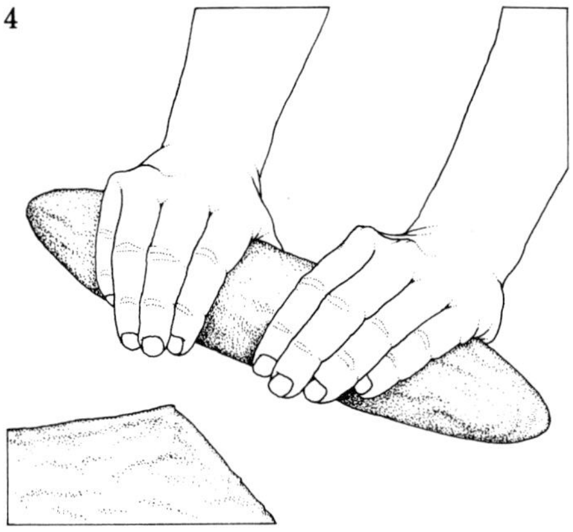

5
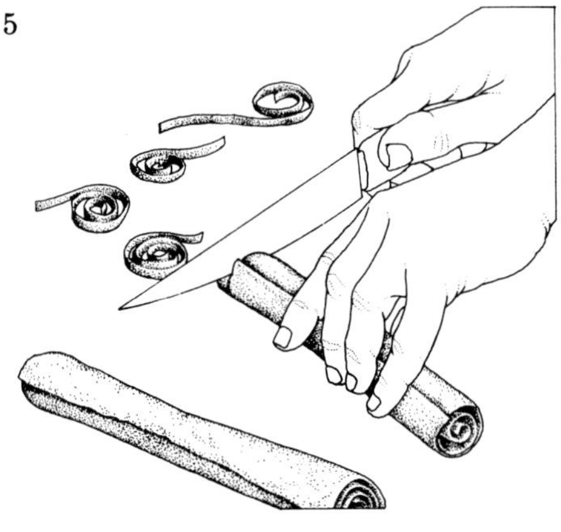

6
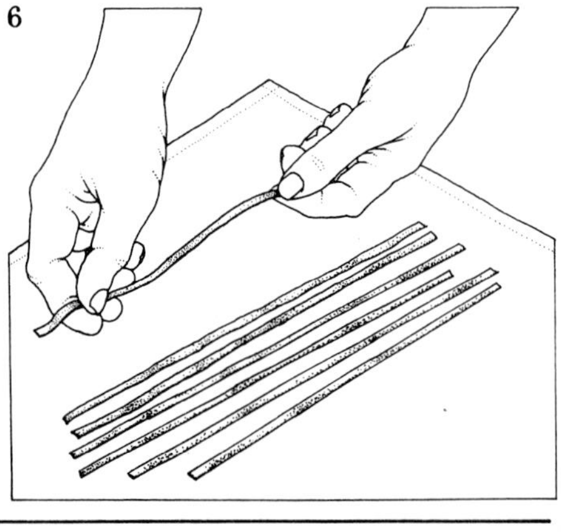

To make Cappelletti

1 Proceed as for Tagliatelle, up to and including stage 4.
2 Cut the dough into 2½ inch squares. Put a little of your chosen filling in the center of each square, then brush the edges with beaten egg.
3 Fold one corner of the dough over the filling to form a triangle, then press the edges firmly to seal. Wind the triangle around your forefinger and pinch the ends together to form the shape of a small 'hat', or cappelletto.

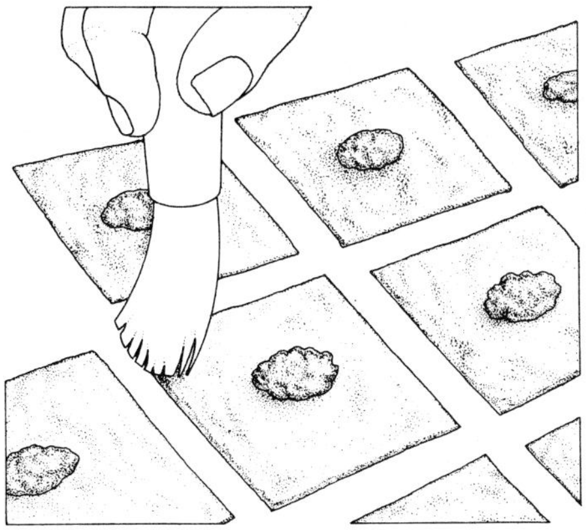

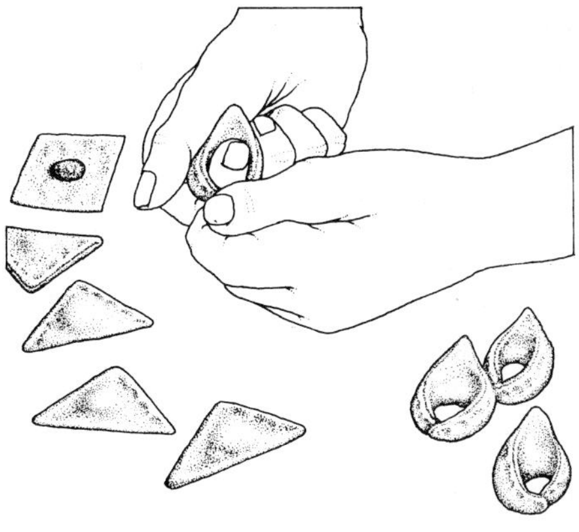

To make Farfalletti

1 Proceed as for Tagliatelle, up to and including stage 4.
2 Cut thin strips of dough about 3 inches long and ¾ inch wide. Squeeze the center of each strip to form a bow and allow to dry completely.

To make frilly bows, use a serrated-edged pastry wheel to cut the dough.

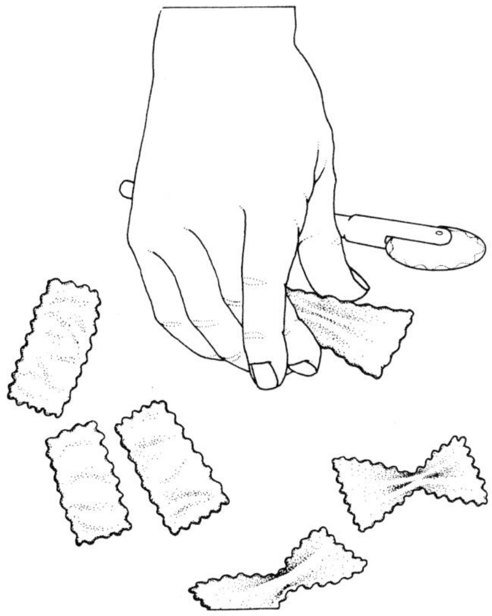

To cook freshly made pasta

Bring 3 quarts of well-salted water to a boil in a large pan. Add 2 tablespoons of oil to prevent the pasta from sticking to itself while cooking, then boil the pasta for 5-7 minutes until *al dente* (tender but firm to bite).

Pour the contents of the pan into a colander and pour boiling water through it. Drain the pasta and toss with pats of butter or a dressing of — preferably — olive oil and finely chopped parsley and garlic. Grated Parmesan cheese can also be served with it, or chopped cooked mushrooms or diced cooked vegetables. In the summer months, when fresh basil is available, serve freshly made pasta with Pesto or Pesto di Formaggio.

Pasta salad

Serves 4
CALORIES PER PORTION: 1202 (5035 kJ)
PROTEIN CONTENT PER PORTION: 27 grams
PREPARATION & COOKING TIME: 1 hour

½ lb wholewheat macaroni or spaghetti, broken into small pieces
5 tablespoons olive or sunflower oil
1 teaspoon paprika
2 teaspoons lemon juice
1 tablespoon wine vinegar
1½ cups thinly sliced button mushrooms
1 tablespoon soy sauce
½ cup finely chopped scallions
1 cup finely chopped celery
2½ tablespoons sunflower seeds
2 hard-cooked eggs, finely chopped
1½ cups coarsely grated Cheddar cheese
2 tablespoons finely chopped basil or parsley
1½ cups garlic-flavored Mayonnaise (page 126)

Cook the pasta in boiling salted water, with 2 tablespoons of the oil added, until *al dente* (tender but firm to bite). Meanwhile mix together the remaining oil, the paprika, lemon juice and vinegar, pour it over the mushrooms and stir until they are evenly coated. When the pasta is cooked, drain it, rinse thoroughly under cold running water and leave until it is quite cold, forking it from time to time so that it does not stick together.

Mix the cold pasta with the soy sauce, scallions, celery, sunflower seeds, eggs, cheese and herbs. Stir in enough Mayonnaise to bind it lightly together, spoon it into a serving dish and scatter the marinated mushrooms over the top before serving.

Pesto

Serves 4
CALORIES PER PORTION: 405 (1670 kJ)
PROTEIN CONTENT PER PORTION: negligible
PREPARATION TIME: about 10 minutes

1½ cups fresh basil leaves
3 cloves of garlic, peeled
salt
1 cup olive oil

Pound the basil and garlic to a pulp with a little salt. Pound in the oil, drop by drop, until the sauce is the consistency of thin cream. Serve with pasta or Minestrone soup (page 37).

Pesto di formaggio

Serves 4
CALORIES PER PORTION: 665 (2780 kJ)
PROTEIN CONTENT PER PORTION: 12 grams

Pound in 1 cup grated Parmesan cheese and ½ to 1 cup pine nuts.

Spaghetti with egg and crispy onion rings

Serves 4
CALORIES PER PORTION:
PROTEIN CONTENT PER PORTION:
PREPARATION & COOKING TIME: 40 minutes

1 lb wholewheat spaghetti
1-2 tablespoons oil
oil for deep frying
1 lb onions, cut into thin rings
½ lb button mushrooms
salt
6 eggs, well beaten
1 clove of garlic, peeled and chopped
coarsely ground black pepper

Cook the spaghetti in a large pan of boiling salted water, with 1-2 tablespoons oil added, for 10-15 minutes until *al dente* (tender, but firm to bite).

Meanwhile, heat the oil in a deep fat fryer to just below 350°F. Put the onion rings and mushrooms in a frying basket, sprinkle very lightly with salt, then lower the basket into the hot oil. Deep fry the onion rings until golden brown and crisp, stirring from time to time to ensure even cooking. Remove the basket from the pan, drain the onions and mushrooms and keep them hot.

Drain the spaghetti in a colander, pour through some boiling water, then drain well and return the spaghetti to the rinsed-out pan. Mix the fried onions and the mushrooms into the spaghetti, then add the beaten eggs and garlic. Cook over gentle heat until the eggs just begin to curdle to a sauce, shaking the pan constantly — try not to let them scramble. Sprinkle with freshly ground pepper and serve.

Note: Tagliatelle can be used instead of the spaghetti, and the onions and mushrooms can be served on top of the egg and spaghetti, if preferred.

Spaghetti al funghi

Serves 4
CALORIES PER PORTION: 915 (3830 kJ)
PROTEIN CONTENT PER PORTION: 18.5 grams
PREPARATION & COOKING TIME: 35 minutes

1 lb wholewheat spaghetti
salt
4-5 tablespoons olive or sunflower oil
4 cups finely chopped mushrooms
8 scallions, sliced in half lengthwise and finely chopped
freshly ground black pepper
1¼ cups heavy cream

Cook the spaghetti in a large pan of boiling salted water, with 1-2 tablespoons of oil added, for 10-15 minutes until *al dente* (tender, but firm to bite). Meanwhile, heat 2 tablespoons of the oil in a pan, add the mushrooms and fry over fairly brisk heat, stirring all the time until they are dark and shiny and most of their juices have evaporated. Remove from the heat and keep hot.

Heat the remaining oil in a small pan, add the scallions and fry over gentle heat until they are just softened.

Drain the spaghetti in a colander and pour some boiling water through it. Drain again, mix it into the mushrooms and season with salt and pepper. Bring the cream to a boil in a separate pan, then pour it over the spaghetti and mushroom mixture. Sprinkle with the onions and serve.

A crisp green salad and a generous sprinkling of Parmesan cheese go well with this dish.

Note: It may seem tedious to use so many pans in this recipe, but you must do so, otherwise the mushrooms will stain the onions or the cream and spoil the appearance of the finished dish.

Spaghetti with eggplant

Serves 4
CALORIES PER PORTION: 730 (3057 kJ)
PROTEIN CONTENT PER PORTION: 25 grams
PREPARATION & COOKING TIME: 1¼ hours, including salting the eggplants

1 lb eggplants, cut into thin strips
1 medium onion, thinly sliced
salt
1 lb wholewheat spaghetti
6 tablespoons olive or sunflower oil
freshly ground black pepper
2 large cloves of garlic, peeled and very finely chopped (optional)
1¼ cups sour cream or plain yogurt (optional)
½ cup grated Parmesan cheese

Mix together the eggplants and onion, sprinkle with salt and leave to drain for 30 minutes. Rinse under cold running water and pat dry with paper towels. Cook the spaghetti in a large pan of boiling salted water with 2 tablespoons of oil for 10-15 minutes until *al dente* (tender, but firm to bite).

Meanwhile, heat 2 more tablespoons of oil in a pan, add half the eggplants and onion and fry over gentle heat until golden brown and crisp. Keep turning them over frequently to ensure they cook evenly. Press them against the sides of the pan to remove any excess oil, then remove, drain well and keep hot.

Heat the remaining oil, add the rest of the eggplants and onion and fry these over gentle heat until they, too, are golden brown and crisp; remove, drain and keep hot.

When the spaghetti is cooked, transfer it to a colander and pour some boiling water through it. Drain well, then pile it in a shallow, warmed serving dish. Add the eggplants and onion, sprinkle with salt and pepper and fold them gently into the spaghetti. Sprinkle the top with garlic, if using, mix in the sour cream or yogurt if you need a sauce, and serve with the grated Parmesan cheese.

Top: a dish of succulent wholewheat spaghetti, ready to use in such culinary delights as Spaghetti with eggplant (center). Try this with sour cream to offset the richness of the vegetables. Front: tasty Brown ravioli squares are filled with a mixture of onion, cheese and parsley, while Gnocchi Romana, made from cornmeal (right) are sprinkled generously with Parmesan and finished under the broiler

Ravioli

It takes practice to make good ravioli; there should be just the right amount of filling for the dough, and the layers of dough should not be too thick. However, it is well worth making your own.

Serves 4
CALORIES PER PORTION: 610 (2555 kJ)
PROTEIN CONTENT PER PORTION: 34 grams
PREPARATION & COOKING TIME: 2 hours

½ quantity of Basic pasta dough (page 74)
1 egg, well beaten
1-2 tablespoons oil
1¼-2½ cups Tomato sauce (page 196)
2-3 tablespoons grated Parmesan cheese

The filling
1½ teaspoons butter
1 tablespoon finely chopped onion
1 cup cottage cheese
1 cup grated Parmesan cheese
¼ cup chopped parsley
a little lemon juice
1 egg, well beaten
salt
freshly ground black pepper

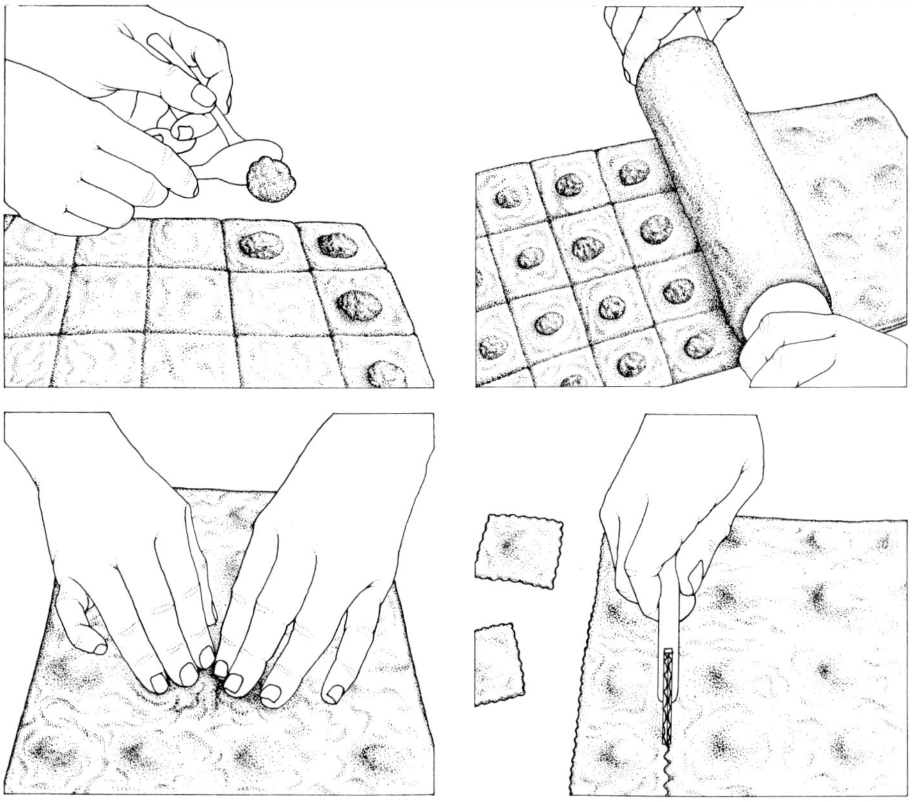

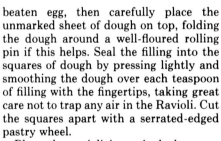

Roll and stretch the dough out on a lightly floured surface until about 20 inches square. Keep both sides of the dough well-floured, then cut the dough in half and mark one half into squares measuring a little less than 2 inches.

To make the filling, melt the butter in a skillet and fry onion until transparent. Put the cooked onion into a bowl with the rest of the filling ingredients and beat well. Place a small teaspoon of filling in the center of each square of dough. Brush the edges of each marked square with beaten egg, then carefully place the unmarked sheet of dough on top, folding the dough around a well-floured rolling pin if this helps. Seal the filling into the squares of dough by pressing lightly and smoothing the dough over each teaspoon of filling with the fingertips, taking great care not to trap any air in the Ravioli. Cut the squares apart with a serrated-edged pastry wheel.

Place the ravioli in a single layer on floured plates, then cover with a dampened floured cloth and leave for at least 30 minutes, or until required.

Cook the Ravioli in a large pan of boiling salted water, with 1-2 tablespoons of oil, for 5-7 minutes until *al dente* (tender, but firm to bite).

Meanwhile, heat the Tomato sauce in a separate pan. Take out the cooked Ravioli with a slotted spoon, drain thoroughly and pile into a warmed serving dish. Pour the hot Tomato sauce over and serve with grated Parmesan cheese.

Cannelloni with spinach

This quantity serves 4 as a main course, 8 as an appetizer.

TOTAL CALORIES: 2330 (9750 kJ)
TOTAL PROTEIN CONTENT: 120 grams
PREPARATION & COOKING TIME: 2 hours

½ Basic pasta dough (page 74)
1-2 tablespoons oil
1¼-2½ cups Tomato sauce (page 196)
1 cup grated Parmesan cheese

The filling
2 tablespoons butter
1 cup finely chopped onion
3 tablespoons wholewheat flour
½ cup milk
2 cups chopped cooked fresh or frozen spinach, thoroughly drained
1 egg, well beaten
salt and freshly ground black pepper

Roll and stretch the dough on a lightly floured surface, as for Tagliatelle, until very thin, then cut out 10 rectangles about 5 × 4 inches. Cook the pasta in a large pan of boiling salted water, with 1-2 tablespoons of oil added, until *al dente* (tender, but firm to bite). Remove from the pan with a slotted spoon, then drain well, turn onto a plate (not paper towels or it will stick) and keep it covered until required.

To make the filling melt the butter over gentle heat, add the onion and fry until golden brown. Sprinkle in the flour and cook for 1-2 minutes, stirring continuously. Remove the pan from the heat, add the milk gradually, stirring well between each addition, then return the pan to the heat. Increase the heat and bring the sauce to a boil, stirring all the time until it thickens.

Add the spinach, stir again, then remove the sauce from the heat and leave it to cool slightly. Add the egg, season with salt and pepper and stir well. Preheat the oven to 400°F.

Pour a thin layer of Tomato sauce on the bottom of a baking dish. Divide the spinach filling among the rectangles of Cannelloni, then roll up to enclose the filling. Place the Cannelloni in the dish side by side with the seams underneath, then coat with the remaining Tomato sauce. Sprinkle with half the Parmesan cheese.

Bake in the preheated oven for 20-30 minutes until the sauce is bubbling and the cheese is golden brown. Serve hot, and pass the remaining Parmesan.

Lasagne verde al forno

Serves 6
CALORIES PER PORTION: 650 (2723 kJ)
PROTEIN CONTENT PER PORTION: 25 grams
PREPARATION & COOKING TIME: 2 hours

1 lb lasagne verde, made from the basic recipe (page 74), cooked and drained
2½ cups Bêchamel sauce (page 196)
1 cup grated Parmesan cheese

The filling
2 tablespoons butter
1 cup finely chopped onion
3 tablespoons wholewheat flour
½ cup milk
2 cups chopped cooked fresh or frozen spinach, thoroughly drained
1 egg, well beaten
salt
freshly ground pepper

The sauce
2 tablespoons olive or sunflower oil
1 cup finely chopped onion
4 cups coarsely chopped mushrooms
2 cloves of garlic, peeled and finely chopped
3 tablespoons wholewheat flour
1¼ cups dry red wine
salt
freshly ground black pepper

Make the filling, following the instructions given on page 78 in the recipe for Cannelloni.

To make the sauce: heat the oil in a pan, add the onion and fry until golden brown. Add the mushrooms and garlic and continue cooking over fairly brisk heat until the mushrooms are dark and shiny and most of their juice has evaporated. Stir them constantly to prevent them sticking and burning.

Mix in the flour, stir in the wine, increase the heat and bring to a boil. Lower the heat and simmer, stirring briskly, until the sauce thickens. Add salt and pepper, then remove the pan from the heat.

Preheat the oven to 350°F. Coat the bottom of a large, well-buttered baking dish about 3 inches deep with a little Béchamel sauce, then layer the dish as follows: lasagne, followed by Béchamel, spinach filling and mushroom sauce. Add a sprinkling of grated cheese and continue layering in the same order until all the ingredients are used up, finishing with a layer of lasagne and a sprinkling of Parmesan cheese.

Bake in the preheated oven for 30 minutes until the top is golden brown and bubbling. Serve hot with some extra Parmesan cheese handed separately, if liked.

Tagliatelle with cream sauce

Serves 4
CALORIES PER PORTION: 785 (3285 kJ)
PROTEIN CONTENT PER PORTION: 17.5 grams
PREPARATION & COOKING TIME: 35 minutes

1 lb wholewheat Tagliatelle, made from the basic recipe
1-2 tablespoons olive or sunflower oil
2 tablespoons butter
1 cup finely chopped onion
1 cup strained cottage cheese
a little light cream
salt
freshly ground pepper
½ cup grated Parmesan cheese

Cook the Tagliatelle in a large pan of boiling salted water with 1-2 tablespoons of oil, until *al dente* (tender, but firm to bite).

Melt the butter over gentle heat, add the onion and fry until soft and pale gold.

Drain the pasta in a colander, pour through some boiling water, then drain again and keep hot. Add the cottage cheese to the onion and stir until melted. (Do not allow the cheese to boil or it will separate and become stringy.) Add the pasta to the cheese mixture, mixing it in well so that each strand of pasta is coated with sauce. Stir in just enough cream to moisten and lighten the texture of the sauce, season with a little salt and plenty of pepper and serve with the Parmesan cheese handed separately.

Note: If you find 1 lb pasta overwhelming for 4, or are serving the dish as an appetizer, use half to three-quarters of the homemade pasta, but remember that the calorie and protein count will alter accordingly.

Tagliatelle with tomato, celery and almond sauce

Serves 4
CALORIES PER PORTION:
PROTEIN CONTENT PER PORTION:
PREPARATION & COOKING TIME: 1 hour

1 lb wholewheat Tagliatelle, made from the basic recipe
7 tablespoons olive or sunflower oil
2 cups finely chopped onions
2 cups finely chopped celery
3 tablespoons wholewheat flour
1 large clove of garlic, peeled and finely chopped
2 cups skinned and roughly chopped tomatoes
1 cup blanched almonds
salt
freshly ground black pepper
½ cup grated Parmesan cheese

Cook the pasta in a large pan of boiling salted water, with 1-2 tablespoons of oil added, until *al dente* (tender, but firm to bite). Meanwhile, fry the onions and celery in ¼ cup of the oil until they are a pale gold; mix in the flour, add the garlic and tomatoes and continue cooking, stirring constantly, until the tomatoes break down to a pulp and the excess liquid has evaporated.

Fry the almonds in 1 tablespoon of the oil until they are golden brown, then shred them coarsely. When the Tagliatelle is cooked, drain it in a colander, pour through some boiling water, then drain again and add it to the sauce. Mix them together gently so that the pasta is thoroughly coated. Season to taste with salt and pepper and pour into a warmed serving dish. Sprinkle with the cheese and scatter the shredded almonds on top before serving.

Note: Spaghetti also goes well with this sauce.

Conchiglie with peas

Serves 4
CALORIES PER PORTION: 930 (3895 kJ)
PROTEIN CONTENT PER PORTION: 32 grams
PREPARATION & COOKING TIME: 45 minutes (a little longer if fresh peas are used)

1 lb conchiglie (pasta shells)
6 tablespoons olive or sunflower oil
2 cups fresh or frozen peas
2 tablespoons butter
2 cups coarsely shredded carrots
2 cups finely chopped onions
1-2 cloves of garlic, peeled and finely chopped
⅔ cup sour cream
¼ cup dried skimmed milk made into a cream with 4-6 tablespoons cold milk
1 cup coarsely grated strong cheese
about ¼ cup hot milk
salt
freshly ground pepper

Cook the pasta shells in a large pan of boiling salted water, with 1-2 tablespoons of the oil added, until *al dente* (tender but firm to bite). Meanwhile, cook the peas gently in the butter, taking care that they do not burn. Fry the carrots and onions in the rest of the oil over moderate heat for 20 minutes, or until they are golden brown.

When the peas are cooked, add them to the carrots and onions, then stir in the garlic, sour cream and the milk solution. Lower the heat and keep the sauce hot, stirring it occasionally. Drain the pasta in a colander and pour some boiling water through it. Drain again thoroughly and add it to the sauce.

Sprinkle over the cheese and stir it in, adding a little of the hot milk if the sauce is too thick. Season well with salt and pepper and serve immediately.

Gnocchi Romana

Serves 4
CALORIES PER PORTION: 330 (1377 kJ)
PROTEIN CONTENT PER PORTION: 15 grams
PREPARATION & COOKING TIME: 1 hour

2½ cups milk
½ small onion, thinly sliced
1 clove of garlic, peeled and finely chopped
1 bay leaf
2 tablespoons butter
½-1 teaspoon salt
⅓ cup polenta or corn meal
1-2 tablespoons melted butter
1 cup grated Parmesan cheese
freshly ground black pepper

Put the milk, onion, garlic, bay leaf, butter and salt in a pan and bring slowly to a boil, so that the flavors infuse into the milk. Strain the milk into a clean pan, bring back to a boil, then pour in the polenta or corn meal. Stir until thick, then simmer for 5 minutes, still stirring constantly to prevent it burning and sticking.

Pour the paste onto a well-oiled marble slab or suitable work surface, then spread it out until about ½ inch thick, keeping the edges straight. Leave until cold, then cut into 2½ inch rounds.

Preheat the oven to 400°F. Arrange the rounds overlapping in a well-buttered baking dish, brush with melted butter, then sprinkle with a little of the Parmesan cheese and plenty of freshly ground black pepper. Bake in the preheated oven for 15-20 minutes until golden. Serve piping hot with the remaining cheese handed separately, and accompanied by a Tomato or Mushroom Sauce (page 196).

Note: If it is very cold and you are using a marble slab, first warm the slab by wiping it with a hot, wet cloth to prevent it from cracking.

Spinach gnocchi

Serves 4
CALORIES PER PORTION: 495 (2067 kJ)
PROTEIN CONTENT PER PORTION: 33 grams
PREPARATION AND COOKING TIME: 1½-2 hours

1 cup chopped cooked spinach, thoroughly drained
1 cup strained cottage cheese
2 eggs
1 egg white
½ cup grated Parmesan cheese
6 tablespoons wholewheat flour
salt
1 tablespoon vinegar
freshly ground pepper

To finish
1-2 tablespoons melted butter
¼ cup grated Parmesan cheese

Put the spinach in a blender with the cottage cheese, eggs, egg white and half the Parmesan cheese. Blend until fairly smooth, then transfer to a bowl and sprinkle in the remaining Parmesan. Add the flour and mix in thoroughly, then leave the dough to stand in a cool place for 30 minutes. Preheat the oven to 400°F.

Bring a large pan of salted water to a boil, then add the vinegar. Season the dough well with salt and pepper, then scoop out spoonfuls and, using 2 spoons, shape the dough gently into balls about the size of golf balls, making the outsides as smooth as possible or the Gnocchi may disintegrate in the pan.

Lower these carefully into the gently simmering water and cook for 2-3 minutes, until they float to the surface, then remove with a slotted spoon and drain thoroughly on paper towels. Cook the Gnocchi in four batches.

Arrange the cooked Gnocchi in a well-buttered baking dish; pour over a little melted butter and sprinkle with the extra Parmesan cheese. Bake in the preheated oven for 10 minutes and serve at once.

Note: A sauce made up of equal quantities of Béchamel and Tomato goes well with Spinach gnocchi.

Main Courses

When planning a dinner party, you should begin by selecting the main course and building all the other dishes around this. If you are cooking for non-vegetarian guests, this is your chance to surprise them with the variety and excellence of vegetarian cuisine.

Make sure that the complete meal is not only enjoyable, but also nutritious enough to provide the necessary protein, vitamins and energy-giving foods. A convenient division of the day's protein intake would be to allow one-sixth for breakfast, two-sixths for lunch and three-sixths for the main meal of the day.

A vegetarian's main sources of protein are the nuts, legumes, eggs, cheese and milk, and my recipes combine these with vegetables, herbs and spices to make dishes that are both delicious and nutritious. Many can be accompanied by a salad or followed by a simple sherbet to clear the palate.

I have included recipes from Chinese cuisine – the Chinese have perhaps the lightest and most delicate touch with vegetables. Indian recipes also feature in my selection – remember that there is an infinite variety to be found in the presentation and cooking of even the most traditional dishes.

Basic crêpe recipe

Serves 4
CALORIES PER PORTION: 260 (1095 kJ)
PROTEIN CONTENT PER PORTION: 9 grams
PREPARATION & COOKING TIME: 1¼ hours, including resting time

2 eggs
½ teaspoon salt
¾ cup plus 2 tablespoons wholewheat flour
1¼ cups milk
oil or clarified butter for frying

Beat the eggs with the salt, then stir in the flour. Pour on the milk and beat it to a thin smooth cream, adding a little extra milk, if necessary. Set aside to rest for 20 minutes. Put a thick-based skillet, about 7 inches diameter, over a moderate heat and brush it with oil or clarified butter. Pour 2 tablespoons of the batter into the pan and swirl it around so that it spreads evenly over the bottom of the pan. When the batter has set and the surface has lost its shiny look, turn it over very gently with a spatula and cook on the other side. If the pan is too hot, the batter will set before it has run thinly enough and the crêpes might burn.

Continue until all the mixture is used up, brushing the pan with a little more oil between each one. Place the crêpes one on top of another on a large, lightly buttered plate over a pan of hot water if you intend to use them immediately; otherwise, put them on a cold plate, cover them with foil or plastic wrap and keep them in the refrigerator until needed.

Note: Crêpes freeze well, if you put a piece of wax paper or foil between each one before packing and storing.

Crêpes Gruyère

Serves 4
CALORIES PER PORTION: 900 (3757 kJ)
PROTEIN CONTENT PER PORTION: 35 grams
PREPARATION & COOKING TIME: 35 minutes

1 pint Béchamel sauce, made with 4 tablespoons butter, 3 tablespoons wholewheat or ¼ cup all-purpose flour and 1 pint milk
1¼ cups finely diced Gruyère cheese
1 tablespoon kirsch
12 crêpes, made from the Basic recipe
¼ cup fresh wholewheat breadcrumbs
½ cup coarsely grated Gruyère cheese
2 tablespoons finely chopped parsley

Preheat the oven to 400°F. Heat the Béchamel sauce gently and stir in the diced cheese and kirsch. Place a little of the warmed mixture on each of the crêpes and roll them up. Place them in a hot, well-buttered baking dish and sprinkle with the breadcrumbs and grated cheese.

Bake the crêpes in the preheated oven for 10-15 minutes until really hot and golden brown. Sprinkle with the chopped parsley and serve with mushrooms, Pommes Lyonnaise or small peas.

Leek and yogurt crêpes

Serves 4
CALORIES PER PORTION: 730 (3045 kJ)
PROTEIN CONTENT PER PORTION: 30 grams
PREPARATION & COOKING TIME: 35 minutes

1½ lb leeks, cut in half, then into ½ inch slices
¼ cup oil
¾ cup plus 2 tablespoons wholewheat flour
2½ cups plain yogurt
1 teaspoon finely chopped marjoram
salt
freshly ground black pepper
12 crêpes, made from the Basic recipe
¼ cup fresh wholewheat breadcrumbs
½ cup grated Cheddar cheese

Preheat the oven to 400°F. Cook the leeks in the oil until they have lost their pungent taste but are still crunchy and just beginning to color. Sprinkle with the flour and mix well. Pour on the yogurt, stir until it is mixed well with the leeks and flour, and bring to a boil, stirring continuously until the mixture thickens. Add the marjoram and season with salt and pepper.

Divide the mixture between the crêpes and roll them up. Place them in a hot, well-buttered baking dish and sprinkle with the breadcrumbs and cheese. Bake them in the preheated oven for 10-15 minutes until they are really hot and golden brown. Serve with plain yogurt as a sauce. Accompaniments: Fennel with orange sauce, Brussel sprouts with peanuts and herb butter or Glazed carrots with cinnamon.

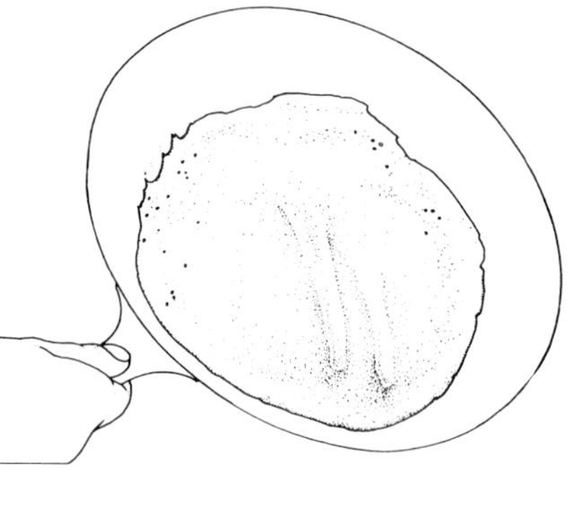

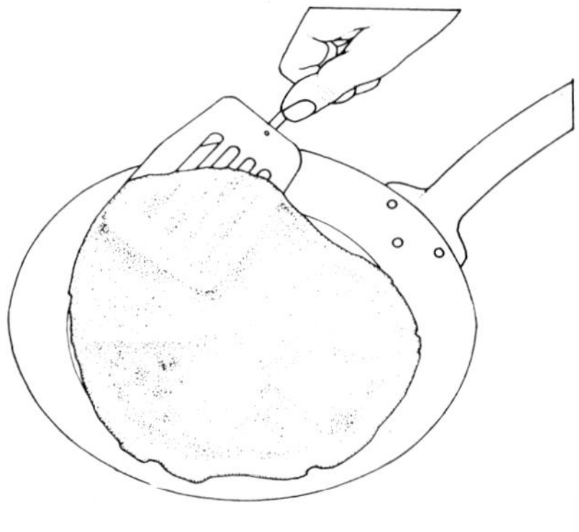

1. Pour a little batter into the pan and quickly tilt the pan to roll the batter evenly over the bottom.

2. When the crêpe is cooked, flip it over with a spatula and briefly cook the second side before filling and rolling.

Corn and lemon crêpes

Serves 4
CALORIES PER PORTION: 860 (3595 kJ)
PROTEIN CONTENT PER PORTION: 36 grams
PREPARATION & COOKING TIME: 35 minutes

4 tablespoons butter or margarine
2 cups finely chopped onions
3 cups cooked corn kernels
7 tablespoons wholewheat flour
1¼ cups milk
2½ cups grated Cheddar cheese
grated rind and juice of 1 lemon
salt
freshly ground pepper
a little freshly grated nutmeg
12 crêpes, made from the Basic recipe
¼ cup fresh wholewheat breadcrumbs

Preheat the oven to 400°F. Melt the butter or margarine in a saucepan over a moderate heat and cook the onions until soft and just beginning to color. Add the corn and cook for a few minutes longer to warm it through. Sprinkle in the flour and mix well. Remove the pan from the heat and gradually stir in the milk. Return to a moderate heat and bring to a boil, stirring continuously until the mixture thickens. Mix in most of the cheese, the lemon rind and juice and stir until the cheese has melted, then season to taste with salt, pepper and nutmeg.

Divide the mixture between the crêpes and roll them up. Place them in a hot, well-buttered baking dish, sprinkle with the breadcrumbs and the remaining cheese and bake in the preheated oven for 10-15 minutes until really hot and golden brown.

Serve with Tomato sauce (page 196).
Accompaniments: Braised celery, green leaf vegetables or a large mixed salad.

Eggplant, onion and tomato crêpes

Makes 12
CALORIES PER PORTION: 570 (2377 kJ)
PROTEIN CONTENT PER PORTION: 18 grams
PREPARATION & COOKING TIME: 1-1¼ hours

1 lb eggplants
salt
¼ cup oil
1 large onion, thinly sliced
2 cups coarsely chopped tomatoes
1½ cups grated Cheddar cheese
1-2 tablespoons wholewheat flour (optional)
1 teaspoon finely chopped oregano
freshly ground black pepper
12 crêpes, made from the Basic recipe
¼ cup fresh wholewheat breadcrumbs

Cut the eggplants into ½ inch cubes and place in a colander. Sprinkle with salt and leave to drain for 30 minutes. Rinse under cold running water and dry well. Preheat the oven to 400°F. Heat half the oil in a thick-based skillet and fry the eggplant cubes until golden brown and soft in the centers. Remove them from the pan and keep hot.

Pour the remaining oil into the pan and fry the onions until golden brown. Add the tomatoes and cook gently until reduced to a pulp. Return the eggplants to the pan, add most of the cheese, and stir until the cheese has melted and the eggplants are hot. If the mixture is too moist to hold its shape, thicken it with the flour dissolved in a very little water. Add the oregano and season with salt and pepper.

Divide the mixture between the crêpes and roll them up. Place in a hot, well-buttered baking dish and sprinkle with the breadcrumbs and remaining cheese. Bake in the preheated oven until really hot and golden brown.
Accompaniments: Red cabbage with apple, Green beans with yogurt and parsley or Greek salad.

Lentil and mushroom crêpes

Serves 6
CALORIES PER PORTION: 320 (1351 kJ)
PROTEIN CONTENT PER PORTION: 15 grams
PREPARATION & COOKING TIME: 1 hour (not including soaking)

1⅓ cups brown lentils, soaked
salt
2 cups finely chopped onions
2 tablespoons vegetable oil
2 cups sliced mushrooms
1 cup coarsely chopped celery
½ teaspoon dried thyme
freshly ground pepper
1-2 eggs, beaten
12 crêpes, made from the Basic recipe

Cook the lentils for 30-45 minutes in 1¼ cups of gently simmering water. Add a little salt when they are nearly cooked — it may be necessary to add a little more water during cooking. Meanwhile, fry the onions in the oil until just beginning to color. Add the mushrooms and celery and cook the mixture gently for about 10 minutes, taking care that it does not burn and that the mixture stays moist. Add a little water, if necessary. Preheat the oven to 400°F.

When the lentils are cooked, drain and add them to the mushroom and onion mixture. Season with thyme and salt and pepper. Quickly stir in one of the eggs so that it binds the mixture together. The texture should be that of soft scrambled eggs, but if it is still too crumbly, add the second egg. Divide the mixture between the crêpes and roll them up. Place them in a hot, well-buttered baking dish and bake in the preheated oven for 10-15 minutes or until really hot.

Serve with Madeira or Tomato Sauce.
Accompaniments: Fried spinach with tomato sauce, squash and tomato casserole or Zucchini provençal.

Cottage cheese and onion croquettes

Serves 4
CALORIES PER PORTION: 445 (1857 kJ)
PROTEIN CONTENT PER PORTION: 10 grams
PREPARATION & COOKING TIME: 1½ hours

1 lb potatoes
1 large bay leaf
1 cup texturized soy protein
1 cup finely chopped onion
1 tablespoon olive or sunflower oil
1 clove of garlic, peeled and crushed
1 cup strained cottage cheese
1 egg, beaten
½ teaspoon finely chopped thyme
½ teaspoon finely chopped marjoram
salt
freshly ground pepper
a little freshly grated nutmeg
wholewheat flour for coating
oil for deep frying

Cook the potatoes with the bay leaf in a little boiling salted water until soft. Drain off and reserve the water, discard the bay leaf, then work the potatoes through a ricer. Pour the reserved potato water over the soy protein and simmer for 3 minutes. Drain and use the liquid, if wished, to make stock for soup. Fry the onion in the oil until soft and golden brown. Add the garlic, potato purée, soy protein, cheese, egg and herbs, and mix well. Season with the salt, pepper and nutmeg and chill for at least 30 minutes until really firm.

Shape the mixture into 12 large croquettes and coat them well with flour. Deep fry the croquettes in oil heated to 350°F until golden brown and crisp. Drain well on paper towels and serve immediately with a Mushroom sauce.
Accompaniments: Leeks with yogurt sauce, Zucchini with sage and cheese sauce, or Green beans with yogurt and parsley, or a protein-rich salad.

Note: These croquettes are also good eaten cold.

Cheese and pepper surprise

Makes 40
CALORIES PER PORTION: 450 (1872 kJ)
PROTEIN CONTENT PER PORTION: 22.5 grams
PREPARATION & COOKING TIME: 1¼-1½ hours

½ lb Edam cheese
4 green peppers, weighing about ½ lb each
a little prepared French-style mustard
a little wholewheat flour
1¼ cups Coating batter (page 194)
oil for deep frying

Cut the cheese into 40 strips about 1½ × ½ inch. Remove cores and seeds from the peppers and cut each one lengthwise into 10 strips. Put the pepper strips in a pan, pour over boiling water to cover and simmer until the peppers are limp but not too soft. Drain and plunge them into cold water, then drain again and dry well with paper towels.

Spread a little mustard on each piece of cheese, then roll a strip of pepper around it and secure with a wooden toothpick. Dip in flour, shake off the excess and then dip in the batter. Deep fry in oil heated to 350°F until golden brown and crisp. Drain well and serve immediately with Tartare sauce.
Accompaniments: Cooked lentils, soybeans or peas, or a Tomato salad.

Eggplant and cheese fricadelles

Makes 8
CALORIES PER PORTION: 816 (3415 kJ)
PROTEIN CONTENT PER PORTION: 37 grams
PREPARATION AND COOKING TIME: 1¼-1½ hours

1 lb eggplants, peeled and chopped
salt
oil for deep or shallow frying
1 cup finely chopped red pepper
1 cup finely chopped onion
2 tablespoons olive or sunflower oil
1 cup texturized soy protein
2 tablespoons water
1 clove of garlic, peeled and finely chopped
3 cups fresh wholewheat breadcrumbs
1½ cups grated Cheddar cheese
1-2 eggs, beaten
freshly ground pepper
2½ cups Brown sauce (page 196)

Place the eggplants in a colander, sprinkle with salt and leave to drain for 30 minutes. Rinse under cold running water and dry well. Fry the eggplants in deep or shallow oil until soft and well browned, then drain and allow to cool. Preheat the oven to 400°F. Fry the pepper and onion in the 2 tablespoons of oil until soft but not browned. Add the soy protein and water and cook gently for 5 minutes until all the excess liquid has been absorbed. Be ready to add a little more water if necessary, to prevent the mixture from sticking.

Remove from the heat, add the eggplant, garlic, breadcrumbs and cheese and bind with the beaten egg. Season with salt and pepper. Shape the mixture into 8 balls, place them in a greased shallow baking dish and flatten them slightly. Bake in the preheated oven for 10 minutes, then pour over half of the Brown sauce and bake the fricadelles for a further 10 minutes, basting once. Serve with the remaining sauce.
Accompaniments: Lyonnaise potatoes or Savory brown rice and a salad.

Left: Eggplant and cheese fricadelles – just one of the splendid range of croquettes that can be made from a variety of vegetables and legumes. Right: Cornish pasties are perfect for picnics. Try them with your homemade pickles, followed by cheese and fresh fruit

Vegetable cakes

Serves 4
CALORIES PER PORTION: 305 (1277 kJ)
PROTEIN CONTENT PER PORTION: 14 grams
PREPARATION & COOKING TIME: about 1 hour

1 lb leeks, shredded
⅔ cup grated carrot
1 cup finely shredded celery
⅔ cup grated turnip
1 tablespoon oil
1 tablespoon cold water
7 tablespoons wholewheat flour
2 cups fresh wholewheat breadcrumbs
1 cup grated Cheddar cheese
1 egg
1 clove of garlic, peeled and finely chopped
½-1 teaspoon finely chopped thyme
½-1 teaspoon finely chopped marjoram
salt
freshly ground pepper
a little oil for brushing

Place all the vegetables in a thick-based pan and add the oil and water. Cover tightly and cook very gently until the vegetables have lost their raw texture, but are still crisp. Shake the pan frequently to prevent the vegetables from sticking and stir the vegetables once or twice. Remove the pan from the heat and allow to cool.

Sprinkle over the flour and mix it in well, then add the remaining ingredients and mix to a fairly firm consistency. Shape into 12 cakes with well-floured hands and place them on a well-oiled baking sheet. Brush the cakes with a little oil and cook under the broiler for 10 minutes on each side, until browned. Serve with Cheese sauce.

Accompaniments: Peas with lettuce and onions, Broccoli surprise or a salad of lentils and tomatoes.

Arancini Siciliani (soybean and rice croquettes)

Makes 8
CALORIES PER PORTION: 450 (1872 kJ)
PROTEIN CONTENT PER PORTION: 21 grams
PREPARATION & COOKING TIME: 45 minutes

1½ cups cooked soybeans
1¼ cups cooked brown short-grain rice
½ cup grated Parmesan cheese
1 clove of garlic, peeled and finely chopped
½-1 teaspoon finely chopped thyme
1-2 eggs, beaten
salt
freshly ground pepper
¼ lb Edam cheese, cut into 8 cubes
beaten egg
fresh or dried wholewheat breadcrumbs for coating
oil for deep frying
8 sprigs of mint to garnish

Mix together the soybeans, rice, Parmesan cheese, garlic, thyme and enough beaten egg to bind. Add salt and pepper to taste.

Divide the mixture into 8 portions and shape each portion into a ball around one cube of cheese. Coat with egg and breadcrumbs, then deep fry in batches in oil heated to 350°F, until crisp and golden brown. Drain well, and garnish each croquette with a sprig of mint. Serve with Tomato sauce.

Accompaniments: A Watercress and tomato salad, or Endive, orange and walnut salad, or a Coleslaw.

Walnut and herb cakes

Makes 12
CALORIES PER PORTION: 590 (2457 kJ)
PROTEIN CONTENT PER PORTION: 17 grams
PREPARATION & COOKING TIME: 1¼ hours

1 cup finely ground walnuts
2 cups fresh wholewheat breadcrumbs
1 cup finely chopped onion
1 clove of garlic, peeled and crushed
½-1 teaspoon finely chopped sage
½-1 teaspoon finely chopped thyme
6 allspice berries, finely ground or about ¼ teaspoon ground allspice
salt
freshly ground pepper
4 tablespoons butter
7 tablespoons wholewheat flour
1¼ cups milk
1 teaspoon brewer's yeast
2 eggs, beaten
Tomato or Brown sauce (page 196) for serving
sprigs of watercress, to garnish

Preheat the oven to 350°F. Mix together the nuts, breadcrumbs, onion, garlic, herbs and allspice, then season the mixture with salt and pepper.

Melt the butter over gentle heat, then stir in the flour. Remove the pan from the heat and gradually add the milk, stirring briskly between each addition. Return the pan to the heat and bring to a boil, stirring continuously until the mixture thickens. Allow to cool slightly before stirring in the brewer's yeast and the eggs, then fold in the nut mixture — the consistency should be firm but moist. Divide into 12 cakes with well-floured hands, adding a little extra flour to the mixture, if necessary.

Place on a well-oiled baking sheet and bake in the preheated oven for 20 minutes, until the cakes are firm and the tops lightly browned. For a darker brown color, brush the cakes with a little oil and put them under the broiler after baking. Arrange them on a serving dish and pour over Tomato or Brown sauce. Garnish with sprigs of watercress and serve immediately.

Accompaniments: Baked carrot loaf, Beets with yogurt or Zucchini provençal and a Green salad.

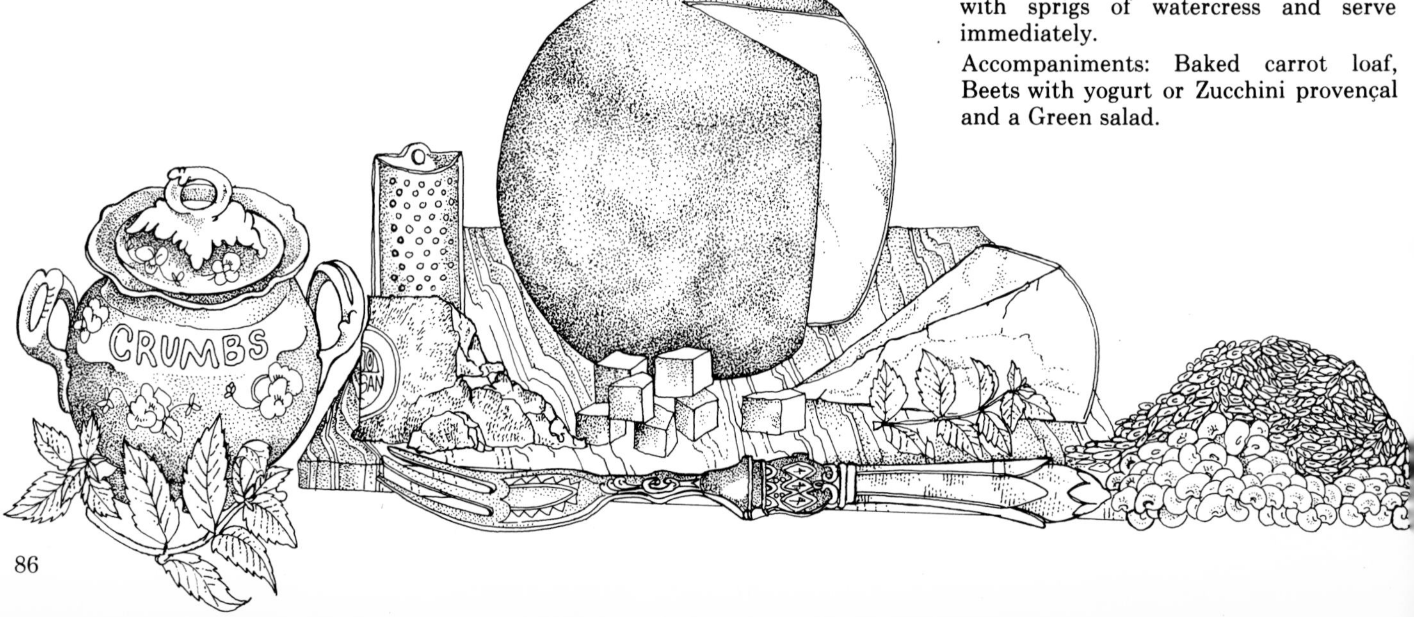

Soybean and nut burgers

Makes 12 thin or 6 fat ones!

Serves 4-6
CALORIES: 1445 (6040 kJ)
PROTEIN CONTENT: 51 grams
PREPARATION AND COOKING TIME: 1-1¼ hours

1½ cups cooked soybeans
2 cups finely ground walnuts
2 cups finely chopped green peppers
2 cups finely chopped onions
2 cloves of garlic, peeled and finely chopped
12 allspice berries, finely ground, or ½ teaspoon ground allspice
2 eggs, beaten
salt
freshly ground pepper
Wholewheat bread rolls (optional)

Preheat the oven to 400°F. Rub the soybeans through a food mill or grinder, or crush in a mortar with a pestle, until coarsely ground. Combine all the ingredients, adding the seasoning to the eggs, and mix together very thoroughly. Shape the mixture into 6 or 12 burgers, pressing each one firmly, so that it will not crumble during cooking.

Place the burgers on a well-oiled baking sheet and cook for 15-20 minutes in the preheated oven, or until they are golden brown on top. Carefully turn them over and cook for a further 10 minutes. Place each one in a split wholewheat bread roll and add a slice of cheese for extra protein, or serve with Tomato sauce (page 196) or tomato and pickles.

Crocchette di spinaci

Serves 4
CALORIES PER PORTION: 285 (1197 kJ)
PROTEIN CONTENT PER PORTION: 21 grams
PREPARATION & COOKING TIME: 45-60 minutes

1 lb cooked spinach
1 cup grated Cheddar cheese
2 cups fresh wholewheat breadcrumbs
2 eggs, well beaten
1 tablespoon lemon juice
7 tablespoons wholewheat flour
salt
freshly ground pepper
1-2 teaspoons chopped thyme or mint (optional)
oil for shallow frying

Drain the spinach well, then chop it finely. Add the cheese, breadcrumbs, eggs, lemon juice and half of the flour and mix thoroughly. Season with salt and pepper and add the chopped herbs, if wished.

Fry about 1 teaspoonful of the mixture in shallow oil to test the consistency; it should hold together. If it doesn't, add a little more flour and keep the croquettes firmly shaped. Don't use too much flour, though, or they will be rather heavy.

When the consistency is right, fry large tablespoonfuls in shallow oil until golden brown on both sides. Take care when you turn them over that they do not break in half. Drain well and serve hot with Tomato sauce.

Accompaniments: Dauphinois potatoes, Paprika beans in sour cream or Rutabaga soufflé.

Salad nut cakes

Makes 8
CALORIES PER PORTION: 113 (475 kJ)
PROTEIN CONTENT PER PORTION: 4 grams
PREPARATION TIME: 30-40 minutes

2 cups finely ground mixed nuts
2 cups fresh wholewheat breadcrumbs
½ cup finely chopped scallions
sprig of mint, finely chopped
½ teaspoon finely chopped marjoram
grated rind of ½ lemon
1 tablespoon lemon juice (optional)
1 egg, beaten
2 tablespoons dry sherry
salt
freshly ground pepper
6-8 tablespoons finely chopped parsley

Combine all the ingredients except the parsley and mix together thoroughly. Shape the mixture into 8 balls and pat into cakes. Roll each one in chopped parsley until well coated. Chill until required. Serve cold with lemon wedges.

Accompaniments: Elona salad, avocado wedges or a Green salad.

Note: A little melted butter can be included if you find the mixture does not bind together as well as it should.

Cornish pasties

Serves 4
CALORIES PER PORTION: 490 (2050 kJ)
PROTEIN CONTENT PER PORTION: 18 grams
PREPARATON & COOKING TIME: ¾ hour

1 medium onion, thinly sliced
4 tablespoons butter
⅓ cup thinly sliced carrot
⅓ cup diced turnip
1 potato, diced
1 cup coarsely chopped mushrooms
1 quantity Wholewheat pie pastry (page 194)
flour for sprinkling
1 teaspoon brewer's yeast
½ cup milk
1 egg, beaten
1 cup grated Cheddar cheese
salt
freshly ground pepper
a little vegetable oil
beaten egg, to glaze

Fry the onion gently in the butter until soft but not browned. Add the carrot, turnip and potato and cook gently for 5 minutes. Add the mushrooms and 2 tablespoons of water; cover the pan and cook over very gentle heat for 10 minutes.

Meanwhile, roll out the dough into a 15 inch square and cut into four. Sprinkle each portion with flour, then cover and put into the refrigerator.

Dissolve the brewer's yeast in the milk and beat in the egg. Pour this over the cooked vegetables and stir until the egg cooks and the mixture thickens. Add the cheese, season with salt and pepper and set aside until cold. Preheat the oven to 400°F. Pour a little oil onto a baking sheet and spread it evenly. There should be a little excess to make the bottoms of the pasties crisp.

Place the squares of dough on the baking sheet and put a quarter of the filling in the center of each. Brush the edges of the pastry with water, fold over diagonally and seal the edges together firmly. Bake in the preheated oven for 30 minutes. After 20 minutes, brush the tops of the pasties with beaten egg to glaze them.

Serve with Coleslaw. They also go well with homemade pickles.

Stuffed cabbage leaves

Serves 6
CALORIES PER PORTION: 570 (2392 kJ)
PROTEIN CONTENT PER PORTION: 23 grams
PREPARATION & COOKING TIME: 1¼ hours

This recipe can also be used with vine leaves, using smaller portions of stuffing.

12 large green cabbage leaves
Basic stuffing
2½ cups Tomato sauce (page 196)

Preheat the oven to 400°F. Trim the thick ends of the stalks from the cabbage leaves, then cook the leaves in boiling water for 5 minutes to blanch them. Drain and rinse under cold running water to cool the leaves. Pat them dry with paper towels.

Place a little of the stuffing at the stalk end of each leaf, fold the sides over the stuffing and then roll up each leaf, completely enclosing the stuffing. Use a wooden toothpick, if necessary, to stop the leaf unrolling. Arrange the stuffed leaves in a double layer in a small baking dish and cover with the Tomato sauce.

Bake in the preheated oven for 45 minutes. Serve hot or cold with rice or lentils.

Stuffed eggplants

Serves 6
CALORIES PER PORTION: 485 (2025 kJ)
PROTEIN CONTENT PER PORTION: 19 grams
PREPARATION & COOKING TIME: 1-1¼ hours, including draining

3 small eggplants, weighing about ¼ lb each
salt
olive or sunflower oil, for brushing
Basic stuffing

Preheat the oven to 400°F. Cut the eggplants in half and scoop out the flesh with a teaspoon, leaving a shell about ¼ inch thick. Roughly chop the eggplant flesh and place in a colander with the shells. Sprinkle liberally with salt and leave to drain for 30 minutes. Rinse and dry well. Brush the eggplant shells with oil and place them in a shallow, ovenproof dish.

Mix the chopped eggplant with the stuffing and pile into the prepared shells. Brush the tops with oil and bake in the preheated oven for 30 minutes. Serve hot with Tomato or Brown sauce (page 197) and green vegetables.

Basic stuffing

TOTAL CALORIES: 1775 (7420 kJ)
TOTAL PROTEIN CONTENT: 76 grams
PREPARATION TIME: 20-30 minutes

2 eggs
1 teaspoon brewer's yeast
2 cups finely ground mixed nuts
2 cups finely chopped onion
1 cup finely chopped celery
1 cup grated Cheddar cheese
salt
freshly ground black pepper
½ teaspoon finely chopped thyme
½ teaspoon finely chopped marjoram
1 clove of garlic, peeled and crushed

Beat the eggs with the brewer's yeast. Mix together all the other ingredients and pour in the eggs. Mix well, and use the stuffing as directed in the following recipes.

Nuts, vegetables, cheese and herbs – all are used in this protein-rich Basic stuffing mixture. Right: this filling Vegetable pudding needs only a Tomato salad as a side dish

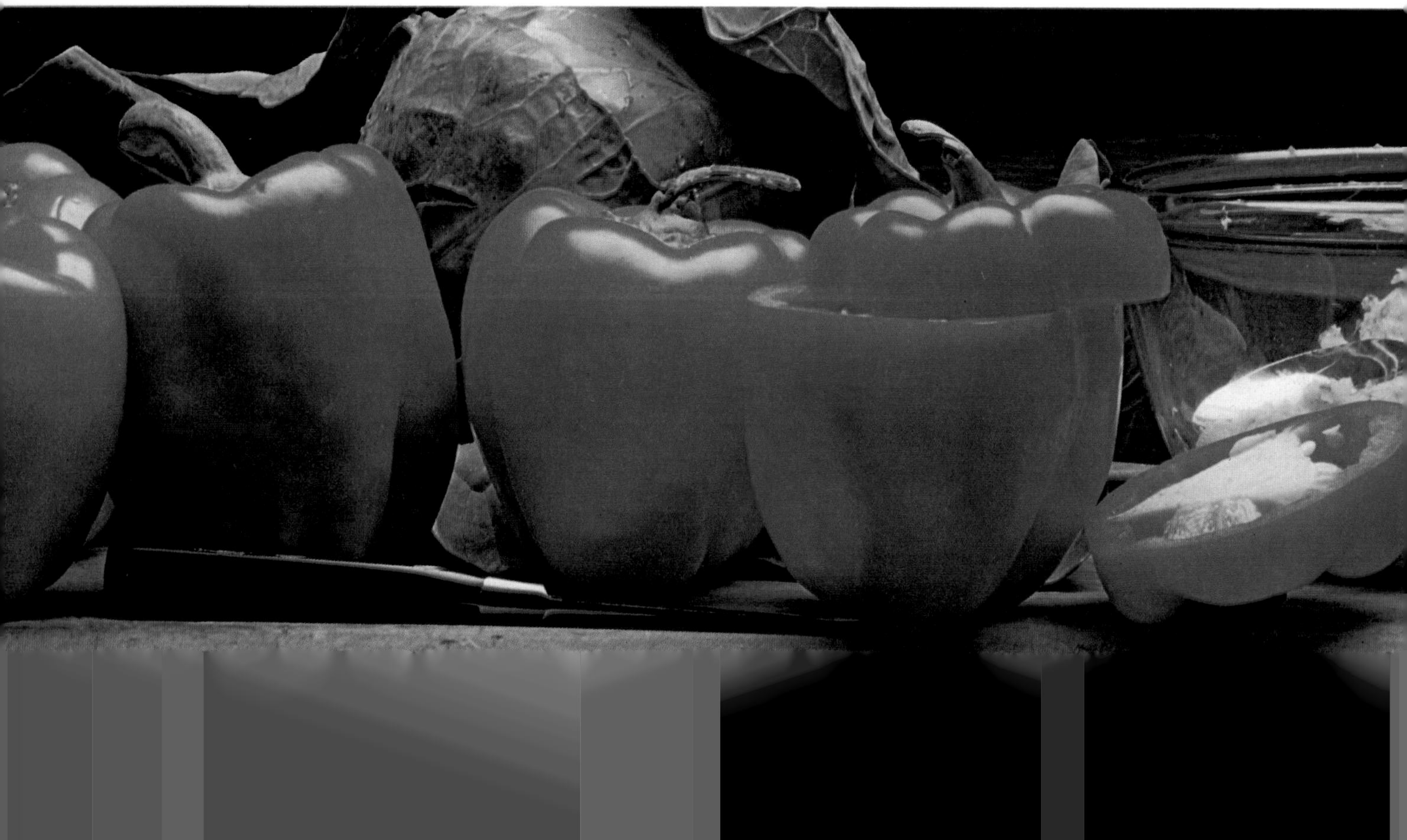

Stuffed peppers

Serves 6
CALORIES PER PORTION: 505 (2125 kJ)
PROTEIN CONTENT PER PORTION: 21 grams
PREPARATION & COOKING TIME: 45 minutes to one hour

6 green or red peppers, weighing about ¼ lb each
Basic stuffing
olive or sunflower oil, for brushing

Preheat the oven to 400°F. Slice the tops off the peppers and remove the cores and seeds. Place them in a baking dish. Fill with the stuffing and brush them liberally with oil.

Bake in the preheated oven for 30-45 minutes, then serve with Tomato sauce or Brown sauce.

Stuffed squash

Serves 4
CALORIES PER PORTION: 485 (2022 kJ)
PROTEIN CONTENT PER PORTION: 21 grams
PREPARATION & COOKING TIME: 2½ hours

1 large summer squash
salt
Basic stuffing

Preheat the oven to 400°F. Cut one end off the squash and use a long-handled spoon to scoop out the pith and seeds. Lightly sprinkle the inside with salt and stand the squash on its end to drain for 30 minutes. Rinse the inside with cold water and dry well.

Fill the squash with the stuffing and replace the end, securing it with wooden toothpicks or small skewers. Place on its side in a well-greased baking dish and bake in the preheated oven for about 1½ hours, or until tender.

Serve hot with Brown sauce and Polish-style cauliflower or broccoli.

Vegetable pudding

Serves 4
CALORIES PER PORTION: 490 (2050 kJ)
PROTEIN CONTENT PER PORTION: 20 grams
PREPARATION & COOKING TIME: 3½-4 hours

The pudding crust
1¼ cups plus 1 tablespoon wholewheat flour
salt
1 teaspoon baking powder
6 tablespoons butter
1 egg, well-beaten
a little water

The filling
½ cup finely chopped onion
⅔ cup diced parsnips
1 cup coarsely chopped mushrooms
1 cup shelled fresh or frozen peas
1½ cups grated Cheddar cheese
2 tablespoons wholewheat flour
½ teaspoon finely chopped marjoram
salt
freshly ground pepper
¼ cup water

To make the pudding crust: sift the flour, salt and baking powder into a bowl and rub in the butter. Add the egg and just enough water to make a fairly firm dough. Divide the dough into one-quarter and three-quarters. Roll out the larger portion and use it to line a 1 pint capacity steaming mold. Roll out the smaller portion to fit the top.

To make the filling: mix together the vegetables and cheese in a large bowl. Sprinkle with the flour, marjoram, salt and pepper and toss well. Place the filling in the lined mold, pressing it well down. Pour on the water and cover with the pastry lid. Cover with wax paper or foil and tie securely.

Lower the pudding into a saucepan and add enough boiling water to come halfway up the sides of the mold. Cover the pan with a lid and simmer the pudding for 3 hours, adding more hot water if necessary during the cooking time. Serve with a Tomato salad.

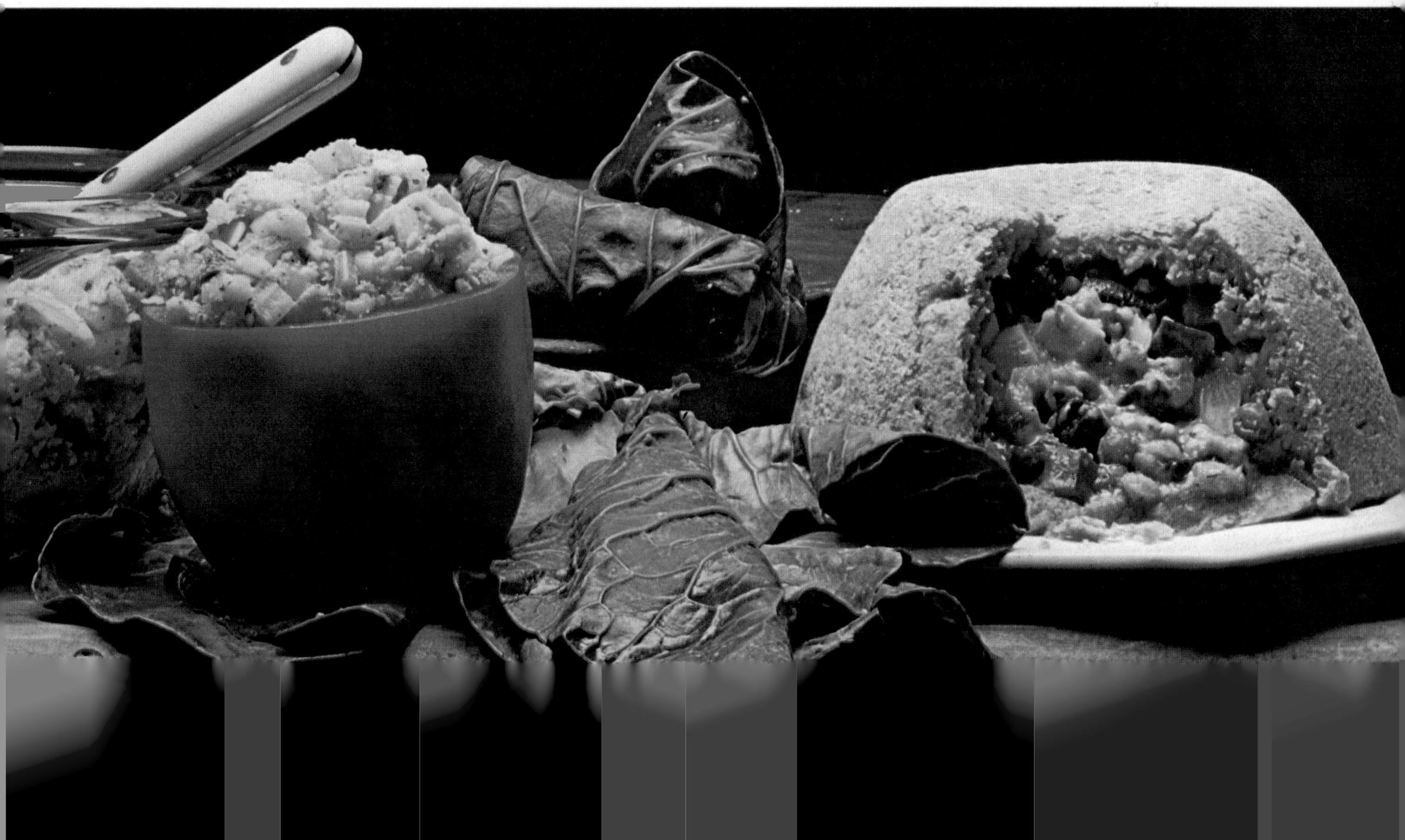

Braised vegetables

Serves 4
CALORIES PER PORTION: 285 (1190 kJ)
PROTEIN CONTENT PER PORTION: 16 grams
PREPARATION & COOKING TIME: 1 hour

¼ cup olive or sunflower oil
1 cup diced turnips
1 cup diced carrots
1¾ cups thinly sliced celery
½ lb red and green peppers, in equal proportions, sliced
1¾ cups shelled fresh or frozen peas
½ lb fresh or frozen green beans
2 tablespoons wholewheat flour
2½ cups water
1 tablespoon brewer's yeast
1 clove of garlic, peeled and crushed
3½ cups shredded white cabbage
salt
freshly ground pepper
½ lb leaf spinach
½ cup coarsely grated cheese

Heat the oil in a thick-based skillet, add the turnips and carrots and cook, stirring continuously, until golden brown.

Add the celery after about 5 minutes cooking time and add the peppers after another 5 minutes. Cook for 5 minutes longer, about 15-20 minutes altogether. Remove the fried vegetables with a slotted spoon and put them into a shallow baking dish about 10 inches in diameter.

Add the peas and beans to the oil in the pan and cook them for about 5 minutes — until they are just browning at the edges. Drain and add them to the other vegetables. Mix them all together.

Stir the flour into the remaining oil — it may be necessary to add a little more oil at this stage — and stir to make a soft paste. Pour in the water, add the brewer's yeast and crushed garlic and bring to a boil, stirring until the sauce thickens. Add the cabbage, bring back to a boil and pour over the other vegetables. Season well.

Preheat the oven to 425°F. Wash the spinach leaves well and remove the central stems. Arrange the stems over the dish. Blanch the spinach leaves in plenty of boiling water, removing them and draining them the moment they have gone limp. Cover the mixed vegetables with overlapping leaves and brush with a little olive oil. Sprinkle the grated cheese over the top and bake in the preheated oven for 20 minutes. Serve with soybeans dressed with finely chopped parsley, butter and lemon juice.

Zucchini and tomato casserole with cheese dumplings

Serves 4
CALORIES PER PORTION: 525 (2190 kJ)
PROTEIN CONTENT PER PORTION: 26 grams
PREPARATION & COOKING TIME: 1½ hours

The casserole
1 lb zucchini, cut into ¼ inch slices
salt
2 medium onions, thinly sliced
2 tablespoons olive or sunflower oil
2 cups chopped tomatoes
2 cloves of garlic, peeled and finely chopped
freshly ground black pepper

The dumplings
1 quart milk
1 tablespoon wine vinegar
1 tablespoon water
2 large eggs, lightly beaten
salt
freshly ground black pepper
a sprinkling of cayenne pepper
½ teaspoon dried thyme
¼ lb Cheddar cheese, cut into small cubes
2½ cups fresh wholewheat breadcrumbs

Sprinkle the sliced zucchini lightly with salt and leave them to drain for 30 minutes while you prepare the dumplings. Bring the milk to a boil, add the vinegar and water, then remove from the heat and stir gently until the curds have more or less separated, leaving an almost clear liquid. Pour through a fine strainer lined with cheesecloth. Return the whey to the saucepan and continue to boil until it is reduced to 2½ cups. Leave on one side.

Allow the curds to cool slightly, then add them to the eggs and season with salt, pepper, cayenne and thyme. Mix well. Add the cheese to the breadcrumbs. Pour on the egg and curd mixture and mix to a firm dough. Form into 10 round dumplings and put on one side.

Meanwhile, fry the onions in the oil, over a medium-to-low heat, until they are golden brown. Drain well and transfer them to an ovenproof casserole. Rinse the zucchini and dry them with paper towels. Increase the heat and fry the zucchini until the edges just begin to brown. Drain them and add to the casserole. Preheat the oven to 400°F.

Fry the tomatoes and garlic until the juices run, season with salt and pepper and continue cooking until they turn to a thick pulp, taking care that they do not burn. Add the whey and bring back to a boil. Pour this mixture over the onions and zucchini in the casserole.

Arrange the dumplings in a single layer in the casserole liquid, taking care to submerge each one, and bake, uncovered, in the preheated oven for 20 minutes. Serve with a mixed salad and soybeans.

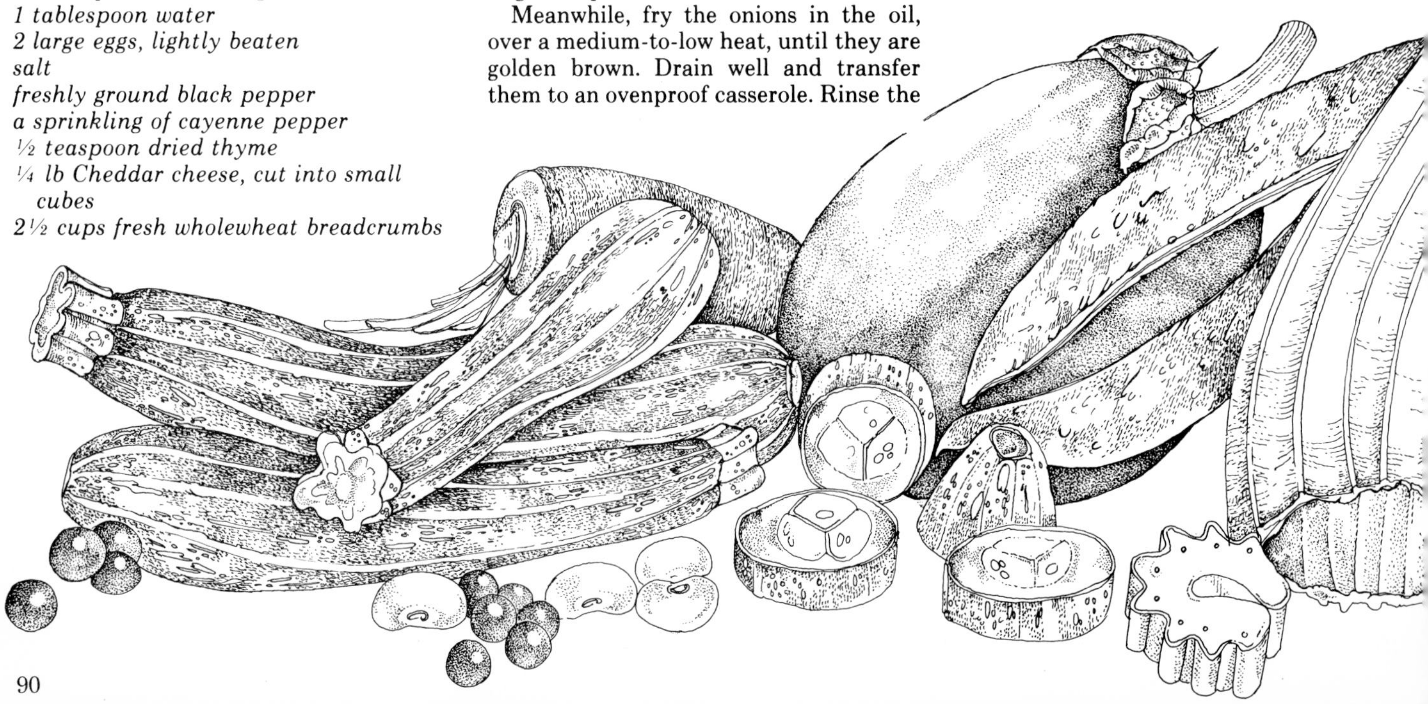

Vegetable moussaka

Serves 4
CALORIES PER PORTION: 435 (1815 kJ)
PROTEIN CONTENT PER PORTION: 21 grams
PREPARATION & COOKING TIME: 1½ hours

1 lb eggplants, sliced
salt
5 tablespoons olive or sunflower oil
2 cups coarsely chopped tomatoes
freshly ground black pepper
1 teaspoon chopped thyme
1 clove of garlic, peeled and finely chopped
2 cups chopped onions
3 cups cooked soybeans, coarsely mashed
1 egg, beaten
1¼ cups milk
⅓ cup dried skimmed milk (optional)

Sprinkle the eggplant slices with salt and allow them to drain for 30 minutes. Rinse and dry them with paper towels. Preheat the oven to 350°F.

Pour 2 tablespoons of oil into a baking dish about 10 inches in diameter, and 3 inches deep. Dip the eggplant slices into the oil and rub them together so that they are evenly coated. Arrange them on a sheet of foil on a baking sheet, not overlapping, and bake them in the preheated oven for 20 minutes or until they are browned.

Meanwhile, put the tomatoes into a saucepan with salt and pepper, the thyme and garlic and cook them gently to a pulp, stirring occasionally to prevent them burning. Set aside. Fry the onions in the remaining 3 tablespoons of oil until golden brown.

Reset the oven to 400°F. Line the baking dish, still slightly oiled, with a layer of cooked eggplant, taking care not to break the pieces when removing them from the foil. Mix the beans well with the tomatoes and onions and spoon into the baking dish. Cover with another layer of eggplant, reserving about 6 good-looking slices.

Mix together the egg, milk, dried milk, if using, and pepper and pour this over the top. Garnish with the 6 reserved slices of eggplant and bake in the preheated oven for 30 minutes. Serve with a Greek salad.

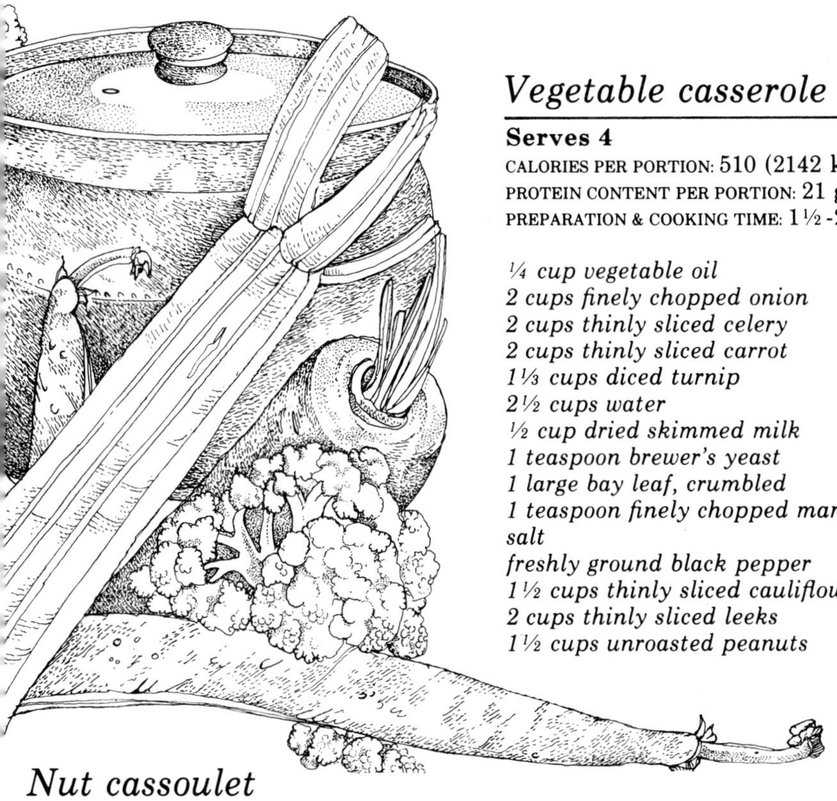

Vegetable casserole

Serves 4
CALORIES PER PORTION: 510 (2142 kJ)
PROTEIN CONTENT PER PORTION: 21 grams
PREPARATION & COOKING TIME: 1½-2 hours

¼ cup vegetable oil
2 cups finely chopped onion
2 cups thinly sliced celery
2 cups thinly sliced carrot
1⅓ cups diced turnip
2½ cups water
½ cup dried skimmed milk
1 teaspoon brewer's yeast
1 large bay leaf, crumbled
1 teaspoon finely chopped marjoram
salt
freshly ground black pepper
1½ cups thinly sliced cauliflower florets
2 cups thinly sliced leeks
1½ cups unroasted peanuts

Preheat the oven to 350°F. Pour the oil into a large, thick-based saucepan and add the onion, celery, carrot and turnip. Place over a moderate heat and cook the vegetables for 20-25 minutes. Shake the pan frequently and stir the vegetables until they begin to color and soften. Transfer the vegetables to an ovenproof casserole. Mix together the water, dried milk powder, brewer's yeast, bay leaf and marjoram, season with salt and pepper, and bring to a boil. Pour this stock over the fried vegetables and add the cauliflower, leeks and peanuts.

Bake in the preheated oven for 1 hour, then serve the casserole with Herb dumplings, baked potatoes and a large Mixed salad.

Nut cassoulet

Serves 6
CALORIES PER PORTION: 755 (3157 kJ)
PROTEIN CONTENT PER PORTION: 32 grams
PREPARATION & COOKING TIME: 2½ hours excluding soaking overnight

1½ cups dried navy beans, soaked
salt
Basic stuffing (page 88), with garlic
¾-1 pint Bêchamel sauce (page 196)
2 cloves of garlic, peeled and crushed
grated rind of 1 lemon
2-4 hard-cooked eggs (optional)
6 tablespoons dried wholewheat breadcrumbs

Cook the drained navy beans gently in plenty of simmering water for about 1 hour or until they are soft but not broken. Add ½-1 teaspoon salt to the cooking water when the beans are almost ready. Drain them well.

Preheat the oven to 400°F. Shape the stuffing mixture into 12 small cakes, pressing them firmly so they will keep their shape. Bring the Béchamel sauce to a boil. Add enough of the sauce to the beans to coat them generously — but not excessively. Add the garlic and grated lemon rind, and pour half of the mixture into a fairly shallow baking dish.

Arrange the cakes with the quartered hard-cooked eggs, if used, on top and cover with the remaining bean mixture. Sprinkle with breadcrumbs and bake in the preheated oven for 20-30 minutes, or until the top is well browned and the cassoulet is bubbling.

This is a substantial dish and should be served hot, accompanied only by a salad.

Vegetable goulash with spätzle

Serves 6
CALORIES PER PORTION: 540 (2266 kJ)
PROTEIN CONTENT PER PORTION: 23 grams
PREPARATION & COOKING TIME: 50 minutes

2 cups coarsely chopped onions
2 cups chopped turnips
¼ cup olive or sunflower oil
2 cups coarsely chopped red peppers
2 cups coarsely chopped white cabbage
2 tablespoons paprika
2 tablespoons wholewheat flour
½ cup dried skimmed milk
1¼ cups water (preferably the water used to soak the soybeans)
salt
freshly ground pepper
1¼ cups dark beer
2 cloves garlic, peeled and crushed
1 tablespoon lemon juice or wine vinegar
3 cups cooked soybeans, very coarsely mashed, leaving a good proportion whole
½ cup sliced pickles
2 hard-cooked eggs, chopped (optional)
⅔ cup sour cream (optional)
2 tablespoons chopped parsley (optional)

The spätzle
1¾ cups wholewheat flour
salt
¼ teaspoon salt
¼ teaspoon grated nutmeg
2 eggs
2 tablespoons milk
4 tablespoons butter, melted

Fry the onions and turnips in the oil in a thick-based pan until golden brown. Add the peppers and cook until any juice has evaporated and the onion has started to brown again. Add the cabbage, then stir in the paprika and wholewheat flour.

Dissolve the milk powder in the water and season with salt and pepper. Pour the beer onto the onions, and when the foaming subsides add the dissolved milk, the garlic and lemon juice or wine vinegar. Put in the soybeans, bring back to a boil and simmer, covered, for 10 minutes, stirring occasionally to prevent burning.

Add half the pickles to the goulash, and mix them well in. Then pour into a heated serving dish and decorate with the chopped eggs, if used and the rest of the pickles. Swirl in the sour cream and sprinkle with the parsley. Serve with spätzle.

To make the spätzle: sift the flour, salt and nutmeg together, keeping the bran apart. Lightly beat the eggs with the milk and 1 tablespoon of the melted butter. Add this to the flour and mix to a soft dough, adding a little extra milk if necessary.

Scoop out small lumps of the dough with a teaspoon or use a pastry bag with a ¼ inch plain round nozzle and cut off ½ inch lengths. Roll these in the bran, if liked.

Drop the spätzle into a large pan of boiling salted water and boil for about 5 minutes: they should be *al dente* (tender, but firm to bite). Drain and serve with the rest of the melted butter poured over them and a little additional grated nutmeg if desired.

Note: Be sure to use fresh paprika. This spice loses its flavor quickly if kept too long.

Vegetable goulash is served here with a swirl of sour cream to counteract the pungency of paprika. Homemade wholewheat Spätzle, with just a hint of nutmeg, go well with this dish

Leipziger allerlei

Serves 4-6
CALORIES PER PORTION FOR 4: 520 (2182 kJ)
PROTEIN CONTENT PER PORTION FOR 4: 20 grams
PREPARATION & COOKING TIME: 1 hour

4-6 tablespoons vegetable oil
2 cups diced celery
1⅓ cups diced carrot
1⅓ cups diced parsnip
2 cups finely chopped onion
1 pint Béchamel sauce (page 196)
1 cup cooked cauliflower florets
2 cups cooked peas
salt
freshly ground pepper
1¼ cups grated Cheddar cheese

Pour the oil into a large thick-based saucepan and add the celery, carrot, parsnip, and onion. Place the pan over moderate heat and cook the vegetables for 20-30 minutes, shaking the pan frequently and stirring the vegetables until they color and soften. Meanwhile, heat up the sauce and cook the cauliflower and peas, if they are not already prepared.

Add about two-thirds of the sauce to the softened vegetables. Pour the mixture into a warmed, shallow flameproof dish, scatter the peas on top and arrange the cauliflower florets down the center. Season with salt and pepper. Cover with the remaining sauce and sprinkle with the cheese. Place the dish under the broiler until the cheese melts and turns a crisp, golden brown.

This is a substantial dish and should be served hot with a salad only.

Chili 'sans' carne

Serves 4
CALORIES PER PORTION: 325 (1375 kJ)
PROTEIN CONTENT PER PORTION: 19 grams
PREPARATION & COOKING TIME: about 2½ hours excluding soaking

1⅓ cups dried red kidney beans, soaked overnight
2 cups coarsely chopped onion
2 tablespoons vegetable oil
1 lb tomatoes, skinned
2 teaspoons finely chopped oregano
1 large clove of garlic, peeled and crushed
1-4 teaspoons chili powder, to taste
1 cup grated Cheddar cheese
salt
freshly ground pepper

Drain the soaked beans, then cook them gently in lightly salted boiling water for about 2 hours, or until they are soft and most of the water has been absorbed. Drain off the excess water and reserve it. Fry the onion in the oil until golden brown, then add the tomatoes and cook them down to a purée. Add the beans with about ¼ cup of the reserved water, the oregano, garlic and chili powder, and mix thoroughly. Sprinkle the cheese over the top and stir until it has melted, then season with salt and pepper.

Serve hot with the traditional Tortillas and a large mixed salad. A lemon-based Rum punch makes a very good 'quencher'.

Peanut curry

Serves 4
CALORIES PER PORTION: 455 (1890 kJ)
PROTEIN CONTENT PER PORTION: 13 gram
PREPARATION & COOKING TIME: 45 minutes

2 teaspoons ground coriander seeds
1 teaspoon ground turmeric
2 tablespoons vegetable oil
1 cup finely chopped onion
1 teaspoon peeled and finely chopped fresh ginger root
1 clove of garlic, peeled and very finely chopped
1½ cups coarsely chopped unroasted peanuts
salt
¼ cup thinly sliced green chili pepper (optional)
1 cup skinned and coarsely chopped tomatoes
½ cup coconut milk
1 cup boiling water
½ cup grated fresh coconut
2 tablespoons finely chopped coriander leaves

Heat the coriander and turmeric in the oil for a few moments. Add the onion, ginger and garlic and cook until the onion is soft. Add the peanuts, salt, chili pepper, if used, tomatoes and coconut milk and cook gently until the tomatoes break down to a pulp. Stir in the boiling water and simmer for 20 minutes. Stir in the coconut and 1 tablespoon of the coriander leaves, increase the heat and boil to a thick purée, taking care that it does not stick or burn. Serve in a warmed bowl, sprinkled with the remaining coriander leaves, and with Cucumber raita as an accompaniment.

Tortillas

Serves 8
CALORIES PER PORTION: 170 (705 kJ)
PROTEIN CONTENT PER PORTION: 5.5 grams
PREPARATION & COOKING TIME: 45 minutes

¾ cup plus 2 tablespoons cornmeal
¾ cup plus 2 tablespoons wholewheat flour
½ teaspoon baking soda
salt
a little hot water
oil for shallow frying

Mix together the cornmeal, flour, baking soda and salt and make into a firm dough with a little hot water. Knead the dough for 3 minutes, then leave it to rest for 30 minutes. Divide it into eight portions, roll each one out into a 'pancake' about 6 inches in diameter and fry on both sides until golden brown and cooked. Turn the Tortillas over two or three times, taking care that they do not break.

Cucumber raita

Serves 4
CALORIES PER PORTION: 35 (150 kJ)
PROTEIN CONTENT PER PORTION: 3 grams
PREPARATION & CHILLING TIME: 1½ hours

3½ cups peeled and diced cucumber
salt
½ teaspoon cumin seeds
1 cup plain yogurt
1 tablespoon finely chopped mint

Sprinkle the cucumber with salt and leave for 20 minutes. Rinse and pat dry. Heat the cumin seeds in a dry saucepan for a few moments until a spicy aroma begins to rise. Crush them in a mortar with a pestle and mix into the yogurt. Add the mint and cucumber and mix thoroughly. Chill well before serving.

Layered brown rice pilau

Serves 4
CALORIES PER PORTION: 730 (3057 kJ)
PROTEIN CONTENT PER PORTION: 22 grams
PREPARATION & COOKING TIME: 2-3 hours, not including soaking

The rice
1 teaspoon finely ground cumin
1 inch cinnamon stick, crushed into small pieces
1 teaspoon clove-based garam masala (page 200)
4 tablespoons clarified butter
1 cup finely chopped onion
¼ cup peeled and finely chopped fresh ginger root
3 cloves of garlic, peeled and very finely chopped
1⅓ cups brown rice, soaked for 1 hour
1 pint boiling water
salt
4 cardamom seeds, split open
¼ cup halved pistachio nuts

The filling
1 teaspoon ground turmeric
½ cup blanched halved almonds
½ cup cashew nuts
½ teaspoon ground cumin
2 tablespoons vegetable oil
1 medium onion, thinly sliced
¼ cup peeled and finely chopped fresh ginger root
2 cloves of garlic, peeled and crushed
1 cup cooked fresh or frozen peas
⅔ cup boiling water
¼ lb panir (page 200), cut into small cubes and fried until golden brown
2-3 red chili peppers, seeded and finely chopped (optional)
¼ cup chopped coriander leaves
salt
2 hard-cooked eggs, quartered

To prepare the rice: heat together the cumin, cinnamon and garam masala in the butter for a few minutes until a spicy aroma begins to rise. Add the onion, ginger and garlic and cook until the onion is soft. Put in the rice and cook briskly for 2-3 minutes, stirring continuously, then add the boiling water, salt, cardamom seeds and pistachio nuts. Cover the pan tightly and cook the rice over very gentle heat for about 45 minutes, or put into a 325°F oven. If the heat is at the right temperature, the rice will be tender and dry. It may be necessary to add a little more water during the cooking, but do not stir the rice or, if possible, lift the lid and allow the steam to escape too often. Use a heatproof glass plate as a cover through which the rice can be clearly seen.

For the filling: heat together the turmeric, nuts and cumin in the vegetable oil until a spicy aroma begins to rise. Add the onion and ginger and continue frying until golden brown. Put in the garlic and cook for a few moments before stirring in the peas and the boiling water. Simmer for 5 minutes, then add the panir, chili peppers, if used, and 3 tablespoons of the chopped coriander and season with salt; cook until thoroughly hot.

Spread half of the rice on a hot serving dish and cover with half of the filling. Spread the remaining rice over the filling and then cover with the remaining filling. Arrange the eggs in the center. Sprinkle with the remaining coriander and serve.

Curried spinach with red lentils

Serves 4
CALORIES PER PORTION: 215 (900 kJ)
PROTEIN CONTENT PER PORTION: 15 grams
PREPARATION & COOKING TIME: 45-60 minutes, excluding soaking

1 lb spinach, well washed
2 tablespoons vegetable oil
1 teaspoon fennel-based garam masala (page 200)
½ teaspoon finely ground cumin
1 cup finely chopped onion
2½ cups water
1 cup red lentils, washed, then soaked for 1 hour
½ teaspoon ground turmeric
1 clove of garlic, peeled and finely chopped
salt
juice of 1 large lemon

Roughly chop the spinach into ½ inch pieces. Pour the oil into a saucepan and heat the garam masala gently with the cumin until a spicy aroma begins to rise. Add the onion and fry gently, stirring until it is soft. Pour on the water, add the drained lentils, turmeric, garlic and salt and cook for 5 minutes. Add the spinach, cover the saucepan and continue cooking for about 20 minutes until nearly all the liquid has been absorbed and the lentils are done. Add a little extra water during the cooking, if necessary. Stir in the lemon juice and serve immediately.

Parsi eggs

Serves 4
CALORIES PER PORTION: 395 (1662 kJ)
PROTEIN CONTENT PER PORTION: 17 grams
PREPARATION & COOKING TIME: 45-50 minutes

1 lb potatoes
oil for shallow frying
1 cup finely chopped onion
¼-½ cup peeled and finely chopped fresh ginger root
2 tablespoons vegetable oil
1 teaspoon ground turmeric
2 green chili peppers, seeded and thinly sliced
1 clove of garlic, peeled and chopped
¾ cup skinned and coarsely chopped tomatoes
salt
8 eggs, well beaten
a sprinkling of freshly grated nutmeg
1 tablespoon chopped coriander leaves

Boil the potatoes in their skins for 10 minutes. Peel when cool and finely dice. Shallow fry until golden brown and crisp. Keep hot.

Meanwhile, fry the onion and ginger in the oil until soft. Add the turmeric, green chili peppers, garlic, tomatoes and salt, and cook gently until the tomatoes have broken down to a pulp. Boil vigorously until any excess juice has evaporated, then lower the heat, add the eggs and cook gently until the mixture is of the consistency of scrambled eggs. Pour into the center of a hot serving dish. Sprinkle the potatoes with salt and a little nutmeg and arrange them around the eggs. Sprinkle the eggs with coriander and serve.

Potato and tomato curry

Serves 4
CALORIES PER PORTION: 275 (1147 kJ)
PROTEIN CONTENT PER PORTION: 4 grams
PREPARATION & COOKING TIME: 45-60 minutes

1 lb potatoes
¼ cup vegetable oil
1 teaspoon ground turmeric
1 teaspoon coriander-based garam masala (page 200)
½ teaspoon chili powder (optional)
¼ cup peeled and finely chopped fresh ginger root
1 cup finely chopped onion
1 clove of garlic, peeled and very finely chopped
salt
2 green chili peppers, thinly sliced
2 cups skinned and coarsely chopped tomatoes
2 tablespoons chopped fresh coriander leaves or parsley

Boil the potatoes in their skins for 10 minutes. Drain and allow to cool slightly, then peel and slice them thickly. Fry the potatoes in the oil in a thick-based skillet until they are golden brown on both sides. Remove them from the pan and set aside until required. Heat the turmeric, garam masala and chili powder for a few moments in the oil in the skillet, then add the ginger and onion and fry until golden brown. Put in the garlic, salt, chili peppers and tomatoes, and cook gently until the tomatoes have broken down to a pulp.

Return the potatoes to the pan, cover and cook very gently until they are tender, stirring occasionally to prevent the mixture from sticking and burning. When the potatoes are cooked, increase the heat if necessary and boil away any excess moisture so that the tomato pulp almost becomes a paste. Shake the pan continually to prevent the mixture from sticking. Serve sprinkled with coriander or parsley.

Turkish pilau

Serves 4
CALORIES PER PORTION:
PROTEIN CONTENT PER PORTION:
PREPARATION & COOKING TIME: 1 hour, not including soaking

1 lb eggplants
salt
2 medium onions, thinly sliced
½ cup olive or vegetable oil
1 cup sliced mushrooms
1⅓ cups long-grain brown rice
2½ cups Brown vegetable stock (page 34)
1 cup skinned and chopped tomatoes
1 cup soy grits
¾ cup unroasted peanuts
1-2 cloves of garlic, peeled and finely chopped
½ teaspoon ground cumin
½ teaspoon ground coriander
½ teaspoon ground cinnamon
freshly ground pepper
2 hard-cooked eggs, finely chopped
8 scallions, finely chopped

Cut the eggplants into ¾ inch cubes, sprinkle them with salt and leave them to drain for 30 minutes. Meanwhile, fry the onions in ¼ cup of the oil until they are golden brown. Add the mushrooms and cook them until they are black and shiny. Stir in the rice and continue stirring for 1-2 minutes until it is thoroughly coated with oil.

Pour on the stock and add the tomatoes, soy grits, peanuts, garlic and spices and season with pepper. Cover and simmer for 5 minutes while you rinse the eggplants and dry them. Fry them in the remaining oil in another pan until they are transparent and beginning to brown. Drain them and scatter them over the pilau.

Cover and continue cooking over low heat for 30-40 minutes, or until the rice is tender — it may be necessary to add a little more water during the cooking time; the pilau should be moist but not mushy. When the rice is ready, turn the pilau into a warm serving dish and sprinkle the chopped eggs and scallions over the top. Serve with a Greek salad.

Lentil and rice kedgeree

Serves 4
CALORIES PER PORTION: 635 (2657 kJ)
PROTEIN CONTENT PER PORTION: 22 grams
PREPARATION & COOKING TIME: 1¼-1½ hours, not including soaking

¼ cup vegetable oil
1 teaspoon ground turmeric
1 teaspoon finely ground cumin
½ teaspoon clove-based garam masala (page 200)
½ teaspoon chili powder (optional)
1-2 green chili peppers, chopped (optional)
¼ cup peeled and finely chopped fresh ginger root
1 cup finely chopped onion
3 cloves of garlic, peeled and finely chopped
1⅓ cups green or brown lentils, soaked for 2 hours
1⅓ cups brown rice
salt
2 hard-cooked eggs, halved
2 bananas, thickly sliced
½ cup halved blanched almonds
2 tablespoons chopped coriander leaves

Pour the oil into a thick-based skillet and add the turmeric, cumin, garam masala and chili powder, if used. Heat gently until a spicy aroma begins to rise, then add the green chili peppers, if used, the ginger and onion and fry until the onion is soft, stirring frequently. Add the garlic, the drained lentils and the rice and fry so that it is evenly coated with oil and spices. Sprinkle with salt and add just enough boiling water to cover.

Cover the pan tightly and simmer very gently for about 45 minutes until the rice and lentils are soft and the water has been completely absorbed. You may have to add a little extra water during cooking — the finished kedgeree should be moist but not mushy. Transfer it to a hot serving dish, garnish with the eggs, banana slices, almonds and coriander and serve immediately.

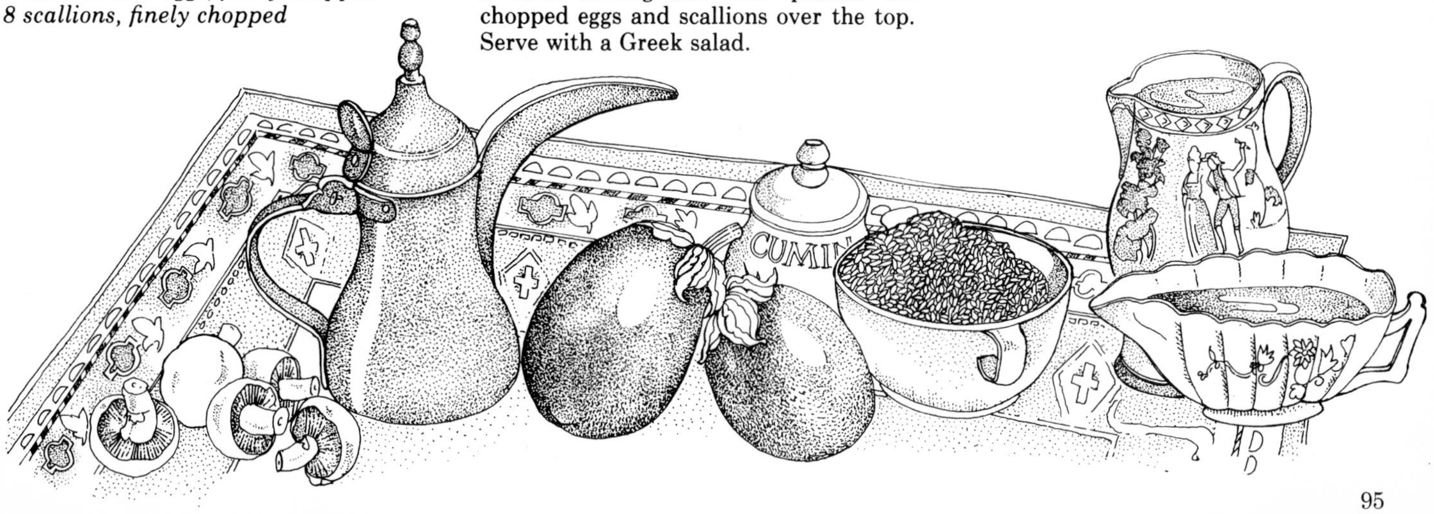

Vegetarian paella

Serves 4
CALORIES PER PORTION: 555 (2328 kJ)
PROTEIN CONTENT PER PORTION: 23.5 grams
PREPARATION & COOKING TIME: 1 hour

½ lb zucchini, thickly sliced
salt
2 cups coarsely chopped onions
¼ cup olive or sunflower oil
1⅓ cups brown long-grain rice
2½ cups White vegetable stock (page 34)
a large pinch of saffron soaked in a little water
1 large clove of garlic, peeled and finely chopped
3-4 red peppers, thinly sliced
1 cup skinned, coarsely chopped and seeded tomatoes
freshly ground pepper
¾ cup coarsely shredded almonds
2 hard-cooked eggs, finely chopped
1½ cups grated Cheddar cheese
¼ cup sliced pimiento-stuffed green olives

Sprinkle the sliced zucchini with salt and leave to drain for 30 minutes. Meanwhile, fry the onions in the oil in a thick-based skillet until they are golden brown. Add the rice and cook over moderate heat for 2 minutes, stirring constantly so that the rice does not stick and is evenly coated with oil. Pour on the stock, the saffron in its water and the garlic and bring to a boil, stirring constantly. Reduce the heat, cover the pan and simmer for 30 minutes.

Rinse the zucchini, pat them dry with paper towels and add them to the pan with the red peppers and tomatoes. Pour on a little more boiling water if the rice is too dry (it should be moist but not mushy). Season with salt and pepper, cover and cook for 10-15 minutes until the rice is soft and the peppers and zucchini are tender.

Turn into a heated flameproof serving dish. Sprinkle over the almonds, chopped eggs and the cheese, garnish with the olive slices and brown under the broiler. Serve with a mixed salad.

Lentil and nut cakes

Serves 4
CALORIES PER PORTION: 345 (1445 kJ)
PROTEIN CONTENT PER PORTION: 11 grams
PREPARATION & COOKING TIME: 35-40 minutes

2-3 tablespoons vegetable oil
1 teaspoon finely ground cumin
1 teaspoon ground turmeric
1 teaspoon clove-based garam masala (page 200)
1 cup finely chopped onion
¼ cup peeled and finely chopped fresh ginger root
1 clove of garlic, peeled and chopped
salt
2 cups cooked brown lentils, coarsely mashed
1 cup finely ground mixed nuts
2 tablespoons wholewheat flour
1 egg, well beaten
oil for shallow frying

Heat the spices in the oil for a few moments. Add the onion, ginger, garlic and salt to taste and fry gently until the onion is soft. Stir in the mashed lentils and nuts; sprinkle in the flour, add the egg and mix thoroughly.

Drop large spoonfuls of the lentil mixture onto a well-floured plate and roll them into 8 balls. Flatten them slightly and fry on both sides until golden brown. Serve with a bowl of plain yogurt.

Vegetable couscous

Serves 4-6
CALORIES PER PORTION: 1085 (4540 kJ)
PROTEIN CONTENT PER PORTION: 38 grams
PREPARATION & COOKING TIME: 2¼ hours, not including soaking

3 cups couscous grains
1⅓ cups dried chick peas, soaked overnight
3 tablespoons peanut oil
2 onions, sliced
2 large cloves of garlic, peeled and crushed
2 green peppers, chopped
4 carrots, sliced
7 oz zucchini, sliced
3 potatoes, quartered
1⅓ cups cubed pumpkin (optional)
2 pints water
⅔ cup seedless white raisins
14 oz canned okra, drained
1 teaspoon cayenne pepper
2 teaspoons ground cumin
1 teaspoon paprika
salt
freshly ground black pepper
⅔ cup harissa sauce
3 tablespoons butter
2 large ripe tomatoes, skinned and quartered
3 hard-cooked eggs, quartered

First make the couscous. Put the grains into a bowl and pour over about 1¼ cups of lukewarm salted water. Stir until mixed, then leave the grains for 30 minutes. Repeat at least once more. Put the chick peas and their soaking liquid into a large saucepan, making sure the peas are well covered. Bring to a boil over high heat, then reduce the heat, cover the pan and simmer for about 1 hour, or until the peas are tender. Drain and set aside.

Heat the oil in a large, deep, thick-based saucepan. Add the onions, garlic, peppers and carrots and fry gently until the onions are soft. Stir in the zucchini, potatoes and pumpkin (if using) and pour on the water. Bring to a boil, reduce the heat, cover the pan and simmer for 20 minutes. Stir in the reserved chick peas, the raisins, okra, cayenne, cumin and paprika and season with salt and pepper, then add about 1 tablespoon of harissa sauce. Bring to a boil again.

Arrange a colander lined with cheesecloth (an open-textured dish cloth will do) on top of the pan containing the vegetables, or over a separate pan of simmering water. Seal the space between the colander and pan, if necessary, with a rolled up dish cloth. Put the couscous grains into the colander, cover tightly and cook the couscous and vegetable mixture over low heat for 15 minutes.

Remove the colander from the pan and stir the butter gently into the grains. Add the tomatoes and eggs to the vegetable mixture. Return the colander to the pan, re-cover and cook both grains and vegetables for a final 5 minutes.

Arrange the couscous on a large, deep serving dish. Spoon over the vegetable mixture with some of the cooking liquid and serve the rest of the harissa sauce separately (you can thin this a little by stirring in some of the remaining liquid from the pan).

Couscous – served with an exotic and imaginative combination of vegetables; the egg adds protein, too

Vegetable kabobs

Serves 4
CALORIES PER PORTION: 557 (2335 kJ)
PROTEIN CONTENT PER PORTION: 11 grams
PREPARATION & COOKING TIME: 1 hour

½ lb zucchini, cut into 1¼ inch cubes
½ lb eggplant, cut into 1¼ inch cubes
salt
10 tablespoons olive or sunflower oil
½ teaspoon ground cumin
1 cup finely chopped onion
2 thin slices of wholewheat bread, cut into 1¼ inch cubes
¼ lb mushrooms
2 green peppers, sliced
2 tomatoes, halved
freshly ground black pepper
1 cup grated Cheddar cheese

Sprinkle the zucchini and eggplant cubes with salt and leave to drain for about 30 minutes to remove any bitterness.

Meanwhile, pour 6 tablespoons of the oil into a skillet, add the cumin and onion and cook over moderate heat until the onion is just beginning to color. Drain the onion and keep on one side. Fry the bread cubes until they are crisp and golden brown, adding a little more oil if necessary. Remove them from the pan and drain on paper towels.

Rinse the zucchini and eggplant cubes and put them into a steamer with the mushrooms and green peppers. Cook them for 5 minutes. Remove the vegetables from the steamer, allow them to cool slightly, then arrange them on skewers alternating zucchini, eggplant, fried bread, pepper and mushroom. Finish each with a halved tomato and lay the completed kabobs on a lightly oiled baking sheet. Pour about 1 teaspoon of the cumin and onion flavored oil over each. Season with salt and pepper and sprinkle with half of the fried onion. Cook them under the broiler for about 5 minutes, until the vegetables are golden brown. Turn the kabobs, spoon over a little more oil, sprinkle with the rest of the fried onion and cover them with the grated cheese. Return the kabobs to the broiler and cook until the cheese has melted. Take care that the kabobs are not too close to the broiler or they will be dry or burnt. Serve with Barbecue sauce and plain boiled rice, or boiled rice flavored with turmeric.

A tomato salad or Tunisian orange salad makes the ideal accompaniment.

Note: If barbecuing the kabobs, add the tomatoes partway through cooking.

Stir-fried one dish meal (with rice)

Serves 4
CALORIES PER PORTION: 420 (1792 kJ)
PROTEIN CONTENT PER PORTION: 21 grams
PREPARATION & COOKING TIME: 30-40 minutes

4 eggs
a little melted butter
¾ lb bean curd, diced
oil for shallow frying
2 cups finely chopped onion
½ cup peeled and finely chopped fresh ginger root
2 cups shredded red pepper
¼ cup vegetable oil
2 cups sliced mushrooms
½ lb bean sprouts
½ lb spinach, coarsely shredded
2 tablespoons miso
2 tablespoons soy sauce
6-8 tablespoons vegetable stock or water
2 tablespoons sweet sherry
½ star aniseed pod, ground
salt

Make an omelet with the eggs, following the basic method on page 66, and cut it into thin strips. Keep hot.

Fry the bean curd in shallow oil until it is golden brown and crisp on the outside. Drain and keep hot.

Fry the onion, ginger and pepper in 3 tablespoons of the oil until they are soft. Add the mushrooms and cook them until they are shiny. Add the bean sprouts, spinach, miso, soy sauce and stock or water with the sherry and ground aniseed. Stir-fry for a few moments until the bean sprouts are hot, adding the remaining tablespoon of oil if necessary. Fold in the omelet strips and fried bean curd and heat through gently. Season to taste with a little salt, if necessary, and serve with plenty of boiled brown rice.

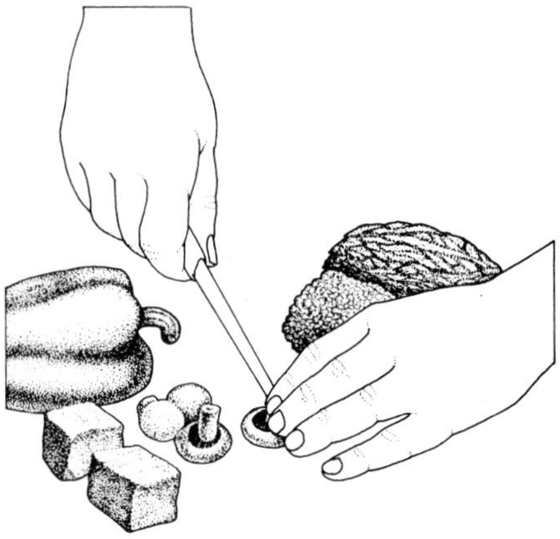

1. Cut all the vegetables into small pieces of a uniform size.

2. Stir-fry, using two forks to lift the vegetables and turn continuously.

Chinese nut cakes

Serves 4
CALORIES PER PORTION: 555 (2310 kJ)
PROTEIN CONTENT PER PORTION: 16.5 grams
PREPARATION & COOKING TIME: 1 hour

½ quantity of Basic stuffing (page 88)
Coating batter (page 194)
oil for deep frying

The sweet and sour sauce
2 medium onions, thinly sliced
2 cups shredded red pepper
2 tablespoons vegetable oil
2 tablespoons soy sauce
¼ cup wine vinegar
1 star aniseed pod, finely ground
2 teaspoons cornstarch
1¼ cups brown stock
3 tablespoons raw brown sugar

Prepare the stuffing and batter.

Fry the onions and pepper in the oil over moderate heat until soft. Stir in the soy sauce, wine vinegar, aniseed, the cornstarch mixed with the stock and the sugar. Bring to a boil, stirring continuously until the mixture thickens, and then lower the heat and simmer for 5 minutes. Keep hot.

Shape the stuffing mixture into eight balls, dip them in the batter and deep fry in hot oil until they are golden brown and crisp. Drain well and then put them into the sweet and sour sauce. Bring the sauce back to a boil and serve immediately with plenty of brown rice.

Kulebiak

This recipe serves 10-12 and is ideal for a buffet party.

TOTAL CALORIES: 4860 (20,340 kJ)
TOTAL PROTEIN CONTENT: 247 grams
PREPARATION & COOKING TIME: 2½ hours

The yeast dough
1 cake compressed yeast (follow the manufacturer's instructions for active dry yeast)
2 teaspoons soft brown sugar
1¼ cups lukewarm milk
3½ cups wholewheat flour
1 teaspoon salt
2 cups finely grated Cheddar cheese
2 eggs, beaten
beaten egg, to glaze

The filling
8 cups finely shredded white cabbage
2 teaspoons salt
⅔ cup cold water
2 cups finely chopped onions
6 tablespoons butter
2 cups coarsely chopped mushrooms
7 tablespoons wholewheat flour
1 cup milk
2 cups grated Cheddar cheese
salt
freshly ground pepper
1 tablespoon finely ground coriander (optional)
3 hard-cooked eggs, chopped

To make the yeast dough: mix the yeast with the sugar, add the lukewarm milk and leave in a warm place for about 10 minutes until it is frothy. Put the flour and salt into a bowl. Sprinkle in the cheese and mix lightly. Make a well in the center, pour the yeast mixture into the flour, add the beaten eggs and mix to a soft but not sticky dough. Add a little more warm milk if necessary. Turn out onto a floured board and knead until completely smooth. Put the dough into a lightly oiled bowl, cover and set aside in a warm place until it has doubled in size.

Meanwhile, make the filling. Put the cabbage in a thick-based saucepan with the salt and water. Bring to a boil and simmer for about 10 minutes until the cabbage has reduced in bulk and is just tender, then continue cooking the cabbage for a further 2-3 minutes until all the water has evaporated. Take care that the cabbage does not burn. Remove from the heat and allow to cool.

Fry the onions in the butter until soft and golden brown. Add the mushrooms and fry until dark and shiny, then remove the pan from the heat and stir in the flour. Add the milk gradually, mixing well between each addition. Return the pan to the heat and bring to a boil, stirring continuously, until the mixture thickens. Remove from the heat, add the cheese and stir until melted. Mix the onion and mushroom mixture into the cabbage and season well with salt, pepper and coriander, if liked. Set aside until completely cold.

To finish the pie, punch down the risen dough and divide it into two portions. Knead each portion well and roll into a rectangle about 10 × 15 inches. Place one portion on a well-oiled baking sheet and cover with the filling, leaving a border of about 2 inches around the edge. Sprinkle over the chopped eggs, brush the edges with water and cover with the second portion of dough. Seal and crimp the edges and make 2 or 3 slits in the top for steam to escape. Leave in a warm place to rise for about 30 minutes. Preheat the oven to 400°F, then bake the Kulebiak in the preheated oven for 20 minutes.

Brush the top with beaten egg to glaze and bake for a further 10-15 minutes until it is golden brown.

Mixed vegetable pie

Serves 4
CALORIES PER PORTION: 555 (2332 kJ)
PROTEIN CONTENT PER PORTION: 18 grams
PREPARATION & COOKING TIME: 1-1¼ hours

double quantity Wholewheat pie pastry (page 194)
1 cup finely chopped onion
2 tablespoons butter
¾ cup cooked soybeans
1 cup cooked peas
1 cup coarsely chopped mushrooms
½ cup dried skimmed milk
1 cup milk
2 tablespoons wholewheat flour
salt
freshly ground pepper
½-1 teaspoon finely chopped marjoram
1 bay leaf, crumbled
1 small clove of garlic, peeled and finely chopped

Keep the dough, well wrapped, in the refrigerator until required. Preheat the oven to 400°F. Fry the onion gently in the butter until it is golden brown. Add the beans, peas, mushrooms and 1 tablespoon of water, and cook over a gentle heat until the mushrooms are dark and shiny. Remove from the heat and leave until cold. If necessary, place the pan in a bowl of cold water to speed up the cooling process.

Stir the dried milk into the fresh milk and then stir in the flour. Stir into the cold vegetables, season with salt and pepper and add the marjoram, bay leaf and garlic.

Roll out half of the dough and line a well-oiled 9 inch pie pan. Fill with the prepared vegetable mixture. Roll out the remaining dough and cover the pie. Seal the two dough layers together and flute the edge. Decorate with dough trimmings and make a hole in the center for steam to escape. Bake in the preheated oven for 30 minutes.

Accompaniments: Polish-style cauliflower, zucchini or broccoli.

Raised vegetable pie

Serves 6
CALORIES PER PORTION: 744 (3113 kJ)
PROTEIN CONTENT PER PORTION: 24 grams
PREPARATION & COOKING TIME: 2-2½ hours

The pastry
2¾ cups wholewheat flour
1 teaspoon salt
12 tablespoons butter
1 egg, well beaten

The filling
1½ cups finely chopped onion
½ lb red peppers, seeded and cut into 1 inch slices
1 cup coarsely chopped celery
1⅓ cups diced turnip
⅔ cup diced carrot
¼ cup olive or sunflower oil
2 cups chopped cabbage
1 clove of garlic, peeled and finely chopped
salt
freshly ground pepper
½ teaspoon finely chopped marjoram
1 bay leaf, crumbled
4 hard-cooked eggs

The binding sauce
2 tablespoons vegetable oil
3 tablespoons wholewheat flour
2 teaspoons agar-agar
1¼ cups milk
1¼ cups grated Cheddar cheese
salt
freshly ground pepper

To make the pastry, put the flour and salt into a bowl and rub in the butter. Add the beaten egg and mix to a firm dough, adding a little cold water, if necessary. Wrap well and keep in a refrigerator until required.

To make the filling, place all the prepared vegetables, except the cabbage, in a large thick-based saucepan. Add the oil and place over a moderate heat. Cook the vegetables, shaking the pan frequently to turn them, until they are just beginning to color and are almost tender. This will take about 20 minutes. Add the cabbage, garlic, seasonings and herbs, and cook quickly for about 5 minutes, shaking the pan continuously. Remove from the heat and leave to cool.

Meanwhile, make the binding sauce. Heat the oil in a small saucepan until just beginning to sizzle. Stir in the flour and mix well. Take the pan off the heat. Mix the agar-agar with a little of the milk to make a creamy mixture. Stir in the remaining milk, then add this gradually to the flour mixture in the pan, mixing well between each addition. Return to the heat, bring to a boil and stir until the sauce thickens. Add the cheese, continue to stir until it has melted and then season well with salt and pepper. Add the sauce to the cooked vegetables and mix very thoroughly.

Preheat the oven to 350°F. Roll out three-quarters of the dough and then line a well-greased 1-quart capacity springform pie pan. Or, alternatively, use a 9 × 5 × 3 inch loaf pan. Put in half the vegetable filling and arrange the eggs on top. Cover with the remaining filling. Roll out the remaining dough to fit the top of the pie, brush the edges with water and seal the two dough layers firmly together. Trim off any surplus and use it to decorate the top of the pie. Make a hole in the center to allow steam to escape, and decorate with dough trimmings. Bake in the preheated oven for 1 hour. Allow the pie to cool completely before removing from the pan.

Serve cold with Mayonnaise or Rémoulade sauce and salads.

Cashew loaf

Serves 4-6
TOTAL CALORIES: 1180 (7580 kJ)
TOTAL PROTEIN CONTENT: 63 grams
PREPARATION & COOKING TIME: 1½ hours

The loaf
2 cups ground cashew nuts
2 cups fresh wholewheat breadcrumbs
1 cup finely chopped onion
2 tablespoons butter
1 clove of garlic, peeled and finely chopped
2 eggs, beaten
⅔ cup milk
grated rind of 1 lemon
½ teaspoon finely chopped marjoram
salt
freshly ground black pepper

The filling
1 cup finely chopped onion
2 cups shredded red pepper
2 tablespoons butter
freshly ground black pepper
salt
1 cup coarsely grated Edam or Cheddar cheese
1 egg, beaten

Preheat the oven to 400°F. Mix together the nuts and breadcrumbs in a bowl. Fry the onion in the butter until soft and golden brown. Add the garlic and fry gently for a few moments longer without allowing it to color. Take out of the pan and add to the mixed nuts and crumbs.

Beat the eggs with the milk, lemon rind, marjoram, salt and pepper. Pour into the nut and crumb mixture and mix thoroughly.

To make the filling: fry the onion and red pepper in the butter until almost soft but not browned. Season liberally with black pepper and a little salt, then remove from the heat and add the cheese and enough beaten egg to bind the mixture.

Line a 9 × 5 × 3 inch loaf pan with wax paper or non-stick parchment paper and press half the nut mixture into the bottom of the pan. Spread the filling mixture on top, then cover with the remaining nut mixture. Bake in the preheated oven for 30-40 minutes, or until firm. Serve hot with Béarnaise sauce (page 195), accompanied by cauliflower or broccoli.

Note: This loaf is also good served cold with salads.

Soybean loaf

Serves 4-6
TOTAL CALORIES: 1040 (4350 kJ)
TOTAL PROTEIN CONTENT: 58 grams
PREPARATION & COOKING TIME: 1-1¼ hours

2¾ cups cooked soybeans
1 cup finely chopped onion
1 cup finely chopped celery
2 tablespoons olive or sunflower oil
2 eggs
1 cup milk
1 clove of garlic, peeled and finely chopped
½-1 teaspoon finely chopped winter or summer savory
salt
freshly ground black pepper

Preheat the oven to 400°F. Thoroughly mash the soybeans. Line a 4½ × 2½ × 1½ inch loaf pan with non-stick parchment paper or wax paper.

Fry the onion and celery in the oil until soft but not browned. Add to the soybeans and mix well. Beat the eggs with the milk, garlic, savory, salt and pepper, and stir into the soybean mixture.

Place the mixture in the prepared pan and bake in the preheated oven for 30 minutes. Allow to cool for a few moments before removing from the pan. Serve with Tomato or Mushroom sauce and a salad.

Curried peanut loaf

Serves 4-6
TOTAL CALORIES: 2185 (9140 kJ)
TOTAL PROTEIN CONTENT: 110 grams
PREPARATION & COOKING TIME: 1¼-1½ hours

The loaf
2 cups ground peanuts
4 cups fresh wholewheat breadcrumbs
2 cups finely chopped onions
1 cup finely chopped celery
1 teaspoon ground cumin
1 teaspoon ground coriander
½ teaspoon caraway seeds
1 teaspoon salt, or to taste
1 teaspoon ground turmeric
1 large clove of garlic, peeled and chopped
1½ inch piece of fresh ginger root, peeled and finely chopped
3 eggs, well beaten

The topping
1 cup milk
2 eggs
¼ teaspoon salt
1 teaspoon curry powder

Preheat the oven to 400°F. To make the loaf, place all the dry ingredients in a bowl and mix very thoroughly. Add the eggs and bind the mixture well. Press it into a 4½ × 2½ × 1½ inch loaf pan lined with non-stick parchment or wax paper or an ovenproof dish, if you are serving the cooked loaf straight from its dish — this way the custard topping will not break. Bake in the preheated oven for 15 minutes.

To make the topping: mix together all the ingredients and pour onto the loaf, then continue baking for 30-35 minutes. At the end of the baking time, when the loaf should be firm and golden brown, allow to cool a little before removing the loaf from the pan, taking care not to break it or the custard on top.

Serve hot with Tomato sauce, subtly flavored with curry powder, and a Mixed salad or Tomato salad. Alternatively, serve cold.

Pizza

Serves 4
CALORIES PER PORTION: 620 (2600 kJ)
PROTEIN CONTENT PER PORTION: 29 grams
PREPARATION & COOKING TIME: 2 hours

3 cups plus 3 tablespoons wholewheat flour
2 teaspoons salt
1 cake compressed yeast (follow manufacturer's instructions for active dry yeast)
1 teaspoon soft brown sugar
1 cup lukewarm milk
¾ lb red peppers, seeded and cut into ½ inch strips
olive or sunflower oil
1 lb tomatoes, skinned, cored and cut into 8 segments
½ lb Mozzarella cheese, thinly sliced
salt
freshly ground black pepper
a sprinkling of fresh or dried oregano
24 black olives, halved and pitted

Sift the flour and salt into a bowl and make a well in the center. Mix the yeast with the sugar and 2 tablespoons warm water. Put in a warm place for about 15 minutes until it is frothy. Add to the warm milk and pour it into the flour. Mix well, adding a little more warm milk if necessary to make a soft but not sticky dough. Knead on a well-floured board until it is completely smooth. Place in a lightly oiled bowl, cover and leave to rise in a warm place until it has doubled in size.

Punch down the dough and divide it into four portions. Shape each portion into an 8 inch round and place on well-oiled baking sheets. Preheat the oven to 400°F.

Cook the peppers in a little oil (preferably olive) and water until they are soft. Arrange strips of pepper, chunks of tomato and slices of cheese on each round of dough. Sprinkle a little oil over them and season generously with salt, pepper and oregano. Garnish with the black olives. Leave the Pizzas in a warm place for 20 minutes, until they are just beginning to rise. Bake in the preheated oven for 30 minutes, and serve with a Mixed or Green salad and a robust red wine or cider.

Top: Curried peanut loaf is served straight from the dish to show the delicate custard topping. Right: savory Cashew loaf has a middle layer of cheese and red peppers; the loaf itself is flavored with marjoram and garlic. Below: ever-popular Pizzas, topped with Mozzarella cheese, olives, tomatoes and – for the authentic Italian touch – oregano

Pea, corn and scallion pie

Serves 6
CALORIES PER PORTION: 480 (3012 kJ)
PROTEIN CONTENT PER PORTION: 27 grams
PREPARATION & COOKING TIME: 1 hour

1 cup texturized soy protein
2¼ cups cooked peas
1⅓ cups cooked corn kernels
2 tablespoons butter
3 tablespoons wholewheat flour
1¼ cups milk
1 cup grated Cheddar cheese
6 large scallions, coarsely chopped
2 eggs, beaten
salt
freshly ground pepper
pre-baked 9 inch pie shell, made with Wholewheat pie pastry (page 194)

Preheat the oven to 400°F. Simmer the soy protein in a little water for 5-8 minutes, adding as much water as necessary to keep the mixture moist — but there should be no excess liquid. Add the peas and corn and leave to cool.

Melt the butter in another pan over gentle heat, then stir in the flour. Remove the pan from the heat and gradually add the milk, stirring well between each addition. Return the pan to the heat and bring to a boil, stirring continuously until the mixture thickens. Add the cheese and stir until it melts, then stir in the scallions and the soy mixture. Allow to cool slightly, then mix in the eggs and season well with salt and pepper.

Pour the mixture into the prepared pie shell and bake in the preheated oven for about 30 minutes or until the filling is set and the top golden brown. Serve hot or cold with a spiced Apricot or Cherry sauce (page 197) and a salad.

Potato, cheese and onion pie

Serves 4
CALORIES PER PORTION: 645 (2707 kJ)
PROTEIN CONTENT PER PORTION: 22 grams
PREPARATION AND COOKING TIME: 1 hour

¾ lb potatoes, thinly sliced
1 cup coarsely chopped onion
1½ cups grated Cheddar cheese
pre-baked 8 inch pie shell, made with Wholewheat pie pastry (page 194)
2 tablespoons finely chopped parsley
1 egg, beaten
1 cup milk
1 clove of garlic, peeled and finely chopped
salt
freshly ground pepper

Cook the potatoes in a little boiling salted water until just soft, then drain. Preheat the oven to 400°F. Put the onion in a pan with just enough water to cover and bring to a boil. Drain the onion and leave to cool. Sprinkle one-third of the cheese over the bottom of the prepared pie shell, cover with half the drained potato slices and sprinkle with half the parsley. Add half the onion, then repeat the layers of potato, cheese, parsley and onion.

Mix the egg with the milk and add the garlic, salt and pepper. Pour this over the layers of filling in the pie shell. Sprinkle with the remaining cheese and bake in the preheated oven for 30-40 minutes, or until the filling is set and the top is golden brown. Serve with a green vegetable or Green or Mixed salad.
Variation: The onion can be fried in 2 tablespoons butter intead of being blanched, if preferred.

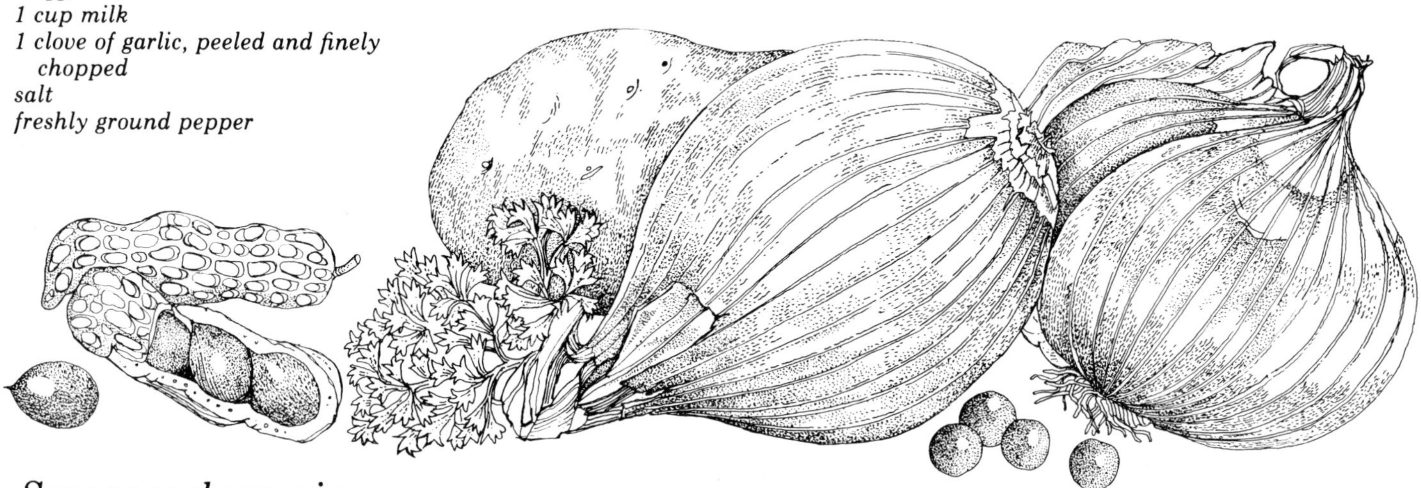

Savory soybean pie

Serves 4
CALORIES PER PORTION: 600 (2517 kJ)
PROTEIN CONTENT PER PORTION: 21 grams
PREPARATION & COOKING TIME: 1 hour

If a smooth-textured filling is required, the soybeans can be worked in a blender before being added to the rest of the ingredients.

1 cup finely chopped onion
2 tablespoons butter
2¼ cups cooked soybeans
½ cup milk
1 clove of garlic, peeled and finely chopped
1 egg, beaten
¼ teaspoon chopped thyme
½ cup grated Cheddar cheese
salt
freshly ground pepper
pre-baked 8 inch pie shell, made with Wholewheat pie pastry (page 194)

Preheat the oven to 400°F. Fry the onion in the butter until soft and golden brown. Mix the soybeans with the rest of the ingredients, using half the cheese. Season with salt and pepper, then add the cooked onion to the soybean mixture. Pour into the prepared pie shell, sprinkle with the remaining cheese and bake in the preheated oven for 30-40 minutes, or until the filling is set and the top is golden brown.

Serve with Okra créole, Beets in sour cream or Leeks in yogurt sauce.

Cauliflower vol-au-vent

Serves 4
CALORIES PER PORTION: 1290 (5865 kJ)
PROTEIN CONTENT PER PORTION: 22 grams
PREPARATION & COOKING TIME: 35-40 minutes

1 large 8 inch diameter vol-au-vent case (patty shell) made from Puff pastry (page 194)
1 tablespoon dried rosemary
¾ lb head cauliflower, broken into florets
2 cups sliced mushrooms
2 tablespoons butter
3 tablespoons wholewheat flour
½ cup dried skimmed milk
1¼ cups milk
salt and freshly ground pepper

Set the oven at 400°F and roll out the pastry on a lightly-floured surface. Cut 2 circles 8 inches in diameter. Cut a 6½ inch diameter lid from the center of one. Brush the edge of the whole circle with beaten egg. Position the ring on top and brush the ring and lid with egg. Bake base and lid, without touching, on a dampened baking sheet for 25 minutes.

Put the rosemary into a pan with 2½ cups water and bring to a boil. Place the cauliflower florets in a steamer over the flavored water and cook for about 10 minutes, or until just tender.

Fry the mushrooms in the butter for 3-4 minutes, then stir in the flour and remove the pan from the heat. Dissolve the skimmed milk in the fresh milk and pour this gradually into the pan, stirring well between each addition. Add the cauliflower, return the pan to the heat and cook over a very gentle heat, stirring frequently, until the mixture thickens. Season with salt and pepper, spoon into the hot vol-au-vent case, cover with the lid, and serve immediately.

Note: Individual vol-au-vents (patty shells) can be made in the same way; bake for 20 minutes. Keep the florets small. A sprinkling of cheese also adds flavor.

Zucchini vol-au-vent

Serves 4
CALORIES PER PORTION: 1530 (6490 kJ)
PROTEIN CONTENT PER PORTION: 25 grams
PREPARATION & COOKING TIME: 1 hour

1 large 8 inch diameter vol-au-vent case (patty shell) made from Puff pastry (page 194) baked as above
1 lb zucchini, thinly sliced
salt
1 cup finely chopped onion
2 tablespoons butter or vegetable oil
2 cups thinly sliced button mushrooms
1-2 cloves of garlic, peeled and finely chopped
3-4 tablespoons water
1¼ cups Bêchamel sauce (page 196)
1 cup grated Cheddar cheese
freshly ground black pepper

Put the vol-au-vent case to heat through for 10 minutes in a 350°F oven. Sprinkle the zucchini with salt and leave to drain for 30 minutes to remove any bitterness. Fry the onion in the butter or oil until it is pale golden. Rinse the zucchini, pat them dry on paper towels and add them to the pan with the mushrooms and garlic. Continue cooking for a few moments until the juices start to run. Add the water, cover the pan and cook over low heat for about 5 minutes, or until the zucchini are cooked but still fairly firm. Check that they do not stick and burn.

Heat the Béchamel sauce and stir in the cheese; add the vegetables, season to taste with salt and pepper and mix thoroughly. Pour the filling into the heated vol-au-vent case and serve immediately.

Note: If you are making individual vol-au-vent cases (patty shells), this mixture should fill about 6-8, depending on size.

Nut and lentil pâté

Serves 6-8
TOTAL CALORIES: 1720 (7208 kJ)
TOTAL PROTEIN CONTENT: 56 grams
PREPARATION & COOKING TIME: 2½ hours, excluding cooling

3 cups ground mixed nuts
3 cups cooked brown lentils
1¼ cups finely chopped celery
2 cups finely chopped onion
2 cloves of garlic, peeled and finely chopped
1¾ cups coarsely chopped tomatoes
8 tablespoons butter
3 eggs, well beaten
½-1 teaspoon finely chopped thyme
1-2 teaspoons finely chopped oregano
salt
freshly ground pepper

Preheat the oven to 400°F. Mix together the nuts, lentils, celery, onion and garlic. Cook the tomatoes very gently until reduced to a pulp, then rub this through a strainer. There should be about 1 cup of tomato purée; if there is more, reduce it by boiling; if less, add a little water. Melt the butter in the tomato purée and allow to cool slightly before adding the eggs, herbs and salt and pepper

Pour this mixture into the ingredients in the bowl and mix thoroughly. Press into a well-oiled 1 quart capacity loaf pan and bake in the preheated oven for 1½-2 hours, or until set. Allow to cool completely before removing the pâté from the pan. Serve chilled with slices of wholewheat toast.

Mushroom and nut loaf

Serves 6
TOTAL CALORIES: 410 (1715 kJ)
TOTAL PROTEIN CONTENT: 12 grams
PREPARATION & COOKING TIME: 2-2½ hours

½ lb chestnuts
2 cups finely chopped onion
2 tablespoons vegetable oil
1 cup sliced mushrooms
1 clove of garlic, peeled and finely chopped
2 cups ground walnuts
2 cups fresh breadcrumbs
7 tablespoons wholewheat flour
½-1 teaspoon finely chopped sage
½-1 teaspoon finely chopped thyme
salt and freshly ground black pepper
1 teaspoon brewers' yeast
⅔ cup warm milk
2 eggs, beaten

Slit the chestnuts and cook in boiling water for about 30 minutes, or until soft. Drain, and while still warm, remove the outer shell and the inner skin. Break the nuts into quarters and place in a bowl.

Preheat the oven to 400°F. Line a 1 quart capacity hinged loaf pan with non-stick parchment paper. Fry the onion in the oil until soft and golden brown. Add the mushrooms and garlic, and fry gently for 3-4 minutes. Add to the chestnuts together with the walnuts, breadcrumbs, flour and herbs and season well.

Dissolve the brewers' yeast in the milk, beat in the eggs and pour into the chestnut mixture, mixing very thoroughly. Spoon it into the prepared loaf pan and bake in the preheated oven for 30-40 minutes or until firm and golden brown.

Serve hot with Tomato or a Brown sauce, accompanied by Peas with lettuce and onions, Pommes Lyonnaise, fried spinach, or cold with salads.

Sformato di piselli

Serves 4-6
TOTAL CALORIES: 1275 (5340 kJ)
TOTAL PROTEIN CONTENT: 60 grams
PREPARATION & COOKING TIME: 2-2½ hours

1 cup finely chopped onion
4 tablespoons butter
3½ cups shelled fresh or thawed frozen peas
3 tablespoons wholewheat flour
1 cup milk
1 cup grated Cheddar cheese
3 eggs, separated
salt
freshly ground black pepper

Fry the onion in the butter until soft but not browned. Add the peas and fry for 1-2 minutes. Sprinkle in the flour and stir well. Take the pan off the heat and gradually add the milk and cheese, stirring well between each addition. Return the pan to a moderate heat and bring to a boil. Continue stirring until the mixture thickens.

Work it in a blender to a smooth purée or pass through a food mill. Transfer the purée to a bowl, add the egg yolks and mix thoroughly and season.

Beat the egg whites until stiff enough to stand in peaks and fold them gently into the purée. Pour it into a well-buttered 7 inch soufflé dish and cover with a well-buttered paper. Place in a pan and pour in enough hot water to come halfway up the sides of the dish. Simmer gently for 1-1½ hours, or until set.

When cooked, either serve from the soufflé dish, or if the mixture is really firm, cool slightly and then unmold onto a serving dish. This can be tricky, as the amount of moisture in the peas can affect the 'set'. Serve with Tomato or Mushroom sauce, accompanied by baked potatoes.

Savory nut roast

Serves 4
CALORIES PER PORTION: 580 (2430 kJ)
PROTEIN CONTENT PER PORTION: 22 grams
PREPARATION AND COOKING TIME: 1¼-1½ hours

2 cups ground mixed nuts
4 cups fresh wholewheat breadcrumbs
1 cup finely chopped onion
2 tablespoons olive or sunflower oil
2 eggs, beaten
salt
freshly ground black pepper
1-2 large cloves of garlic, peeled and finely chopped
1-2 teaspoons brewer's yeast
½-1 teaspoon finely chopped thyme
½-1 teaspoon finely chopped sage
4 tablespoons finely chopped parsley
1 cup grated Edam or Cheddar cheese

Preheat the oven to 350°F. Mix the nuts and breadcrumbs together in a bowl. Fry the onion in the oil until soft but not browned, then add it to the nuts and breadcrumbs. Beat the eggs again with the remaining ingredients, pour into the nut mixture and knead thoroughly together. Leave the mixture to stand for 15 minutes, then shape it into a roll about 6 inches long and place on a well-oiled baking sheet. Bake in the preheated oven for 30-45 minutes until it is firm and golden brown. Serve with a Brown sauce or Mushroom sauce (page 196) and a choice of vegetables.

Vegetable scallops au gratin

Serves 4
CALORIES PER PORTION: 730 (3060 kJ)
PROTEIN CONTENT PER PORTION: 31 grams
PREPARATION AND COOKING TIME: 1 hour

1¼ lb potatoes
1½ cups grated Cheddar cheese
1 egg, beaten
a little milk
2 cups finely chopped onions
2 cups finely chopped green peppers
1 cup finely chopped celery
4 tablespoons butter
1½ cups unroasted peanuts
1 tablespoon chopped parsley
2 tablespoons wholewheat flour
¼ cup dried skimmed milk
⅔ cup milk
salt
freshly ground pepper
a pinch of cayenne (optional)

Boil the potatoes in their skins until tender. Drain and rinse under cold running water until they are cool enough to handle, then peel and mash them with 1 cup of the cheese, the beaten egg and enough milk to make a fairly soft consistency, suitable for piping. Using a pastry bag fitted with a large rose nozzle, pipe a border around four small ovenproof plates or gratin dishes about 5 inches in diameter, and set aside until required.

Preheat the oven to 400°F. Fry the onions, peppers and celery in the butter until they are beginning to brown. Add the peanuts, parsley and flour and mix well. Remove from the heat and allow to cool slightly. Dissolve the dried milk in the fresh milk and pour it onto the vegetables, stirring vigorously. Return the pan to a gentle heat and stir until the mixture thickens.

Season with salt and pepper and divide the filling between the potato rings. Sprinkle with the remaining cheese and dust with cayenne, if used. Bake in the preheated oven for 30 minutes and serve hot.

Croûtes

Serves 4
CALORIES PER PORTION: 239 (990 kJ)
PROTEIN PER PORTION: 2 grams
COOKING TIME: 7 minutes

8 tablespoons butter, preferably clarified, or oil
4 slices of wholewheat bread, crusts removed and quartered diagonally
a little salt, or grated Parmesan cheese

Melt the butter in a thick-based skillet over gentle heat. Put in the slices of bread and fry on both sides until crisp. Drain on paper towels and sprinkle with salt or Parmesan cheese.

Vegetable Accompaniments

It seems to me a pity that the Anglo-Saxon habit of serving all vegetables together with the main course – often on the same plate – has become so widespread. As a result, many people have ceased to appreciate and enjoy a dish of vegetables in its own right, as a separate course after the main dish. This is where I would place the vegetable accompaniment in my menu.
There is a preparation chart on page 202. Follow this, resist the temptation to overcook your vegetables or smother them in sauces – and you, too, will come to love them for themselves again.

Vegetables: preparation and cooking

Most vegetables can be eaten raw; cooking destroys vitamin C and much of the vitamin B complex; vitamin C and the B complex are water-soluble. These three facts provide us with a guide for cooking vegetables. Cook them for the minimum possible time in the minimum amount of water, and serve as soon after cooking as possible. Keeping vegetables warm for any length of time spoils their flavour and completes the vitamin destruction.

Prepare vegetables just before cooking by discarding any discoloured, bruised or damaged portions and then washing them thoroughly to remove any sand or insects. Root vegetables should be scrubbed with a brush. Leaf vegetables such as spinach, kale and most greens should be washed, leaf by leaf, under a running tap. Root vegetables will go brown if they are left in the air after peeling; as the most nutritious part of the root lies just below the skin, it is really much better to cook them unpeeled after thoroughly scrubbing them and removing any blemishes. Old root vegetables with tough skins which need to be peeled should have only the thinnest layer removed and should then be immersed in water. Keep the peelings for use in vegetable stock.

Root and leaf vegetables can often be cooked and served whole, halved or quartered. But for stir-frying or quick cooking they need to be torn, sliced, diced or shredded. This should be done immediately before cooking to minimise vitamin loss. Try, too, not to leave prepared vegetables soaking in water for any length of time.

Refer to the chart on page 202 for more detailed instructions on the preparation of the individual vegetables.

Tearing
Hold the leaf between the index finger and the thumb of one hand and tear off pieces approximately 2 inches square. The advantage of tearing and not cutting is that the leaf is not bruised; when time is short, arrange the leaves one on top of another, cut into slices and then shred the slices into squares.

Slicing
Cut the vegetable in half lengthwise, then holding it down firmly on a chopping board, with the index finger and thumb, use a 5 inch paring knife to cut it down to the board into ⅛-¼ inch slices. Alternatively, you can use a longer knife, 10 inches, with a stiff blade, as the Chinese do; do not cut the vegetable in half, but make the first cut at 30° and roll the vegetable through 180° and cut again at 30° and so on. This produces rather decorative, wedge-shaped slices. You can achieve considerable speed with practice!

Dicing
Cut the slices into strips of the same thickness — ½ inch. Keeping the slices together and flat, cut across into small cubes.

Shredding
Use a coarse grater, preferably made of stainless steel, and rub the vegetable up and down against it, taking care to keep your fingers well out of the way; it might be a good idea to hold whatever is being grated in a thick dish cloth.

There are various gadgets, hand-operated or electric, for shredding and grating, which are well worth the investment as salad making and vegetable preparation become almost instananeous.

You can also shred leaf vegetables by first quartering them, if they are firm like cabbage, and then, holding the wedge firmly on a board and cutting very thin slices. Or pile the individual leaves of loose-leaved vegetables such as spinach one on top of the other and then cut them into very thin strips.

Vegetables can be baked, braised, roasted, boiled, steamed, fried or stir-fried. Each method gives a distinctive quality and flavor to the finished dish, and gives tempting variations to everyday meals. Compare the effect of adding fresh herbs or salt before and after cooking. Serve vegetables with a pat of butter and a vinaigrette dressing made with olive or walnut oil and a herb, wine or cider vinegar.

Cooked vegetables should never be mushy; test them with a sharp skewer — it should penetrate but there should be a slight resistance. Root vegetables should still be firm.

Baking
The basis of baking is that the food is cooked in a dry atmosphere. Root vegetables and vegetable fruits generally have thick enough skins to prevent them from drying out. Try inserting a sliver of garlic into a potato or eggplant before baking it. Other vegetables have to be wrapped in aluminum foil or wax paper to prevent too much water loss; a few drops of oil,

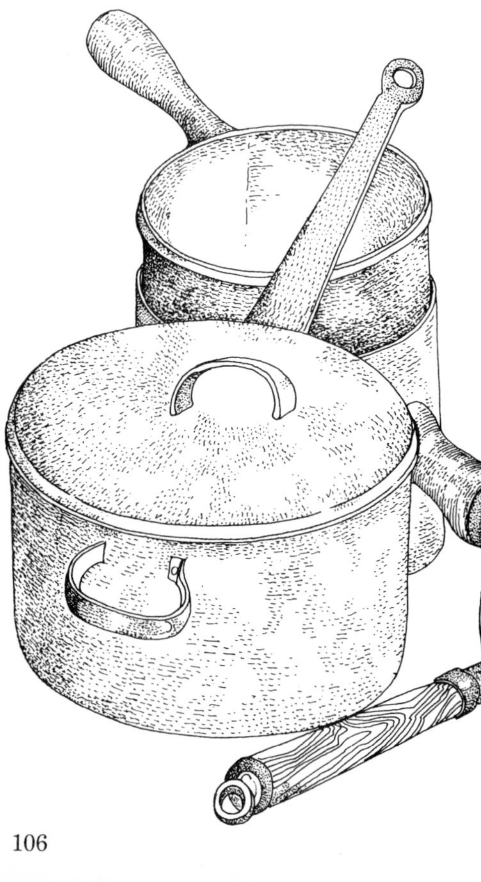
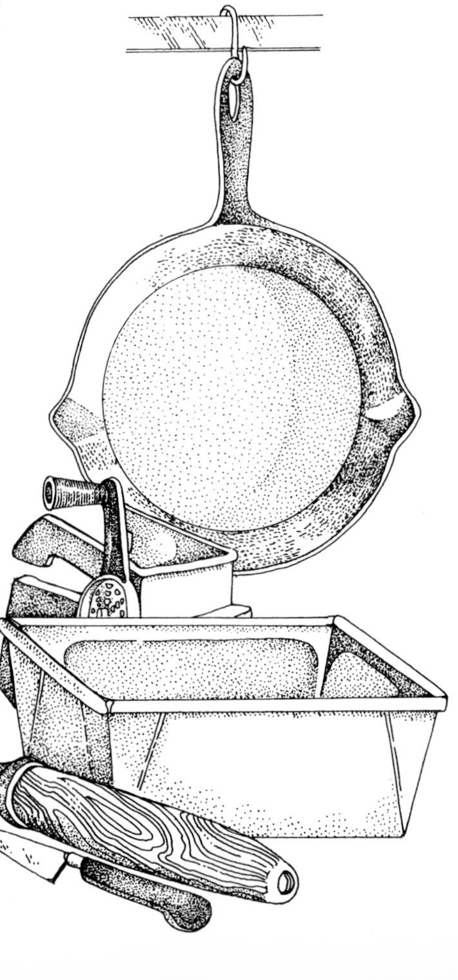
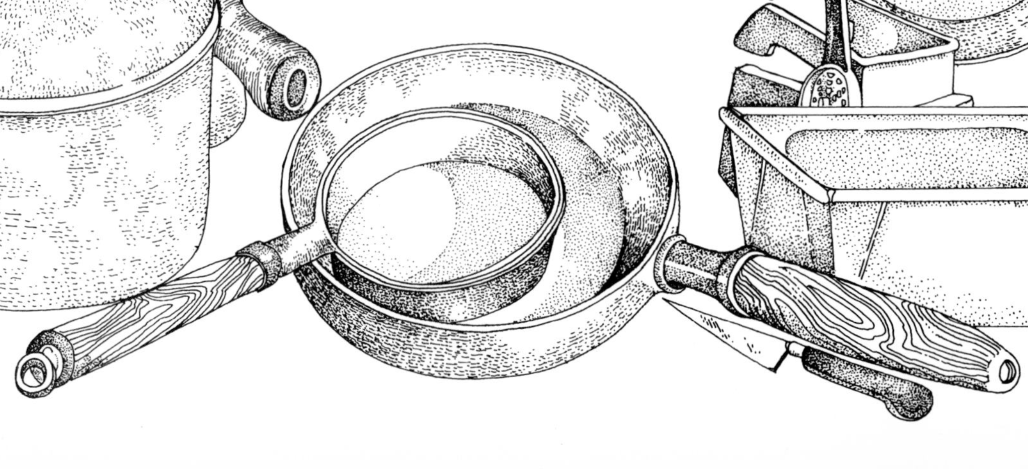

melted butter, wine or stock can be added to increase moisture. Do not forget to prick the skins to prevent bursting.

Spinach, young cabbage leaves or any other tender young greens can be sprinkled with herbs — basil, oregano or summer savory are all good — a little salt and pepper and a dash of oil and melted butter inside, then rolled up into sausages and tied with string. Brush the outsides with oil and bake on a baking sheet in a 425°F oven for 20-30 minutes. The outside leaves become crisp and the inner ones are succulent and delicious.

Braising
Here, the food is cooked in a moist atmosphere surrounded by heat; in earlier days, braising pans had specially shaped lids so that coals and hot ashes could be piled up on top and then the pot placed on the side of the cooking range. Braising is generally understood to mean pre-browning the food in either oil or butter and then continuing the cooking in the oven, in a well-covered pot with a little added liquid. Celery and onions are particularly good when braised.

Roasting
Roasting completes the basic oven methods. The food is cooked at a high temperature in oil or butter. It is really a form of frying; its main advantage is that the food cooks and browns evenly and, as many of the aromatics — spices and herbs — are soluble in oil, the food can be subtly flavored by adding them to the oil in which the food is being roasted. Try cinnamon with roast carrots or mace or nutmeg with parsnips.

Boiling
Use as small a saucepan as possible for boiling green vegetables and make sure it has a tightly-fitting lid. A well-proportioned saucepan should have its height equal to two-thirds of its diameter.

Measure the quantity of water to cover the bottom of the pan to a depth of ¼ - ½ inch and bring it to a boil in another saucepan. Preheat the vegetable pan, then add the prepared vegetables and pour on the boiling water; add salt, cover with the lid and cook for the required time. Experience will show the setting of the heat; ideally there should only be a tablespoon or so of liquid remaining to pour over the vegetables as it is, or slightly thickened with kneaded butter (beurre manié — see the recipe for Cream of leek soup on page 41).

When boiling root vegetables, use enough boiling salted water to cover the prepared vegetables, and cook for the required time. Use the water in which they were cooked to make stock.

Steaming
You can buy specially designed equipment to steam vegetables, ranging from the very attractive Chinese bamboo baskets which stand one on top of another over a saucepan of boiling water, to metal constructions which would not seem out of place in a science fiction movie.

You can easily improvise; the aim is to surround the food with steam at a temperature of 212°F. Try putting a shallow heatproof dish on a trivet in a saucepan containing 1 inch of boiling water and piling the food loosely on it, or packing the food very lightly into a colander and placing it over a saucepan of boiling water, keeping it closely covered.

If using Chinese baskets, make sure they fit snugly one into another and that there is a close fit between the lowest basket and the saucepan. The food requiring the longest cooking is put into the lowest basket; if there is a chance of juices running out of the food, as it does from some fungi, place the food on a small dish or plate but be sure to leave enough space between the plate and the side of the basket for the steam to circulate. When using any of the patent steamers, follow the manufacturer's instructions. All herbs and spices have volatile oils, so by adding them to the water you cook with flavored steam: try squeezing lemon juice, or sprinkling a little soy sauce or wine over first.

Frying
The term frying describes two different methods of cooking in very hot oil(350°F is the safest) or melted clarified butter, or unclarified butter. Though I use butter a great deal, it does burn at a lower temperature than oil, so take care; you can use a mixture of the two.

Unless seasoning is specifically included in a recipe, it is better to season the food after frying.

Shallow frying
The food is cooked in a thick-based skillet with the preheated oil or fat coming just over halfway up the food; whole, parboiled potatoes can be fried in about ½ inch of oil if they are turned over and over until they are evenly cooked. Fry the food on one side until crisp and golden brown and then turn it over with a spatula and a guiding fork and fry the other side. The temperature should be controlled to prevent it rising too high and burning or to prevent it falling and making the food greasy. The food should be completely cooked when both sides are crisp and flecked with brown. Remove from the pan with a slotted spoon and drain on paper towels on a plate in an open hot oven. Serve immediately on hot plates.

Deep-frying
The food is cooked in a deep fat fryer of hot oil (350°F). The fryer should be only just over half full. A frying thermometer is almost essential for good deep-frying. A good test of whether the oil has reached frying temperature is to drop in a cube of day-old bread. It should turn golden-brown in 60 seconds. Deep-frying is the ideal method for cooking croquettes and food in batter and crumbs. Take care not to leave any water drops on the vegetables, as it will cause the hot oil to spatter dangerously.

Do not put too much food in at a time as, if the temperature of the oil drops, the food will not be sealed instantly and will absorb oil or disintegrate. There is also the danger that the oil will froth over onto the hot stove and catch fire.

When the food is done, remove it from the fryer and drain and keep hot as for shallow frying. Allow the oil to regain full frying temperature before putting in the next batch. Remove particles constantly with a small strainer, otherwise they will burn and flavor the food.

Allow the oil to cool down completely before straining it through cheesecloth and returning it to the bottle.

If by mischance, or an ill-timed phone call, the oil catches fire, do not bring water near it! Turn off the heat, cover the pan with the lid, then gently move the pan off the heat. Cover it with a damp dish cloth to quench the flames. The oil cannot be used again.

Stir-frying
This is the ideal way of cooking vegetables. With a little practice, four pans can easily be used at the same time. The vegetables are sliced, diced or shredded, then a little oil or butter is put into a thick-based pan; the Chinese wok is ideal as it was designed for this style of cooking (see page 98). The vegetables are added and stirred over and over with a wooden spoon — the most tender and quickest-cooking ingredients being put in last. Then a little stock, water, wine or soy sauce is added and the food continues cooking. If the vegetables are prepared correctly and cut thinly enough the whole process takes only 5-10 minutes.

Salting
As a rough guide, allow ½ teaspoon of salt to 1 lb of green vegetables and 1 teaspoon to the same quantity of root vegetables; in addition add ½ teaspoon salt to 1¼ cups of water. It is easier to add salt than to remove it. Never add baking soda; it totally destroys the vitamin C content.

Brussels sprouts with peanuts and herb butter

Serves 4
CALORIES PER PORTION: 140 (597 kJ)
PROTEIN CONTENT PER PORTION: 7 grams
PREPARATION & COOKING TIME: 30 minutes

¾ lb Brussels sprouts
½ cup finely chopped onion
6 tablespoons unroasted peanuts
12 large leaves of marjoram, chopped
2 tablespoons butter
2 tablespoons lemon juice

Cook the sprouts in a very little boiling salted water for 10-15 minutes, or until just tender. (If using frozen sprouts, follow the instructions on the package, but undercook them slightly. They will finish cooking in the lemon juice and onion.) Meanwhile, put the onion into another pan of boiling water and cook for 1 minute, then drain. Pour the peanuts into a blender or nut mill and grind them for a few seconds, or chop them with a sharp-bladed knife; they should be fine but not so fine that they bind together. Brush away the red skins. Work the marjoram into the butter, divide it into four pats and chill.

When the sprouts are done, drain them, reserving the water for making stock, and add the onion and lemon juice. Replace the pan of sprouts over the heat and stir them gently, sprinkling the peanuts over as you do so. Turn into a heated dish and put a pat of herb butter on each helping.

Broccoli surprise

Serves 4
CALORIES PER PORTION: 275 (1242 kJ)
PROTEIN CONTENT PER PORTION: 14 grams
PREPARATION & COOKING TIME: 30 minutes

½ lb broccoli spears
salt
2 tablespoons olive or sunflower oil
2 tablespoons wholewheat flour
⅔ cup milk
½ cup grated Cheddar cheese
4 eggs, separated

Cook the broccoli spears in boiling, salted water for 10 minutes, keeping them on the firm side. Drain and keep warm. Preheat the oven to 350°F. Mix together the oil and flour in a small pan over moderate heat, then draw the pan off the heat and stir in the milk. Season with salt. Return to the heat and cook, stirring, until the sauce boils and thickens. Remove the pan from the heat and stir in the grated cheese. Allow to cool slightly, then add the egg yolks and mix well. Butter four small ovenproof soufflé dishes or ramekins and put them into the preheated oven to warm through for 5 minutes.

Meanwhile, beat the egg whites until they hold stiff peaks, then fold in the cheese sauce. Put a large spoonful of the soufflé into each dish and carefully arrange a portion of broccoli on top. Then divide the rest of the soufflé mixture between the four dishes and bake for 10 minutes. The soufflé should not be completely set, but just make a light sauce for the broccoli.

Red cabbage with apple

Serves 4
CALORIES PER PORTION: 80 (365 kJ)
PROTEIN CONTENT PER PORTION: 3 grams
PREPARATION & COOKING TIME: Version 1: 30-40 minutes, Version 2: 1½ hours

1 tablespoon olive or sunflower oil
½ cup chopped onion
1 teaspoon brewer's yeast
1 cup warm water
4 cups shredded red cabbage
2 cups peeled and diced cooking apples
1 tablespoon wine or cider vinegar
¼ teaspoon ground cinnamon (optional)
2 teaspoons wholewheat flour
1 tablespoon cold water
salt

Heat the oil in a large pan and fry the onion until golden brown. Dissolve the brewer's yeast in the warm water. Add the cabbage, apple and yeast solution with the vinegar and cinnamon to the onion and stir so that the apple is evenly mixed with the cabbage. Either continue cooking in a covered pan over low heat until the cabbage is tender but still crisp, or, for a more traditional Middle European flavor, transfer the cabbage to an ovenproof casserole to continue cooking in a 350°F oven for 1-1½ hours. Whichever method is used, the liquid which remains at the end of the cooking time should be thickened as follows: mix the flour to a cream with the cold water in a small pan. Pour on the cooking juices, stirring well, and bring to a boil. Cool until the juices thicken, adjust the seasoning if necessary and pour them onto the cabbage. Stir well and serve.

Vegetable accompaniments can make a meal in themselves. Top left: Carrots with apple and crispy onion rings. Front: a savory Spinach crumble and Right: Zucchini Provençal. Combine a selection of dishes like these for supper

Spinach crumble

Serves 4
CALORIES PER PORTION: 235 (985 kJ)
PROTEIN CONTENT PER PORTION: 8 grams
PREPARATION & COOKING TIME: 30 minutes

1 lb leaf spinach, very thoroughly washed
½ cup finely chopped onion
5 tablespoons olive or sunflower oil
3 tablespoons wholewheat flour
½ cup dry white wine
salt
1 cup fresh wholewheat breadcrumbs

Cut out the thick stems from the spinach and use for stock. Fry the onion in about half the oil in a thick-based pan. Coarsely chop the spinach and, when the onion is transparent, add it to the pan. Lower the heat and cook gently for 10 minutes or until the spinach is just tender. Meanwhile, mix the flour with 1 tablespoon of oil. When the spinach is done, drain the cooking juices onto the oil and flour mixture and stir well. Return it to the spinach in the pan and stir until it thickens. Pour in the wine, add the salt and mix well. Remove the pan from the heat. Preheat the oven to 350°F.

Heat the remaining oil in a separate pan and fry the breadcrumbs until crisp and browned. Pour the cooked spinach into a shallow ovenproof dish, sprinkle the crumbs over the top and bake in the preheated oven for 10-15 minutes.

Note: This also makes a good light lunch or supper dish. For a more substantial meal, make four hollows in the mixture after adding the crumbs, break an egg into each hollow and sprinkle with cheese.

Cauliflower beignets

Serves 4
CALORIES PER PORTION: 500 (2087 kJ)
PROTEIN CONTENT PER PORTION: 20.5 grams
PREPARATION & COOKING TIME: 45 minutes

1 lb head cauliflower, broken into florets
Coating batter (page 194)
oil for deep frying
1 cup grated Parmesan cheese
a sprinkling of cayenne

The spiced apple sauce
1 cup finely chopped onion
2 tablespoons melted butter or vegetable oil
3 cups peeled and chopped cooking apples
4 cloves, finely ground
½ teaspoon ground cinnamon
1 tablespoon raw brown sugar
⅔ cup white wine

Put the cauliflower florets into a pan with a little salted water and bring to a boil. Cover and simmer for 5 minutes. Remove the cauliflower florets from the pan and dry them carefully; allow to cool, then dip them in the batter and deep fry in batches in oil heated to 350°F until they are golden brown and crisp. Drain them on paper towels and keep each batch warm while you cook the rest.

Make the sauce by frying the onion in the butter or oil until golden brown. Add the apples, spices and sugar and cook for a further 2 minutes, then pour in the wine and the same quantity of water and continue cooking until the apples have broken down to a pulp. Rub the sauce through a strainer and reheat it.

Arrange the cauliflower on a warm serving dish and sprinkle over the cheese and cayenne. Serve the sauce separately.

Cauliflower Polish-style

Serves 4
CALORIES PER PORTION: 130 (550 kJ)
PROTEIN CONTENT PER PORTION: 7 grams
PREPARATION & COOKING TIME: 35 minutes

1 lb head cauliflower, broken into florets
2 eggs
½ cup finely chopped onion
2 tablespoons butter
1 cup fresh wholewheat breadcrumbs
¼ cup chopped parsley
salt
freshly ground pepper

Cook the cauliflower florets in boiling salted water to cover for 10-15 minutes, or until they are just done — the stems should still be firm. Hard-cook the eggs, shell them and keep them warm in a pan of hot water. Fry the onion in the butter until golden brown, then add the breadcrumbs and continue frying over moderate heat until slightly crisp. Add the chopped parsley and mix well. Drain the cauliflower and arrange about half the florets on a heated serving dish. Sprinkle a generous half of the crumb mixture over them, season with salt and pepper and arrange the rest of the cauliflower over the crumbs. Sprinkle the rest of the crumbs between the cauliflower florets on the top layer. Roughly chop the eggs, pile them in the center of the dish and serve immediately.

Buttered cabbage with caraway

Serves 4
CALORIES PER PORTION: 187 (785 kJ)
PROTEIN CONTENT PER PORTION: 6.5 grams
PREPARATION & COOKING TIME: 15 minutes

3 cups thickly shredded white cabbage
salt
4 tablespoons butter
freshly ground black pepper
½ teaspoon caraway seeds
¾ cup grated Cheddar cheese
a sprinkling of paprika

Cut the cabbage strips into squares and place them in a saucepan. Bring 1 quart of water to a boil and pour it over the cabbage; add salt and bring back to a boil. Strain off the water immediately and add the butter, pepper and caraway seeds. Continue cooking very gently for 10 minutes, keeping the pan covered.

Stir in the cheese and turn the cabbage over until all the cheese has melted and coated the cabbage. Spoon into a warm dish and sprinkle the top with paprika.

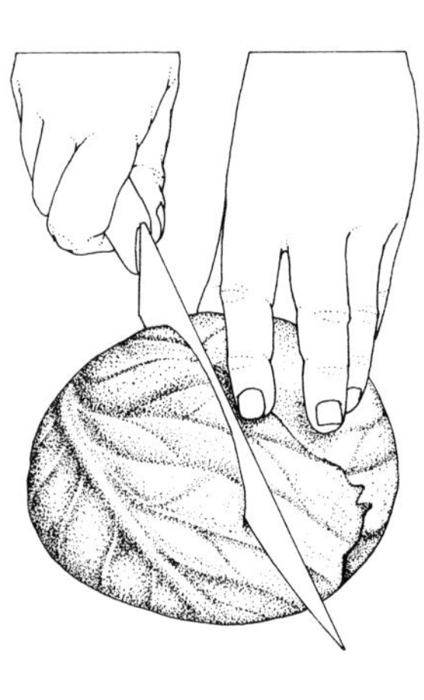

1. Cut the cabbage into quarters.

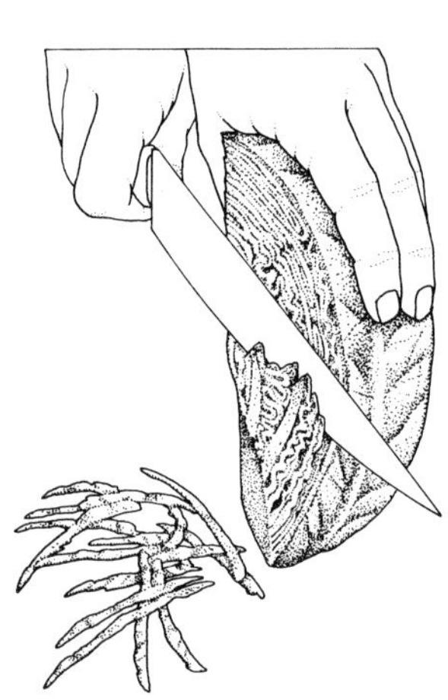

2. Shred very finely, cutting downward.

Colcannon

Serves 4
CALORIES PER PORTION: 300 (1260 kJ)
PROTEIN CONTENT PER PORTION: 4 grams
PREPARATION & COOKING TIME: 30 minutes

1¼ lb potatoes, peeled and sliced
salt
2 cups shredded cabbage
1 medium onion, thinly sliced
3 tablespoons olive and sunflower oil
freshly ground pepper
4 tablespoons butter, or 3 tablespoons extra oil

Cook the potatoes in boiling salted water for 5-10 minutes, or until they can just be pierced with a fork. Put the cabbage in a pan with just enough water to cover, bring it to a boil and then drain. Fry the onion in the oil until it is golden brown and just beginning to crisp. Add the drained cabbage and continue frying until it is also beginning to brown; sprinkle with salt and pepper and keep hot. Fry the parboiled potatoes in the butter or extra oil until they are brown and crisp. Add them to the cabbage and serve at once.

Braised celery

Serves 4
CALORIES PER PORTION: 160 (660 kJ)
PROTEIN CONTENT PER PORTION: 3 grams
PREPARATION & COOKING TIME: 1 hour

¼ cup olive or sunflower oil
1 lb bunch of celery, broken into 2 inch lengths
½ cup coarsely chopped onion
2 tablespoons wholewheat flour
1¼ cups Brown vegetable stock (page 34)
1 teaspoon brewer's yeast
salt and freshly ground pepper

Heat the oil and fry the celery until it is just beginning to brown. Remove the pieces as they do and drain well on paper towels. When the celery is cooked, add the onion to the oil in the pan and fry until well browned. Pour off any excess oil and sprinkle in the flour. Stir until it is smoothly mixed with the onion, then gradually pour on the stock, stirring to prevent lumps, and add the yeast. Bring to a boil, stirring all the time, then lower the heat a little and cook until the sauce is thick and smooth. Meanwhile, preheat the oven to 350°F. Check the seasoning and add salt and pepper if necessary.

Put the celery in a baking dish and pour over the sauce. Cover and bake in the preheated oven for 30-45 minutes; allow extra time if the dish is thick.

Celery with tomato

Serves 4
CALORIES PER PORTION: 65 (267 kJ)
PROTEIN CONTENT PER PORTION: 2 grams
PREPARATION & COOKING TIME: 45 minutes

3 tablespoons butter
1 cup finely chopped onion
1 lb bunch of celery, broken into ½ inch lengths
1½ cups skinned, seeded and chopped tomatoes
salt
freshly ground pepper

Melt the butter over gentle heat and cook the onion for 5 minutes, or until transparent. Add the celery and cook for 5 minutes, taking care that it does not brown. Add the tomatoes and a little salt and pepper and stir over a moderate heat until the tomatoes break down into a pulp. Continue simmering gently for 10 minutes with the pan covered, then remove the lid and increase the heat so the tomato sauce boils and reduces rapidly to a purée. Remove the pan from the heat and serve.

Stuffed artichoke hearts

Serves 4
CALORIES PER PORTION: 230 (960 kJ)
PROTEIN CONTENT PER PORTION: 7 grams
PREPARATION & COOKING TIME: 1½ hours, including chilling

4 medium globe artichokes, soaked and trimmed
salt
2 tablespoons butter
2 tablespoons wholewheat flour
freshly ground pepper
⅔ cup milk
1 egg white
1¼ cups Béchamel sauce (page 196)
2 tablespoons chopped parsley

Cook the artichokes in boiling salted water for 30-45 minutes, or until a leaf will pull out easily. Remove all the leaves, discard the chokes and reserve the hearts. Scrape off the soft lower portion of each leaf with the back of a knife blade, removing any fibers as you go. Melt two-thirds of the butter in a small pan, add the flour, season with salt and pepper and stir together until smooth. Take the pan off the heat and gradually pour on the milk, stirring between each addition. Return the pan to the heat and bring the sauce to a boil, stirring until it thickens. Place over a pan of simmering water and leave for 30 minutes to mature, or transfer the sauce to a double boiler. Beat in the remaining butter.

Meanwhile, rub the artichoke purée from the leaves through a strainer and keep on one side. When the sauce is ready, add the purée first, then the egg white; mix thoroughly and adjust the seasoning. Chill for about 30 minutes.

Twenty minutes before serving, pile the purée onto the artichoke hearts. Put them into a steamer and steam at full boil for 20 minutes. Heat up the Béchamel sauce towards the end of the cooking time. Carefully remove the hearts from the steamer and arrange them in a shallow heated serving dish. Mask them with Béchamel sauce and sprinkle with a little parsley.

Do not be tempted to grate cheese over the dish too, as the flavor of the artichoke is much too delicate.

Italian stuffed artichokes

Serves 4
CALORIES PER PORTION: 210 (882 kJ)
PROTEIN CONTENT PER PORTION: 7 grams
PREPARATION & COOKING TIME: 1¼ hours

4 medium globe artichokes, soaked and trimmed
1¼ cups Tomato sauce (page 196)

The stuffing
1 cup very finely chopped onion
2 tablespoons olive or sunflower oil
1 cup chopped mushrooms
20 leaves of fresh rosemary, finely chopped
salt
½ cup fresh wholewheat breadcrumbs
1 egg, well beaten
freshly ground pepper (optional)

Cook the artichokes in boiling salted water for 30-45 minutes, or until a leaf will pull out easily. Turn them upside down to drain and let them cool slightly. Meanwhile, make the stuffing. Fry the onion in the oil until just transparent, add the mushrooms and continue cooking until the mushrooms are soft and shiny. Remove the pan from the heat, add the rosemary, salt and breadcrumbs and mix well. (If fresh rosemary is not available, use ½ teaspoon dried.) Allow to cool, then pour in the egg and mix thoroughly. Add pepper, if using.

Preheat the oven to 350°F. Open the artichokes and remove the small central leaves and the choke. Fill the center cavities with the stuffing, dividing it equally between the four artichokes. Close up the leaves and put the artichokes into a large ovenproof casserole.

Pour the Tomato sauce over the artichokes, cover the casserole and bake in the preheated oven for 30 minutes.

Note: This dish also makes a substantial appetizer.

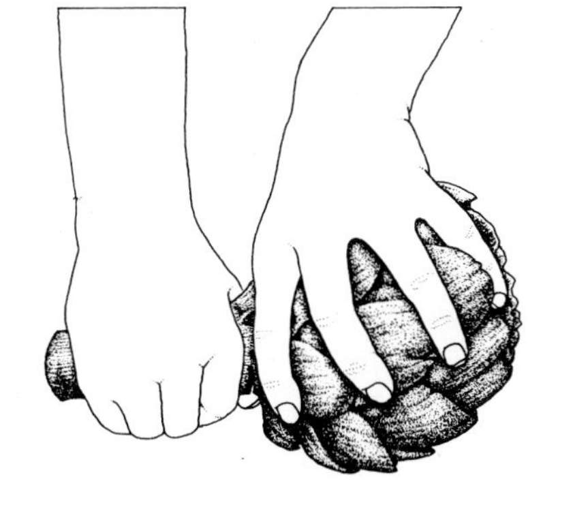

1. Remove the coarse artichoke stalk, breaking as close as you can to the bottom of the leaves.

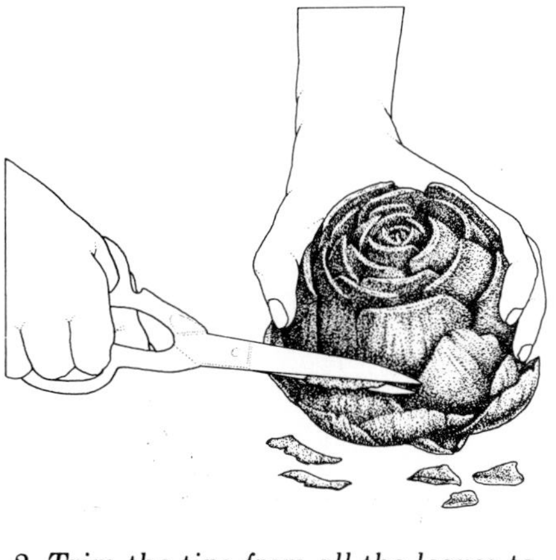

2. Trim the tips from all the leaves to midpoint with the scissors. This makes access to the middle easier.

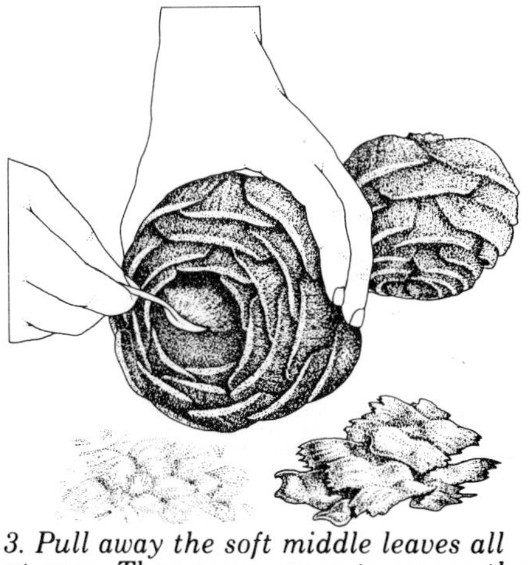

3. Pull away the soft middle leaves all at once. Then use a spoon to scrape the bristly choke off the base. Rinse out.

Braised Belgian endive with cheese sauce

Serves 4
CALORIES PER PORTION: 160 (665 kJ)
PROTEIN CONTENT PER PORTION: 3 grams
PREPARATION & COOKING TIME: 1 hour

1-1½ lb Belgian endive, allowing 1-2 heads per person
2 tablespoons olive or sunflower oil
1 tablespoon lemon juice
⅔ cup vegetable stock
salt
freshly ground pepper
⅔ cup Cheese sauce (page 196)

Preheat the oven to 400°F. Cut off the base of each endive head and discard any bruised or discolored outside leaves. Pour the oil into a baking dish and tilt it so that the oil runs over the bottom. Put in the endive heads and turn them over so that each head is evenly coated with oil. Mix the lemon juice into the stock and pour this over the endive. Season liberally with salt and pepper, cover the dish with aluminum foil or oiled wax paper and bake in the preheated oven for 45 minutes to 1 hour, or until the endive is tender.

Heat up the Cheese sauce toward the end of the cooking time. When the endive is cooked, pour off any cooking liquid into a pan, reduce it to about 1 tablespoon and add it to the hot sauce. Pour this over the endive and serve.

Left: Corn fritters with fried bananas. Right: Green beans with yogurt and parsley. Front: Florence fennel coated with orange sauce

Fennel with orange sauce

Serves 4
CALORIES PER PORTION: 115 (475 kJ)
PROTEIN CONTENT PER PORTION: 4 grams
PREPARATION & COOKING TIME: 20 minutes

2-4 heads of fennel, together weighing about 1 lb
salt
1½ tablespoons butter
2 teaspoons wholewheat flour
½ cup orange juice
grated rind of 2 oranges
1-2 tablespoons chopped parsley

Trim and cut large heads of fennel into quarters, or if using smaller ones, cut them in half. Cook in boiling, salted water until just tender, about 10-15 minutes. Meanwhile, melt the butter in a separate pan, sprinkle in the flour and stir until thick. Pour on the orange juice and stir over gentle heat until the sauce boils and thickens. Remove the pan from the heat and add the orange rind and most of the parsley. Keep warm.

Drain the fennel and arrange the pieces, cut sides uppermost, in a heated serving dish. Spoon over the sauce, opening the leaves of the fennel to allow the sauce to penetrate. Sprinkle with the remaining parsley and serve.

Green beans with yogurt and almonds

Serves 4
CALORIES PER PORTION: 160 (657 kJ)
PROTEIN CONTENT PER PORTION: 4 grams
PREPARATION & COOKING TIME: 10-20 minutes

1 lb fresh or frozen green beans, trimmed
½ cup split blanched almonds
1-2 teaspoons olive or sunflower oil
coarse salt
2 tablespoons butter
½ teaspoon wholewheat flour
½ cup plain yogurt

Cook fresh beans in a little boiling salted water for 10-15 minutes, or until they are just tender. (Cook frozen beans according to the instructions on the package.) Put the almonds in a pan with a very little oil and cook them over gentle heat until they are brown. There should be just enough oil to coat the bottom of the pan, with a little to spare. Take out the almonds and sprinkle them with a little coarse salt.

Melt the butter in a separate pan, sprinkle in the flour and cook gently until the mixture is golden brown and smooth. Add the yogurt and bring to a boil very slowly, stirring all the time. (Middle Eastern cooks say that you should only stir yogurt in one direction as this prevents it curdling.) Continue cooking until the sauce is reduced by about half, then add the beans and turn them until they are evenly coated.

Pile them into a heated dish for serving and either sprinkle the almonds over the top, or serve them separately.

Paprika beans in cream

Serves 4
CALORIES PER PORTION: 115 (487 kJ)
PROTEIN CONTENT PER PORTION: 2 grams
PREPARATION & COOKING TIME: 20 minutes

1 lb green beans, trimmed
1 small onion, thinly sliced
1 cup sour cream
2 tablespoons paprika

Cook fresh beans in a little boiling salted water for 10-15 minutes, or until they are just tender. (Cook frozen beans according to the instructions on the package.) Add the onion slices halfway through the cooking time. Bring the cream to a boil in a small pan, stirring all the time to prevent it burning. When the beans are tender, pour off any remaining water, sprinkle over the paprika and turn the beans until they are evenly coated. Pile them in the center of a heated shallow bowl and pour the cream around them. Serve at once, spooning a little cream over each serving.

Sweet and sour beans

Serves 4
CALORIES PER PORTION: 65 (262 kJ)
PROTEIN CONTENT PER PORTION: 1 gram
PREPARATION & COOKING TIME: 15-20 minutes

1 lb fresh or frozen green beans, trimmed
salt
1 ½ tablespoons butter
½ cup finely chopped onion
¼ cup wine or cider vinegar
1 tablespoon raw brown sugar
6 large mint leaves, chopped almost to a pulp

Cook fresh beans in a very little boiling salted water for 10-15 minutes, or until they are just tender. (If using frozen beans, cook them according to the instructions on the package.) Meanwhile, melt the butter in a pan over gentle heat, add the onion and the vinegar and cook for 5 minutes.

When the beans are tender, there should be little or no water left (drain frozen beans if necessary). Add the sugar, stir until the beans are evenly coated, then add the onion. Stir in the mint and continue stirring gently until the onion and mint are thoroughly mixed into the beans. Spoon into a heated dish for serving.

Corn fritters with fried bananas

Serves 4
CALORIES PER PORTION: 470 (1960 kJ)
PROTEIN CONTENT PER PORTION: 11 grams
PREPARATION & COOKING TIME: 50 minutes

1 large or 2 medium ears of corn or 1 ⅓ cups canned or frozen corn kernels
oil for shallow frying
4 bananas
pinch of ground cinnamon or grated ginger root

The batter
¾ cup plus 2 tablespoons wholewheat flour
½ teaspoon salt
a little freshly ground pepper
1 large egg, beaten
½ cup grated Cheddar cheese
1 cup milk

Cook the ears of corn, if using, in boiling unsalted water for 5-10 minutes, or until they are tender, then rinse under cold running water before scraping off the kernels with a sharp knife. (Cook canned or frozen corn according to the instructions on the can or the package.) Meanwhile, make the batter.

Sift together the flour, salt and pepper, make a well in the center, add the egg, then stir in the cheese and gradually mix in the milk until the batter is smooth. Leave it to rest until the corn is cooked.

Drain the corn well and mix it thoroughly into the batter. Heat ½ inch oil in a thick-based skillet and fry large spoonfuls of the mixture on both sides until golden brown. Drain the fritters on paper towels and keep them hot until the bananas are ready.

Peel the bananas, cut them in half lengthwise, then cut each half into 8 pieces, giving 16 in all. Dust with cinnamon or ginger, reheat the oil and fry the bananas to a golden brown. Pile the fritters in the middle of a warm plate, arrange the banana around the rim and serve immediately while hot.

Succotash

Serves 4
CALORIES PER PORTION: 230 (752 kJ)
PROTEIN CONTENT PER PORTION: 4 grams
PREPARATION & COOKING TIME: 40 minutes

2 cups shelled fresh lima beans
1 large or 2 medium ears of corn or 1 ⅓ cups canned or frozen corn kernels
¼ cup water
2 tablespoons unsalted butter
½ cup heavy cream
2 teaspoons finely chopped parsley
salt

Cook the beans in boiling salted water for 7-10 minutes, or until they are just tender. Strip the corn off the cobs, if using, and simmer the kernels in the water and butter in a small covered pan for 10 minutes without salt, as salt will make them tough. (If using canned or frozen corn, drain it well before heating through in a pan with the water and butter for 4-5 minutes.) When cooked, drain the corn thoroughly, pour on the cream, stir in the parsley and keep hot. Remove the skins from the beans and add to the corn with salt. Stir the mixture gently until it is all mixed together and sprinkle over a little extra parsley.

Puréed peas with cheese croûtes

Serves 4
CALORIES PER PORTION: 250 (1040 kJ)
PROTEIN CONTENT PER PORTION: 10 grams
PREPARATION & COOKING TIME: 25 minutes

3 cups shelled fresh or frozen peas
4 slices of wholewheat bread, crusts removed
4 tablespoons butter
¼ cup grated strong cheese
a sprinkling of cayenne
a little milk
salt
freshly ground pepper
1-2 tablespoons heavy cream
2 large mint leaves, finely chopped

If using fresh peas, cook them in a little boiling salted water until they are tender — about 10-15 minutes. (If using frozen peas, follow the instructions on the package.) Cut each slice of bread into 4 triangles and fry in the butter, turning once, until they begin to crisp and turn brown; drain them on paper towels. Sprinkle with the cheese and dust with cayenne. Put the slices under a hot broiler until the cheese melts and begins to brown.

Meanwhile, pour the peas and the tablespoon or so of remaining water into a blender and work until smooth — it may be necessary to add a few drops of milk from time to time for the purée to have the right consistency. Alternatively, rub the peas through a strainer and add the milk afterwards

Return the purée to the pan and stir over a moderate heat until thoroughly hot. Season with salt and pepper, spoon it into a heated serving dish and pour the cream over. Sprinkle with the finely chopped mint and arrange the cheese croûtes around the edge of the dish.

Mattar Panir

Serves 4
CALORIES PER PORTION: 335 (1395 kJ)
PROTEIN CONTENT PER PORTION: 18 grams
PREPARATION & COOKING TIME: 20 minutes

6 tablespoons ghee or clarified butter
3½ cups cooked fresh or frozen peas
1 teaspoon ground turmeric
1 teaspoon hot chili powder
½ lb panir (page 200)
2 tablespoons chopped fresh coriander
salt
pinch of sugar (optional)

Heat the ghee in a thick-based skillet, add the peas, turmeric, and chili powder and stir together for 3-4 minutes over medium heat.

Add the panir, mix well and cook gently for 2 minutes. Stir in the chopped coriander, season with salt and cook at just below simmering point for about 10 minutes, or until the peas are tender. Add a little sugar if the panir tastes too sour.

Peas with lettuce and onions

Serves 4
CALORIES PER PORTION: 175 (725 kJ)
PROTEIN CONTENT PER PORTION: 6 grams
PREPARATION & COOKING TIME: 20 minutes

5 tablespoons butter
½ cup finely chopped onion
2 cups coarsely torn lettuce
3 cups shelled fresh or frozen peas
1 tablespoon wholewheat flour
½ teaspoon salt
freshly ground pepper

Melt 4 tablespoons of the butter in a pan and cook the onion until transparent. Add the lettuce before the onion colors and cook until the juice runs. Bring to a boil, add the peas, bring back to a boil and continue cooking for 5-10 minutes if fresh peas are used (less time is needed for frozen ones). Add a little extra water if necessary. Combine the flour and salt with the rest of the butter in a bowl, then pour on the liquid from the pan and stir well. Return to the pan, season with salt and pepper and boil until the sauce thickens before serving.

Okra creole

Serves 4
CALORIES PER PORTION: 165 (682 kJ)
PROTEIN CONTENT PER PORTION: 3 grams
PREPARATION & COOKING TIME: 30 minutes

¼ cup olive or sunflower oil
2 cups finely chopped onions
1 cup chopped celery
2 cups diced red peppers
2 cups thinly sliced okra
salt
1 cup water

Heat the oil in a pan, add the onions and cook until they just begin to take color, then add the celery. Cook very gently for 5 minutes before adding the peppers and okra. Season with salt, add the measured water, cover the pan and simmer for 15-20 minutes, or until the okra is tender. Drain before spooning into a heated dish for serving.

Okra in batter

Serves 4
CALORIES PER PORTION: 300 (1255 kJ)
PROTEIN CONTENT PER PORTION: 10 grams
PREPARATION & COOKING TIME: 30 minutes

½ lb trimmed okra
salt
Coating batter (page 194) with ½ teaspoon ground cumin and ½ teaspoon ground cinnamon added to the sifted flour
oil for deep frying

Cook the okra in boiling salted water for 5-10 minutes, or until they are tender but not soft. Drain off the water and refresh them by rinsing in cold water immediately, then drain again and dry.

Make the batter, and mix it thoroughly until smooth, then dip the okra into the batter and deep-fry in batches in oil heated to 350°F until golden brown and crisp. Drain on paper towels and serve hot with a Piquant tomato or Tartare sauce (pages 127 and 196).

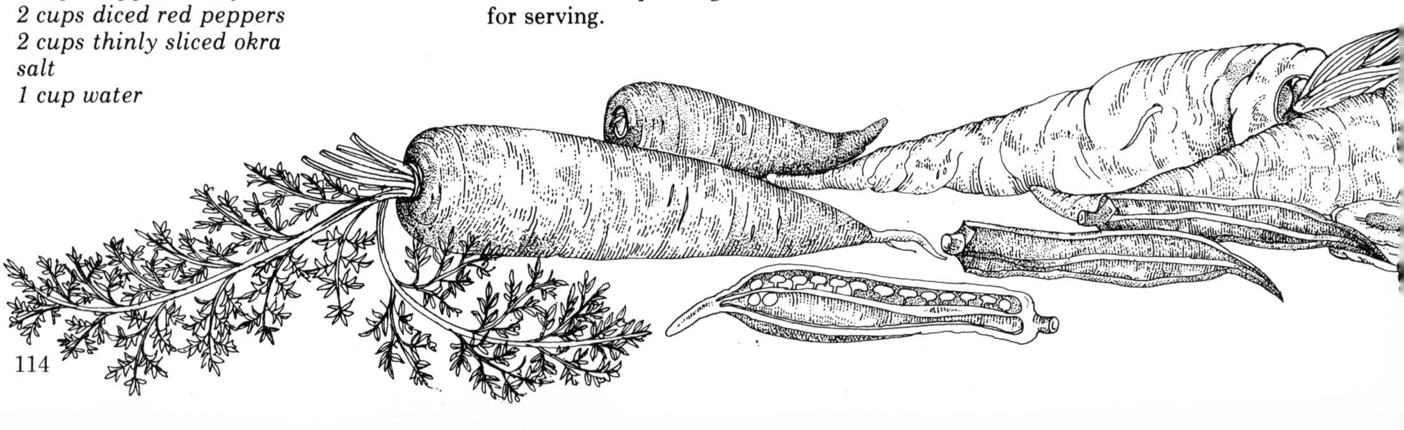

German-style carrots with apple

Serves 4
CALORIES PER PORTION: 175 (726 kJ)
PROTEIN CONTENT PER PORTION: 1.5 grams
PREPARATION & COOKING TIME: 40-50 minutes

1 lb young carrots, scraped
salt
½ lb cooking apples, peeled and cored
a little wholewheat flour
¼ cup olive or sunflower oil
1 medium onion, cut into rings
freshly ground pepper

Cut the carrots lengthwise into thin strips and cook them in very little boiling salted water in a large pan for 10-15 minutes, or until just tender; a stainless steel sauté pan with a lid is ideal — a cast iron one can discolor the carrots. There should be very little water left in the pan by the time the carrots are cooked.

Meanwhile, cut the apples into segments about ½ inch thick. Dip them in the flour and fry in about 3 tablespoons of the oil, turning them over so that they brown on both sides; take care that they do not become mushy, though — the trick is to have the oil hot enough so a crisp skin forms on the outside of the apples. Drain them on paper towels and keep hot while you fry the onion rings in the rest of the oil. Drain the rings when they are crisp and golden. Arrange the carrots interleaved with apple slices on a heated serving dish, with crisp onion rings scattered over the top. Season with salt and pepper before serving.

Rutabaga soufflé

Serves 4
CALORIES PER PORTION: 165 (688 kJ) with cream; 85 (355 kJ) without
PROTEIN CONTENT PER PORTION: 7 grams with cream, 6 grams without
PREPARATION & COOKING TIME: 50 minutes

4 cups chopped rutabaga
salt
2 tablespoons onion juice (see page 55)
¼ teaspoon ground cinnamon
freshly ground black pepper
1 tablespoon wine or cider vinegar
3 eggs, separated
sour cream (optional)

Cook the rutabaga in boiling salted water for about 20 minutes; it should be soft but not mushy. Put into a blender and work it to a purée, or use a food mill — or rub the rutabaga through a strainer. Add the onion pulp, cinnamon, pepper, vinegar and a little salt and mix well. Beat in the egg yolks, one at a time. Preheat the oven to 350°F.

Beat the egg whites until they stand in peaks, then fold them into the purée. Spoon into a hot, buttered soufflé dish of about 1 quart capacity and bake in the preheated oven for 25 minutes. Serve with a little sour cream.

Baked carrot loaf

Serves 4
CALORIES PER PORTION: 83 (349 kJ)
PROTEIN CONTENT PER PORTION: 6 grams
PREPARATION & COOKING TIME: 1 hour

1 lb young carrots, scraped
2 eggs
⅔ cup plain yogurt
salt and freshly ground pepper
¼ teaspoon finely chopped thyme
½ cup finely chopped onion
juice and grated rind of ½ lemon

Cook the carrots in a very little boiling salted water for 10-15 minutes, or until they are tender; ideally there should be almost no water left in the pan when they are done. Preheat the oven to 400°F. Put the carrots into a blender with the rest of the ingredients and blend until smooth. If you do not have a blender, rub the carrots through a strainer or food mill and then mix the other ingredients thoroughly into the purée. Pour into a well-buttered cake pan, 7 inches in diameter and 2½ inches deep, and bake in the preheated oven for about 30 minutes.

Remove the loaf from the oven and allow it to cool for a few minutes before unmolding onto a warm shallow serving dish. Serve with boiled peas or lima beans.

Parsnip cakes

Serves 4
CALORIES PER PORTION: 170 (701 kJ)
PROTEIN CONTENT PER PORTION: 3.5 grams
PREPARATION & COOKING TIME: 40 minutes

4 cups chopped parsnips
salt
½ cup finely chopped onion
1 tablespoon olive or sunflower oil
1 small egg
a little freshly ground pepper
a sprinkling of freshly grated nutmeg
oil for deep frying

Cook the parsnips in boiling salted water for 20-30 minutes, or until they are tender but not mushy. Fry the onion in the tablespoon oil until transparent. Rub the parsnips through a strainer or food mill, or purée them in a blender and put on one side to cool completely. Beat the egg with ½ teaspoon salt, the pepper and nutmeg; add it, with the fried onion, to the parsnip purée and mix well.

Heat the oil to 350°F in a deep fat fryer. Scoop up tablespoonfuls of the purée mixture, each about the size of two walnuts, trim off any untidy bits and gently drop the cakes into the oil. Fry them, 3 or 4 at a time, until golden brown and crisp. Drain them on paper towels. Keep hot.

Glazed carrots with cinnamon

Serves 4
CALORIES PER PORTION: 100 (415 kJ)
PROTEIN CONTENT PER PORTION: 1 gram
PREPARATION & COOKING TIME: 40 minutes

1 ¼ lb carrots, peeled
salt
½ cup finely chopped onion
2 tablespoons olive or sunflower oil
2 teaspoons raw brown sugar
1 teaspoon ground cinnamon

Cut four lengthwise shallow furrows equally spaced around each carrot, using a sharp-pointed knife and cutting at an angle of 45° one way and then making a second at an angle of 90° to the first. Slice the carrots into ⅛ inch slices — these should look like four-petalled flowers — and cook them in a little boiling salted water in a covered pan for about 5 minutes, or until they are just tender.

When the carrots are nearly done, remove the lid, increase the heat and boil until almost dry. Meanwhile, fry the onion in the oil until golden brown, add the sugar and cinnamon and stir until the onion is well coated. Add the carrots and continue stirring until they, too, are well coated with the glaze. Serve at once.

Lyonnaise potatoes

Serves 4
CALORIES PER PORTION: 205 (850 kJ)
PROTEIN CONTENT PER PORTION: 3 grams
PREPARATION & COOKING TIME: 30 minutes

1 ¼ lb potatoes, peeled and thinly sliced
salt
4 tablespoons butter
2 medium onions, cut into thin rings

Lower the potato slices carefully into a pan of boiling, salted water and cook them for 10-15 minutes — the potatoes should still be slightly firm. Meanwhile, melt the butter in a thick-based skillet, add the onion rings and cook gently until transparent, turning them from time to time and taking care they do not burn. Remove the onions from the pan and keep them hot. Strain the butter into a dish to remove any onion specks which would otherwise burn and spoil the flavor of the dish. Wipe out the pan with paper towels and pour back the butter.

Drain the cooked potatoes well, pat them dry with a dish cloth or paper towels, then fry them in the onion-flavored butter on both sides, in two or three batches, until crisp and golden. Arrange the potato and onion in alternate layers on a hot serving dish, and sprinkle with a little salt.

Beets in yogurt

Serves 4
CALORIES PER PORTION: 115 (485 kJ)
PROTEIN CONTENT PER PORTION: 5 grams
PREPARATION & COOKING TIME: 15 minutes

1 tablespoon chopped onion
1 tablespoon olive or sunflower oil
2⅔ cups cooked and diced beets (preferably baked)
1 tablespoon wholewheat flour
½ teaspoon ground cumin
3 tablespoons chopped parsley
salt
freshly ground pepper
1 cup plain yogurt

Fry the onion in the oil until transparent, add the beets and stir gently until they are thoroughly heated and beginning to fry. Sprinkle over the flour, cumin and two-thirds of the parsley and season with salt and pepper. Mix well, then pour on the yogurt and stir over moderate heat until the mixture thickens. Reduce the heat and simmer for a few moments longer before serving with the remaining parsley sprinkled over.

Louisiana sweet potatoes

Serves 4
CALORIES PER PORTION: 190 (807 kJ)
PROTEIN CONTENT PER PORTION: 2 grams
PREPARATION & COOKING TIME: 1 hour 20 minutes

1 ½ lb sweet potatoes
salt
1 tablespoon butter
2 tablespoons finely chopped onion
½ tablespoon wholewheat flour
½ cup vegetable stock
2 tablespoons chopped parsley
1 tablespoon lemon juice

Wash the sweet potatoes and leave them in their skins. Cook them in a pan of boiling salted water for at least 40 minutes, until a skewer can go through them easily, though they should still be fairly firm. Allow to cool slightly, then peel them and, with a melon baller, scoop out balls about the size of small walnuts.

Melt the butter in a skillet and cook the onion over gentle heat until transparent. Sprinkle in the flour and stir until the onion is well coated, then pour on the stock and stir until it boils and thickens. Add half the parsley and the lemon juice, then put in the potato balls, adding a little more stock, if necessary. Heat through quickly, stirring until they are well coated with the sauce and parsley, then spoon into a heated serving dish and sprinkle over the rest of the parsley.

Note: For a stronger lemon flavor, add the grated rind of ½ lemon.

Heaven and Earth (potatoes and apple)

Serves 4
CALORIES PER PORTION: 245 (1016 kJ)
PROTEIN CONTENT PER PORTION: 2.5 grams
PREPARATION & COOKING TIME: 30 minutes

2 cups diced potatoes
salt
4 cups peeled and diced cooking apples
2 medium onions, thinly sliced
½ teaspoon ground cinnamon
¼ cup olive or sunflower oil

Cook the potatoes in well-salted boiling water for about 10 minutes; they should still be firm. Add the apples to the potatoes after 7 minutes — the apples should cook until they are tender but not squashy. Fry the onions in a thick-based skillet with the cinnamon in half the oil until they are golden brown. Remove the onions and keep them hot. Wipe out the pan, return it to the heat and add the rest of the oil.

Drain the potatoes and apple, pat dry with paper towels and put them into the hot oil. Fry until they are just beginning to brown, turning them over gently. Ideally, the potatoes and apples should finish their cooking during the frying. Spoon onto a hot serving dish and sprinkle the fried onions on top.

Dauphinois potatoes

Serves 4
CALORIES PER PORTION: 275 (1150 kJ)
PROTEIN CONTENT PER PORTION: 7 grams
PREPARATION & COOKING TIME: 1 hour

3 tablespoons butter
1 pint milk
1 teaspoon salt
freshly ground black pepper
1 bay leaf (optional)
1 clove of garlic, peeled (optional)
1½ lb potatoes, peeled and thinly sliced

Preheat the oven to 400°F. Butter a baking dish about 9 inches in diameter with about one-third of the butter. Gently heat the milk in a pan, add the rest of the butter, the salt and pepper, and crumble in the bay leaf, if used. Rub the inside of the baking dish with a cut clove of garlic, if liked.

Arrange the potatoes in overlapping layers in the dish, and pour over the milk. Bake in the preheated oven for 45 minutes, until the potatoes are cooked and well browned on top and the milk has become a creamy sauce.

Left: Dauphinois potatoes, the classic French dish, spiked with garlic and cooked in a creamy sauce. Right: crisp and buttery Swiss Rösti turns potatoes into a gourmet treat

Swiss rösti

Serves 4
CALORIES PER PORTION: 145 (602 kJ)
PROTEIN CONTENT PER PORTION: 2 grams
PREPARATION & COOKING TIME: 35 minutes

1¼ lb potatoes, peeled and thickly sliced
2 tablespoons unsalted butter
salt
freshly ground black pepper

Carefully lower the sliced potatoes into a pan of boiling water and cook them for about 10 minutes. Drain well and allow the potatoes to cool.

Melt the butter over gentle heat in a thick-based skillet and shred the potato slices into the butter, using a coarse grater, sprinkling with salt and pepper as you go.

Using two forks, straighten the edges of the potato nest and flatten the top lightly to form a cake measuring about 7 inches in diameter and ½ inch thick. Cover the pan and fry over moderate-to-low heat for about 10 minutes, then remove the lid and gently turn the cake over to cook on the other side for a further 10 minutes. Serve immediately.

Jerusalem artichokes provençale

Serves 4
CALORIES PER PORTION: 90 (383 kJ)
PROTEIN CONTENT PER PORTION: 2.5 grams
PREPARATION & COOKING TIME: 30 minutes

½ cup finely chopped onion
2 tablespoons olive or sunflower oil
1 lb Jerusalem artichokes, peeled and thinly sliced
1 cup skinned and coarsely chopped tomatoes
1 large clove of garlic, peeled and finely chopped
salt
freshly ground black pepper
1 tablespoon finely chopped parsley

Fry the onion in the oil until transparent; add the artichoke slices and continue cooking over a moderate heat for a few minutes, or until the artichokes are just beginning to brown. Add the tomatoes, garlic, salt and pepper and increase the heat. Bring to a boil and cook until the tomatoes have broken down into a pulp and most of the extra liquid has evaporated, leaving the artichoke slices coated with quite a thick purée. Take care that they do not overcook, or stick to the bottom of the pan and burn. Pour into a heated shallow dish, sprinkle with parsley and serve.

Roast winter vegetables

Serves 4
CALORIES PER PORTION: 375 (1576 kJ)
PROTEIN CONTENT PER PORTION: 8 grams
PREPARATION & COOKING TIME: 1 hour 20 minutes

4 medium potatoes
4 parsnips
1 lb slice of pumpkin
4 medium onions
a little olive or sunflower oil
salt
freshly ground pepper
a little ground cinnamon

Wash and peel all the vegetables. Cut the potatoes in half, halve the parsnips lengthwise and slice the pumpkin into four. Put all the vegetables into a pan, cover with hot water and bring it to a boil. Preheat the oven to 400°F. Drain the vegetables immediately, arrange them in a roasting pan with ¼ inch oil in it and brush with more oil. Sprinkle liberally with salt and pepper and sprinkle cinnamon over the parsnips and pumpkin. Roast in the preheated oven for 45 minutes to 1 hour, turning the vegetables over three times during the cooking.

Leeks in red wine

Serves 4
CALORIES PER PORTION: 95 (400 kJ)
PROTEIN CONTENT PER PORTION: 2 grams
PREPARATION & COOKING TIME: 30 minutes

2 tablespoons olive or sunflower oil
1 lb trimmed young leeks, cut to equal lengths and split lengthwise
1 teaspoon crushed coriander
1 cup red wine

Heat the oil in a thick-based pan, place the leeks in it, keeping them all lying in the same direction, and sprinkle with the crushed coriander. Cook over gentle heat for about 5 minutes, or until the leeks just begin to brown. Turn them over carefully and cook on the other side, for the same length of time, then pour on the wine and simmer, covered, for 10 minutes before serving. Served cold, this makes a very good appetizer

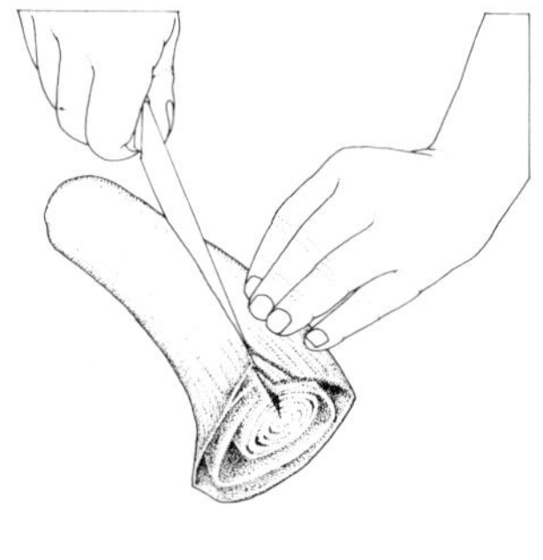

1. Slit the leek along its length and almost to the base.

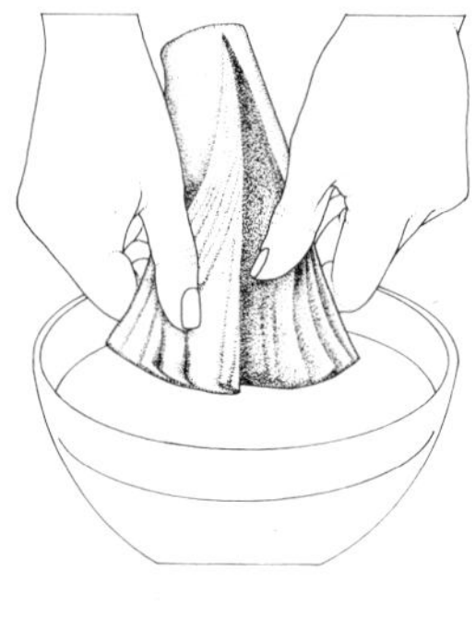

2. Fan it out, upside down, under water, to release any trapped dirt.

Baked spiced onions

Serves 4
CALORIES PER PORTION: 125 (535 kJ)
PROTEIN CONTENT PER PORTION: 3 grams
PREPARATION & COOKING TIME: 35 minutes

4 medium onions, each weighing approximately ¼ lb
2 tablespoons olive or sunflower oil
½ teaspoon ground cumin
½ teaspoon ground coriander
salt
freshly ground black pepper
8 heaping tablespoons fresh wholewheat breadcrumbs

Remove the brown outer skin from the onions and cut each one in half horizontally. Cook in boiling water for 10 minutes, then drain and remove the centers, leaving only two outer layers as a shell. Coarsely chop the onion centers. Preheat the oven to 350°F.

Heat the oil in a small pan and fry the spices with the salt and pepper for about 10 seconds, then add the chopped onion and cook until just golden. Add the breadcrumbs and mix thoroughly. Pile the stuffing into the 8 onion shells and arrange them in a well-oiled baking dish. Bake in the preheated oven for 15-30 minutes, or until tender. Cover the tops with foil if the onions are browning too quickly.

Scallions in butter

Serves 4
CALORIES PER PORTION: 146 (612 kJ)
PROTEIN CONTENT PER PORTION: 2 grams
PREPARATION & COOKING TIME: 15 minutes

3 tablespoons butter
1 lb scallions, trimmed to equal length, leaving about 4 inches of the green tops
a few drops of lemon juice
¼-½ cup fresh wholewheat breadcrumbs
salt
freshly ground pepper

Melt the butter in a thick-based pan and cook the scallions over gentle heat for 5-10 minutes, until the leaves have just gone limp and the scallions have lost their peppery, hot flavor. If you keep all the scallions lying in the same direction as you cook them, it makes all the difference to the appearance of the finished dish.

Squeeze a few drops of lemon juice over the scallions to offset the oiliness of the butter. Sprinkle with enough breadcrumbs to soak up the rest of the butter, season with a little salt and pepper and serve.

This simple dish has a definite air of luxury.

Peperonata

Peperonata also makes a splendid dish served cold.

Serves 4
CALORIES PER PORTION: 110 (473 kJ)
PROTEIN CONTENT PER PORTION: 2.5 grams
PREPARATION & COOKING TIME: 45 minutes

1 lb ripe tomatoes, skinned and quartered
1 cup red wine
2 bay leaves
2 cloves of garlic, peeled and chopped
2 medium onions, thinly sliced
2 tablespoons olive or sunflower oil
¾ lb red peppers, sliced
salt

Put the tomatoes with the wine, bay leaves and garlic into a pan and bring to a boil. Turn down the heat and simmer gently until the tomatoes begin to break down. Fry the onions in the oil until they are just beginning to brown. Add the red peppers and continue frying over a moderate heat for 10 minutes, stirring so that they do not burn. Strain the tomatoes and rub the pulp through the strainer. Return it to the pan and, if necessary, boil to reduce to 1 pint.

Add this sauce to the peppers and onions and simmer in a covered pan for 20 minutes, stirring occasionally to prevent the sauce from sticking and burning. Serve with plenty of plain boiled long-grain rice to soak up the sauce.

Zucchini with sage and cheese sauce

Serves 4
CALORIES PER PORTION: 180 (758 kJ)
PROTEIN CONTENT PER PORTION: 7 grams
PREPARATION & COOKING TIME: 45 minutes (including salting zucchini)

1 lb zucchini, quartered lengthwise
salt

The sauce
2 tablespoons butter
¼ cup finely chopped onion
2 tablespoons wholewheat flour
1¼ cups milk
½ cup grated Cheddar cheese
½-1 tablespoon finely chopped sage
salt
freshly ground pepper
½ cup dry white wine

Sprinkle the zucchini with salt and leave to drain for 30-45 minutes. Meanwhile, make the sauce: melt the butter in a small pan and cook the onion until it just begins to color. Stir in the flour and mix well, then take the pan off the heat and pour on the milk, stirring well between each addition. Return the pan to the heat and bring the sauce to a boil, stirring all the time until it thickens. Add the grated cheese, the chopped sage, or ½ teaspoon dried sage, and season with salt and pepper. Cover the top of the sauce with a piece of buttered wax paper and place the pan in another larger pan containing boiling water, or transfer to a double boiler; keep it cooking very gently for about 30 minutes for the sauce to mature.

Rinse the zucchini, pat them dry and cook them in a very little boiling water, salted if necessary, for 10-15 minutes. Five minutes before serving, add the white wine to the sauce, take the top saucepan out of the larger pan or double boiler and bring to a boil. Adjust the seasoning, if necessary; drain the zucchini, pour the sauce over and serve.

Squash with eggs

Serves 4
CALORIES PER PORTION: 130 (537 kJ)
PROTEIN CONTENT PER PORTION: 7 grams
PREPARATION & COOKING TIME: 20-25 minutes

2 small summer squash, weighing about ½ lb each
salt
4 teaspoons butter
freshly ground pepper
4 small eggs, separated

Cook the squash in boiling salted water until tender — between 10-20 minutes. Drain and cut each in half. Using a teaspoon, scoop out a little of each center and put a teaspoon of butter in each half; when it has melted, sprinkle with a little salt and pepper and prick with a fork to help the butter soak into the flesh. Put an egg yolk into each buttered hollow, taking care not to break it and then cut the whites with two knives, held parallel to each other, until they are liquid and flow easily. Pour in enough egg white just to fill up the cavities and steam the squash for 3-4 minutes or until the eggs are just 'veiled', the whites set and the yolks still runny.

Zucchini provençal

Serves 4
CALORIES PER PORTION: 100 (405 kJ)
PROTEIN CONTENT PER PORTION: 2 grams
PREPARATION & COOKING TIME: 1½ hours (including salting the zucchini)

1 lb zucchini, sliced
salt
1 medium onion, thinly sliced
2 tablespoons olive oil
¾ lb tomatoes, skinned and quartered
1-2 cloves of garlic, peeled and chopped
1 tablespoon chopped parsley

Sprinkle the zucchini slices with salt and leave them for 30-45 minutes. Rinse and pat dry with paper towels. Cook the onion in the oil until golden brown, then remove it with a slotted spoon, taking care not to leave any bits behind to burn and spoil the flavor of the dish. Put the zucchini into the skillet and turn up the heat a little to brown them slightly without burning — do not let them stew in their juices. Once they have browned, lower the heat and allow some juice to collect; add the tomatoes and garlic, season with salt and continue cooking until the zucchini are tender and only a little of the sauce remains. Add the onions, pour into a heated serving dish and sprinkle with parsley. This recipe also works well with okra.

Aubergines au gratin

Serves 4
CALORIES PER PORTION: 170 (721 kJ)
PROTEIN CONTENT PER PORTION: 12 grams
PREPARATION & COOKING TIME: 1½ hours

eggplants, weighing about 1¼ lb
scant cup milk or light cream
2 eggs
salt
1 clove of garlic, peeled and chopped
½ cup fresh wholewheat breadcrumbs
½ cup grated Cheddar cheese

Wipe the eggplants, prick skins and wrap in foil. Bake in a moderate oven, 350°F, for 45 minutes, or until soft. Allow them to cool slightly and scrape pulp out of skins. Work pulp in a blender with milk, eggs, salt and garlic until smooth, or purée by strainer or food mill. Add other ingredients.

Pour purée into shallow ovenproof dish 12 in long. Sprinkle top first with crumbs, then cheese. Bake 20-30 minutes in preheated oven before serving.

Baked savory pumpkin

Serves 4
CALORIES PER PORTION: 125 (510 kJ)
PROTEIN CONTENT PER PORTION: 4 grams
PREPARATION & COOKING TIME: 45 minutes

1 ½ lb pumpkin, peeled and cut into chunks
a little olive or sunflower oil
¼ cup finely chopped onion
1 tablespoon butter or oil
salt
freshly ground pepper
1 egg
1 cup milk
1 tablespoon chopped parsley

Preheat the oven to 400°F. Brush the pumpkin with a little oil and place the chunks in a single layer in a well-oiled baking dish, preferably a metal one. Put it into the preheated oven and bake for 30 minutes. Fry the chopped onion in the butter or oil until it just begins to color.

When the pumpkin is tender, sprinkle it liberally with salt and pepper. Beat the egg with the milk, add the parsley and onion, and season with salt. Pour the mixture over the pumpkin, return it to the oven and bake for another 10 minutes before serving.

Mushroom pudding

Serves 4
CALORIES PER PORTION: 365 (1534 kJ)
PROTEIN CONTENT PER PORTION: 11 grams
PREPARATION & COOKING TIME: 1 hour 20 minutes

½ cup finely chopped onion
2 tablespoons olive or sunflower oil
salt
freshly ground black pepper
4 cups coarsely chopped mushrooms
1 cup fresh wholewheat breadcrumbs
2 eggs, well beaten
⅔ cup sour cream
1 ¼ cup Brown sauce for serving (page 196)

Brown the onion in the oil, season with salt and pepper and add the mushrooms. Continue cooking until most of the juices have evaporated, then remove the pan from the heat and allow the mixture to cool slightly before adding the crumbs, eggs and cream. Mix well and pour into a well-buttered ½ quart capacity steaming mold. Cover the top with wax paper and tie it on firmly. Steam in a pan of boiling water for about 1 hour, adding more water, if necessary. Unmold and serve with a rich Brown sauce.

Mushroom and leek stir-fried with bean curd

Serves 4
CALORIES PER PORTION: 120 (507 kJ)
PROTEIN CONTENT PER PORTION: 7 grams
PREPARATION & COOKING TIME: 20 minutes

½ lb leeks, cut into 1 ½ inch lengths
2 tablespoons vegetable oil
2 cups sliced button mushrooms
1 tablespoon soy sauce
½ lb bean curd, thinly sliced

Cook the leeks in half of the oil in a skillet or wok over moderate heat for a few minutes, until they are just beginning to soften. Add the mushrooms and soy sauce, and continue stir frying until they are cooked. Remove from the pan and keep hot while you fry the bean curd in the remaining oil until crisp and golden brown on both sides. Take care when frying, as the curd may spatter when put into oil. Put the leeks and mushrooms onto a warm serving dish and arrange the bean curd on top. Alternatively, the vegetables can be returned to the pan with the bean curd and stir fried together for a few moments before serving.

Creamed mushrooms with yogurt

Serves 4
CALORIES PER PORTION: 120 (502 kJ)
PROTEIN CONTENT PER PORTION: 6 grams
PREPARATION & COOKING TIME: 20 minutes

1 cup finely chopped onion
2 tablespoons olive oil
1 lb mushrooms, peeled if the skins are tough
1 ¼ cups plain yogurt
¼ teaspoon salt

Fry the onion in the oil until golden brown. Add half the mushrooms broken into pieces about ¾ inch square. Press with a wooden spoon until the juices begin to run and, when the first batch has reduced add the rest. Cook them until they are dark and shiny, then drain off some of the juice and add the yogurt and salt. (I use yogurt which has been left to stand for 2 days as the culture is then fairly strong. Commercial yogurt tends to be too solid and bland.) Continue cooking until all the liquid has evaporated and just a paste is left coating the mushrooms. Spoon into a warm serving dish. This also makes a good filling for patty shells.

Stuffed mushrooms

Serves 4
CALORIES PER PORTION: 265 (1108 kJ)
PROTEIN CONTENT PER PORTION: 17 grams
PREPARATION & COOKING TIME: 40 minutes

1 cup finely chopped onion
6 tablespoons butter
1 lb mushrooms, preferably the large field ones
1 ½ cups cooked lentils
1 clove of garlic, peeled and chopped
2 tablespoons chopped parsley
1 tablespoon lemon juice
salt
freshly ground pepper

Fry the onion in half of the butter until golden brown. Peel the mushrooms and remove the stalks; coarsely chop the stalks, add them to the onions and cook for about 2-3 minutes. Liberally butter a shallow baking dish and cover the bottom with about half of the mushrooms, gills uppermost.

Preheat the oven to 400°F. Add the lentils, garlic and parsley to the cooked onions; mix well and continue cooking until the lentils are really hot. Add a little water to prevent them from burning, if necessary. Put a spoonful or two of the lentil stuffing into each mushroom and sprinkle with lemon juice. Season with salt and pepper, cover the filled mushrooms with the rest of the mushrooms, gills downwards, then melt the rest of the butter and brush this over the tops. Bake for 30 minutes in the preheated oven.

More vegetable accompaniments for the discriminating palate. Top: Baked savory pumpkin. Center: Chinese-style Mushroom and leek stir-fried with bean curd. Bottom: Large field mushrooms, stuffed with lentils and onion

German bread and tomato pudding

Serves 4
CALORIES PER PORTION: 210 (872 kJ)
PROTEIN CONTENT PER PORTION: 9 grams
PREPARATION & COOKING TIME: 40 minutes

1 ½ cups finely chopped onions
2 tablespoons butter
about 8 wafer-thin slices of wholewheat bread
2-3 tablespoons fresh wholewheat breadcrumbs
¼ teaspoon grated nutmeg
1 lb tomatoes, sliced
1 egg
⅔ cup milk
salt
1-2 tablespoons grated Cheddar cheese

Preheat the oven to 400°F. Fry the onions in the butter until they are golden brown. Liberally butter a shallow baking dish about 9 inches in diameter and cover the bottom with slices of the bread, reserving 3 or 4. Fill the spaces between the slices with the crumbs. When the onion is cooked, pour the butter from the pan over the bread and sprinkle with half the onion and the nutmeg. Arrange a layer of tomatoes on top, sprinkle it with the rest of the onion and cover the dish with the rest of the sliced bread. (This time, do not fill the spaces with crumbs.)

Beat the eggs with the milk and a pinch of salt and pour it over the pudding. Sprinkle the top with the cheese and bake in the preheated oven for 30 minutes.

This is a fairly substantial dish and makes a good light lunch or supper if served with a salad.

Red-cooked bean curd with bean sprouts

Serves 4
CALORIES PER PORTION: 235 (992 kJ)
PROTEIN CONTENT PER PORTION: 9 grams
PREPARATION & COOKING TIME: 30 minutes

½ lb bean curd, cut into ½ inch slices
¼ cup vegetable oil
¼ cup soy sauce
1 cup finely chopped onion
¼ lb cucumber, quartered lengthwise, then sliced
2 ½ cups bean sprouts
1 clove of garlic, peeled and very finely chopped
2 tablespoons sweet sherry
2 teaspoons vinegar
1 teaspoon cornstarch
¼ cup water
2 hard-cooked eggs, coarsely chopped

Fry the bean curd in half the oil until the outside is golden brown. Sprinkle with 3 tablespoons of the soy sauce, remove from the heat and leave to marinate, turning it over from time to time.

Fry the onion in the remaining oil until soft. Add the cucumber and the bean sprouts and stir fry for 1 ½ minutes before adding the garlic, the remaining tablespoon of soy sauce, the sherry, vinegar and the cornstarch dissolved in the water. Continue cooking until the sauce has thickened. Add the drained bean curd and cook until hot. Transfer to a warm shallow plate, sprinkle the chopped eggs into the center and trickle over a little of the soy sauce remaining from the marinade. Serve immediately.

Spring rolls

Makes 4
CALORIES PER PORTION: 1155 (4415 kJ)
PROTEIN CONTENT PER PORTION: 13 grams
PREPARATION & COOKING TIME: 1 hour

3 large scallions, finely chopped
½ cup finely chopped mushrooms
2 tablespoons vegetable oil
2 ½ cups bean sprouts
½ cup finely shredded Chinese cabbage (pak choy)
¼ lb bean curd, diced
1 tablespoon soy sauce
1 teaspoon cornstarch
3 cups Basic puff pastry (page 194)

Preheat the oven to 400°F. Stir-fry the scallions and mushrooms in the oil over moderate heat until they soften and the juices evaporate. Add the bean sprouts, cabbage and bean curd and cook for 2 minutes. Add the soy sauce, sprinkle the cornstarch over the vegetables, then stir together until the mixture has thickened. Allow to get quite cold.

Roll out the dough to a thin rectangle, 12 × 16 inches, and cut it into four equally-sized rectangles. When the filling is quite cold, divide it between the four dough pieces. Fold in the sides and roll up. Place on an oiled baking sheet with the dough seam underneath and bake in the preheated oven for about 20 minutes, or until the spring rolls are crisp and brown. Serve hot.

Sweet and sour cabbage

Serves 4
CALORIES PER PORTION: 115 (490 kJ)
PROTEIN CONTENT PER PORTION: 2 grams
PREPARATION & COOKING TIME: 30 minutes

1 tablespoon olive or sunflower oil
½ cup finely chopped onion
8 cloves, finely ground
1-2 pinches of finely ground caraway or aniseed
2 cups shredded white cabbage
1-2 tablespoons honey
½ teaspoon peeled and finely chopped fresh ginger root
2-3 tablespoons cider or wine vinegar
¼ cup halved blanched almonds
⅓ cup coarsely shredded carrot
small piece of preserved ginger, finely chopped (optional)

Heat the oil in a wok or skillet and fry the onion until soft but not browned. Add the finely ground spices and the cabbage and stir fry until the cabbage begins to reduce in bulk and turn moist. Add the honey and ginger root, and when the honey has melted add the vinegar. Continue cooking until the cabbage is limp but still crunchy; this should take about 10 minutes altogether.

Mix in the almonds, carrot and preserved ginger, if used, and serve immediately.

Stir-fried bean sprouts

Serves 4
CALORIES PER PORTION: 250 (1048 kJ)
PROTEIN CONTENT PER PORTION: 4 grams
PREPARATION & COOKING TIME: 15 minutes

½ cup finely chopped onion
¼ cup peeled and finely chopped fresh ginger root
1 clove of garlic, peeled and very finely chopped
3 tablespoons vegetable oil
1 lb bean sprouts
6 water chestnuts, sliced
2 cups coarsely chopped watercress
1 teaspoon salt
2 tablespoons sweet sherry
1 tablespoon soy sauce
½ teaspoon monosodium glutamate — MSG — (optional)
½ tablespoon sesame oil

Fry the onion, ginger and garlic in the oil until soft but not browned. Add the bean sprouts, water chestnuts, watercress and salt and cook for 2-3 minutes, turning frequently. Add the sherry, soy sauce, MSG (if using) and sesame oil and cook for another 2-3 minutes. Serve on a hot shallow plate.

Fried rice dish

Serves 6
CALORIES PER PORTION: 385 (1607 kJ)
PROTEIN CONTENT PER PORTION: 13 grams
PREPARATION & COOKING TIME: 30 minutes

1 cup finely chopped onion
¼ cup vegetable oil
4 eggs
salt
1 cup cooked peas
¾ cup cooked corn kernels
1 cup shredded leeks
1 cup finely chopped mushrooms
2⅓ cups dry cooked rice
2 tablespoons soy sauce
freshly ground pepper
1-2 tablespoons chopped parsley

Fry the onion in 1 tablespoon of the oil until golden brown. Beat the eggs with ½ teaspoon of salt, pour them into the pan with the onion and scramble them lightly. Remove from the pan and keep hot. Pour another tablespoon of oil into the pan and fry the peas and corn for 2 minutes. Add the leeks and fry for a further 1½ minutes, stirring all the time. Finally, add the mushrooms and fry until their juices have almost evaporated. Remove from the pan and keep hot.

Pour the remaining oil into the pan and fry the rice over a gentle heat until hot, turning it over continually with a spatula to prevent it sticking and burning. When it is thoroughly hot, add the vegetables, eggs and soy sauce. Mix together lightly, add salt and pepper, if necessary, and serve sprinkled with chopped parsley.

Washing, soaking and cooking dried legumes and cereals

Washing

Spread the dried legumes or cereals on a clean flat surface and pick out any stones or foreign bodies, then put the legumes or cereals into a bowl of water; throw out any that float, and any bits of wood or leaf.

Soaking

Rinse two or three times in fresh water, then leave to soak for 1-2 hours for lentils and peas and overnight for beans and chick peas. Rice, wheat and cornmeal do not need preliminary soaking.

An alternative method for beans, which also removes some of their flatulent affect, is to cover them with plenty of cold water, bring it to a boil and simmer for 5 minutes before removing from the heat and allowing it to cool. Discard the water, replace it with fresh and then boil them until they are cooked.

Cooking

The age and method of drying affects the cooking time of legumes and cereals so use the following times as a guide only.

Beans, peas and lentils should be cooked in about two to three times their volume of water. Bring the soaked beans, peas or lentils to a boil and simmer, partially covered, until they are soft, adding salt towards the end of the cooking time and extra water if necessary. Use any water left over for stock.

Most beans take 1-2 hours to cook but soybeans take 3-5 hours, as do chick peas. Lentils take 30 minutes to 1 hour. Yellow or green split peas take 30-45 minutes.

Add brown or polished white rice to 2½ times their volume of lightly salted boiling water and simmer in a covered pan over gentle heat. Brown rice will take 35-45 minutes and polished white rice will take 12-15 minutes. Transfer the cooked rice to a colander and pour a jug of boiling water through it to wash away any starch, then drain thoroughly. Put it into a warm serving dish and lightly separate the grains with a fork. The rice should be dry, not mushy, and the grains separate.

If you use a pressure cooker, the cooking times can be reduced by between a half and a third. Cook the food in a bowl on the rack inside the pressure cooker. Pour the recommended quantity of water to make the steam around the bowl. Take care not to release the pressure suddenly or the food may froth out of the bowl.

Cook whole, cracked or crushed wheat and barley as for brown rice; they will take about the same time. Bulgur cooks in 15-45 minutes. Genuine bulgur needs only to be soaked before it is used in salads. See page 124 for polenta or cornmeal.

Savory brown rice

CALORIES PER PORTION: 240 (997 kJ)
PROTEIN CONTENT PER PORTION: 4.5 grams
PREPARATION & COOKING TIME: 1 hour

1½ pints water
½ teaspoon salt
1 cup well washed brown rice
1 cup finely chopped onion
1 tablespoon olive or sunflower oil
a little grated nutmeg
1 tablespoon finely chopped parsley
½ teaspoon very finely chopped thyme
½ teaspoon grated lemon rind

Bring the water to a boil, add the salt then the rice. Bring the water back to a boil, cover the pan, turn down the heat and cook gently for 35-45 minutes. Test a few grains after 30 minutes. Meanwhile, fry the onion in the oil until golden brown.

When the rice is cooked, drain it well if necessary. Sprinkle the nutmeg over the onion and mix well before adding the parsley, thyme and lemon rind. Mix a little of the cooked rice into the onion and herbs, then add the rest of the rice and mix well so that it is evenly distributed. Spoon into a heated serving dish, cover and keep warm for 15 minutes before serving.

Navy beans with yogurt and parsley

Serves 4
CALORIES PER PORTION: 170 (720 kJ)
PROTEIN CONTENT PER PORTION: 14 grams
PREPARATION AND COOKING TIME: 2-3 hours, excluding soaking.

1 cup dried navy beans, washed and soaked overnight
⅔ cup plain yogurt
5 tablespoons finely chopped parsley

Drain the beans and replace with fresh water to cover. Bring to a boil, lower the heat, cover the pan and simmer the beans until they are soft. Add more water if necessary, but by the end of the cooking time most of the liquid should have absorbed. Drain off any excess.

Pour on the yogurt, sprinkle with 4 tablespoons of the parsley and gently mix together. Reheat the beans without allowing them to boil or the yogurt will separate and spoil the appearance of the dish. Pour into a heated serving dish and sprinkle with the remaining parsley.

Red kidney beans with onions and coriander

Serves 4
CALORIES PER PORTION: 225 (947 kJ)
PROTEIN CONTENT PER PORTION: 13 grams
PREPARATION AND COOKING TIME: 2-2½ hours, excluding soaking

1 cup red kidney beans, washed and soaked
1 large onion, cut into rings
2 tablespoons olive or sunflower oil
2 cloves of garlic, peeled and finely chopped
1 teaspoon ground coriander
1 tablespoon chopped parsley
1 tablespoon wine vinegar

Drain the soaking water from the beans and cook them in water to cover in a covered pan for 1½-2 hours or until tender, adding extra water if necessary. Drain the cooked beans and reserve a little of the cooking liquid.

Fry the onion rings in the oil over moderate heat until they are transparent, then add the rest of the ingredients and mix well. Pour in the beans and 1-2 tablespoons of the reserved cooking liquid. Turn the beans over and over with a spatula until they are evenly mixed with the onions. Serve hot or cold.

Soy falafel

Serves 4
CALORIES PER PORTION: 87 (330 kJ)
TOTAL PROTEIN CONTENT: 20 grams
PREPARATION AND COOKING TIME: 1 hour, excluding soaking

1 cup dried soybeans, washed and soaked
1 cup chopped onion
1 teaspoon ground cumin
1 teaspoon ground coriander
salt
a generous pinch of cayenne pepper
2 cloves of garlic, peeled and sliced
¼ cup finely chopped parsley

Drain the beans and mix with the onion. Sprinkle with the spices, salt and cayenne, then add the garlic and parsley and put the mixture through a grinder. Transfer it to a bowl or a mortar and pound with the end of a rolling pin or a pestle to a fairly smooth paste.

Form tablespoonfuls of the mixture into small balls, cover with a cloth and leave for 15 minutes before deep frying in hot oil, 375°F, until brown. Drain well and serve hot.

This makes a good accompaniment to a vegetable casserole or, if made smaller, a perfect cocktail snack.

Whole wheat pilau

Serves 4
CALORIES PER PORTION: 282 (1187 kJ)
PROTEIN PER PORTION: 7 grams
PREPARATION AND COOKING TIME: 1-1½ hours

½ lb eggplant, sliced
salt
2 tablespoons olive or sunflower oil
1 cup very finely chopped onion
½ teaspoon ground cumin
½ teaspoon ground coriander
1 clove of garlic, peeled and finely chopped
freshly ground black pepper
1 cup whole wheat, cooked as for brown rice
⅓ cup seedless white raisins
2 tablespoons orange juice
8 orange segments

Place the sliced eggplant in a colander, sprinkle with salt and leave to drain for 30 minutes. Rinse and pat dry with paper towels. Fry the eggplant slices gently in the oil until they look oily and are just beginning to brown. Add the onion and continue cooking until the onion is transparent.

Add the spices, garlic and pepper, then the cooked wheat, with the raisins. Gently mix into the vegetables and spices, then sprinkle with orange juice. Turn into a shallow dish, arrange the orange segments around it and serve hot.

Polenta

Serves 4
CALORIES PER PORTION: 177 (745 kJ)
PROTEIN CONTENT PER PORTION: 4.5 grams
PREPARATION AND COOKING TIME: 35 minutes

1½ cups polenta (coarsely ground cornmeal)
1½ pints cold water
salt

Pour the water into the top of a double boiler. Add salt and bring the water to a boil. Stir in the polenta and continue stirring over gentle heat until it is thick and smooth. Place over the bottom pan and keep it simmering for 30 minutes. Serve the polenta hot with a rich Tomato sauce (page 196) or a Vegetable casserole (91).

Alternatively, cut cold polenta into slices and fry in hot oil until crisp and golden brown.

Purée of chick peas

Serves 4
CALORIES PER PORTION: 260 (1082 kJ)
PROTEIN CONTENT PER PORTION: 13 grams
PREPARATION AND COOKING TIME: 5½ hours, excluding soaking

1 cup dried chick peas, washed and soaked
1 cup milk
2 tablespoons butter
salt
freshly ground pepper
2 tablespoons finely chopped parsley

Drain the water from the soaked chick peas and replace with enough fresh water to cover completely. Bring to a boil, then lower the heat, cover the pan and simmer for 3-5 hours, or until the peas are very soft.

When the peas are cooked, drain and work a few at a time to a purée in a blender with a little milk. Alternatively, put the chick peas twice through a fine-bladed grinder, or rub through a strainer before stirring in the milk. Melt the butter, add the chick pea purée and seasoning and reheat. Serve sprinkled with chopped parsley.

Salads and Salad Dressings

Salads play a particularly important role in the vegetarian's diet. Not only can they be a valuable source of additional protein and vitamins, but they are extremely versatile and the choice of texture, flavor and color is immense. They can be served as a light meal on their own, as a first course or as an exciting contrast to the main course. They can also be used as 'punctuation' during a meal to clear the palate between courses.

It is said that the secret of a successful salad dressing is similar to successful diplomacy – 'to know just how much oil to put with the vinegar'. The vital point to remember is that the flavor should be a simple harmony. I don't find it a good idea to mix up a large quantity of dressing and store it in the refrigerator; if it is not all used up fairly quickly, the results are very much less than appetizing . . . For greater variety, try using lemon juice instead of vinegar, walnut oil instead of olive oil and add herbs, horseradish, grated orange or lemon rind instead of the now almost obligatory garlic. The salad recipes that follow use fruits and vegetables, dried legumes and nuts; try making one meal of the day entirely of salad and see how much better you feel!

Making Salads

When making a salad choose your ingredients for their contrasting flavors, textures and colors. As a guide, choose something from each of the following:
The lettuces — crisp-hearted; soft round ones, or long, crisp-leaved types.
The other leaves — white or red cabbage, young spinach, beet and mustard greens, Chinese cabbage or dandelion.
The curly leaves — chicory, escarole, corn salad or lamb's lettuce or celery leaves.
The crunchy ones — Belgian endive, celery, crisp dessert apples or cucumber.
The tangy ones — watercress, nasturtium leaves, geranium leaves, red and green peppers, radishes, scallions, Spanish onions and tomatoes.
The herbs — parsley, of course, and basil, tarragon, fennel, thyme, chervil and mint; but also try fresh coriander leaves, bergamot leaves and flower petals, nasturtium leaves or flowers, apple mint or lemon thyme, and balm or lovage.
The other ingredients — can be any fruit, cooked vegetable, dried legume or grain, nut, seed or dairy product that blends or contrasts harmoniously with the rest of the salad.

Having chosen a combination of leaves and herbs, wash them carefully, paying particular attention to the curly leaved ones — grit is not a texture you want in a salad. Discard any damaged or discolored leaves, cut off the roots and root plates of the plants and remove any fibrous cores, stems, strings or membranes from fruits, shoots or leaves.

Dry the leaves thoroughly; there is nothing worse than a watery salad, where the dressing is diluted and runs off the leaves, and all the flavor is lost. Use either a salad basket or centrifugal spinner; failing these, shake the salad gently in a clean dish towel. To ensure that the salad is really crisp, put it in a covered bowl and chill it for an hour or so.

When using tomatoes in a mixed salad, remove the seeds and juice; otherwise they will make it too wet. Also remove all the pith and seeds from red and green peppers as these are very bitter.

The final consideration is the dressing. Bear in mind what you want the dressing to do — provide piquancy, soften otherwise too-strong flavors, add a flavor that is missing in the rest of the ingredients, or is it to provide a cream in which all can blend? Choose from the following:

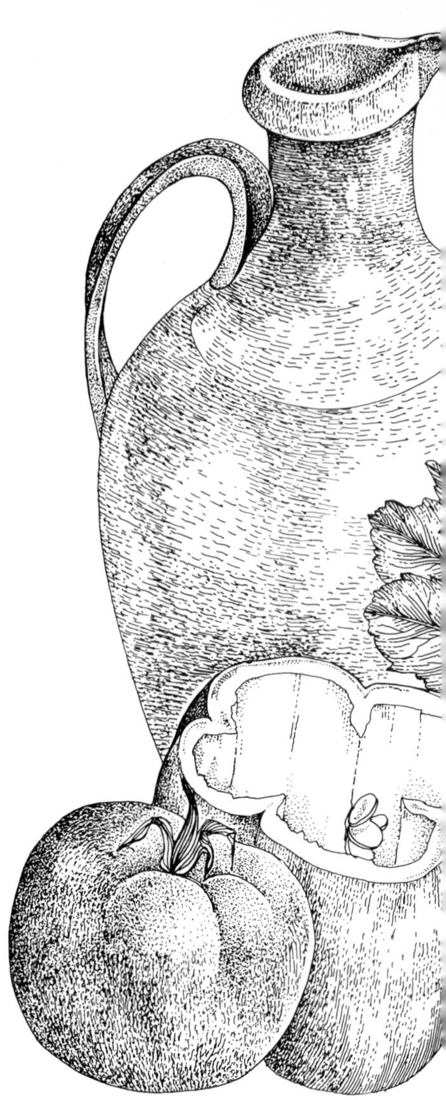

Mayonnaise

Makes about 1½ cups. For 4 servings.

CALORIES PER PORTION: 640 (2667 kJ)
PROTEIN CONTENT PER PORTION: 1 gram
PREPARATION TIME: 20 minutes by hand; 5 minutes in a blender

2 egg yolks
1¼ cups olive or sunflower oil
1-2 tablespoons wine vinegar
salt
freshly ground pepper

By hand

If you have never made mayonnaise by hand before, follow this method exactly. Once you have gained experience you can speed up. The main thing to understand is that when you make mayonnaise, you are making an emulsion: very small globules of oil coated with a layer of egg to prevent them from joining up again. When you add the vinegar at the end to thin the mayonnaise down and give it sharpness, you make the layer of egg more liquid. As you stir the oil into the egg yolks, the movement of the spoon breaks it up into small drops separated by layers of yolk.

Use a bowl that is just large enough to hold the final quantity, about 1½ cups. Put the egg yolks into it and stir until they are mixed together, then add 1 teaspoon of oil and stir 20 times. Repeat with another teaspoon of oil and continue in this way until the mayonnaise begins to thicken. Then add the oil 2 teaspoons at a time. When all the oil has been used, the mixture will resemble a thick, buttery mass. Stir in 1 tablespoon of vinegar and mix well. Add more to give the consistency and piquancy you require, and season.

When you have made mayonnaise several times, you will find you are able to add more oil to the yolks than the amount given above. If the mayonnaise begins to look dry and granular, add no more oil.

In a blender or food mixer

Put the egg yolks into the blender, or a bowl if using a food mixer, and with the beater attachments, beat — or blend — at full speed. Gradually trickle in the oil increasing the flow as the mayonnaise thickens, and add the vinegar at the end.

If the mayonnaise curdles or separates, pour it into another container, clean the bowl and put another lightly beaten egg yolk into it. Follow the above procedure, using the curdled mayonnaise in place of the oil.

Mayonnaise forms the basis of a number of cold sauces; these can be made by adding the following ingredients to the basic recipe:

Green mayonnaise

CALORIES AND PROTEIN CONTENT AS FOR MAYONNAISE

Put the egg and oil mixture into a blender and add 1-2 tablespoons chopped watercress leaves. Blend until uniformly green; add a little vinegar or lemon juice to get the correct consistency and sharpness. The leaves make quite a lot of liquid so be careful not to make the mayonnaise too runny. Blanched spinach is traditionally used in *Mayonnaise verte*, but watercress makes a more piquant sauce.

Aioli

CALORIES AND PROTEIN CONTENT AS FOR MAYONNAISE

Add 2-4 cloves of garlic, chopped to a pulp, to the Mayonnaise and mix thoroughly.

Tartare sauce

CALORIES PER PORTION: 1000 (4197 kJ)
PROTEIN CONTENT PER PORTION: 5.5 grams

Mash 4-5 hard-cooked egg yolks with salt and freshly ground pepper, then gradually work in 1¼ cups olive oil. Add 1 teaspoon vinegar, 2 tablespoons mayonnaise, and mix in 1 tablespoon finely chopped chives.

Thousand Island dressing

CALORIES PER PORTION: 689 (2872 kJ)
PROTEIN CONTENT PER PORTION: 4.5 grams

Add 2 tablespoons chopped olives, 2 finely chopped hard-cooked eggs, 1 teaspoon paprika and a dash or two of chili sauce to taste. Season with salt and pepper.

Roquefort dressing

CALORIES PER PORTION: 680 (2852 kJ)
PROTEIN CONTENT PER PORTION: 4.5 grams

Add ½ cup crumbled Roquefort cheese to a little of the mayonnaise and mash until it is completely smooth. Stir it into the rest of the mayonnaise and sharpen with a little lemon juice. Alternatively, add the same quantity of Roquefort cheese to 1¼ cups of vinaigrette dressing.

Sour cream dressing

CALORIES PER PORTION: 400 (1667 kJ)
PROTEIN CONTENT PER PORTION: 2 grams

Add ⅔ cup sour cream to an equal quantity of mayonnaise and mix together. Alternatively, add the sour cream to an equal quantity of vinaigrette dressing.

Curry mayonnaise

CALORIES AND PROTEIN CONTENT AS FOR MAYONNAISE

Add 1–2 teaspoons of curry powder to the Mayonnaise and mix thoroughly. A hotter sauce can be made by adding a pinch of chili powder or a dash of chili sauce to the curry powder.

Maltese sauce

CALORIES PER PORTION: 647.5 (2733 kJ)
PROTEIN CONTENT PER PORTION: 1 gram

Add the grated rind and 2 tablespoons of juice from an orange, with 1 tablespoon fresh tomato purée and 1 tablespoon vinegar to a firm Mayonnaise.

Cottage cheese dressing

CALORIES PER PORTION: 140 (595 kJ)
PROTEIN CONTENT PER PORTION: 1 gram
PREPARATION TIME: 10 minutes

½ cup strained cottage cheese
1 tablespoon lemon juice
1 tablespoon finely chopped chives
1-2 tablespoons milk
salt
freshly ground pepper

Mash the cottage cheese with the lemon juice and the chives. Pour a little milk into the bowl and continue stirring until the mixture becomes a thick cream, then continue adding milk until the cheese dressing has the consistency of thin cream. Season with salt and pepper and pour over the salad.

French or Vinaigrette dressing

This should be enough for a plain green salad for 4 people.

CALORIES PER PORTION: 210 (890 kJ)
PROTEIN CONTENT PER PORTION: nil
PREPARATION TIME: 5 minutes

salt
freshly ground pepper
2 tablespoons wine or cider vinegar
6-8 tablespoons olive or sunflower oil
1-2 tablespoons chopped fresh herbs (optional)

Add the salt and pepper to the vinegar and mix well. Stir in the oil and beat again until the sauce is smooth textured and creamy; put these ingredients with the herbs, if used, in a screw-topped glass jar and shake vigorously until well mixed, or blend together. Alternatively replace one tablespoon of vinegar with a tablespoon of lemon juice or dry white wine, or use a mixture of all three. Lemon juice and white wine beaten with the oil makes a very good dressing for young lettuce. For a change, use walnut instead of olive oil — excellent with Belgian endive!

Classic green salad

In my opinion, a green salad should contain green or blanched leaves, fresh herbs, a simple dressing of olive or walnut oil, lemon juice, white wine and wine or cider vinegar. Add a suggestion of garlic, a little salt and freshly ground pepper — and that is all.

Serves 4
CALORIES PER PORTION: 300 (1255 kJ)
PROTEIN CONTENT PER PORTION: 1.5 grams
PREPARATION TIME: 25 minutes

¾–1 lb green leaves — choose from lettuce, Belgian endive, mustard and garden cress, watercress, corn salad, young dandelion or spinach leaves, or chicory, but let the main ingredient be the lettuce, preferably a crisp-hearted cabbage type, or a well-grown romaine
1-2 tablespoons chopped fresh herbs (optional)

The dressing
1 tablespoon wine or cider vinegar
1 tablespoon white wine or 2 teaspoons lemon juice
1 teaspoon chopped herbs — chervil, tarragon, basil, or a mixture of these
½ cup olive or walnut oil
salt
freshly ground pepper
1 clove of garlic, cut in half
1 small slice of very dry wholewheat bread or toast, rubbed with garlic and soaked in olive oil — a chapon (optional)

Carefully wash the chosen salad greens, discarding any discolored or bruised leaves. The French rightly claim that a salad should be eaten with a fork only, so tear all the leaves into bite-sized pieces; do not cut them as this will bruise them. Cut Belgian endive into ¾ inch slices.

Make the dressing by beating together the vinegar, wine or lemon juice and fresh herbs, then beat in the oil. Season with salt and pepper. If you have a blender you can pour all the liquids into the bowl and blend for a few moments; or put all the ingredients in a screw-topped glass jar and shake it vigorously — with the lid on! Rub the inside of the salad bowl with the cut clove of garlic or place the *chapon* at the bottom. Pour the dressing into the bowl, but do not dress the salad itself until just before serving, or the leaves — especially the lettuce — will go limp.

Toss the salad by turning it over and over in the bowl until it is evenly coated with dressing. Remove the *chapon*, which should have been tossed with the salad, or keep it on one side while the salad is being tossed; it can then be divided among the garlic-lovers.

Left: thinly-sliced cucumber and strawberries combine to make a cool Elona salad. Right: Javanese salad has onion, celery, red pepper and banana piled on slices of fresh pineapple – a rare combination, and a feast in itself

Mixed salad

The appeal of a mixed salad should be the subtle change of flavor from one mouthful to the next. This is why the sizes of the prepared ingredients should be as equal as possible.

Serves 4
CALORIES PER PORTION: 270 (1120 kJ)
PROTEIN CONTENT PER PORTION: 1.5 grams
PREPARATION & CHILLING TIME: 30-40 minutes

1 large head lettuce or a mixture of salad leaves, torn into small pieces
½ cup finely diced red pepper
1 cucumber, quartered lengthwise, then cut into chunks
½ cup skinned, seeded and roughly chopped tomatoes
¼ cup finely chopped onion
½ cup chopped celery
½ cup thinly sliced Belgian endive
6-12 radishes, thinly sliced (optional)

The dressing
½ cup olive or sunflower oil
1 tablespoon lemon juice
1 tablespoon wine or cider vinegar
salt
freshly ground pepper
1 tablespoon finely chopped fresh herbs

Mix all the salad ingredients together in a bowl and chill well. Beat together the oil, lemon juice and vinegar and season with salt and pepper. Add the herbs to the dressing, then pour it over the salad ingredients and thoroughly toss it just before serving.

Elona salad

Serves 4
CALORIES PER PORTION: 36 (150 kJ)
PROTEIN CONTENT PER PORTION: 1 gram
PREPARATION & CHILLING TIME: 45 minutes

1 tablespoon lemon juice
¼ cup dry white wine
salt
1 lb cucumber, peeled and very thinly sliced
½ lb strawberries (about 16), hulled and sliced

Mix the lemon juice with the wine, season with salt and pour over the cucumber. Leave for 30 minutes, then drain. Arrange a ring of cucumber slices around the outside edge of a large plate; then, working from the outside, continue with rings of alternating slices of cucumber and strawberries. Reserve a few choice strawberry slices for a garnish. Arrange these in the center with 'leaves' cut from the cucumber skin. Chill and serve.

Hawaiian salad

Serves 4
CALORIES PER PORTION: 465 (1940 kJ)
PROTEIN CONTENT PER PORTION: 3.5 grams
PREPARATION & CHILLING TIME: 50 minutes

1 large head romaine lettuce, torn into small pieces
1 cup finely diced red peppers
1 cup seeded and roughly chopped tomatoes
1 cup shredded or grated coconut
1 cup cubed fresh or canned pineapple
1 tablespoon lemon juice
¼ cup dark rum
1 tablespoon wine or cider vinegar
6 tablespoons olive or sunflower oil
salt
freshly ground pepper
1 clove of garlic, peeled and finely chopped
grated rind of 1 small lemon (optional)

Mix together the lettuce, peppers and tomatoes. Sprinkle the coconut over the pineapple cubes, reserving a little, and pour on the lemon juice and rum. Make the dressing by beating together the vinegar, oil, salt and pepper, garlic and lemon rind, if used, and pour this over the lettuce, peppers and tomatoes. Pile the salad in a shallow dish and arrange the pineapple on top. Sprinkle with the reserved coconut and serve slightly chilled.

Javanese salad

Serves 4
CALORIES PER PORTION: 575 (2417 kJ)
PROTEIN CONTENT PER PORTION: 9 grams
PREPARATION & COOKING TIME: 50 minutes

1 cup finely chopped onion
1 tablespoon olive or sunflower oil
¼ teaspoon ground cinnamon
½ teaspoon ground cumin
¾ cup unroasted peanuts
pinch of chili powder
1 tablespoon wine or cider vinegar
½ cup finely chopped celery
1 large banana, sliced
salt
freshly ground pepper
⅔ cup Mayonnaise (page 126)
4 slices of fresh or canned pineapple
2 tablespoons chopped red pepper

Fry the onion in the oil until it is golden brown; add the cinnamon and cumin and fry for a few minutes longer. Add the peanuts, chili powder and vinegar. Stir well, then remove from the heat and leave, covered, to cool. When it is cold, add the celery and banana and season with salt and pepper. Pour the mayonnaise over the salad and stir until thoroughly mixed.

Pile the mixture on the pineapple slices, sprinkle the red pepper over the top and serve.

Creole salad

Serves 8
CALORIES PER PORTION: 210 (887 kJ)
PROTEIN CONTENT PER PORTION: 3 grams
PREPARATION TIME: 30 minutes

½ lb avocados, peeled, cut into chunks and dipped in 2 tablespoons lemon juice
1 cup cubed fresh or canned pineapple
1 cup diced red peppers
1 cup diced celery
salt
freshly ground pepper
1¼ cups boiled brown rice
1 tablespoon lemon juice
1 tablespoon wine or cider vinegar
6 tablespoons olive or sunflower oil

Drain the avocado chunks and mix with the pineapple, peppers and celery; season with salt and pepper.

Gently mix in the rice, taking care not to break the avocado up too much. Beat together the lemon juice, vinegar and oil. Season well with salt and pepper and pour this dressing over the salad.

Roquefort pear salad

This dish can make a very good beginning to a meal — something to whet the appetite.

Serves 4
CALORIES PER PORTION: 805 (3370 kJ)
PROTEIN CONTENT PER PORTION: 10 grams
PREPARATION & CHILLING TIME: 1 hour

4 firm, ripe pears, peeled
1 cup crumbled Roquefort cheese
4 scallions, finely chopped
1 cup Green mayonnaise (page 126)
4 sprigs of watercress to garnish

Cut a small slice off the base of each pear so that it stands upright. Cut each one in half and scoop out the core, leaving a hollow for the filling. Mash the cheese, mix it with the scallions and bind with about 6 tablespoons of mayonnaise to make a firm paste. Fill the pears with this and reshape them. If you do not have a blender, finely chop the watercress leaves before adding them to the mayonnaise. It may be advisable to do this in two stages as the final mayonnaise must be thick enough to hold its shape.

Coat the pears thinly and evenly with green mayonnaise, using a knife to spread the mayonnaise evenly as though frosting a cake. Finally, insert a spray of watercress in each to resemble pear leaves.

Arrange the pears on a plate, taking care that they stay upright and do not split, and chill well before serving.

Florida salad

Serves 6
CALORIES PER PORTION: 440 (1841 kJ)
PROTEIN CONTENT PER PORTION: 3 grams
PREPARATION & COOKING TIME: 45 minutes

¼ cup olive or sunflower oil
4 slices of wholewheat bread, crusts removed and cut into ½ inch cubes
1 cup finely diced red peppers
1 cup cottage cheese
1 lb fresh, firm pears, peeled, cored, cut into ¾ inch cubes and well coated with lemon juice
1 large head crisp lettuce, preferably romaine, torn into small pieces
½ lb cucumber, thinly sliced

The dressing
1 tablespoon lemon juice
1 tablespoon wine or cider vinegar
6-8 tablespoons olive oil
salt
freshly ground pepper
a little grated lemon rind
1 tablespoon finely chopped parsley

Heat the oil in a pan and fry the bread cubes until they are crisp. Drain them on paper towels and leave to get completely cold.

To make the dressing, beat together the lemon juice, vinegar and oil and season with salt and pepper. Add a little grated lemon rind and sprinkle in the parsley.

Mix the peppers with the cottage cheese and marinated pears, but reserve about 12 pieces. Arrange lettuce on a large, round plate and pour over the dressing. Make a ring of cucumber slices around the center and pile the cottage cheese and pear mixture in the middle of this ring. Decorate with the reserved diced pepper and scatter the croûtons around the edge of the salad. Mix it all together at the table just before serving.

Tunisian orange salad

Serves 4
CALORIES PER PORTION: 50 (220 kJ)
PROTEIN CONTENT PER PORTION: 1 gram
PREPARATION & CHILLING TIME: 35 minutes

4 large oranges, peeled and thinly sliced 'across the equator'
2 tablespoons rose water
a little ground cinnamon

Remove every bit of pith from the orange slices and arrange them on a plate in overlapping circles. Pour over the rose water, sprinkle with a little cinnamon and chill.

Just before serving, tilt the plate, carefully pour off the juice into a bowl and pour it again over the orange slices.

Endive, orange and walnut salad

Serves 4
CALORIES PER PORTION: 180 (765 kJ)
PROTEIN CONTENT PER PORTION: 3 grams
PREPARATION TIME: 30 minutes

2-3 oranges, peeled
1 egg yolk
salt
freshly ground pepper
1 teaspoon vinegar
2 tablespoons olive or sunflower oil
orange juice
½ lb Belgian endive, cut into ½ inch slices
½ cup shredded walnuts

Divide each orange into segments, cutting between the flesh and membranes of each segment with a sharp knife to remove all the pith. Cut each segment in half and discard any seeds. Make the dressing by beating the egg yolk with the salt, pepper and vinegar, then beat in the oil and any juice from the orange. Mix together the orange segments and the endive and pour the dressing over them. Pile the salad in a shallow bowl and scatter the walnuts on top before serving.

Orange and apple salad

Serves 4
CALORIES PER PORTION: 345 (1445 kJ)
PROTEIN CONTENT PER PORTION: 3 grams
PREPARATION & CHILLING TIME: 45 minutes

4 large dessert apples, cored, diced and sprinkled with lemon juice
4 oranges, peeled and segmented (see previous recipe)
3 tablespoons chopped dates
½ cup finely chopped red pepper
3 tablespoons pine nuts

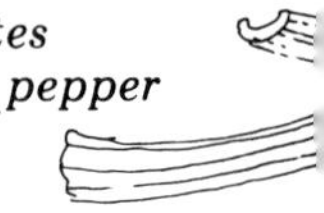

The dressing
1 tablespoon vinegar
1 tablespoon lemon juice
½ teaspoon ground cumin
salt
freshly ground pepper
6 tablespoons olive or sunflower oil

Beat together the vinegar, lemon juice, cumin, salt and pepper with the oil. Stir in the apple chunks. Halve each orange segment and mix these well with the apples. Add the dates and red pepper, and pile the salad in a shallow dish. Scatter with pine nuts and serve well chilled.

Tomato salad

Serves 4
CALORIES PER PORTION: 140 (582 kJ)
PROTEIN CONTENT PER PORTION: 1 gram
PREPARATION TIME: 20 minutes

1 lb tomatoes, thinly sliced
2 tablespoons very finely chopped basil
2 tablespoons very finely chopped onion
¼ cup olive or sunflower oil
1 tablespoon wine or cider vinegar
1 tablespoon lemon juice
salt
freshly ground pepper

Arrange the slices of tomato in overlapping layers on a large flat plate. Sprinkle the chopped basil over half the tomatoes and the onion over the other half. Beat together the oil, vinegar and lemon juice and pour it over the salad, then sprinkle with salt. Grind a little pepper over the onions, not the basil as it may detract from the flavor. Keep the two portions separate when serving.

Tomato, celery and apple salad

Serves 4
CALORIES PER PORTION: 170 (717 kJ)
PROTEIN CONTENT PER PORTION: 4.5 grams
PREPARATION TIME: 20 minutes

1 cup thinly sliced celery
1 cup peeled and diced dessert apple
2 tablespoons lemon juice
1½ cups chopped and seeded tomatoes
½ cup finely diced Cheddar cheese
3 tablespoons olive or sunflower oil
salt
freshly ground pepper

Toss the celery and apple with the lemon juice, making sure that the apple is well coated, otherwise it will turn brown. Add the tomatoes and the cheese, and mix all the ingredients together. Pour on the oil and continue turning the salad, seasoning with salt and pepper as you do so.

Salade Niçoise

This salad should be chunky in texture.

Serves 8
CALORIES PER PORTION: 184 (771 kJ)
PROTEIN CONTENT PER PORTION: 3 grams
PREPARATION TIME: 30 minutes

1 head lettuce, torn into small pieces
½ lb tomatoes, quartered and seeded
1 cup diced cooked potatoes
1 cup thinly sliced celery
1 cup thinly sliced red or green peppers
2 hard-cooked eggs, quartered
12 pitted black olives
6 radishes, thinly sliced (optional)

The dressing
1 tablespoon lemon juice
2 tablespoons wine or cider vinegar
½ cup olive oil
1 clove of garlic, peeled and chopped or pounded to a pulp
salt
freshly ground pepper

Mix together the lettuce, tomatoes, potatoes, celery and peppers, then make the dressing. Beat together the lemon juice, vinegar, oil and garlic and season with salt and pepper. Mix this dressing carefully into the salad and garnish with the quartered eggs, olives and radishes before serving.

Watercress/tomato salad

Serves 4
CALORIES PER PORTION: 336 (1407 kJ)
PROTEIN CONTENT PER PORTION: 2 grams
PREPARATION TIME: 30 minutes

1 lb tomatoes, halved, plus ¼ cup of their juice (see method)
1 large bunch watercress, shredded (scissors are best for this task)

The mayonnaise
1 egg yolk
⅔ cup olive or sunflower oil
salt
freshly ground pepper

Remove the cores and seeds from the tomatoes. Strain the reserved juice. Cut the tomatoes into thin strips and arrange them on a plate. Sprinkle the watercress over.

Make a mayonnaise with the egg yolk and the oil, following the basic recipe on page 126. Take a little more care when adding the oil as it is more difficult to make a mayonnaise with only one egg yolk. When it has thickened, mix in the tomato juice. Sprinkle the salad with salt and pepper and serve the tomato-flavored mayonnaise separately.

Avocado salad

This salad and the Lebanese avocado salad (page 51) both contain garlic, but surprisingly it does not overpower the delicate flavor of the avocado. It is one of a number of unexpected combinations of flavors which complement or develop each other.

Serves 4
CALORIES PER PORTION: 290 (1212 kJ)
PROTEIN CONTENT PER PORTION: 3 grams
PREPARATION & CHILLING TIME: 45 minutes

several small lettuce leaves
1 clove of garlic, peeled
2 tablespoons lemon juice
salt
freshly ground pepper
¼ cup olive or sunflower oil
2 large ripe but firm avocados, peeled and thickly sliced

Arrange the lettuce leaves on a plate to form four small cups. Make the dressing by crushing the clove of garlic with the lemon juice, salt and pepper. Mix thoroughly and pour on the oil as you beat. Strain the dressing over the avocado slices, making sure they are completely coated; otherwise they will discolor. Pile them in the lettuce cups and chill before serving.

Herb loaf

CALORIES: 1895 (7930 kJ)
PROTEIN CONTENT: 40 grams
PREPARATION & COOKING TIME: 40 minutes

Thickly slice a French or wholewheat loaf, but stop cutting each slice just before you get to the bottom. Beat about 8 tablespoons of butter or margarine with 2 tablespoons finely chopped fresh herbs (preferably thyme, sage, tarragon or fennel) until softened and spread each slice with the herb butter. Reshape the loaf, wrap it in foil and warm it in a 350°F oven for about 30 minutes.

Garlic loaf

CALORIES: 1895 (7930 kJ)
PROTEIN CONTENT: 40 grams
PREPARATION & COOKING TIME: 40 minutes

Thickly slice a French or wholewheat loaf, but stop cutting each slice just before you get to the bottom. Soften about 8 tablespoons of butter or margarine with 2 peeled and finely chopped cloves of garlic. Spread this on the cut slices of the loaf, wrap and bake as for Herb loaf.

Mixed bean salad

This salad seems to have an almost universal appeal, as well as being highly nutritious. The three kinds of dried beans should be separately blanched for 5 minutes (page 123), then soaked, preferably overnight, before being cooked in separate pans. This recipe makes enough for 6.

Serves 4
CALORIES PER PORTION: 230 (968 kJ)
PROTEIN CONTENT PER PORTION: 5 grams
PREPARATION & CHILLING TIME: 1 hour

1 cup cooked soybeans
⅔ cup cooked red kidney beans
⅔ cup cooked lima beans
salt
freshly ground pepper
grated rind of 1 lemon
1 clove of garlic, peeled and finely chopped
½ cup finely chopped onion
2 teaspoons paprika
1 tablespoon lemon juice
1 tablespoon wine vinegar
½ cup olive or sunflower oil

Mix the cooked beans together in a bowl, season with salt and pepper and sprinkle with the lemon rind and garlic. Pound the onion almost to a pulp with the paprika, then mix in the lemon juice and vinegar. Gradually stir in the oil and pour the finished dressing over the beans. Mix it in thoroughly. Chill the salad well before serving.

Left: chunks of avocado piled on crisp lettuce leaves, dressed with lemon juice. Front: a protein-rich salad of soy, red kidney and navy beans, tossed in a well-flavored Vinaigrette. Right: Tomato and watercress salad is served with a tomato-flavored Mayonnaise and accompanied by hot Herb loaf

Chick pea salad

Serves 4
CALORIES PER PORTION: 255 (1070 kJ)
PROTEIN CONTENT PER PORTION: 9 grams
PREPARATION TIME: 20 minutes

12 large capers
2 tablespoons finely chopped parsley
3 tablespoons olive or sunflower oil
1 tablespoon lemon juice
3 cups cooked chick peas

Pound the capers with the parsley to a smooth paste. Mix this with the oil and lemon juice and pour over the cooked peas. Serve at room temperature, not chilled, as this deadens the flavor.

Rice and lentil salad

Serves 4
CALORIES PER PORTION: 255 (1070 kJ)
PROTEIN CONTENT PER PORTION: 6 grams
PREPARATION TIME: 15 minutes

1½ cups boiled rice
2¼ cups cooked brown lentils
¼ cup finely chopped onion
1 tablespoon wine or cider vinegar
¼ cup olive or sunflower oil
salt
freshly ground pepper
1 cup seeded and chopped tomatoes

Mix together the rice, lentils and onion. Beat together the vinegar and the oil, season well and pour the dressing over the lentils and rice. Scatter the tomatoes on top. Turn the salad over a couple of times to mix the ingredients thoroughly and coat them with dressing, and serve.

Tabbouleh

This is traditionally made with bulgur, but if you find this difficult to obtain, substitute whole wheat. It's a favorite buffet party dish of mine.

Serves 4
CALORIES PER PORTION: 300 (1262 kJ)
PROTEIN CONTENT PER PORTION: 5.5 grams
PREPARATION & COOKING TIME: 1-2 hours

1½ cups bulgur, soaked in cold water for 45 minutes, or cold cooked wheat
3 cups chopped parsley
2 tablespoons chopped mint
2 tablespoons finely chopped scallions
2 tomatoes, chopped to garnish

The dressing
2 tablespoons lemon juice
4-6 tablespoons olive or sunflower oil
salt
freshly ground pepper

Mix together the drained bulgur or cooked wheat, with the chopped parsley, mint and scallions. Make a dressing by beating together the lemon juice and the oil and seasoning it with salt and pepper. Pour this over the bulgur or wheat and cover the bowl with a plate. Holding them both together firmly, shake them up and down and around and around so that the dressing is thoroughly mixed into the salad. Pile the Tabbouleh in a shallow dish, garnish with the chopped tomatoes and serve.

Egg and lettuce salad

Serves 4
CALORIES PER PORTION: 225 (920 kJ)
PROTEIN CONTENT PER PORTION: 7 grams
PREPARATION & COOKING TIME: 1 hour

4 hard-cooked eggs
4-5 tablespoons olive or sunflower oil
1 tablespoon wine or cider vinegar
salt
freshly ground pepper
1 large head Boston lettuce
6 scallions, cut in half lengthwise, then thinly sliced
1-2 teaspoons finely chopped capers (optional)

Cut the eggs into ¼ inch slices. Carefully remove the yolks and rub them through a strainer into a small bowl, or mash them thoroughly with fork, keeping the white rings on one side. Slowly stir the oil into the mashed yolks using a wooden spoon, then add the vinegar and continue stirring until thoroughly combined. Season with salt and pepper.

Mix together the lettuce and scallions and arrange them in a shallow bowl, reserving a few of the greenest scallion slices. Finely chop the 'solid' pieces of egg white from each end of the egg and add them to the egg yolk dressing.

Pour this into the center of the salad, arrange the egg white rings around this and sprinkle on the green scallion slices. Toss just before serving.

I find this salad is pleasantly bland; however, if you would like a more piquant flavor, add 1-2 teaspoons finely chopped capers to the egg yolks.

Potato and walnut salad

Serves 4
CALORIES PER PORTION: 396 (1650 kJ)
PROTEIN CONTENT PER PORTION: 5 grams
PREPARATION & COOKING TIME: 1½ hours, including cooking the potatoes

¼–½ cup olive or sunflower oil
1–2 tablespoons vinegar
salt
freshly ground pepper
1–1¼ lb potatoes — the firmest available, boiled in their skins
1 medium onion, cut into rings
½ cup shelled walnuts, preferably fresh

Beat together the oil, vinegar, salt and pepper. (The exact quantity depends on how much the potatoes absorb.) Peel and thickly slice the potatoes and put them in a shallow dish. Pour boiling water — the water in which you cooked the potatoes will do — over the onion rings and leave them for a few minutes. Drain and rinse them in cold water, then mix them with the potatoes. Shred the walnuts in a nut mill or blender and scatter them over the salad. Stir the dressing again and pour it over the salad. Allow to cool before serving, though this salad loses flavor if it is served chilled.

Corn and red pepper salad

Serves 4
CALORIES PER PORTION: 405 (1705 kJ)
PROTEIN CONTENT PER PORTION: 3 grams
PREPARATION & CHILLING TIME: 1 hour

2 cups cooked corn kernels
1 cup finely chopped red peppers
1 cup cubed fresh or canned pineapple

The mayonnaise
1 egg yolk
⅔ cup olive or sunflower oil
2 tablespoons lemon juice
salt

Mix together the corn, peppers and pineapple. Make a mayonnaise with the egg yolk, oil and lemon juice, following the basic method given on page 126. Stir this into the salad and adjust the seasoning.

Pile the salad on a plate and chill well before serving.

Arabian bread salad

Serves 4
CALORIES PER PORTION: 170 (727 kJ)
PROTEIN CONTENT PER PORTION: 3 grams
PREPARATION & CHILLING TIME: 45 minutes

4 slices of white or wholewheat toast, about ½ inch thick, crusts removed
3 tablespoons lemon juice
¼ cup finely chopped parsley
2 tablespoons finely chopped mint
1 tablespoon chopped coriander leaves
3-4 tablespoons olive or sunflower oil
1 clove of garlic, peeled and very finely chopped
½ lb cucumber, peeled, quartered and cut into ½ inch slices
1 cup chopped and seeded tomatoes
salt
freshly ground pepper

Cut the slices of toast into small cubes and leave them to cool on a wire rack. Mix together the lemon juice, parsley, mint, coriander, oil and garlic and pour this over the cucumber slices in a bowl. Pat the tomatoes dry, or you will find that the toast absorbs their juice and this spoils the flavor of the oil and lemon juice. Add the tomatoes to the salad bowl and mix well, then add the cubes of toast. Mix these in, season the salad with salt and pepper and serve it well chilled.

Red bean salad

Serves 4
CALORIES PER PORTION: 205 (855 kJ)
PROTEIN CONTENT PER PORTION: 15 grams
PREPARATION TIME: 15 minutes

2 cups cooked or canned red kidney beans
½ cup chopped celery
2 pickles, thinly sliced
½ cup seeded and roughly chopped tomatoes
1 small onion, finely chopped
⅔ cup sour cream or Mayonnaise (page 126)
salt
freshly ground pepper
2 tablespoons finely chopped parsley

Combine all the vegetables with the sour cream or mayonnaise and adjust the seasoning. Pile the mixture in a shallow dish and sprinkle the parsley over the top.

Italian green bean salad

Serves 4
CALORIES PER PORTION: 265 (1107 kJ)
PROTEIN CONTENT PER PORTION: 4.5 grams
PREPARATION TIME: 15 minutes

½ onion (preferably Spanish), cut into rings
1 lb green beans, cooked
2 hard-cooked eggs, finely chopped

The dressing
1 tablespoon wine or cider vinegar
1 tablespoon lemon juice
6-8 tablespoons olive or sunflower oil
salt
freshly ground pepper
1 clove of garlic, peeled and finely chopped
½-1 teaspoon finely chopped fresh oregano or winter savory

Mix together the vinegar, lemon juice, oil, salt, pepper, garlic and herbs. Gently mix the onion rings with the beans, pouring over the dressing at the same time. Pile the mixture in a shallow dish and sprinkle the chopped eggs on top.

Note: If you like a milder onion flavor, or Spanish onions are not available, blanch the onion slices lightly by pouring boiling water over them and leaving them to stand for 5 minutes. Drain, refresh them by rinsing them in cold water and pat dry before adding to the salad, or follow the method given in the recipe for Onion ring salad below.

Onion ring salad

Blanched onion rings also make a very good addition to other salads.

Serves 4
CALORIES PER PORTION: 115 (490 kJ)
PROTEIN CONTENT PER PORTION: 1 gram
PREPARATION & COOKING TIME: 15 minutes

1 lb mild-flavored onions, preferably Spanish, cut into rings
½ teaspoon wine vinegar
3 tablespoons olive or sunflower oil
salt
freshly ground pepper
1 tablespoon chopped parsley

Bring a large pan of water to a boil. Fill a bowl with plenty of ice cubes or iced water. Put the onion rings into a blanching basket and lower it into the boiling water. Use a slotted spoon to keep the onion rings below the surface, and the moment the water comes back to a boil, remove the basket and plunge it into the iced water. Shake the basket a little so that all the onions cool immediately, then drain them well on paper towels. If you have a centrifugal salad shaker, use this. Arrange the onions in a shallow dish.

Beat together the vinegar and oil and pour it over the onions. Season with salt and pepper and sprinkle with parsley.

Greek salad

Serves 4
CALORIES PER PORTION: 315 (1330 kJ)
PROTEIN CONTENT PER PORTION: 7 grams
PREPARATION TIME: 20 minutes

1 large head crisp lettuce, preferably romaine, torn into small pieces
12 small pitted black olives, sliced
½ cup finely chopped tomatoes
6 scallions, thinly sliced
1 cup diced green and red peppers
6-8 tablespoons olive or sunflower oil
1 tablespoon wine or cider vinegar
1 tablespoon lemon juice
a little grated lemon rind
1 clove of garlic, peeled and finely chopped
1 tablespoon chopped coriander leaves or parsley
salt
freshly ground pepper
¼ lb Feta cheese, cut into ½ inch cubes

Mix together the lettuce, olives, tomatoes, scallions and peppers in a wide, shallow bowl. Beat together the oil, vinegar, lemon juice and rind, garlic and coriander or parsley, and season with salt and pepper. Pour the dressing over the salad and turn over until the whole salad is evenly coated and glistening. Scatter the cheese over the top and serve.

Caesar salad

Serves 4
CALORIES PER PORTION: 380 (1600 kJ)
PROTEIN CONTENT PER PORTION: 9 grams
PREPARATION & COOKING TIME: 45 minutes

¼ cup olive or sunflower oil
4 slices of wholewheat bread, crusts removed and cut into ½ inch cubes
2 heads crisp lettuce, preferably romaine, torn into small pieces
½ cup freshly grated Parmesan cheese

The dressing
1 egg
¼ cup olive or sunflower oil
1 teaspoon wine vinegar
salt
freshly ground pepper
1 small clove of garlic, peeled and finely chopped
1 teaspoon lemon juice

Heat the oil in a skillet and fry the bread cubes over moderate heat until they are crisp; drain them on paper towels and allow to get completely cold.

Meanwhile, make the dressing by beating together the egg, oil, vinegar, salt and pepper, garlic and lemon juice until well blended, or put in a blender and work until smooth. Put the lettuce into a salad bowl and strain the dressing over; toss it well. Arrange the croûtons of bread in the center and sprinkle the Parmesan around them. Mix them all together at the table.

The vegetarian chef's salad

This popular salad must have been invented by a chef in a hurry, who had to produce something for late arrivals in a restaurant, using only the ingredients on hand. It makes a very good light lunch or supper dish with a bowl of soup and some fresh fruit to follow.

Serves 4
CALORIES PER PORTION: 920 (3855 kJ)
PROTEIN CONTENT PER PORTION: 19.5 grams
PREPARATION & COOKING TIME: 30 minutes

4 eggs
1 tablespoon olive or sunflower oil
salt
freshly ground pepper
1 large head Boston or Bibb lettuce, torn into small pieces
½ cup finely chopped scallions
1 cup watercress leaves
2 cups thinly sliced celery
2 cups thinly sliced Belgian endive
¼ lb cheese, preferably Emmenthal, cut into thin strips
1½ cups Mayonnaise (page 126)
a little light cream

Make an omelet with the eggs and oil, then season it with salt and pepper and leave it to get cold. You can speed up this process by putting it on a cold plate over some ice cubes. Meanwhile, mix the salad greens, celery and endive in a bowl with the cheese.

Cut the cooled omelet into strips about ½ × 3 inches, and add these to the salad, mixing them in well but taking care not to break up the cheese sticks or the omelet more than you can help.

Pour in the mayonnaise, thinned with a little cream, and continue turning the salad, checking the seasoning as you do so. Pile it on a flat plate to serve.

Cole slaw 1

Serves 4
CALORIES PER PORTION: 540 (2275 kJ)
PROTEIN CONTENT PER PORTION: 17 grams
PREPARATION TIME: 20 minutes

3 cups shredded white cabbage
½ cup olive or sunflower oil
2 tablespoons wine or cider vinegar
salt
freshly ground pepper
1 cup coarsely grated Cheddar cheese
1 cup peeled and shredded dessert apple, sprinkled with 2 tablespoons lemon juice
¾ cup sunflower seeds

Put the cabbage into a bowl. Beat together the oil, vinegar, salt and pepper. Sprinkle the cheese over the cabbage with some of the dressing, mixing it in gradually, otherwise the cheese will stick together in lumps. Add the apple, lemon juice and sunflower seeds, then pour in the remainder of the dressing and mix thoroughly. Serve in a shallow bowl.

Cole slaw 2

Serves 4
CALORIES PER PORTION: 492 (2062 kJ)
PROTEIN CONTENT PER PORTION: 12 grams
PREPARATION TIME: 20 minutes

3 cups shredded white cabbage
½ cup olive or sunflower oil
1 tablespoon wine or cider vinegar
1 tablespoon clear honey
salt
freshly ground pepper
1 egg, lightly beaten
1 cup peeled and shredded dessert apple, sprinkled with 2 tablespoons lemon juice
½ cup finely chopped onion
¾ cup unroasted peanuts

Put the cabbage in a bowl. Beat together the oil, vinegar, honey, salt, pepper and the egg. Strain this dressing over the cabbage and add the apple, lemon juice and onion. Work the peanuts in a blender for a few seconds, or put them through a nut mill — or crush them coarsely in a mortar with a pestle. Add them to the salad and mix thoroughly. Serve in a shallow bowl.

Cole slaw 3

Serves 4
CALORIES PER PORTION: 455 (1872 kJ)
PROTEIN CONTENT PER PORTION: 8 grams
PREPARATION TIME: 20 minutes

2 cups shredded white cabbage
2 cups cooked brown lentils
1 cup peeled and shredded dessert apple, sprinkled with 2 tablespoons lemon juice
½ cup olive or sunflower oil
1 tablespoon wine or cider vinegar
1 tablespoon clear honey
1 teaspoon curry powder
1 small clove of garlic, peeled and very finely chopped
salt
freshly ground pepper
1 egg, lightly beaten
½ cup cottage cheese

Put the cabbage in a bowl with the lentils, apple and lemon juice. Beat together the oil, vinegar, honey, curry powder, garlic, salt and pepper and the egg. Stir this slowly into the cottage cheese to make a smooth cream. Pour this dressing over the cabbage, lentils and apple and mix well.

More salad suggestions

Try the following salad mixtures, served with Mayonnaise or a French or Vinaigrette dressing:

Cold cooked macaroni with chopped unroasted peanuts, sliced tomatoes and blanched and chopped onions.
Grated raw carrot, diced red pepper and pineapple cubes.
Thinly sliced cooked zucchini, cooked diced potatoes and thinly sliced or whole radishes.
Large beefsteak tomatoes stuffed with julienne strips of cheese, cooked potatoes and scallions.
Thin slices of cheese interleaved with layers of blanched or raw onion rings and sliced tomatoes.
Cottage cheese with chopped raw or pickled cucumber piled up on a plain cole slaw with a little grated strong cheese and a pinch of cayenne sprinkled over the top.
Grated raw carrot, finely chopped celery, peanuts and a little finely chopped onion on slices of dark rye bread.
Cooked soybeans with chopped onion and grated cheese and covered with sliced raw mushrooms marinated in lemon juice.
Fresh peaches, halved and filled with finely chopped celery and red peppers on a bed of torn lettuce leaves; dress the lettuce with a vinaigrette dressing and the peaches with mayonnaise.
Shredded celery root with diced apples, cucumber and watercress.
Thinly sliced Jerusalem artichokes with sliced tomatoes, celery and chopped parsley.
Diced cooked beets in sour cream flavored with caraway seeds and lemon juice and rind.

Desserts

However successful your dinner party so far, and however well-received the main course, it is the dessert which really gives you the chance to shine. It is the crowning point of the meal and even if your guests pretend not to like puddings or rich, cream-filled cakes, you will be surprised at how many change their minds once your pièce de résistance is on the table.

This is the course where your favorite flavors can come into their own, where fruits can shine, softly whipped syllabubs, luscious filled crêpes and heart-warming sponge cakes can rule the day. Choose something that will complement the main course and remember that a cold pudding can be very refreshing after a hot, spicy main course, even in winter. Whether you serve your cheeseboard before the dessert in the French style, or to round off the meal in the English manner, try to have at least one representative of each of the main cheese 'families'.

A well-balanced cheeseboard should include one of the soft, creamy cheeses – a Bel Paese, Port Salut, a Camembert or Brie; then a blue-veined Dolcelatte, a Roquefort or Stilton and a hard cheese such as a mature Cheddar, a Gruyère, an Edam or Gouda.

Apricot soufflé

Serves 4
CALORIES PER PORTION: 200 (845 kJ)
PROTEIN CONTENT PER PORTION: 9 grams
PREPARATION & COOKING TIME: 1 hour, excluding soaking

½ lb dried apricots, soaked overnight in cold water to cover
1 vanilla bean
3 to 6 tablespoons raw brown sugar, according to taste
3 tablespoons heavy cream
3 egg yolks
a little melted butter
5 egg whites

Drain the apricots, then put them in a pan with the vanilla bean, sugar and enough water just to cover. Bring to a boil, cover the pan, then lower the heat and simmer for 15-20 minutes, until the apricots are soft but not falling apart.

Meanwhile, prepare a 6 inch diameter soufflé dish: cut a strip of doubled wax paper long enough to go around the outside of the dish overlapping by 1-2 inches, and standing 2-3 inches higher than the rim. Tie the paper securely around the outside of the dish.

When the apricots are soft enough to purée, remove the vanilla bean and work the apricots to a smooth purée in a blender, or rub them through a strainer. Stir in the cream and egg yolks and mix well. Preheat the oven to 350°F and put in the prepared soufflé dish to warm.

Remove the soufflé dish from the oven and brush the inside and the inside of the paper collar with melted butter. Beat the egg whites until stiff enough to stand in peaks. Fold the beaten egg whites into the apricot purée and pour it into the prepared soufflé dish. Bake in the preheated oven for about 20 minutes until the soufflé is well risen, but still slightly soft in the center. Carefully remove the paper collar, then serve immediately with cream.

Baked orange soufflé

Serves 4
CALORIES PER PORTION: 300 (1257 kJ)
PROTEIN CONTENT PER PORTION: 10 grams
PREPARATION & COOKING TIME: 35 minutes

1½ tablespoons butter
3 tablespoons all-purpose flour
1¼ cups milk
½ cup sugar
grated rind of 3 oranges
4 eggs, separated
a little melted butter

Melt the butter in a pan over gentle heat and add the flour. Stir until thick, then allow to cook for 1 minute. Take the pan off the heat and gradually stir in the milk. Return the pan to the heat, add the sugar and continue stirring until the sauce thickens. Remove the pan from the heat.

Add the grated orange rind to the sauce and stir well, then allow to cool.

Stir the egg yolks into the sauce. Preheat the oven to 375°F. Tie a paper collar onto the outside of a 6 inch diameter soufflé dish (see previous recipe) and put it in the oven to warm.

Liberally brush the inside of the hot soufflé dish with melted butter. Beat the egg whites until stiff enough to stand in peaks and fold them into the sauce. Pour into the soufflé dish. Bake for 20 minutes, until the soufflé is well risen, and serve immediately.

Chocolate soufflé

Serves 4
CALORIES PER PORTION: 250 (1080 kJ)
PROTEIN CONTENT PER PORTION: 9 grams
PREPARATION & COOKING TIME: 30 minutes

4 squares (4 oz) dark chocolate, broken into small pieces
2 tablespoons brandy
3 tablespoons raw brown sugar
4 egg yolks, well beaten
a little melted butter
6 egg whites

Preheat the oven to 350°F. Put the chocolate pieces in a double boiler with the brandy and sugar. Heat gently until the chocolate has melted, stirring occasionally with a warm spoon — if you do not warm the spoon, the chocolate will set around it. Make a collar of double wax paper long enough to go around the outside of a 6 inch diameter soufflé dish, overlap by 1-2 inches and stand 2-3 inches higher than the rim. Tie the paper securely in place around the outside of the dish and put the dish in the oven to heat through.

Leave the chocolate to cool slightly, then add the egg yolks a little at a time, stirring well after each addition. Remove the soufflé dish from the oven and brush the inside and the inside of the paper collar with melted butter. Beat the egg whites until stiff enough to stand in peaks, then fold them into the chocolate mixture. Pour into the soufflé dish, then bake in the preheated oven for 15-20 minutes until the soufflé is well risen. Carefully remove the paper collar and serve immediately with cream and Almond cookies (page 164).

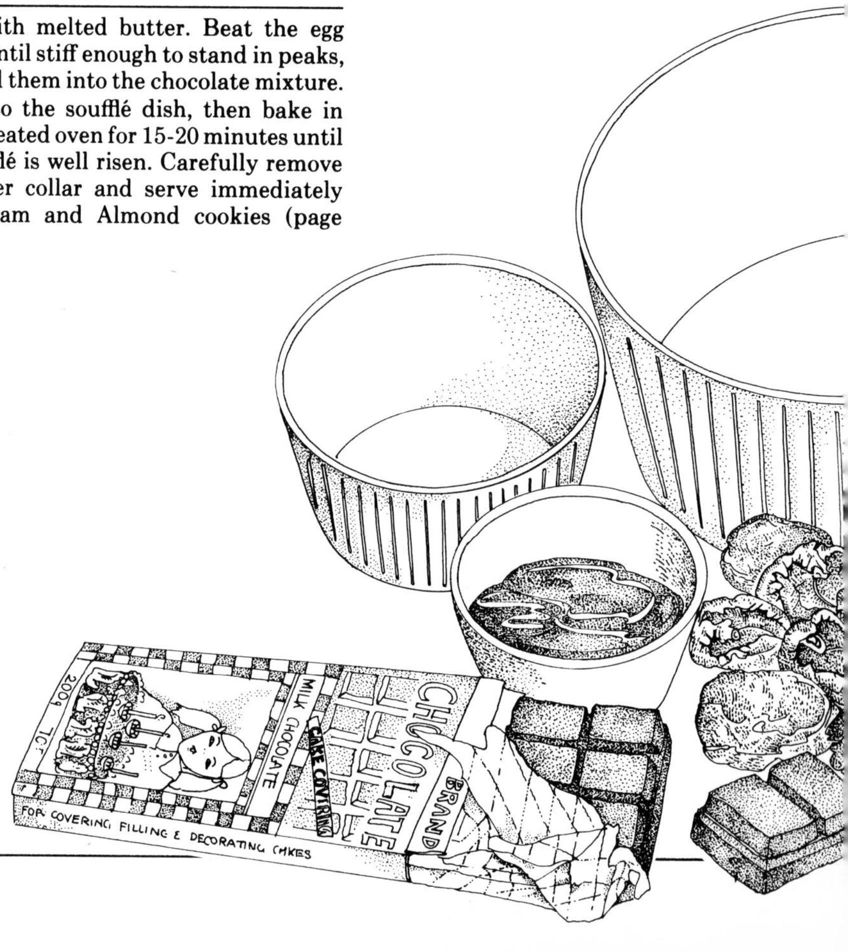

Lemon amber

Serves 4
CALORIES PER PORTION: 185 (780 kJ)
PROTEIN CONTENT PER PORTION: 5 grams
PREPARATION & COOKING TIME: 1 hour (longer if beating by hand)

finely grated rind and juice of 1 large lemon
2 eggs, separated
½ cup sugar
a little melted butter
¼ cup all-purpose flour
⅔ cup milk

Put the lemon rind and juice, egg yolks and sugar in a bowl and beat together until the mixture leaves a ribbon trail across the top when the beater is lifted.

Preheat the oven to 350°F. Butter an 8 inch layer cake pan and set aside. Sift the flour into a bowl and mix with a little of the milk, then gradually stir in the remaining milk.

Beat the egg whites until stiff enough to stand in peaks. Stir the milk mixture into the lemon and egg yolks, then fold in the egg whites. Pour the mixture into the prepared pan, stand the pan in a roasting pan and pour in just enough boiling water to come halfway up the sides of the cake pan. Bake in the preheated oven for 45 minutes and serve hot with cream or a fruit purée.

Almond surprise

This is a very rich dessert, but 4 people will finish it without much effort.

CALORIES PER PORTION: 655 (2950 kJ)
PROTEIN CONTENT PER PORTION: 12 grams
PREPARATION & COOKING TIME: 1 hour (longer if beating by hand)

4 eggs, separated
½ cup sugar
1¼ cups heavy cream
1 cup ground almonds
finely grated rind of 1 orange
large pinch of freshly grated nutmeg
a little melted butter

Prepare a 6 inch diameter soufflé dish: cut a strip of doubled wax paper long enough to go around the outside of the dish, overlap by 1-2 inches and stand 2-3 inches higher than the rim. Tie the paper securely around the outside of the dish.

Beat together the egg yolks and sugar until the mixture leaves a ribbon trail across the top when the beater is lifted. Add the cream and continue beating until thick, then stir in the almonds, orange rind and nutmeg.

Beat the egg whites until stiff enough to stand in peaks, then fold them into the almond mixture. Pour mixture into the well-buttered soufflé dish, stand the dish in a large pan and pour in enough boiling water to come halfway up the side of the dish. Cover and simmer for 45 minutes. Remove the paper collar, and serve hot, with Caramel sauce (page 198).

Crêpes pralinées

Serves 4
CALORIES PER PORTION: 625 (2615 kJ)
PROTEIN CONTENT PER PORTION: 14 grams
PREPARATION & COOKING TIME: 50 minutes

1 cup unblanched almonds
¼ cup granulated sugar
12 thin crêpes made from the Basic mixture (page 82)
6 tablespoons unsalted butter
2 tablespoons dark rum, or to taste

To make the praline: cook the almonds with the sugar in a thick-based pan over moderate heat until the sugar melts and coats the almonds. Stir constantly to prevent it burning. Remove the pan from the heat and pour the praline onto a lightly oiled plate, or a sheet of non-stick parchment paper. Leave until cold and set, then crush finely with a rolling pin, or work to a powder in a blender.

Warm the crêpes between two heatproof plates over a pan of boiling water. Cream the butter in a bowl with a wooden spoon until soft, add the praline and work it in well. Add the rum a few drops at a time, beating well after each addition until the mixture is light and fluffy. Spread a little of the praline mixture on each crêpe, then fold it over to enclose the filling. Arrange the crêpes on a warm serving plate and serve with cream and an apple purée flavored with cinnamon or vanilla.

Crêpes with cottage cheese and raisins

Serves 4
CALORIES PER PORTION: 775 (3255 kJ)
PROTEIN CONTENT PER PORTION: 13 grams
PREPARATION & COOKING TIME: 45 minutes

1 cup strained cottage cheese
1 teaspoon grated lemon rind
¼-½ cup raw brown sugar
2 tablespoons lemon juice
⅓ cup raisins
12 thin crêpes made from the Basic mixture (page 82)
2 tablespoons unsalted butter, melted

Preheat the oven to 400°F. Beat the cottage cheese well, then add the lemon rind and 2-4 tablespoons of the sugar, half the lemon juice and the raisins and mix thoroughly. Divide the mixture between the crêpes, roll them up and arrange the filled crêpes side by side on a well-buttered baking sheet.

Brush each one with melted butter, sprinkle with the remaining lemon juice and sugar and warm in the preheated oven for 10 minutes, until they are really hot and sizzling. Serve with wedges of lemon and a bowl of brown sugar.

As a variation, flavor the sugar with a little ground cinnamon.

Crêpes aux cerises

Serves 4
CALORIES PER PORTION: 715 (2997 kJ)
PROTEIN CONTENT PER PORTION: 14 grams
PREPARATION & COOKING TIME: 45 minutes

12 thin crêpes made from the Basic mixture (page 82) with a few drops of almond extract added
2 cups pitted black cherries, cooked and coarsely chopped
⅓ cup raw brown sugar
¼ cup water
¼ cup Kirsch
1¼ cups heavy cream
¼ cup shredded blanched almonds

Keep the crêpes warm between two heatproof plates over a pan of boiling water. Put the cherries, sugar and water in a pan and heat gently until the sugar has dissolved. Remove from the heat and stir in the Kirsch.

Preheat the oven to 400°F. Put a spoonful of the cherry mixture on each crêpe, then roll them up and arrange side by side in a baking dish. Pour over any remaining cherry juice and half the cream, then sprinkle with the almonds. Bake in the preheated oven for 10 minutes. Serve hot with cream — the remaining cream — lightly whipped.

Note: Cook pitted fresh cherries by simmering them in a little water with sugar to taste — until they are just soft, but not squashy. Canned cherries can also be used.

Lemon meringue pie

Serves 6
CALORIES PER PORTION: 1150 (4815 kJ)
PROTEIN CONTENT PER PORTION: 26 grams
PREPARATION & COOKING TIME: 45 minutes

pre-baked 9 inch pie shell, made with Wholewheat pie pastry (page 194)
2 tablespoons apricot jam, heated and strained
finely grated rind of 2 lemons
1 cup lemon juice
4 eggs, separated
2½ cups sweetened condensed milk
1 cup sugar

Preheat the oven to 300°F. Brush the inside of the pie shell with the warm apricot jam. Put the lemon rind and juice in a bowl with the egg yolks and condensed milk and mix well. Pour this filling into the pie shell.

Beat the egg whites until stiff enough to stand in peaks, then fold in the sugar. Spread this meringue mixture over the top of the lemon filling, making sure that the filling is completely covered. Swirl the meringue mixture into a pattern with a fork.

Bake in the preheated oven for 20-30 minutes or until the meringue is crisp and browned. Allow to cool slightly before serving.

Apricot meringue pie

Serves 4
CALORIES PER PORTION: 500 (2095 kJ)
PROTEIN CONTENT PER PORTION: 9 grams
PREPARATION & COOKING TIME: 1 hour, excluding soaking time

½ lb dried apricots, soaked overnight in cold water to cover
about ⅓ cup raw brown sugar, or to taste
1 vanilla bean
1 cup water
pre-baked 8 inch pie shell, made with Wholewheat pie pastry (page 194)
2 tablespoons apricot jam, heated and strained
2 egg whites
¼ cup granulated sugar

Drain the apricots, then put them in a pan with the brown sugar, vanilla bean and water. Bring to a boil, cover the pan, then lower the heat and simmer for 15-20 minutes, until the apricots are soft but not falling apart. Remove the apricots from the heat, drain off any excess liquid, remove the vanilla bean and leave them to cool slightly. Taste for sweetness and add more brown sugar if necessary.

Preheat the oven to 300°F. Lightly brush the inside of the pie shell — still in its pan — with the warm apricot jam. Arrange the drained apricots in the pie shell. Beat the egg whites until they are stiff enough to stand in peaks, then fold in the granulated sugar. Spread the meringue mixture over the top so that it covers the apricots completely and swirl it into a pattern with a fork.

Bake in the preheated oven for about 30 minutes or until the meringue is crisp and browned. Allow to cool slightly before serving with rum-flavored whipped cream or Chantilly cream (page 198).

A luscious selection of hot puddings and desserts. Top left: Apricot meringue pie with its crispy topping. Top right: steamed Lemon pudding with Raspberry sauce. Below left: thin crêpes filled with black cherries and sprinkled with almonds. Below right: Chinese sugar apples in sesame-flavored syrup

Cheesecake

Serves 4
CALORIES PER PORTION: 695 (2910 kJ)
PROTEIN CONTENT PER PORTION: 14 grams
PREPARATION & COOKING TIME: about 1 hour

1½ cups Wholewheat pie pastry (page 194)
2 tablespoons apricot jam, warmed and strained
½ cup raw brown sugar
2 eggs, separated
1 cup strained cottage cheese
3 tablespoons seedless white raisins
finely grated rind and juice of 1 lemon

Roll out the dough and line a 7 inch diameter pie pan. Brush the bottom with warm apricot jam. Put the sugar and egg yolks in a bowl, then cream together until light. Add the cheese, raisins and lemon rind and juice and beat until well mixed.

Preheat the oven to 350°F. Beat the egg whites until stiff and standing in peaks, then fold these into the cheese mixture. Pour into the pie shell, then bake in the preheated oven for 45 minutes until set. Leave to cool slightly before serving.

Alsatian apple tart

Serves 6
CALORIES PER PORTION: 630 (2620 kJ)
PROTEIN CONTENT PER PORTION: 12 grams
PREPARATION & COOKING TIME: 1 hour

2 lb cooking apples
pre-baked 10 inch pie shell, made with Wholewheat pie pastry (page 194)
2 tablespoons apricot jam, heated and strained
½ cup sugar
½ teaspoon ground cinnamon
½ cup half-and-half
½ teaspoon vanilla extract
2 eggs, well beaten
1 tablespoon raw brown sugar

Preheat the oven to 400°F. Peel and core the apples, then cut them into segments about ½ inch thick. Put these in a pan with boiling water to cover, simmer for 2 minutes, then drain and rinse under cold running water. Pat them dry.

Lightly brush the inside of the pie shell with the warm apricot jam. Arrange the blanched apple segments in overlapping layers in the pie shell, then mix the sugar with the cinnamon and sprinkle this over the apple layers. Bake in the preheated oven for 15-20 minutes, or until the apples are soft when pierced with a skewer.

Mix together the half-and-half, vanilla, eggs and brown sugar and pour this over the apples. Return the tart to the oven and bake for a further 15 minutes until the custard has set. Serve with cream or Custard sauce (page 198).

Chinese sugar apples

These apple fritters are a specialty of Peking cuisine. They can be dipped into syrup at the table and then 'set' in iced water.

Serves 4
CALORIES PER PORTION: 540 (2265 kJ)
PROTEIN CONTENT PER PORTION: 7.5 grams
PREPARATION AND COOKING TIME: 1 hour

¾ lb cooking apples
Coating batter (page 194)
oil for deep frying
⅔ cup sugar
¼ cup sesame oil
2 tablespoons sesame seeds

Peel and core the apples, then cut them into chunks. Put them in a bowl with the batter and stir them to make sure they are well coated.

Heat the oil in a deep-fat fryer to 350°F. Put 6-8 apple chunks into the frying basket and deep fry in the hot oil for 1-2 minutes until golden. Remove from the oil, drain on paper towels and keep hot while frying the remainder.

Melt the sugar in a thick-based pan without letting it brown. Pour in the sesame oil and heat for a moment or two longer. Prepare a bowl of iced water.

Put the apple fritters into the pan a few at a time and turn them over to coat them well in the sugar and oil. Plunge immediately into the iced water with oiled spoons. Sprinkle with sesame seeds and serve immediately.

Spiced beignets

Serves 4
CALORIES PER PORTION: 385 (1615 kJ)
PROTEIN CONTENT PER PORTION: 9 grams
PREPARATION & COOKING TIME: 1 hour

1 cup milk
6 tablespoons unsalted butter
1 cup all-purpose flour
¼ teaspoon ground cinnamon
pinch of salt
1 teaspoon raw brown sugar
2-3 eggs
oil for deep frying
a little confectioners' sugar

Bring the milk to a boil in a pan with the butter. Sift together the flour, cinnamon and salt and stir in the sugar.

When the milk comes to a boil, take the pan off the heat and pour in the flour mixture all at once. Beat vigorously and return the pan to the heat. Continue beating until the mixture comes away from the sides of the pan, then remove the pan from the heat again and leave the mixture to cool slightly before beating in the eggs one at a time until the mixture is firm, smooth and glossy. If the eggs are large, it may not be necessary to add all of the third egg.

Heat the oil in a deep-fat fryer to 350°F. Drop teaspoonfuls of the mixture into the hot oil and deep fry for 1-2 minutes until golden brown. Remove the beignets from the pan with a slotted spoon and drain on paper towels. Keep each batch hot while frying the remainder. If there is any moisture in the oven, the beignets will lose their crispness.

Pile the beignets on a warmed serving plate, sprinkle lightly with confectioners' sugar and serve hot with Honey and orange sauce.

Honey and orange sauce

CALORIES PER PORTION: 115 (490 kJ)
PROTEIN CONTENT PER PORTION: 0.25 grams
PREPARATION & COOKING TIME: 10 minutes

½ cup thick honey
1 cup hot water
2 teaspoons cornstarch
finely grated rind of 2 oranges

Heat together the honey and water in a pan, stirring constantly until the honey has melted. Mix the cornstarch to a paste with a little cold water, then stir in a little of the hot honey mixture and return it to the pan. Bring the sauce to a boil, then simmer until the sauce thickens, stirring constantly. Add the orange rind, pour the sauce into a warmed jug and serve hot.

Note: Omit the cornstarch to make a thin sauce.

Cottage cheese with strawberries and kirsch

Serves 4
CALORIES PER PORTION: 320 (1345 kJ)
PROTEIN CONTENT PER PORTION: 4 grams
PREPARATION & CHILLING TIME: 2½ hours

1 cup strained cottage cheese
2 egg whites
¾ lb strawberries, hulled
4 teaspoons kirsch or lemon juice
sugar, for serving

Work the cheese in a bowl with the back of a wooden spoon until smooth. Beat the egg whites until stiff enough to stand in peaks, then fold these into the cheese. (If the cheese is too firm, first stir in a little egg white.)

Put the mixture in a fine strainer, place it over a bowl, then leave to drain in the refrigerator for 2 hours.

Unmold the cheese onto a serving plate, arrange the strawberries around it and sprinkle with the kirsch or lemon juice. Serve sugar separately.

Compôte of dried fruit

Serves 4
CALORIES PER PORTION: 275 (1160 kJ)
PROTEIN CONTENT PER PORTION: 3.5 grams
PREPARATION & COOKING TIME: 3 hours
SOAKING TIME: overnight

⅔ cup dried apricots
⅔ cup prunes
⅔ cup dried apple rings
2½ cups water
1 vanilla bean
¼ cup halved blanched almonds
⅓ cup currants
a sprig of mint
½ cup raw brown sugar
3 tablespoons thinly sliced candied ginger, in syrup
1 teaspoon rose water
1-2 tablespoons kirsch

Wash the apricots, prunes and apple rings carefully and put them into separate bowls with one-third of the water in each. Leave to soak overnight. The following morning, transfer the fruit and water to separate pans, adding a little more water if necessary; the fruit should just be covered. Put the vanilla bean and almonds with the apricots, the currants with the prunes and the mint with the apples.

Divide the sugar between the fruits and bring each to a boil. Simmer, covered, until the fruit is tender, stirring occasionally. The apricots and prunes should take about 30 minutes and the apple rings about 10 minutes. Add a little more water, if necessary.

Allow to cool and then mix the fruits and their syrups together. Stir in the ginger, rose water and kirsch and chill for 1 hour. Serve with lightly whipped cream.

Jamaican bananas

Serves 4
CALORIES PER PORTION: 720 (2997 kJ)
PROTEIN CONTENT PER PORTION: 1 gram
PREPARATION & COOKING TIME: 10 minutes

4 ripe but firm bananas
2 tablespoons butter
3 tablespoons soft brown sugar
2 large pinches of freshly grated nutmeg
½ cup rum
1¼ cups cranberry sauce

Peel the bananas and cut them in half lengthwise. Fry them gently in the butter in a chafing dish (or flameproof dish which can be taken to the table) until golden brown. Sprinkle on the brown sugar and grated nutmeg and, by gently shaking the pan from side to side and with a spatula, cover the bananas with the sugar and nutmeg. Pour over the rum and light.

Serve, while still flaming, with a little cranberry sauce between the two halves of each banana.

Fruit fool

Serves 4
CALORIES PER PORTION: 410 (1717 kJ)
PROTEIN CONTENT PER PORTION: 11 grams
PREPARATION & CHILLING TIME: 2½ hours (not including preparing the fruit)

½ lb fresh or dried fruit — apples, apricots, gooseberries, peaches, plums or prunes, cooked
1¼ cups thick Custard sauce (page 198)
⅔ cup heavy cream (optional)

Put the fruit in a blender and work to a smooth purée, or work through a food mill or strainer. Mix the purée thoroughly into the Custard sauce. Whip the cream until thick, if using, then fold into the purée. Chill in the refrigerator for about 2 hours, then serve with Langue de chat cookies (page 164).

Orange sherry syllabub

Serves 4
CALORIES PER PORTION: 775 (3238 kJ)
PROTEIN CONTENT PER PORTION: 6 grams
PREPARATION & CHILLING TIME: 1½ hours

2½ cups heavy cream
grated rind of 2 oranges
1-2 tablespoons honey
2 eggs, separated
2 tablespoons lemon juice
½ cup cream sherry

Whip the cream with the orange rind and honey until it holds its shape. Beat the egg yolks until light and foamy, then add the lemon juice and sherry and mix them into the cream. Beat the egg whites until they form soft peaks and fold into the cream. Pour the syllabub into eight tall glasses and serve chilled. Sweet Almond cookies (page 164) go well with this dessert.

Coffee Marquise

Serves 4
CALORIES PER PORTION: 575 (2400 kJ)
PROTEIN CONTENT PER PORTION: 10 grams
PREPARATION & CHILLING TIME: 3-4 hours

2½-3 teaspoons agar-agar
1 pint milk
2 teaspoons instant coffee powder
⅓ cup raw brown sugar
2 egg yolks, well beaten
8 ladyfingers
2 tablespoons sweet sherry

To finish
1¼ cups heavy cream, whipped
2 squares (2 oz) dark chocolate, coarsely grated

Sprinkle the agar-agar over the milk in a pan, leave for 5 minutes, then stir well. Add the coffee powder and sugar, then bring to a boil over moderate heat, stirring constantly to prevent sticking. Lower the heat and simmer for 2 minutes, then remove from the heat and leave to cool slightly.

Beat a little of the hot liquid into the egg yolks, then gradually beat in the remaining liquid. Pour the mixture into an 8 inch layer cake pan, then dip the ladyfingers into the sherry and press them in a layer on top of the mixture, radiating from the center like the spokes of a wheel.

Leave to cool, then chill in the refrigerator for 2-3 hours, or until set. Invert a serving plate over the pan, then unmold the Marquise onto the plate. Spread the cream over the Marquise to mask it completely, then sprinkle with the chocolate. Serve chilled.

Summer pudding

Serves 6
CALORIES PER PORTION: 350 (1472 kJ)
PROTEIN CONTENT PER PORTION: 11 grams
PREPARATION & CHILLING TIME: at least 8 hours, preferably overnight

1 ¼ lb mixed summer fruit — raspberries, hulled strawberries, pitted red or black cherries, red or black currants
⅓ cup honey
8-10 slices of freshly made, but cold, wholewheat bread, about ½ inch thick, crusts removed

Put the washed fruit into a saucepan with the honey and bring it gently to a boil. Poach just until the fruit begins to break up and the juice starts to run.

Cut eight pieces of bread, shaping them into triangles to cover the bottom of a 6 inch diameter soufflé dish. Cut more bread into rectangles to line completely the sides of the dish, spreading over a little of the fruit to hold the bread in place. Then pour in the rest of the fruit, keeping about ½ cup of the juice to one side. Cover the top of the dish with the remaining bread, cut into triangles.

Put either a plate or the rust-proof loose base of a round cake pan which fits inside the soufflé dish on top of the bread and press it down with a heavy weight. Chill overnight or for at least 8 hours. Keep the reserved juice in the refrigerator.

Remove the plate or cake pan base and gently unmold the pudding, taking care that it does not distintegrate. If the slices of bread have been arranged without any gaps between them there should be no problem. Pour the reserved juice over any dry areas. Serve with a light Custard sauce (page 198) or lightly whipped cream.

Caramel oranges

Serves 4
CALORIES PER PORTION: 210 (885 kJ)
PROTEIN CONTENT PER PORTION: 1 gram
PREPARATION & CHILLING TIME: about 4 hours

4 large oranges, preferably seedless
¾ cup granulated sugar
1 cup warm water

Carefully remove the outer skin (zest) of 2 oranges with a sharp knife, then cut this into matchstick strips. Put the strips in a small pan, cover with water and bring to a boil. Boil for 10 minutes to remove any bitterness, then drain and rinse under cold running water.

Remove the peel and pith from all 4 oranges, together with the outer skin from the segments. Discard the seeds, if any. Slice the orange flesh thinly into rounds, then arrange in overlapping circles in a shallow serving bowl.

Put the sugar in a heavy pan and heat very gently until the sugar has melted, stirring constantly and breaking up any lumps with the back of the spoon. Continue cooking until the syrup turns golden brown, stirring all the time.

Pour in about one-quarter of the water and stir vigorously, taking care to cover your hands, as the caramel will spatter. Add the remaining water one-quarter at a time, stirring constantly, then add the strips of orange rind and simmer until transparent.

Remove the orange strips from the syrup with a slotted spoon and sprinkle them over the orange slices in the serving bowl. Pour over the syrup and leave to cool. Chill well, then serve on their own, or with cream.

Left: The best of summer's fruits in an irresistable Summer pudding. Right: Caramel oranges – serve them on their own or with cream. Front and back: Lemon and orange posset is a light, airy dessert

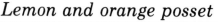

Scottish posset

Serves 4
CALORIES PER PORTION: 848 (3550 kJ)
PROTEIN CONTENT PER PORTION: 7.5 grams
PREPARATION & CHILLING TIME: 1 hour

2 eggs, separated
grated rind and juice of 1 lemon
2 tablespoons honey
¼ cup whiskey
2½ cups heavy cream
¼ cup oatmeal

Beat together the egg yolks, lemon rind and juice, honey and whiskey. Whip the cream until it holds its shape, and beat the egg whites until they are stiff enough to stand in peaks.

Combine the egg yolk mixture with the cream, then fold in the beaten egg whites. Pour into four tall glasses.

Toast the oatmeal in a clean saucepan, shaking it from side to side continuously over a medium heat until it is a good nut-brown color. Allow it to cool, then sprinkle a tablespoon over each glass. Serve chilled.

Lemon and orange posset

The eggs and cream should be well chilled for making this dessert.

Serves 4
CALORIES PER PORTION: 750 (3142 kJ)
PROTEIN CONTENT PER PORTION: 5 grams
PREPARATION & CHILLING TIME: 1 hour

finely grated rind and juice of 2 large lemons
⅔ cup dry white wine
2-3 tablespoons raw brown sugar
finely grated rind of ½ orange
2½ cups heavy cream, chilled
3 egg whites, chilled

Put the lemon juice, half the wine and the sugar in a pan and heat gently until the sugar has dissolved, stirring occasionally. Remove from the heat, stir in the lemon and orange rinds, and remaining wine, then leave until cold.

Whip the cream until thick, then stir in the wine mixture until evenly distributed. Beat the egg whites until stiff enough to stand in peaks, then fold these into the cream mixture.

Divide the mixture equally between four serving glasses, then chill in the refrigerator for about 45 minutes before serving with Langue de chat cookies (page 164).

Zabaglione

If possible, use a hand-held electric beater to make this dessert. The Italians use a balloon whisk, but this requires practice and experience and you will probably have more success with the electric beater at first.

Serves 4
CALORIES PER PORTION: 142 (597 kJ)
PROTEIN CONTENT PER PORTION: 3 grams
PREPARATION & COOKING TIME: 15 minutes

4 egg yolks
¼ cup light brown sugar
¼ cup Marsala wine

Put all the ingredients in a heatproof bowl, then stand the bowl in a shallow pan of gently simmering water. Beat for about 5 minutes until the mixture is thick and foamy, taking care not to allow the mixture to get too hot or it will cook (it should feel hot to the touch, but not hot enough to scald).

Remove the bowl from the pan and continue beating until the mixture cools slightly so that the surface does not set. Serve immediately with ladyfingers or Langue de chat cookies (page 164).

Steamed lemon pudding

Raw brown sugar should not be used in this recipe as it will spoil the color of the finished pudding.

Serves 6
CALORIES PER PORTION: 375 (1571 kJ)
PROTEIN CONTENT PER PORTION: 7.5 grams
PREPARATION & COOKING TIME: 2-2½ hours

1 cup all-purpose flour
2 teaspoons baking powder
pinch of salt
4 cups fresh white breadcrumbs
8 tablespoons butter or margarine
½ cup sugar
2 eggs, beaten
finely grated rind and juice of 1 large lemon
approx ½ cup milk

Sift the flour, baking powder and salt into a bowl, then add the breadcrumbs and mix well.

Cream the butter or margarine with the sugar in a separate bowl until light and fluffy. Add the eggs a little at a time, beating well after each addition, then stir in the lemon rind and juice.

Stir the dry mixture gradually into the creamed mixture, adding enough milk to give a soft dropping consistency. Butter the inside of a 1 quart capacity steaming mold, then pour in the mixture. Cover with a piece of well-buttered wax paper or foil, making a pleat in the center to allow the pudding to rise. Tie securely with string.

Put the mold in a steamer or pan with enough boiling water to come halfway up the sides of the mold and steam or boil for 1½-2 hours, topping up with more boiling water as necessary during steaming. Take the mold carefully out of the pan, then untie and remove the wax paper or foil. Unmold the pudding onto a warmed serving plate and serve hot with plain or Tipsy custard, or a Raspberry sauce (page 199).

Pineapple upside-down cake

Serves 6
CALORIES PER PORTION: 650 (2723 kJ)
PROTEIN CONTENT PER PORTION: 7.5 grams
PREPARATION & COOKING TIME: 1 hour 10 minutes

The filling
12-14 oz canned pineapple chunks, drained
⅔ cup raw brown sugar
½ cup water
4 tablespoons butter or margarine
1 teaspoon ground cinnamon
2 teaspoons cornstarch
finely grated rind and juice of 1 lemon

The topping
¾ cup plus 2 tablespoons wholewheat flour
2 teaspoons baking powder
1 teaspoon ground cinnamon
8 tablespoons butter or margarine
⅔ cup raw brown sugar
2 large eggs, well beaten
2-4 tablespoons milk

To make the filling: put the pineapple in a pan with the sugar, water, butter or margarine and cinnamon. Bring to a boil, stirring until the sugar has dissolved, then lower the heat. Mix the cornstarch to a paste with a little cold water, then pour on some of the syrup, stirring constantly. Add the lemon rind and juice and return to the pan. Simmer until it thickens, stirring all the time, then remove from the heat and keep warm.

To make the topping: mix together the flour, baking powder and cinnamon in a bowl. Cream together the butter or margarine and sugar in a separate bowl until light and fluffy. Add the eggs a little at a time, beating well after each addition. Stir the dry mixture gradually into the creamed mixture, adding just enough milk to give a soft, dropping consistency. Preheat the oven to 400°F. Butter a 9 inch layer cake pan, then arrange the pineapple chunks in a single layer in the bottom of the pan. Pour over enough of the sauce to come halfway up the pineapple, then spread the cake mixture over the top.

Bake in the preheated oven for 30 minutes, then turn out the pudding carefully onto a warmed serving plate. Warm through the remaining sauce and pour it over the pudding. Serve hot with Custard sauce.

Almond castles

Serves 6
CALORIES PER PORTION: 250 (1046 kJ)
PROTEIN CONTENT PER PORTION: 6 grams
PREPARATION & COOKING TIME: 1 hour 10 minutes

1 cup ground almonds
7 tablespoons wholewheat flour
1 teaspoon baking powder
a pinch of salt
4 tablespoons butter or margarine
⅓ cup raw brown sugar
2 eggs, well beaten
1 tablespoon milk
1 tablespoon brandy
6 dates, finely chopped (optional)

Mix the almonds, flour, baking powder and salt in a bowl and set aside.

Cream the butter or margarine with the sugar in a separate bowl until light and fluffy. Add the eggs a little at a time, beating well after each addition.

Stir the dry ingredients gradually into the creamed mixture, adding the milk and brandy to give a soft, dropping consistency. Add the dates, if using.

Butter the insides of six dariole molds, then divide the mixture equally between them, filling them not more than three-quarters full. Cover each mold with a piece of wax paper or foil, making a pleat in the center to allow the pudding to rise. Tie the paper securely with string. Put the molds in a steamer or pan with enough boiling water to come halfway up the sides of the molds and steam for 35 minutes, topping up with more boiling water as necessary during steaming.

Take the molds carefully out of the pan, then untie and remove the wax paper, or take off the foil. Unmold the puddings onto warmed serving plates and serve hot with a Caramel or Custard sauce (page 198).

Bread and butter pudding with rum

This is a sophisticated version of a children's favorite. Use day-old white bread, preferably homemade.

Serves 4
CALORIES PER PORTION: 307 (1287 kJ)
PROTEIN CONTENT PER PORTION: 8 grams
PREPARATION & COOKING TIME: 1 hour 10 minutes

a little melted butter
8 slices of white bread, crusts removed and quartered
2 tablespoons unsalted butter
⅓ cup seedless white raisins
1¼ cups milk
1 vanilla bean or ½ teaspoon vanilla extract
⅓ cup raw brown sugar
finely grated rind of 2 oranges
2 eggs, well beaten with 1 tablespoon dark rum

Brush the inside of a shallow baking dish with a little melted butter. Spread the slices of bread with the unsalted butter and arrange in the dish in overlapping circles, sprinkling the raisins in between the slices.

Preheat the oven to 350°F. Heat the milk gently in a pan with the vanilla bean, if using, then set aside for a few minutes for the flavor to infuse. Remove the vanilla bean, return the pan to the heat, then stir in half the sugar and the orange rind. Continue stirring until all the sugar has dissolved.

Stir in the eggs and rum, and the vanilla extract if using this instead of the vanilla bean, then pour over the bread in the dish. Sprinkle the remaining sugar over the top and bake the pudding in the preheated oven for 40 minutes, or until the custard is set and the top is well browned. Serve hot.

Chocolate nut pudding

Serves 4
CALORIES PER PORTION: 510 (2125 kJ)
PROTEIN CONTENT PER PORTION: 11.5 grams
PREPARATION & COOKING TIME: 2 hours

2 cups fresh white breadcrumbs
7 tablespoons wholewheat flour
½ cup finely ground mixed nuts
2 teaspoons baking powder
¼ teaspoon salt
4 squares (4 oz) semisweet chocolate
4 tablespoons butter or margarine
⅓ cup raw brown sugar
2 eggs, beaten
⅔ cup milk

Put the breadcrumbs, flour, nuts, baking powder and salt in a bowl, then grate in the chocolate. Mix well and set aside.

Cream together the butter or margarine and sugar in a separate bowl until light and fluffy. Add the eggs a little at a time, beating well after each addition.

Stir the dry mixture gradually into the creamed mixture, adding just enough milk to give a soft, dropping consistency. Butter the inside of a 1 quart capacity steaming mold, then pour in the mixture. Cover with a piece of well-buttered wax paper or foil, making a pleat in the center. Tie the paper securely with string.

Put the mold in a steamer or pan half filled with enough boiling water to come halfway up the sides of the mold and steam for 1½ hours, topping up with more boiling water as necessary. Take the mold carefully out of the pan, remove the wax paper or foil and unmold the pudding onto a warmed serving plate. Serve hot with Chocolate sauce (page 199).

College pudding

Serves 6
CALORIES PER PORTION: 500 (2087 kJ)
PROTEIN CONTENT PER PORTION: 9 grams
PREPARATION & COOKING TIME: 1¾ hours

7 tablespoons wholewheat flour
2 cups fresh wholewheat breadcrumbs
1 teaspoon baking powder
⅓ cup currants
⅓ cup seedless white raisins
pinch each of ground cloves, ground allspice, freshly grated nutmeg and cinnamon
8 tablespoons butter or margarine
⅓ cup raw brown sugar
2 eggs, well beaten
3-4 tablespoons milk

Mix together the flour, breadcrumbs, baking powder, fruit and spices in a bowl. Cream together the butter or margarine and sugar in a separate bowl until light and fluffy. Add the eggs a little at a time, beating well after each addition.

Stir the dry mixture gradually into the creamed mixture, adding just enough milk to give a soft, dropping consistency. Butter the inside of a 1 quart capacity steaming mold, then pour in the mixture. Cover with a piece of well-buttered wax paper or foil, making a pleat in the center to allow the pudding to rise. Tie securely with string.

Put the mold in a steamer or pan with enough boiling water to come halfway up the sides of the mold and steam for about 1½ hours, topping up with more boiling water as necessary during steaming. Take the mold carefully out of the pan, then untie and remove the wax paper or foil. Unmold the pudding.

Christmas pudding

This recipe makes two 1-quart puddings.

TOTAL CALORIES: 3480 (14,560 kJ)
TOTAL PROTEIN CONTENT: 69 grams
PREPARATION & COOKING TIME: 10-11 hours

¾ cup plus 2 tablespoons wholewheat flour
1½ teaspoons baking powder
2 cups fresh wholewheat breadcrumbs
¼ cup ground almonds
½ teaspoon salt
¼ teaspoon freshly grated nutmeg
¼ teaspoon ground allspice
¼ teaspoon ground cinnamon
⅔ cup currants
⅔ cup seedless white raisins
⅔ cup raisins
⅔ cup coarsely chopped candied cherries
½ cup halved blanched almonds
8 tablespoons unsalted butter
⅓ cup raw brown sugar
3 eggs, beaten
finely grated rind and juice of 2 oranges
6 tablespoons brandy
1 cup milk

Put all the dry ingredients in a large bowl and mix well. Add the fruit and nuts and stir until evenly distributed. Set aside.

Cream together the butter and sugar in a separate bowl until light and fluffy. Add the eggs a little at a time, beating well after each addition. Stir in the orange rind and juice and ¼ cup of the brandy.

Stir the dry mixture gradually into the creamed mixture, adding enough milk to give a soft, dropping consistency. Liberally butter the insides of two 1-quart capacity steaming molds, then divide the mixture equally between them, pressing it down well. Cover each mold with a piece of well-buttered wax paper or foil, making a pleat in the center to allow the pudding to rise. Tie securely.

Put each mold in a steamer or pan half filled with boiling water and steam for 6 hours, adding more boiling water as necessary during steaming.

Take the molds carefully out of the pans and immediately remove the wax paper or foil. Pour 1 tablespoon of brandy over the top of each pudding, leave until cold, then cover with clean wax paper or foil, pleated as before. Tie securely with string, then store in a cool, dry place until required.

Before serving either of the Christmas puddings, steam for 4 more hours. Remove the mold carefully from the pan, then untie and discard the wax paper or foil. Unmold the pudding onto a warmed serving plate, pour over the remaining warmed brandy and set alight. Serve with brandy butter.

Bavarois with brown sugar meringues

Serves 4
CALORIES PER PORTION: 380 (1602 kJ)
PROTEIN CONTENT PER PORTION: 9 grams
PREPARATION & CHILLING TIME: 3½ hours

2 teaspoons agar-agar
2 tablespoons cold water
1 pint milk
1 tablespoon honey
grated rind of 2-3 oranges
3 egg yolks, well beaten
⅔ cup heavy cream
2 oranges, peeled and sliced (optional)

The meringues
2 egg whites
⅔ cup soft brown sugar

Mix together the agar-agar and water. Bring the milk, honey and orange rind to a boil and pour this onto the agar-agar. Stir well.

Return to the saucepan and boil for 2 minutes. Add the hot milk mixture to the egg yolks, stirring continuously to prevent curdling. Return to the saucepan and heat gently, stirring all the time, until it has formed a thin custard. Strain off the orange rind at this point if you want a very smooth cream. Pour into a 2½ cup capacity mold and leave to cool, then refrigerate for 2 hours.

To make the meringues: preheat the oven to 225°F. Beat the egg whites until they are stiff enough to stand in peaks. Add the sugar gradually while beating and continue to beat until all the sugar is mixed in and the mixture holds its shape. Using a teaspoon, dot walnut-sized pieces of meringue onto a well-buttered baking sheet, or one lined with non-stick parchment paper. Bake in the cool oven for about 2 hours. To test when they are done, remove one from the oven and allow it to cool, then break it in half. It should be crisp when broken.

Whip the cream. Unmold the Bavarois and spread thinly with the whipped cream. Dot meringues over the cream just before serving, and serve with slices of fresh orange, if liked, and the extra meringues. Or sandwich the extra meringues together with orange-flavored whipped cream and serve with coffee.

Make Brown sugar meringues to accompany the Bavarois, or sandwich them with orange-flavored whipped cream and serve with coffee

Mont blanc

Serves 4
CALORIES PER PORTION: 435 (1825 kJ)
PROTEIN CONTENT PER PORTION: 3 grams
PREPARATION & CHILLING TIME: 2 hours

1 lb chestnuts
1¼ cups heavy cream
1-2 tablespoons sugar, according to taste

Put the chestnuts in a pan, cover with water and boil for 30 minutes. Drain, then remove the peel and inner brown skin. Mash the chestnuts, then work in a blender or rub through a strainer. Leave to cool.

Put the chestnut purée in a bowl with half the cream, then beat until thick and light. Beat in sugar to taste. Turn the mixture out onto a serving plate and fork into a pyramid shape. Whip the remaining cream until just thick, then swirl it over the chestnut pyramid. Chill in the refrigerator for 1 hour, then serve with Almond cookies (page 164).

Breads, Cakes and Pastries

How wonderful to be grown up, and no longer subject to the sensible childhood law of 'bread and butter before cakes and cookies'. Even so, there could be something of a dilemma . . . .

If the bread is freshly home-baked, filling the kitchen with the glorious aroma of loaves straight from the oven, and there is a dish of pale, creamy farmhouse butter waiting to be spread over each still-warm slice – who could possibly leave room for cakes and cookies? And if the bread and butter were spread with a delicious, homemade preserve (see the next chapter), then the cakes may go back into their tins for another day.

If bread is the staff of life, cakes and pastries must be the rose in the buttonhole. And you can enjoy them at any time of day – a slice of Madeira or rich fruit cake with a glass of sherry (or Madeira, of course), instead of morning coffee or afternoon tea; sweet wholewheat crackers with your cheeseboard; tiny cream-filled éclairs or palmiers for your special guests – my recipes will suit all tastes. This is an indulgent selection, with as many of my favorite recipes as we had room to include. Choose the ones you will enjoy . . .

Breads, cakes and cookies

Read the recipe right through before you start; preheat the oven to the required temperature and allow enough time for it to reach it before you need to use it. Measure out all the ingredients and arrange them at the back of your work surface in order of use. If you follow this routine you will work much more efficiently and you won't have to go searching for some missing ingredient with your hands covered in dough.

Flour: Most of my recipes specify wholewheat, or graham, flour. If you like a smooth-textured result some of the bran can be removed by putting it through a coarse sifter, or by mixing it with a proportion of all-purpose flour. If the bran is sifted out, don't forget to measure it and make up the quantity with extra sifted flour to the quantity originally specified.

Butter: If butter is to be creamed, bring it to room temperature first and, if it is still too hard, cut it into small pieces and leave it in a bowl in a barely warm oven for a few minutes to soften. Take care that it does not melt or turn oily. Butter for rubbing-in should be cold and hard so that it will not melt with the heat of your hands. If you are inclined to have warm hands, use a pastry cutter or two knives and cut it with these.

Sugar: I have used raw brown sugar in most of the recipes because I like its flavor and value its mineral content. If you do not favor brown sugar, or feel it masks the flavor of any other ingredients, use white granulated sugar instead. The texture of the finished cake or cookie will be different, though.

Dried fruit: Choose good-quality dried fruit.

Pans: When greasing pans, I use clarified butter. I also line the pans with non-stick parchment paper to prevent any chance of the cake sticking; it also helps prevent the cake burning if your oven is inclined to be 'hot'.

Yeast: Yeast is a living vegetable organism which requires moisture and sugar or carbohydrate to grow. The temperature of the milk or water in which it is mixed should be close to body temperature; any hotter and the yeast will be killed. Ensure that the liquid is no hotter than 100°F. If due attention is paid to these requirements, yeast cooking is as easy as any other form of cooking. If you are using active dry yeast, follow the manufacturer's instructions to obtain the equivalent of compressed yeast. Otherwise, I would suggest adding it to the warm liquid with ½ teaspoon of sugar per 1¼ cups of water and leaving it in a warm place until frothy. This can take up to 20 minutes.

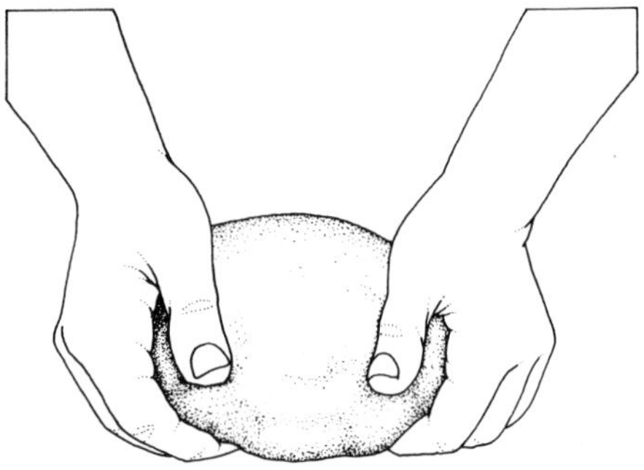

1. Roll the bread dough into a ball in the bowl and turn out onto a lightly-floured surface.

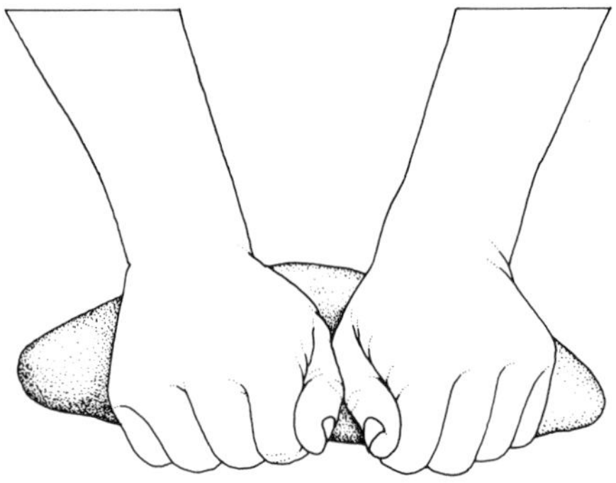

2. Working away from you, and always in the same direction, flatten the dough with the palms of your hands.

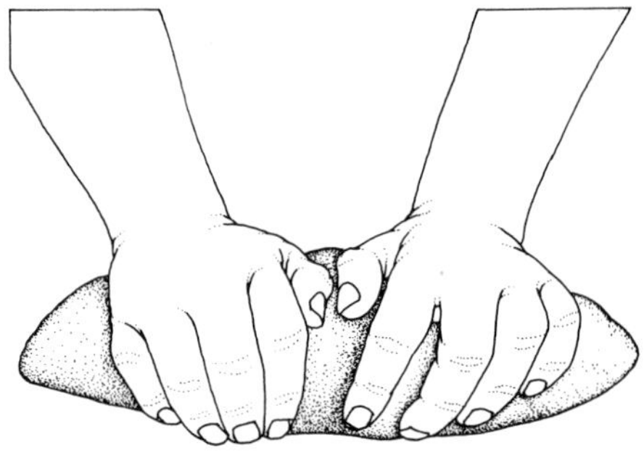

3. Using the 'heels' of your hands, push out the dough to form a long sausage shape.

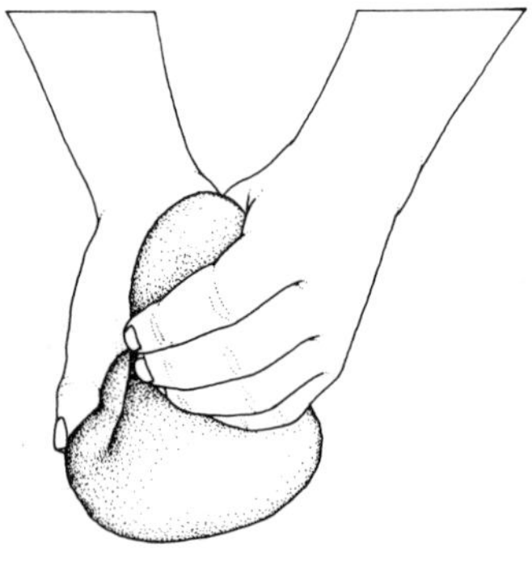

4. Roll up the dough, overlapping it in three layers, to make a ball again. Turn the dough ball sideways.

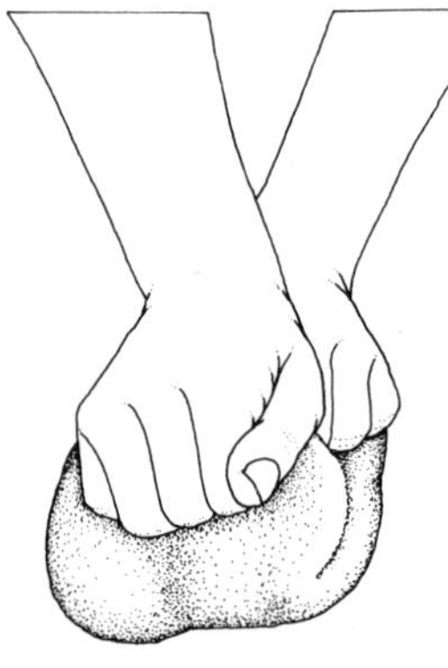

5. Flatten the ball and push it out again in front of you. This will stretch the dough again in a different direction.

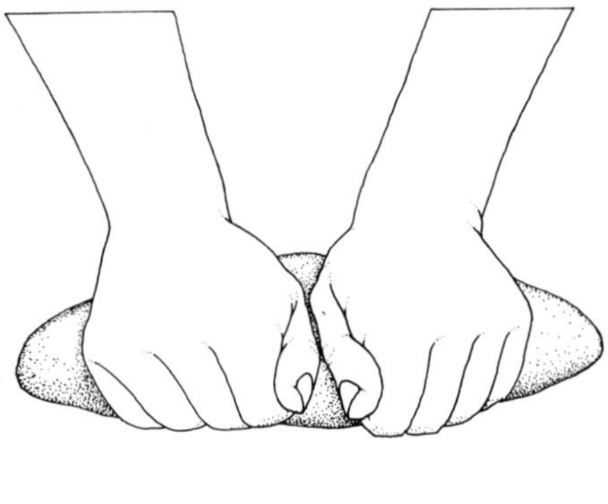

6. Continue pushing out, folding and turning, with a rhythmic rocking action, until the dough is elastic.

Basic quick bread

Makes 2 loaves

CALORIES PER LOAF: 1762 (7375 kJ)
PROTEIN CONTENT PER LOAF: 78 grams
PREPARATION & COOKING TIME, INCLUDING RISING: 1½-2 hours

1 tablespoon soft brown sugar
3 cakes compressed yeast (follow manufacturer's instructions for active dry yeast)
2½ cups lukewarm water
8 cups wholewheat flour, or half wholewheat and half all-purpose or bread flour
2 teaspoons salt
½ cup dried skimmed milk (optional)
1 tablespoon honey (optional)

Add the brown sugar and dry yeast to the warm water and mix well; compressed yeast should be first mixed into a paste with the brown sugar and a little of the water and then added to the rest of the warm water. Leave in a warm place for about 15 minutes until the liquid is frothy. Sift the flour and salt together into a bowl, keeping the bran for dusting the baking pans and the tops of the loaves. Add the dried skimmed milk and honey (if used) to the yeast liquid and stir until dissolved. (The honey helps to keep the bread moist.) Pour the liquid into the flour and mix well with a spoon to a fairly firm dough, adding extra water if necessary.

Turn the dough out onto a floured board and knead with floured hands for 3-5 minutes, or until the dough becomes elastic. Divide the dough in half and place each half in a 4½ × 2½ × 1½ inch loaf pan. The pans should be well-buttered and dusted with some of the bran from the flour. Press the dough well down into the corners — it should come about halfway up the pan. Brush the top of the dough with a little milk and sprinkle over the remaining bran.

Cover the pans with a sheet of foil or wax paper and leave in a warm place until the dough has doubled in size. The time this takes will vary, depending on the temperature of the room and the quality of the yeast.

Preheat the oven to 400°F. Place the loaves in the preheated oven, and bake for 10 minutes, then reduce the temperature to 350°F and continue baking for 20-30 minutes, or until the loaves sound hollow when taken out of their pans and tapped. The loaves can be turned upside down for the last few minutes if the undersides are not quite done. Allow to cool on a cake rack.

Rye bread

CALORIES PER LOAF: 1715 (7165 kJ)
PROTEIN CONTENT PER LOAF: 66 grams
PREPARATION & COOKING TIME, INCLUDING RISING: 2 hours

Use 4½ cups wholewheat flour, or all-purpose or bread flour, and 3¾ cups finely ground rye flour; if coarsely-ground rye flour is used it may be necessary to reduce the liquid or add more flour to get a firm dough. Add ¼ teaspoon caraway seeds if liked. Rye flour dough needs longer kneading and should be put into the oven when it reaches the top of the pans, i.e. a little before it has doubled in size. Follow the recipe for Basic quick bread.

Soda bread

Makes 1 loaf

CALORIES: 1795 (7500 kJ)
PROTEIN: 69 grams
PREPARATION & COOKING TIME: 40 minutes

3½ cups wholewheat flour
2 teaspoons baking soda
2 teaspoons cream of tartar
1 teaspoon salt
2 tablespoons butter
1 tablespoon honey
1¼ cups buttermilk

Sift the flour, soda, cream of tartar and salt together, keeping the bran left in the sifter to one side. Melt the butter and honey in a pan over gentle heat, then remove the pan from the stove and stir in the cold buttermilk. Pour this into the flour and mix to a soft dough, adding a little water if necessary. Preheat the oven to 400°F.

Turn the dough onto a floured board and shape into a round 9 inches in diameter. Mark the loaf into four triangular sections with the back of a knife and sprinkle the bran over the top. Place on a well-floured baking sheet and bake in the preheated oven for 30 minutes. Serve warm or cold.

Soy and wholewheat bread

CALORIES PER LOAF: 1750 (7320 kJ)
PROTEIN CONTENT PER LOAF: 98 grams
PREPARATION & COOKING TIME, INCLUDING RISING: 1½-2 hours

Use 2 cups soy flour and 5¼ cups of wholewheat flour; a little more liquid might also be required. Follow the recipe for Basic quick bread.

Sourdough rye bread

CALORIES: 3425 (14330 kJ)
PROTEIN CONTENT: 132 grams
PREPARATION & COOKING TIME: overnight plus 1 hour

4½ cups wholewheat flour, or sifted all-purpose or bread flour
3¾ cups finely ground rye flour
2½ cups lukewarm water
3 cakes compressed yeast (follow manufacturer's instructions for active dry yeast)
1 tablespoon soft brown sugar
½ cup dried skimmed milk
1 tablespoon honey (optional)
2 teaspoons salt

Mix the flours in a bowl, divide in half and set aside one half. Mix the other into a soft dough with a little more than half the water and cover the bowl. Leave in a warm place overnight, or up to 24 hours if a more sour dough is wanted.

Cream the yeast with the sugar, stir in the rest of the water and leave until it is frothy, about 15-20 minutes. Add the dried skimmed milk and honey, if used, and stir until dissolved. Add the salt to the remaining flour and pour in the yeast solution; stir until the liquid has been absorbed and then add the sour dough. Turn out onto a lightly floured board, and knead the two doughs together with well-floured hands, mixing them thoroughly until they are smooth and elastic. Follow the recipe for Basic quick bread.

Croissants

Makes 12 croissants

CALORIES: 2875 (12030 kJ)
PROTEIN CONTENT: 61 grams
PREPARATION & COOKING TIME (INCLUDING RISING AND RESTING): 4 hours

1 ¼ cakes compressed yeast (follow manufacturer's instructions for active dry yeast)
1 teaspoon soft brown sugar
1 ¼ cups lukewarm water
4 cups all-purpose or bread flour
2 teaspoons salt
10 tablespoons butter
2 eggs, lightly beaten
1 tablespoon water

Add the yeast and sugar to the warm water and leave in a warm place until frothy; this will take 15-20 minutes. Sift the flour and salt into a bowl and, using a pastry cutter or 2 knives, cut 2 tablespoons of the butter into the flour so that the mixture resembles coarse breadcrumbs.

Add one lightly beaten egg to the yeast liquid and pour it into the flour. Stir with a wooden spoon until most of the flour is mixed in.

Turn out onto a well-floured board and knead for about 5 minutes, or until the dough is completely smooth and elastic. Add a little more water or flour if necessary to make a firm dough. Roll out to a rectangle, 16 × 10 inches. Dust with flour and fold into three; wrap in wax paper or foil and put into the freezer for 10 minutes.

Dust the remaining butter with flour and cut it into three equal pieces; *dust again with flour and cut the first butter portion into 16 even-sized cubes. Take the dough out of the freezer and unfold it — if necessary pressing it out to its original size. Place the cubes of butter, evenly spaced, over two-thirds of the rectangle, leaving a ½ inch border around the edges without butter.

Fold the unbuttered section over one-third of the length of the dough, then fold the double sections over the remaining buttered portion and seal the open edges with a slight pressure of the rolling pin. Turn the dough 90° and flatten it out with the hands or by making a series of presses with the rolling pin. Then roll out to the original measurements.** Repeat from * to ** with the two remaining portions of butter.

Fold the dough in three and wrap in wax paper or foil. Return to the freezer for 30 minutes. Remove from the freezer, remove the paper or foil and roll the dough to the same rectangular shape as before. Then turn the dough 90° again and roll out to a rectangle 18 × 12 inches. Dust with flour, fold in three, wrap in wax paper and return to the freezer for a further 30 minutes. (This makes a total of five rollings.)

Remove the dough from the refrigerator, unfold it and mark it into six equal squares [each 6 inches square]. Cut each one into two triangles and brush lightly with some of the remaining eggs, well beaten with the tablespoon of water.

Roll each triangle up, starting from the base, and place on a baking sheet with the apex of the triangle underneath. Gently ease the dough into crescents, leaving plenty of room between them to allow for rising. Leave them at room temperature for 45 minutes to rise, then brush with a little more beaten egg. Bake in a preheated 425°F oven for 15-20 minutes. Serve warm.

Corn bread muffins

Makes 12 muffins

CALORIES: 835 (3490 kJ)
PROTEIN CONTENT: 30 grams
PREPARATION & COOKING TIME: 30 minutes

1 cup plus 3 tablespoons corn meal
1 teaspoon baking powder
½ teaspoon baking soda
½ teaspoon salt
1 cup milk
1 egg, well beaten

Preheat the oven to 400°F. Mix the dry ingredients together and pour in the milk. Add the egg, mix thoroughly, and pour into 12 patty pans brushed with melted butter or margarine. Bake in the preheated oven for 15-20 minutes until well risen and golden brown.

Serve immediately. Muffins make a very good accompaniment to fried eggs, sausages and bacon for a hearty breakfast or brunch.

In the basket: a fine selection of stone-ground wholewheat loaves and rolls. Left: brown Poppy seed braid. Right: this Fruit and honey loaf is delicious toasted and Front: wholewheat flour can also be used for making Croissants

Poppy seed braid

Makes 1 loaf

CALORIES: 2230 (9330 kJ)
PROTEIN CONTENT: 76 grams
PREPARATION & COOKING TIME: 2 hours

¾ cake compressed yeast
1 teaspoon raw brown sugar
1¼ cups lukewarm milk
3½ cups wholewheat flour
½ teaspoon salt
4 tablespoons butter, softened
1 tablespoon poppy seeds

The glaze
2 tablespoons raw brown sugar
1 tablespoon milk

Cream the yeast with the sugar and pour on half the milk. Leave for 15-20 minutes until frothy. Sift the flour with the salt and pour in the yeast mixture. Add enough milk to make a soft dough, then add the softened butter. Knead until the dough is smooth and elastic. Place in a bowl lightly brushed with melted butter, cover and leave in a warm place until the dough has doubled in size. Take it out and knead it for a few moments, then divide it into three. Roll each portion into a 'sausage' about 12 inches long and braid them together. Carefully place on a baking sheet brushed with melted butter, with the ends tucked underneath, and leave in a warm place to rise (about 1 hour).

Meanwhile, make the sugar glaze by dissolving the sugar in the milk over moderate heat. Preheat the oven to 400°F. When the loaf is ready for baking, lightly brush the top with glaze and sprinkle with poppy seeds. Bake in the preheated oven for 15-20 minutes, or until the braid is well risen and sounds hollow when the base is tapped with the knuckles.

French bread and rolls

Makes 1 loaf or 18 rolls

CALORIES: 1995 (8340 kJ)
PROTEIN CONTENT: 52 grams
PREPARATION & COOKING TIME (INCLUDING RISING AND RESTING): 4½ hours

⅔ cup lukewarm milk
¾ cup lukewarm water
1 teaspoon soft brown sugar
1 cake compressed yeast (follow manufacturer's instructions for active dry yeast)
4 cups all-purpose or bread flour
1 teaspoon salt
3 tablespoons butter, melted

Mix together the milk, water, sugar and yeast and leave in a warm place for about 15 minutes, or until frothy. Add this to the sifted flour and salt and stir until most of the flour is mixed in. Turn out onto a floured board and knead, with floured hands, for 10 minutes to a soft dough. Add more liquid, if necessary.

Pour a tablespoon of melted butter into a warm bowl and put the dough into it, turning it to coat it all over with the butter. Cover and leave in a warm place for 1 hour or until it has doubled in size.

Turn the dough out of the bowl and knead on a floured board for another 3 minutes. Pour another tablespoon of melted butter into the bowl and leave the dough in it, after turning it over, for a further hour or until it has once again doubled in bulk. Knead again for 3 minutes.

Shape the dough into a long sausage and, unless you have a special French loaf pan, place it on a well-buttered baking sheet and leave in a warm place until well risen (about 2 hours). Bake for 20 minutes in a preheated 425°F oven. I make a foil trough, with a flat base and walls of rolled-up foil, brush it liberally with melted butter and put the sausage-shaped dough in it; this gives the final loaf a better shape. Glaze the top with the remaining butter during the last 5 minutes of cooking; it may also be necessary to increase the temperature in order to get an attractive brown top.

Alternatively, shape the dough into 18 rolls. Put them on a well-buttered baking sheet and leave them to rise in a warm place for 1½-2 hours, or until they have doubled in size. Bake in a preheated 425°F oven for 15-20 minutes.

Cheese and herb bread and rolls

CALORIES: 2300 (9600 kJ)
PROTEIN CONTENT: 72 grams
PREPARATION & COOKING TIME: 4½ hours

Add ¾ cup finely grated dry cheese and ½ teaspoon dried mixed herbs to the flour and salt and follow the recipe above.

Pita

Makes 8 small or 4 large pita

CALORIES: 850 (3560 kJ)
PROTEIN CONTENT: 31 grams
PREPARATION & COOKING TIME: 2-2½ hours

1¾ cups wholewheat flour
½ teaspoon salt
½ cake compressed yeast (follow manufacturer's instructions for active dry yeast)
½ teaspoon raw brown sugar
⅔ cup warm water
1 tablespoon olive oil

Sift the flour and salt into a bowl. Cream the yeast with the sugar, pour on the water and leave in a warm place for about 20 minutes until frothy. When the yeast mixture is ready, add to the flour and mix to a soft dough. Turn onto a lightly floured surface and knead until the dough is elastic and completely smooth. Pour the olive oil into a warm bowl and turn the dough in it until it is coated all over. Cover and leave in a warm place for about 40 minutes or until it has doubled in size. Punch down the dough on a lightly floured surface and knead until the oil is mixed in.

Preheat the oven to 400°F. Divide into eight equal portions for small pita or four for large ones and roll each portion into an oval shape about ¼ inch thick. Place on greased baking sheets and bake in the preheated oven for 7-10 minutes until they are well risen and just about to color. Remove them from the baking sheet and cool on a cake rack.

Serve warm as an accompaniment to eggplant and olive mousse, Greek salad or Vegetable kabobs, or slit them open at one end, cut through the dough to make a sort of pouch and fill with a vegetable curry.

Wholewheat biscuits

Makes about 6 biscuits

CALORIES: 1305 (5460 kJ)
PROTEIN CONTENT: 45 grams
PREPARATION & COOKING TIME: 30 minutes

1¾ cups wholewheat flour
½ teaspoon salt
1 teaspoon baking powder
4 tablespoons butter
1 egg, well beaten
⅔ cup milk
beaten egg for glazing (optional)

Sift the flour, salt and baking powder into a bowl and rub in the butter until the mixture resembles fine breadcrumbs. Add the egg and two-thirds of the milk and mix to a soft dough, adding more milk if necessary.

Preheat the oven to 400°F. Turn out onto a lightly floured surface and knead very lightly until smooth. Roll out to about 1 inch thick and cut into rounds or triangles. Place on a floured baking sheet and bake in the preheated oven for about 10-15 minutes until well risen and browned. Glaze the tops if desired with a little beaten egg before putting the biscuits into the oven.

Fruit biscuits: Mix 1 tablespoon of raw brown sugar with the flour and add ⅓ cup currants, raisins or chopped dates after the butter has been rubbed in.

Cheese biscuits: Add 2 tablespoons of dry grated Cheddar cheese to the rubbed-in mixtures and a pinch of cayenne, if desired.

Fruit and honey loaf

Makes 1 loaf
CALORIES: 2190 (9160 kJ)
PROTEIN CONTENT: 62 grams
PREPARATION & COOKING TIME: 2 hours

1 cake compressed yeast (follow manufacturer's instructions for active dry yeast)
3 tablespoons raw brown sugar
⅔ cup lukewarm milk
2¾ cups wholewheat flour
½ teaspoon salt
4 tablespoons butter
2 tablespoons honey
1 egg, well beaten
⅓ cup currants
⅓ cup seedless white raisins

Cream the yeast with 1 teaspoon of the sugar, stir in the milk and leave in a warm place for about 20 minutes until frothy. Meanwhile, sift the flour and salt into a bowl and rub in the butter. When the yeast mixture is ready, stir in the honey, the egg and the remaining sugar. Pour into the flour and mix thoroughly.

Turn out onto a lightly floured board and knead with well-floured hands until the dough is smooth, adding the fruit as you do so; the dough should be fairly soft and almost sticky. Put the dough into a greased 9 × 5 × 3 inch loaf pan and leave to rise in a warm place for about 45 minutes, or until it has doubled in bulk. Preheat the oven to 400°F.

Bake the loaf in the preheated oven for 15 minutes, then reduce the heat to 350°F and continue baking for a further 20 minutes. Allow to cool slightly in the pan, then place the loaf on a cake rack to continue cooling.

Fruit and honey loaf is particularly delicious toasted.

Bagels

Makes about 8 bagels

CALORIES: 1225 (5130 kJ)
PROTEIN CONTENT: 42 grams
PREPARATION & COOKING TIME: 2½ hours

1¾ cups wholewheat flour
½ teaspoon salt
¾ cake compressed yeast (follow manufacturer's instructions for active dry yeast)
1½ tablespoons raw brown sugar
½ cup lukewarm milk
1 egg, well beaten
3 tablespoons butter, melted

Sift the flour and salt into a bowl. Cream the yeast with the sugar, then add three-quarters of the milk and leave in a warm place for about 20 minutes until frothy. When the yeast solution is ready, add the beaten egg and melted butter. Pour this into the flour and mix to a fairly soft dough, adding the rest of the milk, if necessary.

Turn the dough onto a lightly floured surface and knead until smooth. Put it into a warm, buttered bowl and leave in a warm place until the dough has doubled in size. Punch down the dough and knead it for a few minutes.

Take pieces of dough about the size of a golf ball and form into thin rolls about 5 inches long by ½ inch in diameter. Form them into circles and pinch the ends together. Lay them on a well-floured baking sheet or board, cover with a floured cloth and leave in a warm place for 30 minutes until they have risen a little. Preheat the oven to 400°F. Lift the bagels gently and drop them one at a time into gently simmering water. Cook until they float to the surface.

Remove from the pan with a slotted spoon and lay on a well-oiled baking sheet. Bake in the preheated oven for 20-30 minutes until the bagels are golden brown and crisp.

Popovers

Makes 4 or 6
CALORIES: 1490 (6230 kJ)
PROTEIN CONTENT: 70 grams
PREPARATION & COOKING TIME: 45 minutes

1¾ cups wholewheat flour
½ teaspoon salt
4 eggs, well beaten
1 pint milk
2 tablespoons butter, melted

Preheat the oven to 400°F. Sift the flour and salt into a bowl. Mix the eggs with the milk and melted butter, pour into the flour and beat until the mixture is thick, creamy and completely smooth. Half-fill well-oiled patty pans with the mixture and bake in the preheated oven for 20-30 minutes, or until they are well risen and golden brown.

When cooked, the centers will be hollow. They are delicious filled with a vegetable ragoût or lightly cooked chopped vegetables in a cheese sauce, and served hot.

Madeira cake

Serves 8
CALORIES: 2750 (11510 kJ)
PROTEIN CONTENT: 54 grams
PREPARATION & COOKING TIME: 1½ hours

10 tablespoons butter or margarine
⅔ cup raw brown sugar
1 teaspoon finely grated lemon rind
3 eggs
1¾ cups wholewheat flour
½ teaspoon salt
1½ teaspoons baking powder
a little milk
2 inch piece of candied peel, cut into thin slices

Line a 9 × 5 × 3 inch loaf pan with non-stick parchment or wax paper. Brush this with a little melted butter or margarine. Cream the butter or margarine with the sugar and lemon rind until light and fluffy. Add the eggs one at a time, beating the mixture well after each addition.

Preheat the oven to 350°F. Sift the flour with the salt and baking powder, using a sifter which only removes the coarser bran. Fold the sifted flour into the creamed mixture, adding a little milk, if necessary, to make a soft dropping consistency. Transfer the mixture to the prepared pan and bake in the preheated oven for 20 minutes. Take out the pan, lay the slices of peel down the center to decorate, and continue baking for a further 40 minutes, until the cake is well-risen, golden brown and firm. Test it by inserting a toothpick or skewer into the center; it should be clean when it is removed.

Remove the pan from the oven, allow to cool for 5 minutes, then unmold the cake onto a cake rack. Carefully remove the paper and leave the cake to cool completely.

Layer cake

Serves 8
TOTAL CALORIES: 2890 (12100 kJ)
PROTEIN CONTENT: 45 grams
PREPARATION & COOKING TIME: 55 minutes

1½ cups plus 2 tablespoons wholewheat flour
1½ teaspoons baking powder
½ teaspoon salt
12 tablespoons butter or margarine
⅔ cup raw brown sugar
3 eggs, well beaten
½ teaspoon vanilla extract
a little milk
3-4 tablespoons homemade jam, or Brown sugar butter cream (page 199)
a little confectioners sugar

Brush the insides of two 8 inch diameter layer cake pans with melted butter or margarine. Sift together the flour, baking powder and salt. Cream together the butter or margarine and sugar until light and fluffy, then gradually add the eggs, beating well after each addition.

Preheat the oven to 350°F. Add the vanilla to the creamed mixture, then fold in the sifted ingredients, adding a little milk, if necessary, to make a soft, dropping consistency. Divide the mixture equally between the two prepared pans and level the surfaces.

Bake the cakes in the preheated oven for 25-30 minutes until they are well risen and just beginning to shrink away from the edges. Unmold onto a cake rack to cool. Sandwich the two layers together with jam or Brown sugar butter cream and sprinkle the tops with confectioners sugar, or fill with flavored Butter cream.

Variations: for a coffee-flavored cake, use light brown sugar and sift instant coffee powder into the dry ingredients, then follow the method for Layer cake. Fill with coffee or chocolate-flavored butter cream and spread the top with chocolate glacé icing.

For a chocolate version, use light brown sugar and sift cocoa powder into the dry ingredients. Sandwich with Raspberry jam and top with Peanut butter icing.

Cherry cake

Serves 8
CALORIES: 3115 (13020 kJ)
PROTEIN CONTENT: 55 grams
PREPARATION & COOKING TIME: 1½ hours

Follow the basic recipe for Madeira cake, but replace the lemon rind with ½ teaspoon vanilla extract and omit peel.

Dust 1 cup candied cherries with some of the flour mixture, stir them in with the the flour, bake as Madeira cake.

Cut-and-come-again cake

Serves 8
CALORIES: 2690 (11260 kJ)
PROTEIN CONTENT: 59 grams
PREPARATION AND COOKING TIME: 2¼ hours

1¾ cups wholewheat flour
3 tablespoons baking powder
1 teaspoon ground allspice
1 teaspoon salt
8 tablespoons butter or margarine
½ cup ground almonds
⅓ cup currants
⅓ cup seedless white raisins
3 tablespoons honey
⅔ cup milk
2 eggs, well beaten

Preheat the oven to 325°F. Brush a 6 inch round deep cake pan with a little melted butter or margarine and cut a round of wax paper or non-stick parchment paper to line the bottom. Brush this, too, with a little melted butter or margarine.

Mix together the flour, baking powder, allspice and salt in a bowl and rub in the butter or margarine until the mixture looks like fine breadcrumbs. Stir in the ground almonds and dried fruit. Warm the honey over gentle heat until melted, remove the pan from the heat and stir in the milk and eggs. Pour this into the dry ingredients in the bowl and mix thoroughly.

Spoon the mixture into the prepared cake pan and bake in the preheated oven for about 1¾ hours until well risen and firm — a toothpick or skewer inserted into the center should come out clean. Leave the cake in the pan for about 10 minutes, then unmold onto a cake rack to cool.

Cut into two layers when cool and sandwich together with Almond paste (page 199). For a special occasion, the top can be covered with a frosting.

Genoese sponge cake

Serves 8
CALORIES: 1150 (4810 kJ)
PROTEIN CONTENT: 31 grams
PREPARATION & COOKING TIME: 50-60 minutes

3 eggs
½ cup raw brown sugar
½ teaspoon vanilla extract
4 tablespoons butter/margarine, melted
10 tablespoons wholewheat flour

Preheat the oven to 350°F. Lightly brush the inside of a 7 inch square deep cake pan with melted butter or margarine. Line the bottom with a square of wax paper or non-stick parchment paper and lightly brush this, too, with butter or margarine.

Beat the eggs and sugar in a bowl until thick and mousse-like and the beater leaves a trail on top of the mixture when lifted. Add the vanilla to the melted butter or margarine, then pour it onto the eggs while still beating. Sift the flour into the mixture with a sifter that removes the coarser bran and fold it in gently.

Pour into the prepared cake pan and bake in the preheated oven for 30 minutes, or until the cake is firm when lightly pressed with the fingertips. Carefully unmold the cake onto a cake rack, peel off the paper and leave to cool. Dust with confectioners sugar before serving.

Variations: Make double the quantity, bake in two 7-inch diameter layer cake pans and sandwich the cooled cakes together with jam and whipped cream. Cover the top and side with Brown sugar frosting (page 199) or plain or flavored Glacé icing.

For Coffee Genoese cake, flavor the basic mixture by adding instant coffee powder to the eggs and sugar while beating, and cover the finished cake with coffee flavored Brown sugar frosting or Glacé icing. Use light brown sugar if you find the darkest raw brown sugar masks the coffee flavor.

Try making double the quantity of Genoese cake, adding cocoa powder to the eggs and sugar, sandwiching the finished cakes with chocolate-flavored butter cream and topping with chocolate icing or frosting.

Behind left: a rich-tasting, fruit-filled Cut-and-come-again cake, sandwiched with Almond paste. Behind right: this Cherry cake will soon become a family favorite. Right: crisp, satisfying wholewheat pastry makes a special Apple pie and Front: homemade Black cherry jam fills this Wholewheat sponge cake

Old-fashioned sponge cake ring

Serves 8
CALORIES: 1795 (7520 kj)
PROTEIN CONTENT: 61 grams
PREPARATION AND COOKING TIME: 1½ hours

6 eggs, separated
1 cup plus 3 tablespoons raw brown sugar
1 cup plus 2 tablespoons wholewheat flour
1 teaspoon baking powder
½ teaspoon salt
½ cup boiling water
a little confectioners sugar

Beat the egg yolks with the sugar until the mixture is thick and mousse-like and will leave a trail when the beater is lifted.

Preheat the oven to 325°F. Sift the flour with the baking powder and salt using a sifter which only removes the coarser bran. Beat the egg whites until they stand in peaks. Fold the flour into the beaten egg yolks, adding a little of the boiling water after each addition. Lastly, fold in the egg whites and pour the mixture into an unbuttered 10 inch diameter deep tube pan with a removable base (you can butter just the base).

Bake in the preheated oven for about 65 minutes, or until the mixture is firm to the touch. To prevent the cake from sinking, turn the pan upside down and place it over the neck of a bottle. When the cake is quite cold, remove the bottle and unmold the cake — you may have to use a sharp knife to cut between cake and pan for the best results. Dust the top with confectioners sugar.

Alternatively, slice the cake into two layers and sandwich them together with jam and whipped cream. Frost the top and sides with Brown sugar frosting (page 199) or plain or flavored Glacé icing.

Jelly roll

Serves 6
CALORIES: 1580 (6610 kJ)
PROTEIN CONTENT: 45 grams
PREPARATION & COOKING TIME: 1 hour, excluding cooling

3 large eggs
6 tablespoons raw brown sugar
10 tablespoons wholewheat flour, bran sifted out

Preheat the oven to 350°F. Line a 14 × 9½ inch shallow baking pan or jelly roll pan with wax paper or non-stick parchment paper. Brush with a little melted butter or margarine.

Put the eggs and sugar into a bowl and beat until light and foamy, and the beater, when lifted, leaves a thick trail or ribbon on the surface. Fold in the flour, turn the mixture into the prepared pan and bake for 20-30 minutes, or until the cake is just firm when pressed lightly with the fingertips.

Remove from the oven and unmold onto a piece of wax paper or non-stick parchment paper. Peel off the lining paper and immediately roll up the cake. Leave to get quite cold and then carefully unroll and spread with jam, or jam and whipped cream, or Brown sugar butter cream (page 199). Sprinkle a little confectioners sugar over the top, or frost the top with Glacé icing, if wished.

Sour cream lemon cake

Serves 6
CALORIES: 1950 (8150 kJ)
PROTEIN CONTENT: 51 grams
PREPARATION & COOKING TIME: 1½ hours

1¼ cups plus 1 tablespoon wholewheat flour
1 teaspoon baking powder
½ teaspoon baking soda
½ teaspoon salt
2-3 eggs
1 cup raw brown sugar
1 cup sour cream
1 teaspoon grated lemon rind
1 tablespoon confectioners sugar

Preheat the oven to 350°F. Brush the inside of a 7 inch square deep cake pan with melted butter or margarine. Sift the flour into a bowl with the baking powder, soda and salt.

Beat the eggs with the sugar until very frothy and thick enough to leave a trail when the beater is lifted. Stir in the cream and lemon rind. Fold in the flour and pour into the prepared cake pan.

Bake in the preheated oven for 35-45 minutes until the cake is risen, golden brown and just firm when pressed lightly with the fingertips. Leave the cake in the pan for 5 minutes, then unmold onto a cake rack to cool. Dust the top with the confectioners sugar.

Boston molasses cake

Serves 6
CALORIES: 3140 (13140 kJ)
PROTEIN CONTENT: 47 grams
PREPARATION & COOKING TIME: 1¾ hours

8 tablespoons butter or margarine
⅓ cup light corn syrup
⅓ cup molasses
½ cup raw brown sugar
1¾ cups wholewheat flour
½ teaspoon salt
1 teaspoon ground allspice
2 teaspoons baking powder
2 eggs, well beaten
⅔ cup raisins

Preheat the oven to 325°F. Line a 7 inch square deep cake pan with wax paper or non-stick parchment paper and brush with a little melted butter or margarine.

Warm the butter or margarine, syrup, molasses and sugar in a pan over gentle heat until the butter has melted, stirring occasionally to prevent the sugar from sticking. Remove the pan from the heat. Sift together the flour, salt, allspice and baking powder, then stir the eggs into the melted mixture, followed by the sifted ingredients and, lastly, the raisins. Mix thoroughly and pour the mixture into the prepared cake pan.

Bake in the preheated oven for 1¼-1½ hours, or until the cake is just beginning to shrink away from the edges of the pan. Unmold carefully onto a cake rack to cool.

Honey spice cake

CALORIES: 2770 (11560 kJ)
PROTEIN CONTENT: 45 grams
PREPARATION AND COOKING TIME: 1¾ hours

Follow the recipe for Boston molasses cake, but replace both syrup and molasses with ⅔ cup honey and omit the raisins.

Spiced apple cake

Serves 8
CALORIES: 4120 (17240 kJ)
PROTEIN CONTENT: 68 grams
PREPARATION & COOKING TIME: 1 hour

1¾ lb cooking apples, peeled and cored
1 cup hot water
1¾ cups plus 3 tablespoons raw brown sugar
8 tablespoons soft butter or margarine
2 eggs, well beaten
½ teaspoon finely grated orange rind
2¾ cups wholewheat flour
½ teaspoon baking powder
1½ teaspoons baking soda
1½ teaspoons salt
½ teaspoon ground cinnamon
½ teaspoon ground cloves
½ teaspoon ground allspice
½ cup walnut pieces
⅔ cup raisins

Preheat the oven to 350°F. Line two 9 inch diameter layer cake pans with wax paper or non-stick parchment paper. Brush with a little melted butter or margarine.

Cook the apples in half the water until they are soft; rub them through a strainer and mix in the sugar, butter or margarine, the eggs, orange rind and remaining water. Sift together all the dry ingredients and stir them into the apple mixture. Beat the mixture thoroughly, then stir in the nuts and raisins

Pour the mixture into the two prepared cake pans and bake in the preheated oven for 35-40 minutes, or until the cakes are well risen, golden brown and firm. Unmold them onto a lightly greased cake rack, carefully remove the paper and leave the cakes to get quite cold.

Sandwich them together with Brown sugar butter cream (page 199), using one third as a filling and the rest for covering the top and sides.

Apple strudel

Serves 6
CALORIES PER PORTION: 740 (3107 kJ)
PROTEIN CONTENT PER PORTION: 9.5 grams
PREPARATION & COOKING TIME: 2 hours

The pastry
2 cups all-purpose flour
10 tablespoons unsalted butter
⅔ cup warm water
a little confectioners sugar

The filling
2 cups fresh wholewheat breadcrumbs fried in 4 tablespoons unsalted butter until just beginning to crisp
1 lb cooking apples, peeled, cored, chopped and soaked in the juice of 2 lemons
⅓ cup raw brown sugar
¼ cup slivered blanched almonds
⅓ cup seedless white raisins
¼ teaspoon freshly grated nutmeg
1 teaspoon ground cinnamon

1. Put your hands under the dough on the cloth and lift, moving outward.
2. Roll up the dough with the filling and crumbs, using the cloth to help.

Sift the flour into a warmed bowl. Melt 4 tablespoons of the butter in the water and pour it, little by little, into the flour, stirring all the time. Knead until you have a smooth dough. Take it out of the bowl and knead it for 10 minutes — the dough should be soft and pliable, so add a little more warm water if it feels dry. Return to the warmed bowl, cover and leave it for 30 minutes.

Lay a clean cloth about 3 ft square on a table which you can walk around. Sprinkle the cloth with flour and place the rested dough in the center. Gently roll it out to a square and then place your hands under the dough and carefully stretch it outwards. Melt the remaining butter and brush a little of it over the dough if it looks as though it is getting dry. Continue stretching until the dough is so thin you can almost read through it. Try to keep it the same thickness all over with slightly thicker edges to work on.

When all the dough is of a uniform thickness, brush it lightly all over with most of the melted butter and cut off the thick outer edges. Preheat the oven to 350°F. Straighten shape and sprinkle the breadcrumbs along one side, followed by the apples, the sugar, the almonds, the raisins and the spices, keeping the filling neatly along one end of the strudel. Then, by lifting up the cloth, gently roll the strudel up so that the filling is trapped between layers of very thin buttery dough. Form the roll into a horseshoe and gently ease it onto a well-buttered baking sheet. Brush the top liberally with the remaining melted butter and bake in the preheated oven for 30-40 minutes, or until the pastry is golden brown and crisp.

Remove from the baking sheet, sprinkle the top with confectioners sugar and serve hot or cold with lightly whipped cream.

While this recipe seems rather a performance, it is not nearly as difficult as it might appear at first sight. Practice the first time with half quantities; if holes appear in the dough, repair them by making a patch with a piece from the edge, otherwise the hole will grow. Some cooks work section by section; I work from the center outwards, and in Austria it is generally done by four people working around a square table. When you have mastered it, you will realize why the strudel is one of the most popular pastries in Europe.

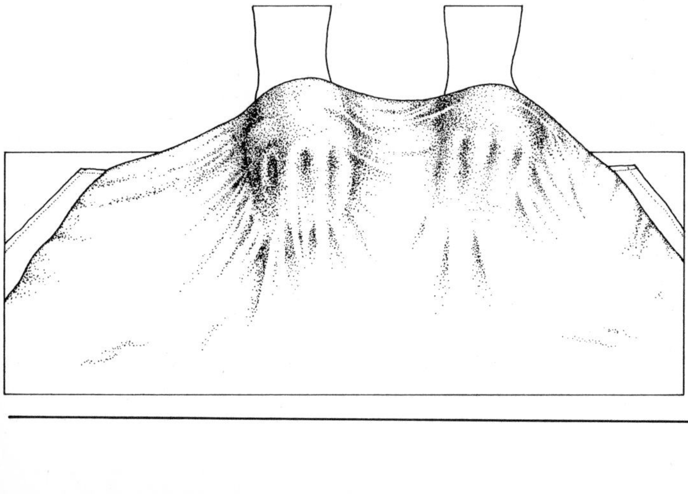

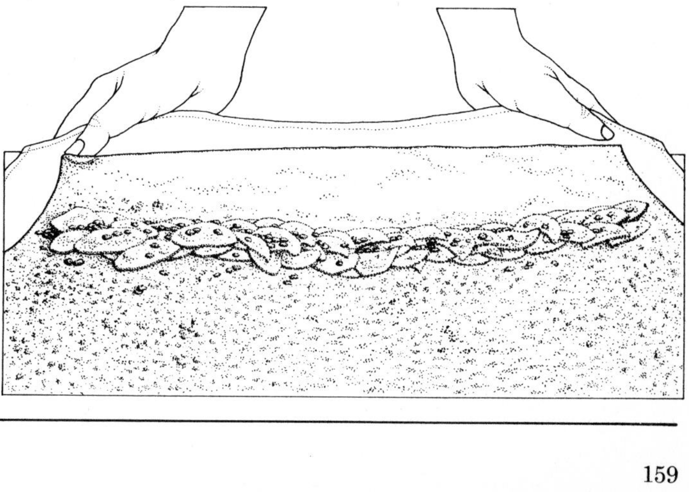

Chocolate nut cake with Ricotta filling

Serves 8
CALORIES PER PORTION: 710 (2972 kJ)
PROTEIN CONTENT PER PORTION: 10 grams
PREPARATION & COOKING TIME: 1 hour
CHILLING TIME: overnight

10 tablespoons butter
¾ cup plus 1 tablespoon soft brown sugar
3 eggs
1 cup chopped walnuts
1 cup plus 2 tablespoons wholewheat flour
1 teaspoon baking powder
1 tablespoon cocoa powder
½ teaspoon salt
½ cup orange juice
¼ cup raspberry jam, heated and strained
1¼ cups heavy cream
about ⅔ cup Ricotta or cottage cheese
a few walnut halves

Preheat the oven to 350°F. Cream together the butter and sugar until light and fluffy. Add the eggs, one at a time, beating well after each addition. Add the chopped walnuts. Sift together the flour, baking powder, cocoa and salt. Fold this into the creamed mixture, adding a little more milk if necessary to give a soft dropping consistency.

Divide the mixture evenly between two well-buttered 7 inch layer cake pans and bake in the preheated oven for 30 minutes. Turn out onto a cake rack to cool.

Slice each cake into two layers and sprinkle 2 tablespoons of orange juice over each layer, then spread a thin layer of raspberry jam on three of the layers. Cover and leave in the refrigerator overnight.

A few hours before serving, whip the cream and mix the Ricotta or cottage cheese with 2 tablespoons of it; spread this over each layer of raspberry jam. Sandwich the four layers together with the plain one on top; spread the rest of the whipped cream over the top of the cake and decorate with walnut halves. Serve well chilled.

Hazelnut cake

Serves 6
CALORIES PER PORTION: 460 (1930 kJ)
PROTEIN CONTENT PER PORTION: 5.5 grams
PREPARATION & CHILLING TIME: 2½ hours

The cake
4 egg whites
1⅓ cups raw brown sugar
½ teaspoon cider vinegar
1¼ cups finely ground hazelnuts
a little melted butter

The filling
2 squares (2 oz) dark chocolate, broken into small pieces
2 cups water
1¼ cups heavy cream

To make the cake: beat the egg whites until stiff enough to stand in peaks, then add the sugar one-third at a time, beating well after each addition. Beat in the vinegar, then continue beating until the mixture is completely smooth and stiff. Fold in the hazelnuts.

Preheat the oven to 350°F. Line two buttered 8 inch layer cake pans with non-stick parchment paper, then brush the parchment liberally with melted butter. Divide the cake mixture equally between the pans, then bake in the preheated oven for 15 minutes.

Reduce the heat to 250°F and dry out the cakes for a further 1 hour, or until the tops are firm when lightly pressed with the fingertips. Cover the cakes with wax paper or foil if the tops become too brown during baking. Unmold the cakes onto a cake rack, remove the parchment, then leave to cool.

To make the filling: put the chocolate and water in a small, heavy pan and heat very gently, stirring constantly, until the chocolate has melted, then remove the pan from the heat and allow to cool. Whip the cream until thick, then stir in the melted chocolate until evenly mixed.

Spread about three-quarters of the cream filling over one of the cakes, then place the other cake on top and sandwich together. Swirl the remaining cream over the top of the cake, then chill in the refrigerator before serving.

Mille feuilles

Serves 6
CALORIES PER PORTION: 525 (2203 kJ)
PROTEIN CONTENT PER PORTION: 3 grams
PREPARATION & COOKING TIME: 45 minutes
CHILLING TIME: 1 hour

1 cup basic Puff pastry (page 194)
1 cup confectioners' sugar
½ cup raspberry jam
1¼ cups whipping cream

Preheat the oven to 450°F. Roll out the dough into a 10 inch square and cut it in half. Place the two rectangles on a lightly oiled baking sheet and bake in the preheated oven for 15-20 minutes or until well risen and golden brown. Remove from the oven and carefully transfer to a cake rack to cool.

Sift the confectioners sugar into a bowl and gradually stir in just enough water to make a coating frosting.

When the pastry is quite cold, cut each rectangle crosswise in half. Spread three of the pastry slices with a layer of jam and whipped cream, then carefully lift one on top of the other. Finish with the plain slice of pastry. Spread with the frosting and serve chilled.

Chocolate éclairs

Makes 12
CALORIES PER PORTION: 460 (1920 kJ)
PROTEIN CONTENT PER PORTION: 6 grams
PREPARATION & COOKING TIME: 1½ hours

1 quantity basic Choux pastry (page 194)
1¼ cups whipping cream
1 tablespoon raw brown sugar (optional)
3 squares (3 oz) semisweet chocolate

Preheat the oven to 350°F. Using a ¾ inch plain nozzle, pipe 3 inch fingers of the dough onto well-oiled baking sheets. Use a dampened knife to cut off the dough at the end of each finger and leave about 1½ inches between each to allow for rising. Place in the preheated oven and increase the temperature to 425°F. Bake for 20 minutes then check by removing one éclair and breaking it in half. If it is not cooked in the middle, continue baking the rest at the original, lower temperature for 10-15 minutes more.

Remove from the oven, slice the éclairs halfway through to allow the steam to escape and leave on a cake rack to cool.

When the éclairs are completely cold, whip the cream with the sugar, if used, and pipe into the éclairs. Melt the chocolate in a bowl set over hot water. Coat the tops and allow to set.

Palmiers

Makes 6-8

CALORIES PER PORTION: 110 (457 kJ)
PROTEIN CONTENT PER PORTION: 1 gram
PREPARATION & COOKING: 30 minutes

1 cup basic Puff pastry (page 194)
2 tablespoons sugar, mixed with ½ teaspoon ground cinnamon (optional)

Sprinkle a marble slab or work surface lightly with flour and roll out the dough to a 12 × 10 inch rectangle. Brush it lightly but evenly with water, then sprinkle over half the sugar mixture and gently press it in. Fold the edge of each long side into the center. Brush again lightly with water, sprinkle with half the remaining sugar mixture and press it in gently. Fold the edge of each long side into the center again, making a narrow rectangle about 12 × 2½ inches. Fold in half and cut crosswise into 12 thick slices.

Preheat the oven to 400°F. Lay each slice flat on the work surface and roll it out lightly and carefully to about ¼ inch thick, taking care that the folded layers are spread out by the pressure of the rolling pin. Place on a well-oiled baking sheet, leaving about 1 inch between each one to allow space for spreading. Brush the tops lightly with water, sprinkle with the remaining sugar mixture and bake in the preheated oven for about 15 minutes, taking care that the sugar does not burn. If the Palmiers are not completely crisp after 15 minutes baking, transfer to a cake rack and return to the oven to bake for a few more minutes.

Serve cold, singly, or sandwiched together with lightly whipped cream.

Eccles cakes

Makes 12 small cakes

CALORIES PER PORTION: 145 (610 kJ)
PROTEIN CONTENT PER PORTION: 1.5 grams
PREPARATION & COOKING TIME: 45 minutes

2 tablespoons unsalted butter
3 tablespoons raw brown sugar
3 tablespoons finely chopped mixed candied peel
⅓ cup currants
grated rind and juice of 1 small lemon
¼ teaspoon ground allspice
1 cup Rough puff pastry (page 194)

Preheat the oven to 400°F. Melt the butter in a small saucepan; add the brown sugar, peel, currants, lemon rind and juice and allspice and allow to cool.

Meanwhile, roll out the dough to about ¼ inch thick and cut into 3 inch rounds. Place the dough trimmings one on top of the other, re-roll them and cut into rounds as before. There should be about 12 in all. Divide the cooled filling between the dough rounds and, gathering up the edges, form them into little balls.

Place on an oiled baking sheet with the seams underneath and flatten them with gentle hand pressure until they are about ½ inch thick. Using a sharp knife, mark the tops with a lattice pattern, then chill in the refrigerator for 20 minutes. Brush the tops with beaten egg and sprinkle with a little sugar. Bake in the preheated oven for 15-20 minutes until golden brown and well risen. Serve hot or cold.

Eccles cakes, Palmiers sandwiched with whipped cream and Chocolate éclairs – why not have one of each?

To prepare, bake and glaze a pie shell

For a really crisp pie, bake the shell unfilled, or 'blind', before adding any filling. This also helps eliminate the possibility of the filling breaking through the pastry before it is cooked.

To line the pie pan, roll out the dough into a round, about 3/16 inch thick and about 2 inches bigger in diameter than the pan. If the pie pan has a removable base, place it on a baking sheet. Lift the dough on the rolling pin and gently lay it over the pan. Without stretching it, carefully ease the dough into the pan, pressing it down well so no air gets trapped underneath; this will cause the pastry to rise in bubbles during cooking. Press the dough to the sides, then trim the excess from the edges. Line with a sheet of foil or wax paper and half-fill with dried beans.

To bake the pie shell, place in a preheated 400°F oven and bake for 15 minutes. Remove the baking beans and foil or paper lining. Lower the heat to 350°F and bake for a further 10-15 minutes, or until the pastry is crisp and beginning to brown. If bubbles do form in the pastry, prick with a skewer to release the air.

To glaze the pie shell, while still hot, brush the pastry with egg white for a savory pie, or with strained, melted apricot jam for a sweet pie.

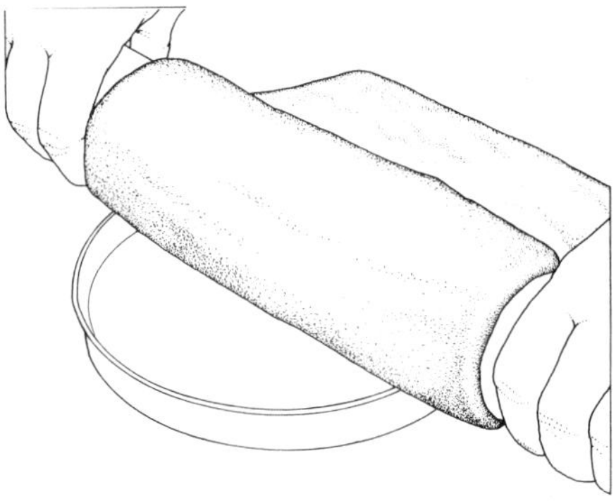

1. Wrap the rolled dough around the rolling pin to lift it then unroll over the pie pan.

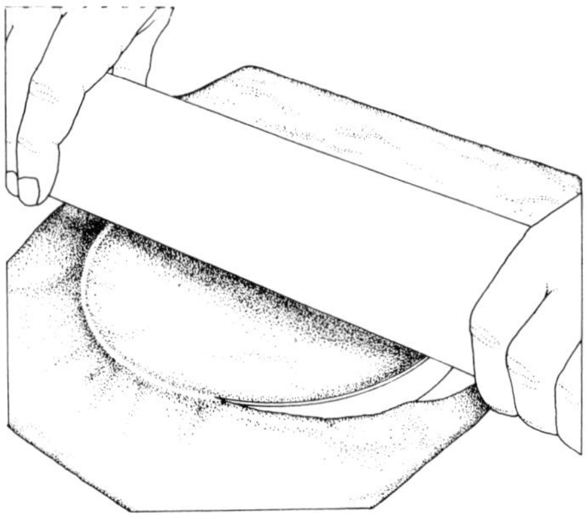

2. Press the dough into the pan to fit, using a bent forefinger. Roll the pin across to remove excess.

3. Line with foil then dried beans, filling to the sides. Bake first with the lining and then without to crisp it.

Old-fashioned custard pie

Serves 6

CALORIES PER PORTION: 595 (2482 kJ)
PROTEIN CONTENT PER PORTION: 17.5 grams
PREPARATION & COOKING TIME: 1 hour
COOLING & CHILLING TIME: 2 hours

pre-baked 8 inch pie shell, made with Wholewheat pie pastry (page 194) and glazed with apricot jam
3 eggs
1 egg yolk
⅓ cup raw brown sugar
¼ teaspoon grated nutmeg
¼ teaspoon salt
2½ cups milk
½ teaspoon vanilla extract

Preheat the oven to 350°F. Place the pie shell on a baking sheet. Beat the eggs and egg yolk with the sugar, nutmeg and salt until light and creamy. Bring the milk to a boil and pour it slowly onto the eggs, stirring continuously. Return the mixture to the saucepan and cook, stirring, until the custard thickens to coating consistency. Do not allow it to boil. Stir in the vanilla and pour the filling into the pie shell. Bake in the preheated oven for 30-45 minutes, or until the custard has set. Take care not to overcook the pie, or the custard will become watery. Allow to cool, then chill for 1 hour before serving.

Peanut butter pie

Serves 6

CALORIES PER PORTION: 865 (3617 kJ)
PROTEIN CONTENT PER PORTION: 22 grams
PREPARATION & COOKING TIME: 30 minutes
COOLING & CHILLING TIME: 1½-2 hours

pre-baked 8 inch pie shell, made with Wholewheat pie pastry (page 194) and glazed with apricot jam
⅔ cup raw brown sugar
3 tablespoons cornstarch
½ teaspoon salt
2½ cups milk
½ cup crunchy unsalted peanut butter
2 eggs, well beaten
1 teaspoon vanilla extract

Place the pie shell on a serving plate. Mix together the sugar, cornstarch and salt in a saucepan and gradually stir in the milk. Stir in the peanut butter a teaspoonful at a time. Place the pan over a moderate heat and bring to a boil, stirring continuously. Simmer until the mixture thickens and the peanut butter is well mixed in. Pour slowly onto the eggs, stirring vigorously, then return the mixture to the pan and bring back to a boil, stirring. Lower the heat and simmer the filling for 1 minute. Allow to cool for a few minutes, then stir in the vanilla. Pour into the pie shell, leave to cool, then chill the pie for about 1 hour before serving.

Pumpkin pie

Serves 6

CALORIES PER PORTION: 542 (2272 kJ)
PROTEIN CONTENT PER PORTION: 13 grams
PREPARATION & COOKING TIME: 1 hour

pre-baked 8 inch pie shell, made with Wholewheat pie pastry (page 194)
1½ cups cooked pumpkin
¼ teaspoon salt
1¼ cups milk
2 eggs, well beaten
½ cup raw brown sugar
1 teaspoon ground cinnamon
½ teaspoon ground ginger
½ teaspoon grated nutmeg
6 cloves, finely ground, or ¼ teaspoon ground cloves
1 teaspoon grated orange rind

Preheat the oven to 400°F. Place the pie shell on a well-oiled baking sheet. Mix all the remaining ingredients together thoroughly and pour into the pie shell. Bake in the preheated oven for 45 minutes until the filling has set, then serve hot or cold.

Linzer torte

Serves 6
CALORIES PER PORTION: 725 (3025 kJ)
PROTEIN CONTENT PER PORTION: 12 grams
PREPARATION & COOKING TIME: 1½ hours

1 cup ground hazelnuts
¾ cup plus 2 tablespoons wholewheat flour
½ teaspoon ground cinnamon
¼ teaspoon salt
1 teaspoon grated lemon rind
8 tablespoons unsalted butter
⅓ cup raw brown sugar
3 eggs, well beaten
⅔ cup raspberry jam

Preheat the oven to 350°F. Mix together the nuts, flour, cinnamon, salt and lemon rind. Cream the butter with the sugar until very soft and fluffy, then gradually add about three-quarters of the eggs, beating thoroughly between each addition. Add the nut mixture and mix to a firm dough, adding a little more egg, if necessary. Put a little less than a quarter of the dough on one side.

Oil an 8 inch pie pan and place the larger portion of dough in the center. Press it out so that it covers the bottom and sides of the pan evenly, and spread it with the raspberry jam. Roll out the remaining dough and cut into strips about ½ inch wide. Use to make a lattice over the jam. Bake in the preheated oven for 1 hour, until lightly browned and crisp.

Cool on a cake rack and serve with lightly whipped cream.

Pecan pie

Serves 6
CALORIES PER PORTION: 900 (3770 kJ)
PROTEIN CONTENT PER PORTION: 14 grams
PREPARATION & COOKING TIME: 1¼ hours

pre-baked 8 inch pie shell, made with Wholewheat pie pastry (page 194) and glazed with apricot jam
⅓ cup raw brown sugar
2 eggs, well beaten
4 tablespoons butter, melted
⅔ cup light corn syrup, heated until liquid
¼ teaspoon ground ginger (optional)
¼ teaspoon ground cinnamon (optional)
1¼ cups halved pecans

Preheat the oven to 350°F. Place the pie shell on a baking sheet. Mix together the sugar, eggs, butter and syrup with the spices, if used. Fold in the nuts, making sure they are thoroughly and evenly mixed. Pour the filling into the pie shell, taking care not to spill any over the side as it may run underneath the pie shell and burn.

Bake in the preheated oven for 45 minutes to 1 hour or until the filling is set and is golden brown. Allow to cool slightly before serving, or serve cold.

Strawberry or raspberry shortcake

Serves 6
CALORIES PER PORTION: 675 (2820 kJ)
PROTEIN CONTENT PER PORTION: 12 grams
PREPARATION & COOKING TIME: 1-1¼ hours

1 lb strawberries or raspberries, hulled
3-4 tablespoons sugar
1¼ cups whipping cream

For the Shortcake
1¾ cups wholewheat flour
½ teaspoon ground cinnamon (optional)
1 tablespoon baking powder
1 teaspoon salt
6 tablespoons butter, margarine or shortening
1 cup milk

Preheat the oven to 400°F. Set aside about 6 whole berries for decoration. Sprinkle the remaining fruit with sugar, crush lightly and then set aside while you make the shortcake.

Sift the flour with the cinnamon, if used, baking powder and salt into a bowl through a coarse strainer to extract the bran. Discard this. Rub in the butter, margarine or shortening until the mixture resembles fine breadcrumbs. Add the milk and mix to a very soft dough. Divide the dough in half, roll it out and line two well-oiled 8 inch layer cake pans. Bake in the preheated oven for 15 minutes. Remove the shortcakes from the oven and cool for 5 minutes, then turn them out onto a cake rack and allow to cool completely.

Place one shortcake on a serving plate and cover with a layer of crushed fruit. Place the second shortcake on top and cover with the remaining crushed fruit. Decorate with some of the whipped cream and the reserved whole berries and serve immediately with the remaining cream. Alternatively, spread the shortcake layers with whipped cream before covering with fruit and decorate as before.

Apple pie

Serves 6
CALORIES PER PORTION: 610 (2557 kJ)
PROTEIN CONTENT PER PORTION: 8 grams
PREPARATION & COOKING TIME: 1½ hours

⅔ cup raw brown sugar
1 tablespoon wholewheat flour
½ teaspoon ground cinnamon
½ teaspoon grated orange rind
1¾ lb cooking apples, peeled and cored
1 tablespoon orange juice
⅓ cup seedless white raisins
1 quantity Wholewheat pie pastry (page 194)

Preheat the oven to 450°F. Mix the sugar with the flour, cinnamon and grated orange rind. Cut the apples into slices about ½ inch thick. Immediately stir them into the sugar mixture to prevent discoloration. Add the orange juice and raisins.

Roll out three-quarters of the dough and line an 8 inch pie pan. Fill with the apple mixture and dampen the edges of the dough. Roll out the remaining dough into a round to fit the top and place this over the apples. Seal the edges well and make two leaf-shaped slits in the top to allow the steam to escape. Bake in the preheated oven for 15 minutes, then reduce the temperature to 350°F and bake for a further 30 minutes.

Serve hot or cold with cream or custard sauce.

Wholewheat shortbread

Serves 6
TOTAL CALORIES: 1835 (7680 kJ)
TOTAL PROTEIN CONTENT: 20 grams
PREPARATION & COOKING TIME: 1¼ hours
CHILLING TIME: 1 hour

1 cup plus 2 tablespoons wholewheat flour
½ teaspoon salt
⅓ cup raw brown sugar
8 tablespoons butter
¼ cup sugar

Mix the flour and salt in a bowl and stir in the brown sugar. Rub the butter into the dry ingredients until the mixture begins to stick together, then press lightly to form a stiff dough. Knead carefully on a floured surface until fairly smooth and then press the mixture into an 8-inch diameter loose-bottomed fluted tart pan. Chill for about 1 hour.

Preheat the oven to 300°F and bake the shortbread for 45-60 minutes until firm and just beginning to brown. Remove from the oven and sprinkle the top with half of the sugar. Cool in the pan for 5 minutes, then unmold onto a cake rack and sprinkle the other side with sugar. When cold, break into fingers or triangles and store in an airtight tin.

Langue de chat cookies

Makes about 30

TOTAL CALORIES: 750 (3150 kJ)
TOTAL PROTEIN CONTENT: 13 grams
PREPARATION & COOKING TIME: 30-40 minutes

4 tablespoons butter or margarine
⅓ cup raw brown sugar
2 egg whites
7 tablespoons wholewheat flour
½ teaspoon salt

Preheat the oven to 350°F. Cream the butter or margarine and sugar together until soft and fluffy. Beat the egg whites until they stand in peaks and fold them into the creamed mixture together with the flour and salt.

Using a pastry bag fitted with a ½ inch nozzle, pipe the mixture in 2 inch lengths on a baking sheet brushed with melted butter. Keep them about 2 inches apart and fairly flat in shape. Bake them in the preheated oven for 10 minutes.

Remove the baking sheet from the oven, take off one cookie and allow it to cool; if it is not completely crisp, return the remainder to the oven, reduce the heat to 250°F and cook for a little longer until the cookies are crisp when cold.

Almond or hazelnut cookies

Makes about 4 dozen

TOTAL CALORIES: 830 (3470 kJ)
TOTAL PROTEIN CONTENT: 13 grams
PREPARATION & COOKING TIME: 30 minutes

4 tablespoons soft butter
⅓ cup raw brown sugar
2 egg whites, stiffly beaten
½ cup ground almonds or hazelnuts

Preheat the oven to 350°F. Line two baking sheets with non-stick parchment paper.

Cream together the butter and sugar until light and fluffy, then fold in the egg whites. Stir the nuts lightly into the mixture. Drop teaspoonfuls of the mixture onto the prepared baking sheets, leaving plenty of space between them, and bake in the preheated oven for about 10 minutes, or until they are beginning to turn golden brown around the edges. Remove the cookies from the oven and allow to cool.

Savory cheese bits

Makes about 4 dozen

TOTAL CALORIES: 1975 (8250 kJ)
TOTAL PROTEIN: 59
PREPARATION & COOKING TIME: 45 minutes

¾ cup plus 2 tablespoons wholewheat flour
salt
freshly ground pepper
8 tablespoons butter
1¼ cups grated Cheddar cheese
egg, well beaten
cayenne

Preheat the oven to 400°F. Mix the flour and seasoning together in a bowl and rub in the butter. Add 1 cup of the cheese and knead the mixture until it is a smooth paste. Turn out onto a lightly floured board and roll out to about ¼ inch thick. Cut into squares about 2 inches wide and then cut the squares into triangles. Lay them on a well-greased baking sheet and brush lightly with the egg. Sprinkle over the remaining cheese and a little cayenne. Bake for 10-15 minutes until golden brown and firm. Allow to cool slightly before removing from the sheet. Serve warm as a cocktail snack or as an accompaniment to soup or casseroles.

Honey oatcakes

TOTAL CALORIES: 2400 (10050 kJ)
TOTAL PROTEIN CONTENT: 32 grams
PREPARATION & COOKING TIME: 45 minutes

2 tablespoons honey
2 tablespoons corn syrup
6 tablespoons butter or margarine
⅔ cup raw brown sugar
2 cups rolled oats

Set oven at 350°F. Brush 8 in square cake pan with melted butter or margarine, line base with non-stick parchment paper.

Put honey, syrup, butter or margarine and brown sugar into saucepan, melt over gentle heat. Add oats, mix well. Turn mixture into pan, bake in preheated oven 20-30 minutes, until golden brown. Cut into strips while warm. Allow to cool. Turn out and store in airtight container.

Preserving, Pickling and Freezing

There is nothing quite as satisfying as a shining row of jars of homemade jams, jellies, pickles and chutneys standing on the pantry shelves.

Although freezing has become the most convenient way of storing fruit and vegetables straight from the market or garden, the sheer pleasure of opening a jar of fragrant, full-fruit strawberry jam or the first, pungent aroma of your favorite pickle will convince you that nothing can quite take its place. I make my jams when the fruit is at its best – you will find the yields of my recipes vary. Lemon curd, for instance, will not keep well once made, though it is so delicious that the contents will vanish within hours of the jar being opened. Pepper relish is one of my favorite pickles and I like to make lots and lots at a time . . .

I include some basic guidelines on freezing, with instructions on the preparation of fruit and vegetables, and the storing of made-up dishes. Though I prefer to prepare my food fresh for each meal, it is sometimes more convenient to cook ahead of time.

Canning fruit

Recent research has suggested that the home cook should not attempt to can fruit lacking in acid, e.g. dessert apples, and ripe peaches, and that when canning suitable ingredients such as gooseberries or rhubarb, a pressure canner must be used to achieve the correct sterilizing temperatures.

While fruit can be canned in water, the flavor and color is better preserved if it is covered in a syrup made by boiling 1 cup sugar in 2½ cups of water for about 2-3 minutes. More sugar may be needed if the fruit is very acid.

Prepare the fruit by washing it carefully and removing any stalks, stems or leaves. Cherries should be pitted, gooseberries should have tops and bottoms removed and rhubarb cut into short, even lengths. Apples and pears should be peeled and cored; peaches and apricots should be peeled and halved and the pits removed. Plums can be left whole, or halved and the pits removed.

Pack the fruit closely, but do not squash together, in clean, sterilized wide-necked canning jars and cover with the syrup, releasing any air bubbles with a sterilized spatula, toothpick or skewer. Leave about ½ inch space between the syrup and the top of the jar as the fruit may make some juice and if the jar is filled to the top it may boil out. Put on the sterilized lid, then screw down the screwband firmly tight.

Put the jars into a large pressure canner on top of the rack and see that they do not touch the sides of the canner or each other. Pour in more hot water enough to bring the level 2 inches above the tops of the jars. Put on the lid, leaving the vent open and bring the water to a boil. Allow steam to escape for a couple of minutes, then close the vent. Bring the pressure to whatever the manufacturer recommends and hold it for the time they suggest.

Leave to cool before releasing the pressure, otherwise the jars might burst. Remove the lid of the pressure canner, take out the jars and cool quickly in cold water. Test them after 48 hours cooling to see if the seals have taken. The lids should have snapped down on the jars; if they have, label and store in a cool, dark place.

Jam-making

One of the most satisfying sights in any pantry is a row of homemade jams, jellies, chutneys and preserves. However, as already mentioned, recent research has suggested that you should restrict your efforts at preserving to tomatoes and the acid fruits and leave most vegetables to the professionals.

Wide-necked jars make the removal of the contents much easier. For preserving, make sure that the jars are not cracked or the top edges chipped. Wash the jars in hot water with a little detergent, rinse thoroughly in clean water and drain. For jams, jellies, chutneys and pickles, stand the jars upside down on a baking sheet in 250°F oven for 30 minutes before filling them.

Choose ripe but not overripe fruit for jam-making. Wash it carefully and remove hulls, stems and leaves where appropriate. Cut out any blemishes or bruised parts, using a stainless steel or silver knife to avoid a metallic taste.

Soft berry fruits such as raspberries and strawberries should be soaked in salt water for 20-30 minutes to remove any insects. Use 2 tablespoons salt to every 1 quart of water. Rinse the fruit thoroughly under cold running water.

Use an aluminum, stainless steel or tin-lined copper pan and simmer the fruit *before* adding sugar if a soft-textured jam is required, as the sugar can toughen the skin. To make a firm-textured strawberry jam, sprinkle the strawberries with the measured sugar and leave them in a bowl overnight. Always allow the sugar to dissolve completely, stirring constantly, before allowing the jam to come to a boil, then boil rapidly until setting point is reached. I use lemon juice instead of pectin as an aid to setting.

To test for setting, take a small spoonful of the boiling jam and pour it onto a cold saucer. Chill rapidly and push the jam lightly with a fingertip; if the jam wrinkles and a drop picked up on a knife does not run off, the jam is ready. Alternatively, run the edge of a spoon through the middle of the jam on the saucer. If the jam stays divided, it is at setting point. Allow the jam to cool for 20-30 minutes, then stir it to distribute the fruit evenly just before filling the warmed canning jars. Leave a little over ½ inch between the jam and the top of the jar.

Seal the jars as soon as they have been filled and the outsides wiped clean. Process the jam in a boiling water bath (212°F), following the instructions of the manufacturer of your pressure canner, and cool. Don't forget to label the jar and write on it the date the jam was made.

Preserving

Fruit and tomatoes for preserving should be ripe but firm. Wash the fruit and prepare as for jam. Plums and apricots should be halved and the pits removed. If a few of the pits are cracked open and the kernels added to the fruit, this will give the preserved fruit a faint almond flavor. Peaches should be peeled, halved and pitted; do not include any kernels as their flavor will be too strong.

Fruit should be canned in a syrup made by dissolving 2 cups sugar to each 1 quart boiling water. Simmer gently until the sugar has dissolved, stirring constantly, then strain and allow to cool completely before using.

Rinse the canning jars — there is no need to dry them off in the oven — then pack in the fruit carefully, without squashing it. Leave a space of about 1 inch between the top of the fruit and the rim of the jar. Pour in enough syrup to come about ½ inch above the fruit and use a

1. Simmer the fruit until tender. Add warmed sugar, stirring until it dissolves.

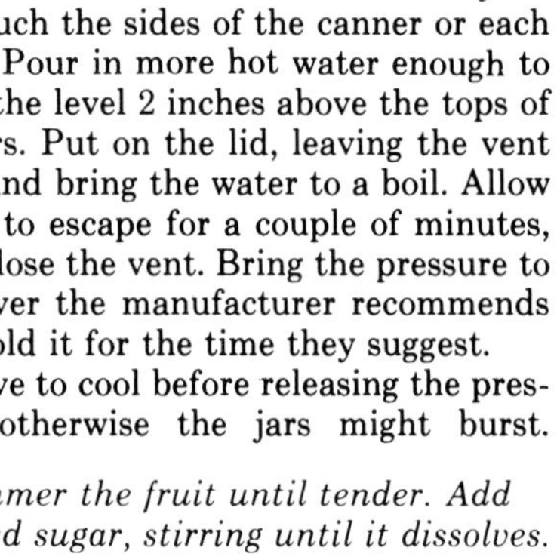

2. Boil at a rolling boil. Test for set on a saucer: jam should stay separated.

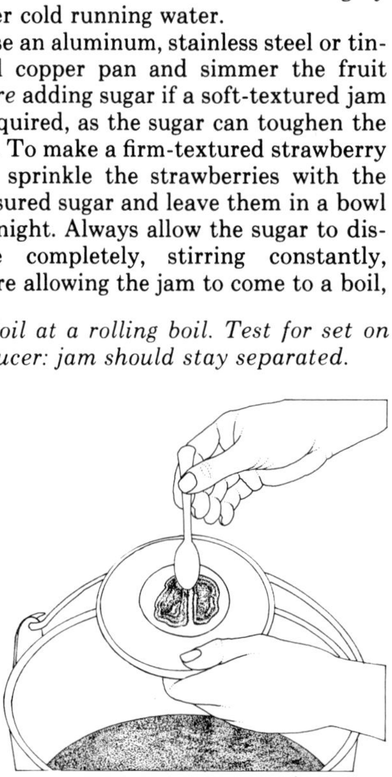

3. When setting point is reached, remove pan from heat and skim off any scum.

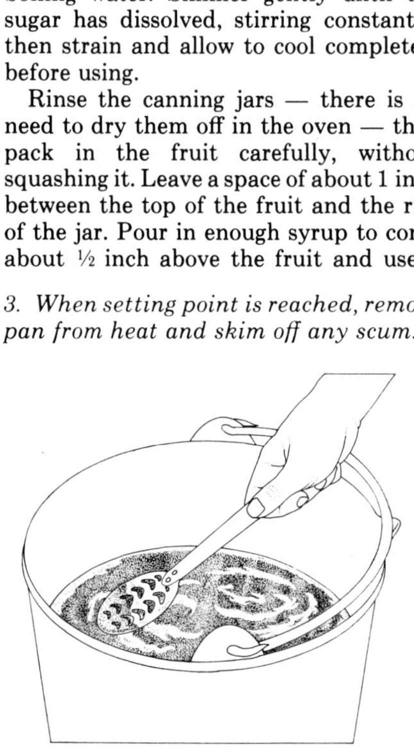

clean skewer or toothpick to release any trapped air bubbles.

Tomatoes can be canned whole, skinned or unskinned, or as a purée. Skin them by dropping them into boiling water for a minute and then transferring them to a bowl of iced water to prevent them continuing to cook. Cut the skin into quarters with a sharp pointed knife and peel off carefully. If the tomatoes are to be canned unskinned, prick the skins thoroughly to prevent them from bursting. Pack them into the jars, replacing the sugar syrup with a mild brine made by dissolving ¼ cup salt in every 1 quart of water, releasing any air bubbles with a clean skewer or toothpick, as for fruit.

To make a tomato purée for canning, boil coarsely chopped tomatoes, seasoned with salt, pepper and herbs if liked, until reduced to a pulp. Rub through a strainer and pour into warmed jars, as for jam, leaving about ½ inch between the purée and the rim of the jar, then seal.

Stand the filled jars on a rack in a large pressure canner and follow the manufacturer's instructions for processing.

When the jars are quite cold and properly sealed, store them in a cool, dry, dark, well-ventilated place. If mold appears on jam soon after it has been made, it is generally a sign that the jam was canned before reaching setting point, or the fruit was too low in pectin (the substance that makes jams and jellies set). In the case of chutneys or pickles, perhaps it is a sign that the vinegar was not up to strength. Provided the mold has not penetrated below the surface, it can generally be scraped off, but the contents should be eaten up as soon as possible.

4. Let whole fruit jam stand ½ hour then stir. Pour liquid jam directly into jars.

Gooseberry jam

CALORIES: 5100 (21340 kJ)
PROTEIN CONTENT: 11 grams
PREPARATION & COOKING TIME: 1¼ hours

¼ cup lemon juice plus the pith and seeds of 3 lemons
2½ lb gooseberries, washed well, tops and bottoms removed
1 pint water
7⅓ cups raw brown sugar
finely grated rind of 1 large lemon

Tie the pith and seeds from the lemons in a small piece of cheesecloth. Put the gooseberries, lemon juice and water into a saucepan or preserving pan, add the cheesecloth bag and bring to a boil. Simmer for 20 minutes, then gradually stir in the sugar with the lemon rind, stirring until the sugar has dissolved. Continue boiling, stirring from time to time, until jell point is reached. Discard the cheesecloth bag, pack into jars and process. Yields about 4 lb.

Note: Try putting a dozen or so heads of elderflowers into the cheesecloth bag with the lemon. They give the jam a delicate muscatel flavor.

Apricot jam

CALORIES: 4190 (17530 kJ)
PROTEIN CONTENT: 6 grams
PREPARATION & COOKING TIME: 2 hours

2½ lb apricots, washed well, any stem ends and leaves removed, halved and pitted
juice of 1 large lemon
1¼ cups water
5⅔ cups raw brown sugar

Put the apricots into a saucepan or preserving pan with the lemon juice and the water, bring to a boil and simmer until the fruit is soft. Add the sugar, stir to dissolve and continue boiling, stirring constantly, until jell point is reached. Pack into jars and process.

Note: If wholefruit jam is desired, add the sugar at the same time as the fruit, as it will slightly toughen the skin and flesh; take care when stirring the jam not to break the fruit.

A dozen or so kernels from the pits can be added to the jam at the same time as the fruit to give a slightly almond flavor. Blanch them in boiling water for 5 minutes and split them in half before adding them. Yields about 3 lb.

For Plum jam, follow the above method, use the same quantity of fruit, water and sugar as for Apricot jam, but omit the lemon juice.

Strawberry jam

CALORIES: 4205 (17590 kJ)
PROTEIN CONTENT: 6 grams
PREPARATION & COOKING TIME: 1½ hours

2¼ lb strawberries, washed well and hulled
6⅔ cups raw brown sugar
3 tablespoons lemon juice plus the pith and seeds of 3 large lemons

Make sure you have discarded any strawberries that are moldy or over-ripe. Put the rest into a saucepan, or preserving pan, over moderate heat and bring to a boil, breaking some berries with a spoon to release the juice. Add the sugar and the lemon juice and stir to dissolve. Tie the pith and seeds from the lemons in a piece of cheesecloth and suspend this in the boiling liquid. Continue boiling, stirring from time to time to prevent the fruit sticking and burning, until jell point is reached. Discard the cheesecloth bag. Pack into jars and process. Yields about 3 lb.

Note: If wholefruit jam is required, sprinkle the hulled strawberries with the sugar, leave them in a bowl overnight and then put them into a saucepan or preserving pan. Bring them to a boil and follow the recipe, taking care, however, not to break the fruit when you are stirring the jam.

A satisfying variety of fresh-fruit jams and jellies for the pantry – choose the best of the season's fruits to enjoy all year round

Raspberry jam

CALORIES: 4190 (17540 kJ)
PROTEIN CONTENT: 9 grams
PREPARATION & COOKING TIME: 1 hour 15 minutes

2¼ lb raspberries
5½ cups raw brown sugar
2 tablespoons lemon juice plus the pith and seeds of 2 lemons

Wash the raspberries by putting them into a bowl of cold water and agitating them gently, then lift them out into another bowl of clean water. By repeating this process with clean water once more, any dust or grit is left behind and the raspberries are not damaged. Discard any that are moldy or bruised. Put the berries in a saucepan or preserving pan. Stir over gentle heat until the juices begin to run, then follow the method given for Strawberry jam. Yields about 3 lb.

Black cherry jam

CALORIES: 3480 (14570 kJ)
PROTEIN CONTENT: 7 grams
PREPARATION & COOKING TIME: 2½ hours

3 lb black cherries, washed well, any stems and leaves removed, and pitted
4 large or 6 small lemons, enough to give 1 cup of juice
2½ cups water
4⅔ cups raw brown sugar

Discard any blemished cherries. Squeeze the lemons and measure the juice. Remove the seeds and the pith and put them into a pan with the cherry pits and 1 pint of the water. Bring to a boil, simmer for 30 minutes, then strain into a clean saucepan, rubbing any pulp through the strainer. Add the rest of the water, the lemon juice and the cherries and bring to a boil. Lower the heat and simmer gently for about 30 minutes. Add the sugar, stir to dissolve, increase the heat and boil, stirring occasionally, until jell point is reached. Pack into jars and process.

If a wholefruit jam is required, add half the sugar with the pitted cherries as the sugar will toughen the skins and fruit slightly. Yields about 3 lb.

Lemon curd

CALORIES: 2065 (8640 kJ)
PROTEIN CONTENT: 30 grams
PREPARATION & COOKING TIME: 1 hour

2 heaping teaspoons finely grated lemon rind
½ cup lemon juice
1 cup granulated sugar
3 eggs, well beaten
8 tablespoons unsalted butter

Put the lemon rind and juice and sugar into a heatproof bowl and stand it in a large saucepan of gently boiling water. Stir until the sugar has dissolved, then stir the beaten eggs thoroughly into the mixture. Divide the butter into four, add one portion to the mixture in the bowl and stir until it melts. Add the rest of the butter piece by piece, stirring all the time and making sure each piece has melted into the mixture before adding the next.

Continue cooking and stirring, scraping the sides and bottom of the bowl from time to time until the curd has the consistency of thick cream, pour into warmed, sterilized jars. Cool before covering; store in a cool, dry place. Eat within four weeks. Yields about 1 lb.

Apple jelly

CALORIES: 5010 (20960 kJ)
PROTEIN CONTENT: 2 grams
PREPARATION & COOKING TIME: 3 hours

2¼ lb cooking apples, washed well and stalks removed
2 quarts water
4¼ cups granulated sugar
juice of 1 large lemon

Cut each apple into 8 segments and put them into a saucepan with the water. Bring to a boil, then reduce the heat, cover and simmer for 2 hours. Stir occasionally to break the apples up. When they have cooked to a pulp, rub them through a strainer and pour the purée into a jelly bag. Drain overnight into a bowl. Pour juice into a clean saucepan, add sugar and lemon juice, stir to dissolve. Bring to a boil; reduce heat and simmer until jelly reaches jell point. Skim to remove scum; pack into jars. Yields about 5 lb.

Note: Apple jelly can be flavored with mint leaves, rose petals or lemon rind added with the sugar. Tie in cheesecloth, remove before pouring into jars.

Black currant jelly

CALORIES: 4220 (17660 kJ)
PROTEIN CONTENT: 9 grams
PREPARATION & COOKING TIME: 1½ hours

2¼ lb black currants, washed well
1 quart water
6⅔ cups raw brown sugar

Remove any leaves from the black currants but leave the stems. Put them into a saucepan with three-quarters of the water. Bring to a boil and simmer for 20 minutes, stirring occasionally. Strain through a fine strainer into a clean saucepan. Return the pulp to the original pan with the rest of the water and boil for 5 minutes. Strain as before, pressing the pulp gently with the back of a spoon to release any extra juice. Add it to the rest of the juice and bring to a boil. Add the sugar, stir to dissolve and continue boiling until jell point is reached. Pack into jars. Yields about 6 lb.

Note: To make Red currant jelly use red currants instead of black currants and granulated sugar instead of brown so it does not mask the flavor of the fruit.

Three fruit marmalade

CALORIES: 5642 (23580 kJ)
PROTEIN CONTENT: 4 grams
PREPARATION & COOKING TIME: 3½ hours

1½ lb mixed citrus fruit (2 oranges, 1 grapefruit and 1 lemon)
1½ quarts water
8 cups raw brown sugar

Scrub the fruit in hot water, cut into quarters and then into thin slices, taking care to save all the juice. Remove the seeds and tie them loosely in a piece of cheesecloth. Pour the water into a saucepan, or preserving pan, and add the fruit and juice, suspending the cheesecloth bag containing the seeds in the liquid. Bring to a boil, cover the pan and simmer for 1½ hours. Remove the cheesecloth bag and weigh the juice and fruit; if it is much over 3 lb, return it to the pan and boil rapidly until it is reduced. Weigh the juice and fruit, add 2⅔ cups of sugar to each pound, return it to the saucepan and stir to dissolve. Boil rapidly until jell point is reached. Skim the marmalade, remove the pan from the heat and leave for 20-30 minutes until it has thickened slightly. Stir to distribute the fruit evenly, then pack into jars and process. Yields about 5 lb.

Chunky marmalade

CALORIES: 8140 (34070 kJ)
PROTEIN CONTENT: 6 grams
PREPARATION & COOKING TIME: 4 hours

2¼ lb Seville oranges
juice, pith and seeds of 2 large lemons
2 quarts water
11 cups raw brown sugar

Scrub the fruit in hot water to clean them thoroughly. Cut them first into quarters, then into small chunks, taking care to catch all the juice. Remove the central pithy core and seeds and keep them on one side. Put the chunks of orange, lemon juice and water into a saucepan, or preserving pan, with the lemon and orange pith and seeds tied loosely in a piece of cheesecloth and suspended in the liquid. Bring to a boil, then reduce the heat and simmer for about 1½ hours until the skin of the oranges is soft and can be pierced easily with a fork. Now add the sugar, stir to dissolve and boil rapidly until jell point is reached. Discard the cheesecloth bag. Skim the marmalade, remove the pan from the heat and leave for 20-30 minutes until the marmalade has thickened slightly. Stir to distribute the fruit evenly, pack into jars and process. Yields about 8 lb.

Seville orange jelly

CALORIES: 3665 (15330 kJ)
PROTEIN CONTENT: 3 grams
PREPARATION & COOKING TIME: 4 hours

1 lb Seville oranges
1 quart water
juice, pith and seeds of 2 lemons
4 cups granulated sugar

Shred the orange rind into thin strips and tie it in a cheesecloth bag. Peel the white pith off the oranges and keep it on one side; chop the flesh into small pieces, catching all the juice. Remove the orange seeds and add them to the pith. Pour the water into a saucepan and add the small chunks of fruit with the orange and lemon juice. Tie the lemon pith and seeds in a cheesecloth bag with the orange pith and seeds and suspend this in the liquid. Add the other cheesecloth bag containing the shredded rind. Bring the liquid to a boil, reduce the heat, cover the pan and simmer for 2 hours. Discard the cheesecloth bag containing the pith and seeds, strain the liquid through a fine strainer, or strainer lined with cheesecloth, and return it to the pan. Add the sugar and the shredded rind from the bag, stir to dissolve the sugar and boil rapidly, stirring occasionally, until jell point is reached. Skim the jelly, remove from the heat and allow to stand for 20-30 minutes until it has thickened slightly. Stir to distribute the rind evenly, then pack into jars. Yields about 4 lb.

Damson cheese

CALORIES: 4280 (17910 kJ)
PROTEIN CONTENT: 4 grams
PREPARATION & COOKING TIME: 1½ hours

2½ lb damsons, washed well, any stalks or leaves removed, and pitted
2½ cups water
about 4¼ cups granulated sugar

Put the damsons and the water into a thick-based saucepan and bring to a boil. Reduce the heat, cover and simmer until the fruit is completely soft. Rub through a strainer, measure the pulp and measure out the same amount of sugar. Pour the pulp into a clean saucepan and boil, stirring constantly, until it has begun to thicken. Add the sugar, stir to dissolve and continue cooking, stirring occasionally until it is a thick purée. Pack into jars and process. Yields about 2 lb.

Orange preserve

CALORIES: 8230 (34430 kJ)
PROTEIN CONTENT: 8 grams
PREPARATION & COOKING TIME: 4 days

2¼ lb oranges
1½ quarts water
11⅓ cups raw brown sugar

Wash the oranges carefully, remove the stem ends and cut the oranges into quarters. Put these into a saucepan with the water and bring to a boil. Cover the pan, reduce the heat and simmer for 2½-3 hours until the skin is soft and can be pierced easily with a fork. Remove from the heat, keep covered and leave overnight. The following morning, add enough boiling water to make up the original quantity of liquid. Bring it to a boil, add the sugar and stir until it has dissolved, then reduce the heat, cover and simmer for 30 minutes, stirring occasionally. Make sure that the orange skins are immersed in the liquid as they are inclined to turn over and float to the top. Remove the pan from the heat, keeping it covered, and leave until the following morning.

Make up the liquid to the original quantity with a little boiling water as before, bring to a boil and simmer for a further 30 minutes, then leave overnight. Repeat the process the following day, simmer for 30 minutes then boil to a syrup just short of jell point. Skim the top and spoon the orange pieces into jars. Pour over the boiling syrup and process. Yields about 10 lb.

Note: If you dislike finding the occasional seed, remove seeds before cooking; tie them in a piece of cheesecloth and suspend them in the liquid during the whole of the cooking time.

Spiced pickled peaches

CALORIES: 860 (3610 kJ)
PROTEIN CONTENT: 6 grams
PREPARATION & COOKING TIME: 1 hour

2½ lb small, ripe firm peaches, peeled, halved and pitted
2½ cups wine vinegar
1 teaspoon ground allspice
2 inch stick of cinnamon, crumbled
1 teaspoon coriander seeds
2 bay leaves, crumbled
⅔ cup raw brown sugar

Put the halved peaches into a saucepan with the vinegar, spices and bay leaves and bring to a boil. Simmer for 10 minutes, or until the peaches are tender, then remove them from the pan with a slotted spoon and keep on one side. Add the sugar to the pan, stir to dissolve and return the peaches to the pan. Cook for a further 5 minutes. Remove the peaches from the saucepan with the slotted spoon and place them in jars. Boil the vinegar until reduced by one-third, pour this over the peaches, making sure it covers them completely, and process. Yields about 3 lb.

Note: This recipe can also be used to make Spiced pickled apricots or plums, replacing the peaches with the same quantity of apricots or plums.

Lemon chutney

CALORIES: 3310 (13840 kJ)
PROTEIN CONTENT: 8 grams
PREPARATION & COOKING TIME: 4 hours

1½ lb lemons, cut into ¼ inch slices
1¼ cups wine vinegar
2 medium onions, thinly sliced
2 cloves of garlic, peeled and thinly sliced
2 inch stick of cinnamon, crumbled
6 cloves
1 teaspoon cumin seed
2 bay leaves, crumbled
½ teaspoon chili powder
3⅔ cups raw brown sugar

Put the lemon slices into a pan, cover them with water and bring to a boil. Cover the pan, turn down the heat and simmer for 2 hours, adding a little more water, if necessary, during the cooking time. Measure the liquid and make it up to 1¼ cups with additional water. Return it to the saucepan with the lemon slices, add the rest of the ingredients, except the sugar, and bring back to a boil. Add the sugar, stir until it has dissolved, then continue cooking until the juice thickens slightly when a little is put on a cold plate; it should not be quite thick enough to jell. Pack into jars and process. Yields about 4 lb.

Spiced cherries

CALORIES: 1850 (7740 kJ)
PROTEIN CONTENT: 6 grams
PREPARATION AND COOKING TIME: 30 minutes, excluding maturing time: 4 weeks

1 quart wine vinegar
12 cloves, coarsely crushed
2 inch stick of cinnamon, crumbled
2 bay leaves, crumbled
2 cups raw brown sugar
2½ lb ripe black cherries, well washed and pitted

Pour the vinegar into a saucepan, add the spices, bay leaves and sugar and bring it to a boil. Stir until the sugar has dissolved before adding the cherries. Bring back to a boil and simmer for 5 minutes, then pour the spiced cherries into jars and process. Yields about 5 lb.

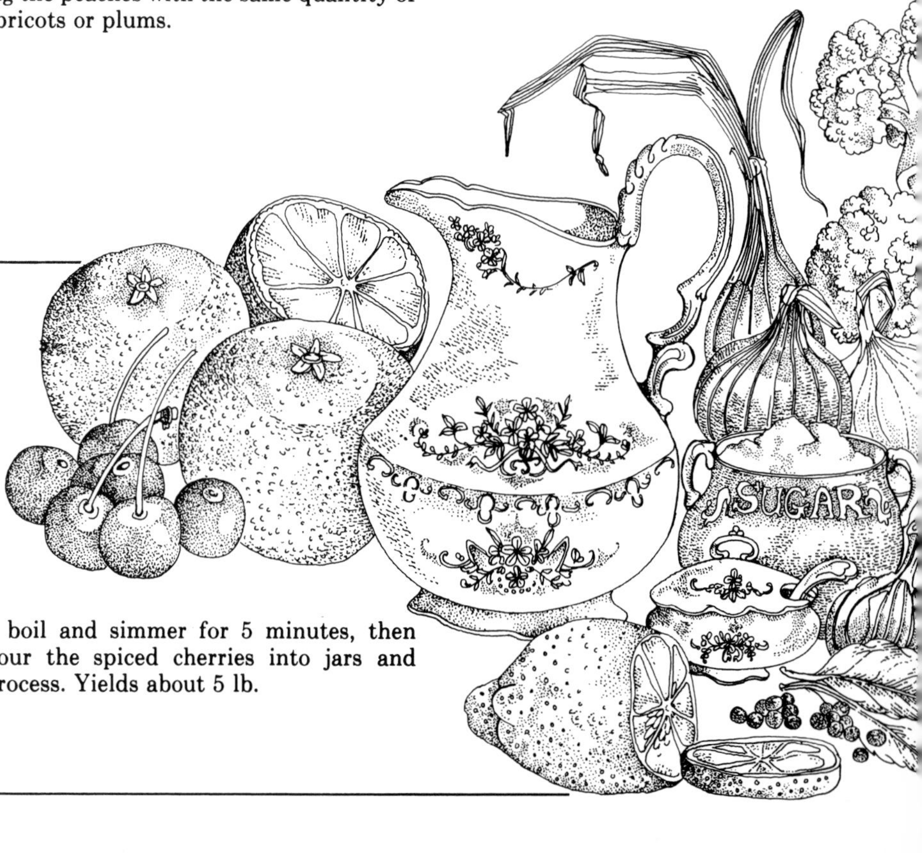

Piccalilli

CALORIES: 450 (1880 kJ)
PROTEIN CONTENT: 12 grams
PREPARATION & COOKING TIME: 2 days

2¼ lb mixed vegetables — cauliflower, pearl onions, green beans, red and green peppers, cucumbers — and unripe pears and apples
apples
⅓ cup salt
1½ quarts vinegar
½ cup coarsely crushed mustard seed
1 cup thinly sliced green ginger root
½ teaspoon ground cinnamon
½ teaspoon freshly ground black pepper
8 cloves of garlic, peeled and finely chopped
⅓ cup raw brown sugar
1 tablespoon wholewheat flour

Cut the vegetables into small chunks, sprinkle them with the salt and leave them to drain for 24 hours, stirring four times during the draining period. Rinse and dry them thoroughly. Put the vinegar, spices, garlic and sugar into a saucepan, bring to a boil and add the vegetables. Bring back to a boil and simmer for 10 minutes, then allow to cool and leave in the pan, covered, for 24 hours. Drain off the vinegar and mix 1-2 tablespoons of it to a smooth paste with the flour. Put this into a saucepan with the rest of the vinegar and bring to a boil, stirring until it thickens. Add the vegetables, bring back to a boil and simmer for 5 minutes. Pack into jars and process. Yields about 2 lb.

Sweet cucumber pickle

CALORIES: 745 (3120 kJ)
PROTEIN CONTENT: 14 grams
PREPARATION & COOKING TIME: 6 hours

2¼ lb cucumbers, coarsely chopped
¾ lb onions, thinly sliced
½ lb green peppers, halved
3 tablespoons salt
⅔ cup raw brown sugar
1½ tablespoons mustard seed
1 teaspoon grated lemon rind
½ teaspoon ground mace
1¼ cups wine vinegar

Put all the vegetables into a bowl, sprinkle them with the salt and leave for 4 hours. Rinse them and drain thoroughly. Put all the other ingredients into a saucepan and bring to a boil, stirring until the sugar has dissolved. Simmer for 5 minutes before adding the vegetables, then bring back to a boil and cook for 10 minutes, stirring occasionally. Pack into jars and process. Yields about 4 lb.

Pepper relish

CALORIES: 1590 (6640 kJ)
PROTEIN CONTENT: 32 grams
PREPARATION & COOKING TIME: 2 hours

8½ cups finely chopped red peppers
8½ cups finely chopped green peppers
8½ cups finely chopped onions
2½ cups wine vinegar
1⅓ cups raw brown sugar
2-4 cloves of garlic, peeled and finely chopped
2 bay leaves, crumbled
1 teaspoon ground allspice
1 teaspoon mustard seed
2 teaspoons salt

Blanch the peppers in enough boiling water to cover them. Drain immediately, put them into a saucepan with the onions and cover again with water. Bring to a boil, pour off the water, drain the vegetables thoroughly and keep on one side. Put the vinegar into the rinsed out pan and bring to a boil. Add the sugar, garlic, bay leaves, allspice, mustard seed and salt. Stir until the sugar has dissolved, then add the peppers and onions and bring back to a boil. Boil the mixture vigorously for 2-3 minutes, stirring constantly, then pack into jars and process. Yields about 8 lb.

Tomato chutney

CALORIES: 1270 (5310 kJ)
PROTEIN CONTENT: 22 grams
PREPARATION & COOKING TIME: 2½ hours

4½ lb tomatoes, skinned and cored
4 cups finely chopped onions
1¼-2½ cups wine vinegar
1 tablespoon salt
1⅓ cups raw brown sugar
2 inch stick of cinnamon, crumbled
2 bay leaves
4 cloves of garlic, peeled and chopped
½ teaspoon chili powder
2 teaspoons ground allspice

Quarter the tomatoes and put them in a stainless steel or enamel saucepan with the rest of the ingredients. Bring to a boil and simmer to a thick purée. Stir occasionally to begin with, and almost constantly toward the end of the cooking time to prevent the chutney sticking and burning. When it is ready, pack into jars and process. Yields about 7 lb.

Note: This recipe can be used for making Green tomato chutney but increase the amount of sugar to 2 cups.

Pickled walnuts

CALORIES: 2625 (10980 kJ)
PROTEIN CONTENT: 53 grams
PREPARATION & MATURING TIME: 8 weeks

2¼ lb young green walnuts
2 cups salt
2 quarts water
3 tablespoons black peppercorns
3 tablespoons small allspice berries
1½ quarts wine vinegar
½ teaspoon freshly grated ginger root
2 inch stick of cinnamon, crumbled

The walnuts must be freshly picked and should be young enough to be pierced easily with a very thick needle, even through the stem end; the outer covering should be firm and juicy.

Prick the walnuts all over with a carpet needle, holding them in a cloth, or wear rubber gloves, as the juice stains almost indelibly.

Dissolve half the salt in half the water and pour it over the walnuts in a bowl. Do not use a lead-glazed container as the solution and, later, the vinegar will dissolve the lead. If the solution does not quite cover the walnuts then make up a little extra, using the same proportion of salt to water. Cover and leave the nuts for 5 days in a cool place, stirring twice a day to ensure even brining. Drain them, then mix the rest of the salt and water, and any additional brine required, and pour this over the walnuts. Leave for another 5 days, stirring twice a day as before. Drain the walnuts and spread them out in a single layer on a flat dish. Let them dry in the sun until they are black. Crush the peppercorns and allspice berries in a mortar with a pestle — do not grind them or the flavor will be too strong. Simmer the vinegar with the spices for 15-20 minutes until it is well flavored. Allow to cool and strain. Fill sterilized wide-necked canning jars three-quarters full with walnuts and pour in the spiced vinegar, adding extra if necessary to cover the walnuts. Process and leave in a cool place for 6 weeks before using. Yields about 2 lb.

Homemade pickles delight the eye and tickle the palate. From left to right: Pepper relish; Tomato chutney; Spiced cherries; more Pepper relish; Pickled red cabbage and Piccalilli – the English mustard pickle. Behind: make your own herb vinegars – rosemary, sage and bay leaf – and add their piquancy to salads and vegetable dishes

Pickled red cabbage

CALORIES: 200 (840 kJ)
PROTEIN CONTENT: 2 grams
PREPARATION & MATURING TIME: 6 days

8½ cups shredded red cabbage
⅓ cup salt
1 quart wine vinegar
1 teaspoon ground allspice
1 teaspoon ground cinnamon
2 teaspoons ground coriander
½ teaspoon ground black pepper
2 bay leaves, crumbled

Sprinkle the cabbage with the salt in a bowl, cover and leave for 24 hours. Rinse and pat dry. Simmer the vinegar with the spices and bay leaves for 10 minutes, then allow to cool. Pack the cabbage lightly into sterilized wide-necked canning jars and strain the spiced vinegar over. Cover the jars, process and leave for 5 days. The cabbage should now be ready to eat; it softens if kept too long, so use it up in the next 2-3 weeks. Yields about 3 lb.

Pickled onions

CALORIES: 230 (960 kJ)
PROTEIN CONTENT: 9 grams
PREPARATION TIME: 30 minutes
SALTING TIME: 24 hours
MATURING TIME: 2 months

2¼ lb pearl pickling onions
¼ cup salt
1 pint wine vinegar
½-1 teaspoon ground allspice
1 teaspoon coarsely ground coriander
¼-½ teaspoon ground cloves
½ teaspoon freshly ground pepper
2 inch stick of cinnamon, crumbled

Drop the onions into a pan of boiling water, bring the water back to a boil and transfer the onions immediately to a bowl of cold water. Using a sharp knife, remove tops and tails, cutting just enough of the onion to allow you to remove the outer skin. Put them into a glass bowl and sprinkle with salt, turning them so that they are covered. Cover the bowl and leave for 24 hours, stirring about every 6 hours Rinse and dry them thoroughly.

Pour the vinegar into a saucepan, add the spices and bring to a boil. Cover and allow to cool. Pack the onions loosely into sterilized canning jars and cover with the vinegar, tapping the side of the jar to release any bubbles. Process and store in a cool place for 2 months before using. Yields about 2 lb.

Note: If a milder flavor and a softer texture are required, put the onions into warmed, sterilized jars, pour the boiling vinegar over them and seal when cold.

Pickled eggs

CALORIES: 1015 (4240 kJ)
PROTEIN CONTENT: 93 grams
PREPARATION & COOKING TIME: 1 hour, excluding storage time

1 quart wine vinegar
1 teaspoon ground allspice
1 teaspoon ground coriander
½ teaspoon coarsely ground black pepper
2 inch stick of cinnamon, crumbled
6 cloves, coarsely ground
2 hot red chili peppers, or green chili peppers if a milder flavor is preferred
1 teaspoon salt
2 bay leaves, crumbled
1 clove of garlic, peeled and finely chopped
1 medium onion, thinly sliced
12 freshly cooked hard-cooked eggs

Put the vinegar into a saucepan with the spices, salt, bay leaves, garlic and onion. Bring to a boil, then reduce the heat, cover the pan and simmer for 10 minutes. Shell the eggs and place them in sterilized wide-necked canning jars. Allow the vinegar to get cold, then strain it over the eggs — they must be completely immersed. Cover and store for 10 days in the refrigerator before using them.

Herb vinegars

CALORIES: nil
PROTEIN CONTENT: nil
MATURING TIME: 3-4 weeks

Herb vinegars are delicious, so it is worth making the effort to obtain fresh herbs in the required quantity. Use wine or cider vinegar as the basic liquid. You will require approximately the same volume of loosely packed leaves and young stems of tarragon or mint as vinegar. Carefully wash, dry and bruise the leaves before you immerse in the liquid. Store in screw-topped bottles for 3-4 weeks for the flavors to infuse before using the vinegar in salad dressings or add it in small quantities to soups, casseroles or vegetable dishes.

Spiced vinegar

Add 6 cloves of garlic and 2-4 red chili peppers, all thinly sliced, to 2½ cups of boiling vinegar. Leave to steep for 2 weeks. This makes a fiery and piquant seasoning.

Freezing

The main advantages of freezing are convenience and economy. It allows the busy cook the luxury of planning ahead, preparing and cooking food for future consumption so that it only needs thawing and reheating when required. By buying frozen food in bulk, freezing fresh food when it is plentiful and cheap, and by freezing home-grown fruit and vegetables, a considerable saving can be made.

Choose a freezer best suited to your requirements. A vertical cupboard type takes up less floor area and is easier to load and unload. The horizontal chest-type ones are not so convenient but are generally slightly cheaper. Go to a reputable, specialist dealer and discuss your requirements and available budget, and once you have bought a freezer, make sure that you know what to do if it breaks down. The manufacturer's instruction booklet will help here.

Good quality wire baskets make storage easier and more efficient in top loading freezers, as you do not have to move a lot of individual packages to find a particular item. It is advisable to keep foods of one type together in one basket. Choose stainless steel or plastic covered rust-proof baskets.

The inside of the freezer should be cleaned at least twice a year. Run the stocks down beforehand and wrap the rest in layer upon layer of newspaper to prevent them thawing; keep them tightly packed in a cool place — preferably a freezer or refrigerator — while you clean the interior.

Switch off the power supply and leave the doors or lid of the freezer open. You can accelerate the defrosting by standing bowls of hot water on the shelves. Scrape off the frost from the sides, top and bottom, being careful not to damage the surface. Wipe all inside surfaces with a weak solution of baking soda or mild detergent and water, or follow the directions of the manufacturer. Rinse the inside surfaces carefully with a clean cloth wrung out in fresh water, dry thoroughly and turn the power back on. Set the temperature control to its lowest setting or quickest freezing rate, or use the fast-freezing switch and reload it with the food as soon as the normal storage temperature of 0°F has been reached. Do not forget to turn the control back to its normal setting once the correct temperature is reached.

Freeze food in heavy-duty plastic bags or food containers with well-fitting lids. Use foil containers, obtainable from freezer centers or counters in the larger department stores, for cooked food that you wish to reheat without removing from the container.

Make sure that all food is hermetically sealed and that as much air as possible is removed from the container to avoid oxidation of the contents. Use a drinking straw to suck the air out of the partially closed bag before sealing. When using rigid containers, cover the surface of the food with wax paper or freezer foil. Remember that liquids expand by approximately $\frac{1}{10}$ of their volume when they freeze, so leave enough head space to allow for this, otherwise you will have accidents. When you freeze casseroles or foods in a sauce, ensure that all the food is covered with sauce, then cover the surface with wax paper or freezer foil. Freeze convenient portions of food in separate containers; it is annoying and wasteful to find that you have to thaw enough soup for 8 when you only need enough for 2. Separate individual turnovers, crêpes, etc. with layers of plastic wrap or foil to prevent them sticking together.

Label all food clearly with waterproof ink; record what it is, when it was frozen, and the quantity. It is surprising how the memory can play tricks!

Remember that the quality of the frozen food depends on the quality of the food before freezing. Ensure that all food preparation is done under hygienic conditions and that the food is cooled and frozen as quickly as possible after blanching or cooking.

When freezing precooked food, it is advisable to undercook it slightly to allow for the extra time it will cook for when it is reheated. Be generous with sauces so that the food does not dry out when it is being reheated.

Season lightly, adding extra, if necessary, when the food is reheated as freezing can concentrate flavoring. Garlic is inclined to develop a musty flavor so add on reheating the dish. Add cream or egg liaisons when reheating as freezing can make them separate, and you may find you have to thicken flour-based sauces at this point.

The general principle to remember when freezing fresh vegetables is to choose the best available quality of fresh-picked, unblemished produce and blanch and cool it immediately in ice-cold water to prevent enzyme action taking place while it is stored.

Fruit in prime condition can be frozen whole, though it is often more convenient to peel it and remove any cores or seeds before freezing. If it is at all over-ripe, cook it and then freeze it as pie filling or fruit purée. Strawberries and similar fruit can be frozen spread out on trays before being packed in bags. This ensures that they do not freeze into a clump and can easily be separated on thawing.

Herbs freeze well and should be stripped or chopped and frozen in small containers, or in water in ice cube trays. Pack the flavored ice-cubes in plastic bags for storing.

The following charts give more detailed instructions on freezing the more common vegetables, prepared fruits and some cooked foods.

Thawing

The best way to thaw raw frozen food is also the slowest. Take it out of the freezer and leave it in the refrigerator; allow enough time for it to thaw completely; 1 lb will take approximately 6-8 hours. If you are in a hurry, thaw it out at room temperature, which will halve the time. Remember that vegetables should be cooked from frozen and not be thawed first. Loaves and cakes can be left to thaw in the refrigerator overnight.

Once the food is thawed, cook it as soon as possible to prevent any growth of bacteria.

Heating and cooking

Frozen casseroles, stews and pies should be heated as rapidly as possible to achieve the best results. Preheat the oven to 400°F and transfer the food to a baking dish if it has not been frozen in a foil container. A shallow casserole holding 1 quart will take about an hour to heat up. Leave the lid off for quicker cooking; as the food thaws, gently separate the pieces.

If the food has a sauce it may be necessary to strain it off and beat it vigorously to make it smooth. It may also be necessary to mix it together again if it has separated or to thicken a flour-based sauce.

Soups and sauces can be thawed from frozen in a saucepan over moderate heat, but stir them constantly to prevent them sticking and burning, and heat them thoroughly.

Blanching and freezing vegetables

If frozen vegetables are going to be stored for more than 2 months, the raw vegetables should be blanched first to prevent enzyme action changing the flavor. Use a frying basket placed inside a larger pan filled with boiling water for blanching fruit and vegetables. Allow 4 quarts of boiling water per 1 lb. See that the heat under the pan is sufficient to bring the boiling water back to a boil within 1 minute of the vegetables being plunged in, and do not attempt to blanch too much at a time. Time blanching from the moment the water comes back to a boil. When the time is up, plunge the vegetables immediately into ice-cold water to stop them cooking further. Replace the water and keep adding more ice to ensure that it really is ice cold.

Once the vegetables have cooled — and

this should be done as quickly as possible hence the ice-cold water — drain them. Pack them in heavy-duty plastic bags, freezer foil or rigid, lidded containers and freeze them as quickly as possible. Follow the manufacturer's instructions on how much fresh food your freezer can freeze and store at a time. The key to successful freezing and the least damaging to nutrition and flavor is *how fast* you can freeze and *how much air you can remove* from the container. Full details for different types of vegetables are given on pages 206 –207.

Keeping times
Most vegetables and fruit will keep for up to 12 months, if properly frozen. However, beets and onions will only keep up to about 6 months and puréed potatoes to about 3 months.

Fruit
Fruit can be frozen after blanching — as for vegetables. It can be frozen separately and packed into bags when frozen, or it can be frozen in syrup, or as a purée. If you are using syrup, make sure that you have enough; allow about 1¼ cups to every 1 lb of fruit. Dissolve 2 cups sugar in 5 cups hot water and bring to a boil. Allow to cool and then refrigerate before using. Keep the fruit below the surface of the liquid with a piece of wax or parchment paper. Add about ⅛ teaspoon ascorbic acid to the syrup for each 1 lb of those fruits which might otherwise discolor. Do not forget to leave room for expansion when using syrup.

Thaw the fruit just before using and keep it submerged in the syrup for as long as possible.

Apples Peel, core and cut into quarters or ½ inch slices. Blanch for 1-2 minutes depending on the firmness of the fruit and cool quickly. Pack in rigid containers and cover with syrup. Alternatively, peel and core the apples and cook to a purée with a little sugar. Freeze, when cold, in rigid containers.

Apricots Drop them into boiling water, leave for 30 seconds to loosen the skins, then drain and peel them. Cut them in half and remove the pits. Pack in rigid containers and cover with syrup plus ascorbic acid. Cover with wax paper and the lid and freeze.

Berries
Blackberries; black currants; blueberries; boysenberries; cherries; gooseberries; raspberries; red currants; strawberries.

Wash carefully and dry. Pick over the fruit and remove any stems, leaves or hulls; remove tops and bottoms of gooseberries. Freeze by any of the following methods:

1 Freeze separately on trays covered with non-stick paper and pack them together in bags, when frozen.
2 Sprinkle them with sugar, allowing ½-¾ cup to 1 lb fruit. Mix well; pack into bags and freeze.
3 Pack into rigid containers, cover with syrup and the surface of the liquid with a piece of non-absorbent, wax paper.
4 Reduce to a purée in a blender, then sweeten and freeze in rigid containers.

Grapes Freeze seedless grapes whole; seeded grapes should be cut in half and the seeds removed. Pack into rigid containers, cover with syrup and a piece of non-absorbent wax paper and freeze.

Grapefruit and oranges Peel, removing all the pith; separate into segments and pack in rigid containers. Cover with syrup and a piece of non-absorbent, wax paper and freeze. Alternatively, squeeze out the juice and strain. Freeze into cubes in an ice cube tray, putting the cubes into bags when they are frozen.

Lemons and limes Squeeze and freeze the juice as for grapefruit and oranges above, or cut them into thin slices and interleave with plastic wrap. Pack them flat in plastic bags before freezing.

Peaches Peel the peaches, if ripe, without any preliminary immersion in boiling water to loosen the skins, as the heat will cause some discoloration. Cut them in half, remove the pits and pack the peaches as they are, or cut into ½ inch thick slices, in rigid containers. Cover with syrup and a piece of non-absorbent or wax paper and freeze.

Pears These do not freeze as well as other fruits. Choose pears that are slightly under-ripe, poach them in syrup, add ascorbic acid and pack into rigid containers. Cover with the poaching syrup and a piece of non-absorbent wax paper before freezing.

Plums Wash, cut in half and remove the pits. Pack into rigid containers, cover with syrup plus ascorbic acid and a piece of non-absorbent wax paper, and freeze.

Rhubarb Wash, trim and cut into 1 inch lengths. Blanch for 1½ minutes. Cool quickly, pack into rigid containers and cover with syrup to freeze. Use in pies or cook from frozen.

Cream ices and sorbets
The following recipes will serve 4-6 people. It is well worth making them in even larger quantities, however, as they are quite time-consuming to make, but keep well in the freezer.

Orange sorbet

Serves 4
CALORIES PER PORTION: 210 (867 kJ)
PROTEIN CONTENT PER PORTION: 2 grams
PREPARATION & COOKING TIME: 4 hours

¾ cup sugar
1¼ cups water
finely grated rind of 2 oranges
1¼ cups fresh orange juice
2 egg whites

Put the sugar and water in a pan and heat gently until the sugar has dissolved, stirring occasionally. Remove the pan from the heat and leave until cold.

Stir in the orange rind and juice, then pour the mixture into a freezing tray. Cover and place in the freezer. Freeze for about 1 hour until the mixture becomes slushy and the edges are solid, then remove from the freezer and stir well. Replace and freeze for another hour. Remove the tray from the freezer again, stir the mixture well to break up any lumps and mix the frozen parts into the rest of the mixture. Beat the egg whites until stiff enough to stand in peaks, then fold the mixture into them. Return the sorbet to the freezer and freeze again for 2-3 hours, or until firm and set.

Note: To make lemon sorbet, substitute lemon rind and juice for the orange.

Raspberry sorbet

Serves 4
CALORIES PER PORTION: 230 (955 kJ)
PROTEIN CONTENT PER PORTION: 2.5 grams
PREPARATION & FREEZING TIME: 3-4 hours

1 cup sugar
1 pint water
1 lb fresh or thawed frozen raspberries
2 egg whites

Put the sugar and water in a pan and heat gently until the sugar has dissolved, stirring occasionally. Remove the pan from the heat and pour over the raspberries. Leave until cold.

Rub the mixture through a strainer, then make the purée up to 3¼ cups with water. Pour the mixture into a freezing tray, cover and place in the freezer. Freeze for about 1 hour until the mixture becomes slushy and the edges are set.

Beat the egg whites until stiff enough to stand in peaks. Remove the tray from the freezer, stir well to break up any lumps, and mix the frozen bits into the rest of the mixture, then fold the mixture into the egg whites. Return to the freezer and freeze again for 2-3 hours until firm.

Black currant ice

Serves 4
CALORIES PER PORTION: 370 (1547 kJ)
PROTEIN CONTENT PER PORTION: 3.5 grams
PREPARATION & FREEZING TIME: about 5 hours

½ lb fresh or frozen black currants
⅔ cup raw brown sugar
1¼ cups water
1 teaspoon lemon juice
1¼ cups heavy cream
2 egg whites

Put the black currants, sugar and water in a pan and heat gently until the sugar has dissolved, stirring occasionally. Bring to a boil, then boil for about 10 minutes or until the black currants are soft. Remove from heat and leave until cold.

Rub the mixture through a strainer, then stir in the lemon juice. Pour the mixture into a freezing tray, cover and place in the freezer. Freeze for about 1 hour until the mixture becomes slushy and the edges are solid.

Whip the cream until thick. Remove the tray from the freezer, stir the mixture well to break up any lumps, then fold into the whipped cream. Return to the freezer and freeze again for about 1 hour, until thick.

Beat the egg whites until stiff enough to stand in peaks. Remove the ice from the freezer, then fold into the egg whites. Return to the freezer and continue freezing for 2-3 hours until the ice is firm and set.

Champagne ice

Serves 4
CALORIES PER PORTION: 790 (3315 kJ)
PROTEIN CONTENT PER PORTION: 3.5 grams
PREPARATION & FREEZING TIME: about 5 hours

⅔ cup sugar
½ cup water
juice of 2 oranges
finely grated rind of 2 lemons
juice of 3 lemons
2½ cups Champagne
2½ cups heavy cream
2 tablespoons brandy

Put the sugar and water in a pan and heat gently until the sugar has dissolved, stirring occasionally, then remove from the heat and leave until cold.

Stir in the orange juice, lemon rind and juice and the Champagne, then pour the mixture into a freezing tray. Cover and place in the freezer. Freeze for about 1 hour until the mixture becomes slushy and the edges are solid.

Remove the tray from the freezer and stir the mixture well to break up any lumps, and mix the frozen parts well into the rest of the mixture. Whip the cream until thick. Fold the frozen mixture into the whipped cream with the brandy. Return to the freezer and freeze again for 2-3 hours, or until firm and set.

Vanilla ice cream

Serves 4
CALORIES PER PORTION: 710 (2957 kJ)
PROTEIN CONTENT PER PORTION: 10.5 grams
PREPARATION & FREEZING TIME: about 5 hours

1¼ cups milk
1 vanilla bean or ½ teaspoon vanilla extract
3 eggs, separated
⅔ cup raw brown sugar
2½ cups heavy cream

Heat the milk gently in a pan with the vanilla bean (if using), then set aside for a few minutes for the flavor to infuse. Beat together the egg yolks and sugar in a bowl, strain in the hot milk and continue beating until all the sugar has dissolved. Add the vanilla extract at this stage, if using this instead of the vanilla bean.

Pour the mixture into the rinsed-out pan, return to the heat and simmer gently until the sauce thickens, stirring constantly. Remove the pan from the heat and leave to cool.

Pour the mixture into a freezing tray, cover and place in the freezer. Freeze for about 1 hour until the mixture looks slushy and the edges are solid.

Whip the cream until thick. Remove the tray from the freezer, stir the mixture well to break up any lumps, then fold in the whipped cream. Return to the freezer and freeze again for about 1 hour, or until the mixture is thick.

Beat the egg whites until stiff enough to stand in peaks, then remove the ice cream from the freezer and fold it into the beaten egg whites. Return to the freezer again and freeze for 2-3 hours until the ice cream is firm. Serve sprinkled with chopped nuts and a Chocolate or Butterscotch sauce.

Chocolate ice cream

Serves 4
CALORIES PER PORTION: 1000 (4112 kJ)
PROTEIN CONTENT PER PORTION: 13 grams
PREPARATION & FREEZING TIME: about 5 hours

8 squares (8 oz) dark chocolate

Follow the basic recipe for Vanilla ice cream, melting the chocolate in half the milk, then adding the remaining milk before continuing.

Coffee ice cream

Serves 4
CALORIES PER PORTION: 710 (2980 kJ)
PROTEIN CONTENT PER PORTION: 11.5 grams
PREPARATION & FREEZING TIME: about 5 hours

2-3 tablespoons instant coffee powder

Follow the basic recipe for Vanilla ice cream, dissolving the instant coffee powder in the milk before continuing.

Ice creams and sorbets make a refreshing interlude between spicy or strongly flavored dishes at a dinner party. They are not difficult to make in quantity if you have a freezer or ice cream maker. Top left: Strawberry ice cream. Top right: Lemon sorbet. Bottom left: Champagne ice. Bottom right: a Raspberry ice

Brown bread ice cream

Serves 4
CALORIES PER PORTION: 850 (3547 kJ)
PROTEIN CONTENT PER PORTION: 15 grams
PREPARATION & FREEZING TIME: 5-6 hours

2 cups fresh wholewheat breadcrumbs
2 tablespoons sugar
½ teaspoon ground cinnamon
2 tablespoons sweet sherry

Sprinkle the breadcrumbs with the sugar and cinnamon, spread them out on a baking sheet and bake them in a 375°F oven until well browned. Allow to cool. Sprinkle the sherry over them and stir them into the Vanilla ice cream just before folding in the egg whites. Serve with a Caramel or Raspberry sauce (pages 198 and 199).

Praline ice cream

Serves 4
CALORIES PER PORTION: 850 (3547 kJ)
PROTEIN CONTENT PER PORTION: 15 grams
PREPARATION & FREEZING TIME: 5-6 hours

1 cup unblanched almonds
¼ cup sugar

Cook the almonds with the sugar in a thick-based pan over moderate heat until the sugar melts and coats the almonds. Stir constantly to prevent it burning. Continue cooking until the sugar has caramelized slightly, then pour the praline onto an oiled plate, or a large sheet of non-stick parchment paper. Leave until cold, then work to a powder in a blender, or crush finely with a rolling pin.

Follow the recipe for Vanilla ice cream above, omitting the vanilla bean and using only half the quantity of sugar given. Fold in praline powder with whipped cream.

Freezing prepared and cooked food

Food	Storage time	Preparation	Freezing	Thawing and cooking
Soups and Sauces (except egg-based sauces)	2-3 months	Go carefully with the seasoning.	Freeze in convenient amounts in freezer bags.	Warm bag in water, then pour sauce into a pan. Melt over moderate heat, avoiding burning. Adjust seasoning and add extra liquid, if necessary.
Casseroles and food cooked in sauces (except egg-based sauces)	2 months	Season lightly and omit the garlic if the food is going to be stored for the maximum time. Cook for a slightly shorter time to allow for the extra cooking when it is reheated. Allow to cool, then pour into foil or freezer bags, lined casserole dishes, or into rigid containers with lids. Make sure the sauce covers the surface of the food, lay a piece of freezer paper on top and seal.	Freeze lined casserole dishes until firm; then remove the dish and wrap the frozen casserole in a freezer bag for storage.	Thaw in room for 4-6 hours. Pour into dish, add garlic if required. Bake at 400°F for 1 hour, until boiling. Alternatively remove foil and place in original dish. Bake at 400°F for 1 hour then 350°F for ½ hour. Heat fully. Thicken if necessary.
Crêpes	1-2 months	Add one tablespoon of olive or sunflower oil to every 1 cup flour in the recipe. Cook and allow to cool.	Interleave with lightly oiled wax paper and seal in a freezer bag.	Thaw in refrigerator overnight or in room 2-3 hours. Remove paper, wrap in foil. Bake at 375°F for ½ hour. Or roll up with hot filling. Bake in covered dish for ¼ hour.
Croquettes (uncooked)	1 month	Make up the mixture	Wrap mixture in foil or a freezer bag and seal it.	Thaw in room. Mix and form into croquettes. Cook as in recipe.
Pizzas (cooked)	2 months	Bake as usual, and allow to cool.	Wrap cooled pizzas, interleaved with wax paper and seal in foil or freezer bags to freeze.	Bake from frozen at 400°F for 20 minutes, or thaw in room for 2 hours. Reheat for ¼ hour.
Vegetable loaves and terrines (uncooked)	1 month	Season lightly; omit the garlic for maximum storage. Line a loaf pan with foil and pour in the filling.	Freeze until hard, remove the loaf pan. Wrap in more foil, or seal in freezer bag.	Put bag in water until foil loosens. Remove foil and return loaf to original well-oiled tin. Bake as in recipe.
Vegetable loaves and terrines (cooked)	2 months	Cook as in recipe but season lightly. Omit garlic for maximum storage. Cool completely.	Wrap in foil or a freezer bag and seal.	Thaw in room for 4-6 hours, Serve cold.
Cookie dough	6 months	Shape dough into cylinders, wrap in foil or freezer wrap.	Freeze dough cylinders wrapped in the chosen covering; freeze shapes on non-stick paper, pack in rigid containers.	Thaw in room. Slice and bake as usual. Shaped biscuits can be baked from frozen; allow an extra 5-10 minutes.
Cookies (cooked)	6 months	Bake as usual and allow to cool.	Pack in rigid containers.	May be crisped at 350°F when thawed.
Bread	4 weeks	Bake in the usual way and allow to cool.	Freeze, sealed in freezer bags or foil.	Thaw in bag or foil in room; allow 2½-3 hours for small loaf. Make toast from frozen bread slices.
Cakes	4-6 months	Bake as usual and cool. Roll up jelly rolls with wax paper inside. Fill and frost cakes after thawing.	Wrap in foil or seal in freezer bags.	Thaw in room; allow sandwich cake layers 3-4 hours, small cakes 1-2 hours, large fruit cake 4-6 hours.
Pastry (dough) Shortcrust Puff	 3 months 3-4 months	Roll out; trim to fit pie pans or foil dishes. Puff pastry can be made into vol-au-vent cases.	Freeze unwrapped until hard. Leave in foil dishes, or remove any pie pans and interleave pastry with wax paper. Seal in freezer bags.	Thaw in room for 3-4 hours. Fit into oiled or buttered quiche or pie pans. Proceed as for fresh pastry.
Pastry (cooked)	6 months	(see recipes)	Allow to cool before freezing with care, seal in foil or freezer bags.	Thaw unfilled pie shells in room for 1 hour, filled case for 2-4 hours. Reheat at 350°F for 15-20 minutes.

Do not over-season curries of hot, spiced dishes as flavorings intensify during freezing. You will soon know how much to add.

Planning a Menu

The first consideration when planning a lunch or dinner party is to choose food that you think will appeal to your guests. Try and find out beforehand whether there are any foods which your guests will not enjoy; nothing spoils an occasion more than if a guest is forced to refuse something the host or hostess has taken a great deal of time and trouble to prepare. Choose the food as far as possible to match the occasion, but remember that the best and most enjoyable meals are often the simplest ones. Never strain your own capabilities or the resources of your kitchen. The best cooking is always done when you are confident and relaxed and not in a state of nervous exhaustion.

Winter Dinner Party for 8

Cream of Leek Soup	41
Mushrooms in Garlic Butter	62
Cheese and Pepper Surprise	84
with Tartare Sauce	127
Paprika Beans in Cream	112
Glazed Carrots with Cinnamon	116
Tabbouleh	133
Hazelnut Cake	160

CALORIES PER PORTION: 1925 (8055kJ) approx.
PROTEIN CONTENT PER PORTION: 50 grams approx.

Make double quantity of all the recipes except the Hazelnut Cake.

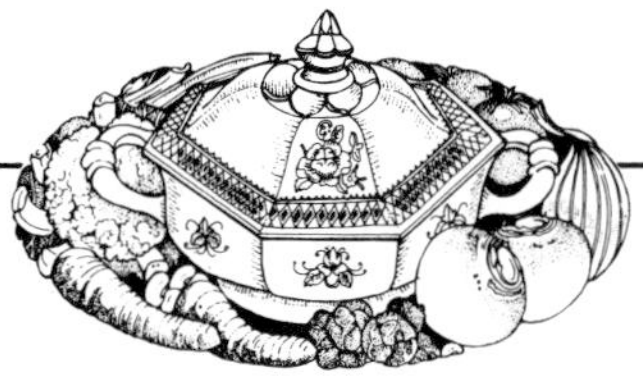

Summer Buffet for 12

CALORIES PER PORTION: 3980 (16650kJ) approx.
PROTEIN CONTENT PER PORTION: 83 grams approx.

Make double quantity of the soup, both Vol-au-vents, and – for guests with a sweet tooth – two Shortcakes.

Winter Lunch for 4

Spinach Ramekins	54
Chili 'sans' Carne	93
with Tortillas	93
Tunisian Orange Salad	130
Tomato, Celery and Apple Salad	131
Pineapple Upside-down Cake	146

CALORIES PER PORTION: 1205 (5070kJ) approx.
PROTEIN CONTENT PER PORTION: 37 grams approx.

Barbecue Supper for 4

Vegetable Kabobs	98
with Barbecue Sauce	197
Soybean and Nut Burgers in Rolls	87
Coleslaw 1	136
Mixed Salad	128
Baked Potatoes with Sour Cream	
Pumpkin Pie	162
Fresh Fruit	

CALORIES PER PORTION: 2710 (11360kJ) approx.
PROTEIN CONTENT PER PORTION: 70 grams approx.

Method for baking potatoes is given in the recipe for Stuffed Potatoes on page 50. Wholewheat Rolls are made from the Basic Quick Bread recipe on page 151.

Indian Supper for 4

CALORIES PER PORTION: 2570 (10750kJ) approx.
PROTEIN CONTENT PER PORTION: 95 grams approx.

We assume you will have a portion of each dish.

Chinese Meal for 4

Corn, Chinese Cabbage, Mushroom and Trailing Egg Soup	39
Fried Rice	123
Red-cooked Bean Curd with Bean Sprouts	122
Sweet and Sour Cabbage	122
Stir-fried Bean Sprouts	122
Spring Rolls	122

CALORIES PER PORTION: 2905 (12170kJ) approx.
PROTEIN CONTENT PER PORTION: 71 grams approx.

Chinese Sugar Apples (page 142) would make a delicious dessert for this menu, should one be required; otherwise, serve fresh lychees.

Summer Picnic for 6

For the Pâté menu:
CALORIES PER PORTION: 1530 (6425kJ) approx.
PROTEIN CONTENT PER PORTION: 44 grams approx.

For the Quiche menu:
CALORIES PER PORTION: 1510 (6325kJ) approx.
PROTEIN CONTENT PER PORTION: 43 grams approx.
(not including bread, cheese and fruit)

Basic Recipes

Without basic recipes, no cook can proceed, while the vegetarian cook will want to look again at the staples of the domestic kitchen. In this section you will find not only a Shortcrust pastry made from wholemeal flour, but also successful brown Puff pastry, Rough puff and Choux as well, for delicious light creations.

Sauces are given for all occasions: a Barbecue sauce or a piquant fruit sauce will lend distinction to a meatless main course. There are also sweet sauces for tempting desserts or you could try the original Brown sugar frosting or Peanut butter icing on a Sunday cake.

Yogurt is easy to make at home – and it is an improvement on the commercial variety. If you have not tried sprouting your own seeds, instructions are given for four different types for fresh, vitamin-packed salads. You will also find invaluable information on vegetables: helpful charts giving cooking and serving instructions which preserve the maximum flavor of fresh vegetables. If you want to freeze them to delay the pleasure of eating, you will also find comprehensive freezing instructions.

Wholewheat pie pastry

Makes 1¾ cup quantity
TOTAL CALORIES: 1720 (7200 kJ)
TOTAL PROTEIN CONTENT: 33 grams
PREPARATION & CHILLING: 40 minutes

1¾ cups wholewheat flour
½ teaspoon salt
8 tablespoons unsalted butter
2-3 tablespoons water

Mix the flour and salt in a bowl. Rub in the butter until the mixture resembles fine breadcrumbs. Gradually add the water, with a little extra if necessary, and mix to a firm dough. Knead lightly on a floured surface until smooth, then wrap the dough in aluminum foil or plastic wrap and chill in the refrigerator for about 30 minutes before using.

Note: This recipe makes enough pastry to line an 8 inch diameter tart or pie pan with some over for a lattice topping, or a 9 inch tart or pie pan. For a rich pie pastry, increase the butter to 10 tablespoons.

Puff pastry

Makes 4 cup quantity
TOTAL CALORIES: 4905 (20539 kJ)
TOTAL PROTEIN CONTENT: 46 grams
PREPARATION TIME: 2 hours

1 lb unsalted butter
4 cups all-purpose flour
2 teaspoons salt
1½ cups ice-cold water with 2 teaspoons lemon juice added

You should have no difficulty in making puff pastry as long as you realize that success depends on keeping the layers of butter and dough separate. The butter and dough must be of the same consistency. Take care to keep the ingredients and utensils as cool as possible. Use a marble slab for preference when rolling out the dough.

Knead 28 tablespoons (3 sticks plus 4 tablespoons) of the butter until pliable and shape into a 5 inch square.

Sift the flour and salt into a bowl and rub in the remaining 4 tablespoons of butter. Add the water and mix with a knife to a firm dough. Knead lightly on a floured surface until smooth. Roll the dough into an oblong, about 16 × 9 inches. Place the butter in the center and fold over the two sides, slightly stretching the dough to overlap a little in the center. Dampen the edge of the top layer to seal it. Fold over both ends, completely enclosing the fat, and press very lightly with the rolling pin to seal the layers of dough together. Wrap the dough in aluminum foil or plastic wrap and chill in the refrigerator for 10 minutes.

On a lightly floured surface, gently roll out the dough into an oblong, about 16 × 9 inches. To begin with, gentle pressure with the rolling pin, rather than actual rolling, will prevent the dough splitting and the butter coming through. Fold the bottom third of the oblong up and the top third down, press the edges lightly to seal and turn the top fold to the right-hand side. Repeat the rolling and folding five more times. Wrap the dough and place in the refrigerator to relax for 20 minutes after the second, fourth and sixth rolling and folding. Use as required, or divide into portions and freeze (see chart on page 207).

Rough puff pastry

Makes 2¼ cup quantity
TOTAL CALORIES: 2170 (9080 kJ)
TOTAL PROTEIN CONTENT: 25.2 grams
PREPARATION TIME: 1½-2 hours

12 tablespoons well-chilled unsalted butter
2¼ cups all-purpose flour
½ teaspoon salt
¾ cup ice-cold water with 1 teaspoon lemon juice added

Knead the butter until it is pliable but not soft or oily. Sift the flour and salt into a bowl and rub in a quarter of the butter. Cut the remaining butter into ¾ inch cubes and add to the flour. Toss lightly in the flour with the fingertips until well coated, taking care not to squash them. Add enough of the water and mix with a knife to make a fairly soft, lumpy dough. Turn out onto a floured surface and flour the dough but do not knead. Shape it into a rectangle about 4 × 6 inches with gentle hand pressure, then roll out to a 12 × 5 inch rectangle. Fold the bottom third up and the top third down.

Press the edges lightly by hand or with a rolling pin to seal. Turn the top fold to the right-hand side. Repeat the rolling and folding once and then wrap the dough well and place in the refrigerator for about 30 minutes to chill. Roll and fold twice more and chill it for a further 30 minutes. Use as required.

Choux pastry

Makes 1 cup quantity
TOTAL CALORIES: 1280 (5360 kJ)
TOTAL PROTEIN CONTENT: 37 grams
PREPARATION TIME: 15 minutes

1 cup all-purpose flour
1 cup milk
6 tablespoons butter
¾ teaspoon salt
3 eggs, well beaten

Sift the flour. Put the milk, butter and salt into a saucepan and place over a moderate heat until the butter melts. Increase the heat and bring to a boil, then remove the pan from the heat and immediately add the flour all at once, stirring vigorously. Return the pan to the heat and continue stirring until the mixture thickens and comes away from the sides of the pan. Allow to cool very slightly, then add the eggs a little at a time, beating very well between each addition. The mixture should be glossy and firm enough to hold its shape and, you may not need to use all the egg. There should be enough dough to make about 40 small Profiteroles or 24 Eclairs.

Coating batter

TOTAL CALORIES: 660 (2760 kJ)
TOTAL PROTEIN CONTENT: 28 grams
PREPARATION & RESTING TIME: 35 minutes

1 cup plus 2 tbls wholewheat flour
1 teaspoon salt
1 tablespoon butter, melted
2 egg yolks, beaten
⅔ cup milk
1 egg white

Sift flour into bowl with salt. Discard bran. Mix butter and egg yolks into milk, pour on flour. Mix well; stand 30 minutes. Stir in stiffly beaten egg white, add milk to dilute, if necessary. Use immediately.

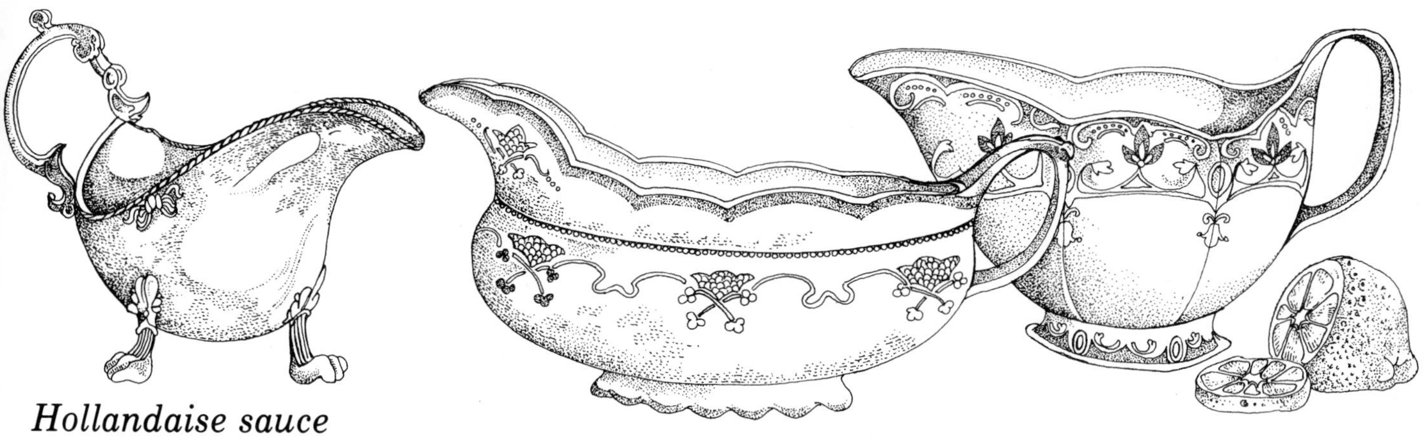

Hollandaise sauce

Serves 4
CALORIES PER PORTION: 225 (1060 kJ)
PROTEIN CONTENT PER PORTION: 2 grams
PREPARATION & COOKING TIME: 10 minutes

2 egg yolks
1 tablespoon lemon juice
8 tablespoons unsalted butter
salt

Beat the egg yolks with the lemon juice in the top of a double boiler until they are completely smooth. Add about a sixth of the butter and beat it into the egg yolks. Increase the heat under the pan, but never allow the water to boil, otherwise the sauce will curdle. Add another piece of butter and continue beating. Continue in this way until all the butter has been added and the sauce has begun to thicken. It should be thick enough to leave a trail when the spoon is moved across the surface.

Remove the top pan immediately from the lower pan of water and continue beating until the sauce has cooled down slightly and there is no danger that it will go on cooking. (The pan can be placed in a large bowl of cold water to hasten the process.) Season very lightly with salt and serve. Hollandaise sauce should be served lukewarm. If it has to be kept, place the pan in a saucepan of warm water, but do not let it boil.

Mousseline sauce: Stir 2-3 tablespoons lightly whipped cream into the basic Hollandaise sauce just before serving.

Butter sauce

This sauce is delicious served with vegetables where the richness of Hollandaise is not required.

Serves 4
CALORIES PER PORTION: 635 (2560 kJ)
PROTEIN CONTENT PER PORTION: 3 grams
PREPARATION & COOKING TIME: 20 minutes

6 tablespoons unsalted butter
1½ tablespoons all-purpose flour
1¼ cups boiling water
1-2 teaspoons lemon juice
a good pinch of grated lemon rind
salt
freshly ground pepper

Melt half of the butter in a saucepan over gentle heat, then remove the pan from the heat and mix in the flour. Pour on the boiling water, stirring vigorously. Do not return the pan to the heat. When the sauce is completely smooth, beat in the rest of the butter in four separate portions; add the lemon juice and rind and season with salt and pepper.

Do not allow this sauce to cook at all, or the flavor will be spoiled.

Béarnaise sauce

Serves 4
TOTAL CALORIES: 1080 (4510 kJ)
PROTEIN CONTENT PER PORTION: 13 grams
PREPARATION & COOKING TIME: 20 minutes

¼ cup wine vinegar
¼ cup finely chopped onion
1 bay leaf
1 tablespoon finely chopped mixed herbs
6 peppercorns, coarsely crushed
2 large egg yolks
8 tablespoons unsalted butter

Put the vinegar, onion, bay leaf, mixed herbs and peppercorns into a small saucepan and simmer it over very, very gentle heat until only 1 tablespoon is left. Strain it into a double boiler, add the egg yolks and mix thoroughly. Add about a sixth of the butter. Increase the heat slightly but do not let the water boil and continue beating until the butter has melted and is mixed into the eggs. Add another sixth of the butter and continue beating. Carry on in this way until all the butter has been added and the sauce is thick and foamy.

Béchamel sauce

Serves 4
CALORIES PER PORTION: 120 (500 kJ)
PROTEIN CONTENT PER PORTION: 3.5 grams
PREPARATION & COOKING TIME: 40 minutes

2 tablespoons butter
½ cup finely chopped onion
3 tablespoons wholewheat or ¼ cup all-purpose flour
1 ¼ cups milk
bay leaf
a blade of mace or a pinch of grated nutmeg
salt
freshly ground black pepper

Melt the butter over gentle heat and fry the onion until transparent. Stir in the flour and cook for a few moments longer, stirring all the time. Remove the pan from the heat and gradually add the milk, stirring well after each addition. Return the pan to the heat, add the bay leaf and mace or nutmeg and bring the sauce to a boil, stirring until it thickens. Transfer it to a double boiler, cover with a piece of buttered wax paper and simmer for 30 minutes. Strain the sauce and thin with a little hot milk if necessary. Adjust the seasoning and serve.

Béchamel sauce is the basis of a number of other sauces:

Cheese sauce: Add ½ cup grated sharp Cheddar cheese to the Béchamel sauce before straining. Stir until it has melted into the sauce, then strain as above and adjust the seasoning, adding a pinch of cayenne if liked.
Onion sauce: Cook 1 cup finely chopped onion in 1 tablespoon of butter until just transparent and add to the sauce before it is put into the double boiler. Rub some of the onion through the strainer with the sauce if you like a stronger onion flavor.
Parsley sauce: Stir 2 tablespoons of finely chopped parsley into the sauce after straining it and add a little lemon juice as well, if liked.
Caper sauce: Add 2-3 tablespoons finely chopped capers and a little wine or cider vinegar, or some of the vinegar from the capers, if liked, after straining the sauce.
Polonaise sauce: Add 1-2 tablespoons freshly grated horseradish, after straining. Then stir in 2 tablespoons heavy cream and a little lemon juice, if liked.
Mustard sauce: Stir in 1-2 teaspoons prepared French mustard and a little wine, or cider, vinegar after straining.
Sauce allemande: Stir a little of the basic Béchamel, after straining, into 2 well-beaten eggs in a bowl. Mix well, pour in the rest of the sauce and return it to a clean saucepan. Sprinkle with a pinch of grated nutmeg, add 1 teaspoon of lemon juice and stir well. Reheat the sauce, taking care that it does not boil or the eggs will curdle, and serve.
Lyonnaise sauce: Cook 1 cup finely chopped onion in 2 tablespoons butter until golden brown, then add them, with the butter in which they have been cooked, to the Béchamel sauce after straining.

Brown sauce

Serves 4
CALORIES PER PORTION: 140 (590 kJ)
PROTEIN CONTENT PER PORTION: 3.5 grams
PREPARATION & COOKING TIME: 30 minutes

1 cup finely chopped onion
2 tablespoons olive or sunflower oil
2 tomatoes, coarsely chopped
1-2 tablespoons wholewheat flour
1 ¼ cups brown vegetable stock
a pinch of dried thyme
bay leaf
¼ cup red wine
1 teaspoon brewer's yeast
salt
freshly ground pepper

Fry the onion in the oil until golden brown; add the tomatoes and continue cooking, stirring constantly, until all the liquid has evaporated and they have started to brown. Sprinkle over the flour, stir it well, then pour on the stock and bring to a boil, stirring all the time until the sauce thickens. Add the thyme, bay leaf, red wine and brewer's yeast and simmer the sauce for 20 minutes, stirring occasionally. Strain into a clean pan, adjust the seasoning, reheat and serve.

The following sauces are based on Brown sauce.

Mushroom sauce: Cook 1 cup finely chopped mushrooms in 2 tablespoons butter until soft and shiny and add them to the brown sauce after straining it. If a smoother textured sauce is required, add the mushrooms before straining the sauce and rub them through the strainer. Season well with pepper and a little cayenne, if desired.
Paprika sauce: Add 2 tablespoons of fresh paprika to the basic Brown sauce recipe with the flour. A little wine vinegar or lemon juice can also be added, if liked.
Madeira sauce: Add 2-4 tablespoons well-flavored dark Madeira to the basic Brown sauce after straining. Adjust the seasoning and serve as it is, or simmer the sauce for 5-10 minutes to evaporate the alcohol.
Piquant sauce: Pour 3 tablespoons wine vinegar into a saucepan with 3 coarsely crushed peppercorns, a bay leaf and a sprig of thyme or rosemary. Reduce it to 1 tablespoon, then strain it into the finished sauce. Add 1 tablespoon very finely chopped dill pickle.

Tomato sauce

Serves 4
CALORIES PER PORTION: 60 (247 kJ)
PROTEIN CONTENT PER PORTION: 1.5 grams
PREPARATION & COOKING TIME: 40 minutes

½ cup finely chopped onion
1 tablespoon olive or sunflower oil
1 tablespoon wholewheat flour
⅔ cup water
2 cups coarsely chopped tomatoes
1 bay leaf
1 clove of garlic, peeled and finely chopped (optional)
salt
freshly ground pepper

Fry the onion in the oil until transparent, stir in the flour, then add the water. Stir well, then put in the tomatoes with the bay leaf and garlic, if used. Bring to a boil, stirring all the time, then simmer the sauce for 30 minutes, stirring from time to time. Rub the sauce through a strainer, adjust the seasoning and reheat before serving.

For a more piquant sauce, add 1 tablespoon wine or cider vinegar to the water and stir ½ tablespoon finely chopped capers into the sauce after straining.
Bigarade sauce: Add the thinly pared and sliced rind of 2 Seville oranges, with their juice, to the basic Tomato or Brown sauce.

Catalane sauce

CALORIES PER PORTION: 130 (540 kJ)
PROTEIN CONTENT PER PORTION: 3 grams
PREPARATION AND COOKING TIME: 20 minutes, using prepared basic sauces

⅔ cup Brown sauce
⅔ cup Tomato sauce
½ cup finely chopped red peppers
1 tablespoon butter, melted
1 tablespoon lemon juice
½ teaspoon grated orange rind
½ clove of garlic, peeled and finely chopped

Heat up the two sauces together. Fry the peppers in the butter over moderate heat until they are soft; add the lemon juice, orange rind and garlic and cook for a few minutes, then pour on the sauces. Stir well and simmer for a further 5 minutes before serving.

Piquant cherry sauce

CALORIES PER PORTION: 47 (195 kJ)
PROTEIN CONTENT PER PORTION: 1 gram
PREPARATION & COOKING TIME: 45 minutes

6 tablespoons wine vinegar
2 tablespoons finely chopped onion
1⅔ cups pitted morello or Bing cherries
⅔ cup water
grated rind and juice of 1 orange
salt
freshly ground pepper
½ teaspoon freshly ground allspice
¼ teaspoon ground cinnamon

Put the vinegar and onion into a small saucepan and simmer over gentle heat until the liquid is reduced by half. Add the cherries, water and the orange rind and juice and increase the heat slightly. Simmer until the cherries are soft, about 15-20 minutes, then remove from the heat and rub through a strainer. Adjust the seasoning, add the cinnamon and reheat the sauce, if necessary, before serving.

Horseradish sauce

CALORIES PER PORTION: 175 (725 kJ)
PROTEIN CONTENT PER PORTION: 1 gram
PREPARATION TIME: 10 minutes

2-3 tablespoons peeled and freshly grated horseradish
1 teaspoon wine vinegar or lemon juice
⅔ cup heavy cream
salt

Mix together the horseradish and vinegar or lemon juice. Lightly whip the cream, then fold in the horseradish and season with salt.

For a change, try using sour cream instead of heavy cream.

Barbecue sauce

CALORIES PER PORTION: 145 (610 kJ)
PROTEIN CONTENT PER PORTION: 2 grams
PREPARATION & COOKING TIME: 20 minutes

1¼ cups finely chopped onion
2 tablespoons sunflower or olive oil
1¼ cups Tomato sauce
1 clove of garlic, peeled and finely chopped
½ cup finely diced canned pineapple
½ cup finely diced dill pickles
2 tablespoons wine vinegar
salt
freshly ground pepper
a pinch of cayenne

Fry the onion in the oil until transparent, then add all the other ingredients except the salt, pepper and cayenne and simmer for 5 minutes. Adjust the seasoning and serve the sauce hot or cold.

Spiced apricot sauce

CALORIES PER PORTION: 115 (485 kJ)
PROTEIN CONTENT PER PORTION: 1.5 grams
PREPARATION & COOKING TIME: 10 minutes

3 cups cooked or canned apricots
⅔ cup Brown vegetable stock (page 34)
½ teaspoon ground cinnamon
½ teaspoon ground ginger
a dash of Tabasco sauce
3 tablespoons sweet sherry
salt
freshly ground pepper

Rub the apricots through a strainer or food mill into a saucepan and thin the purée with some of the stock.

Add the rest of the ingredients, season well with salt and pepper and bring the sauce to a boil over moderate heat, stirring constantly to prevent it from sticking. Lower the heat and simmer for another 5 minutes, stirring occasionally. Pour into a jug and serve.

The sauce can also be served cold.

Green gooseberry sauce

CALORIES PER PORTION: 110 (460 kJ)
PROTEIN CONTENT PER PORTION: 1 gram
PREPARATION & COOKING TIME: 30 minutes

1 cup halved green gooseberries
2 tablespoons butter
1 tablespoon wholewheat flour
⅓ pint water
1 tablespoon white wine
salt
freshly ground pepper

Cook the gooseberries in very little water until they are tender, about 10-15 minutes, then press them through a strainer. Melt the butter in a pan over gentle heat and stir in the flour, then remove the pan from the heat, pour on the water and mix until smooth. Return the pan to the heat, bring to a boil and simmer the sauce for 10 minutes, stirring occasionally to prevent it burning. Add the gooseberry purée and wine and mix well. Adjust the seasoning, if necessary, and cook for a few minutes longer before serving.

Herb butter

CALORIES PER PORTION: 100 (412 kJ)
PROTEIN CONTENT PER PORTION: nil
PREPARATION & CHILLING TIME: 1 hour

Beat ¼ cup finely chopped herbs, such as parsley, tarragon, chervil or watercress, or a mixture of all of these into 8 tablespoons unsalted butter. Form the herb butter into a roll and chill well before cutting it into 4 slices, one for each portion.

Clarified butter

CALORIES PER PORTION: 415 (1472 kJ)
PROTEIN CONTENT PER PORTION: 0.25 grams
PREPARATION TIME: 10 minutes

16 tablespoons (2 sticks) butter

Put the butter into a small pan over gentle heat and warm until it has melted and begun to bubble. Continue cooking until the bubbling subsides, but do not allow the sediment at the bottom of the pan to color. Strain the melted butter through a cheesecloth-lined strainer and store in a covered jar. Discard the milk solids that are left after straining. This quantity should give about ¾ cup of clarified butter.

Montpelier butter

CALORIES PER PORTION: 100 (412 kJ)
PROTEIN CONTENT PER PORTION: nil
PREPARATION & CHILLING TIME: 1 hour

1 clove of garlic, peeled and cut in half
1 tablespoon chopped chervil
1 tablespoon chopped tarragon
1 tablespoon chopped chives
2 tablespoons chopped watercress
1 teaspoon finely chopped capers
1 teaspoon finely chopped dill pickle
8 tablespoons unsalted butter

Rub the inside of a small bowl with the cut clove of garlic. Put in the herbs, watercress, capers and pickle and mix well. Beat in the softened butter and form it into a roll. Chill well before cutting into 4 portions for serving.

Sweet Sauces

The sweet sauces have been chosen to complement the cakes, puddings, ices and desserts in this book.

These are followed by one or two of my favorite icings, frostings and fillings for cakes.

Chantilly cream

CALORIES PER PORTION: 335 (1465 kJ)
PROTEIN CONTENT PER PORTION: 4 grams
PREPARATION TIME: 5 minutes

1¼ cups heavy cream
3 tablespoons soft brown sugar
1 egg white, stiffly beaten

Lightly whip the cream with the brown sugar until it just holds its shape, then fold in the stiffly beaten egg white.

Butterscotch sauce

CALORIES PER PORTION: 157 (660 kJ)
PROTEIN CONTENT PER PORTION: negligible
PREPARATION & COOKING TIME: 20 minutes

2 tablespoons light corn syrup
2 tablespoons butter
½ cup raw brown sugar
1½ tablespoons cornstarch
1¼ cups water

Put the syrup, butter and sugar into a pan and cook over medium heat until the sugar has started to caramelize; mix the cornstarch to a cream with a little of the water, then add the rest of the water and mix well. Remove the pan from the heat and pour the cornstarch mixture onto the caramel. Stir well, return the pan to the heat and cook, stirring, until it is well combined and the sauce has thickened.

If a richer sauce is required, use half milk and half water.

Caramel sauce

CALORIES PER PORTION: 185 (780 kJ)
PROTEIN CONTENT PER PORTION: negligible
PREPARATION & COOKING TIME: 20 minutes

1 tablespoon cornstarch
1¼ cups water
¾ cup sugar

Mix the cornstarch to a cream with a little of the water and then add the rest. Melt the sugar in a thick-based pan, stirring continuously, and continue cooking until it has turned a rich golden brown. Take the pan off the heat and gradually stir in the water and cornstarch mixture, taking care that the hot sugar does not spatter onto your hand. Return the pan to the heat and cook, stirring well, until the caramel has dissolved and the sauce has thickened. Pour it into a jug and serve hot or cold.

Custard sauce

CALORIES PER PORTION: 210 (872 kJ)
PROTEIN CONTENT PER PORTION: 5 grams
PREPARATION & COOKING TIME: 40 minutes

4 tablespoons butter
3 tablespoons wholewheat or ¼ cup all-purpose flour
1¼ cups milk
3 tablespoons raw brown sugar
1 vanilla bean
1 egg, well beaten

Melt the butter in a saucepan over gentle heat, stir in the flour and cook for a few moments without allowing the flour to color. Remove the pan from the heat and stir in the milk. Return the pan to the heat, add the sugar and bring the sauce to a boil, stirring until it thickens. Add the vanilla bean, pour the sauce into a double boiler, cover it with a piece of buttered wax paper and let it simmer over boiling water for about 30 minutes. Remove from the heat and allow to cool slightly before pouring it slowly onto the egg, stirring vigorously as you do so. Strain the sauce and thin with a little extra milk, if necessary, to make it up to 1¼ cups.

Tipsy custard

CALORIES PER PORTION: 210 (872 kJ)
PROTEIN CONTENT PER PORTION: 5 grams

Follow the recipe (left), but add 1-2 tablespoons of brandy before straining the sauce.

Raspberry sauce

CALORIES PER PORTION: 250 (1045 kJ)
PROTEIN CONTENT PER PORTION: 1 gram
PREPARATION & COOKING TIME: 30 minutes

1 lb raspberries
1⅓ cups raw brown sugar

Put the raspberries into a saucepan with the sugar and place over gentle heat. Break some of the fruit with a wooden spoon to release some of the juice, and simmer over gentle heat for about 20 minutes. Rub the sauce through a strainer and serve hot or cold.

Chocolate sauce

CALORIES PER PORTION: 265 (1115 kJ)
PROTEIN CONTENT PER PORTION: 1.5 grams
PREPARATION & COOKING TIME: 15 minutes

1 cup plus 3 tablespoons raw brown sugar
2 tablespoons butter
1 cup water
2 tablespoons cocoa powder

Put the sugar, butter and water into a pan and bring to a boil, stirring continuously. Simmer until all the sugar has dissolved, then sift in the cocoa powder and continue stirring. Boil until the sauce thickens slightly when a drop is put onto a cold plate. If it is boiled for too long it will turn into toffee.

For a special occasion add 1 teaspoon of brandy just before serving. The above recipe will make about 1 cup of sauce.

Brown sugar frosting

TOTAL CALORIES: 520 (1054 kJ)
TOTAL PROTEIN CONTENT: 7 grams
PREPARATION & COOKING TIME: 30 minutes

⅔ cup raw brown sugar
3 tablespoons boiled water
2 egg whites, stiffly beaten
½ teaspoon vanilla extract

You need a candy thermometer to make this frosting successfully.

Put the sugar and water into a very clean, small, thick-based saucepan and bring to a boil over fairly high heat. Boil until the temperature reaches 225°F. As soon as the syrup reaches the correct temperature, pour it slowly into the egg whites while beating vigorously. Add the vanilla and continue beating until the frosting is thick enough to coat the top and sides of a cake.

If the syrup goes grainy as it gets near to the correct temperature, it shows that the saucepan was not quite clean and grease-free or perhaps that the sugar was not of good enough quality. Try not to let any sugar crystallize around the edges of the pan as it will encourage graining to occur.

Chocolate frosting: Add 1 tablespoon of sifted cocoa powder toward the end of beating.

Coffee frosting: Add 1-2 teaspoons of instant coffee powder toward the end of beating.

Orange frosting: Add 1-2 teaspoons finely grated orange rind toward the end of beating.

Brown sugar butter cream

TOTAL CALORIES: 2565 (10740 kJ)
TOTAL PROTEIN CONTENT: 4 grams
PREPARATION & COOKING TIME: 20 minutes plus cooling time

⅔ cup plus 3 tablespoons raw brown sugar
8 tablespoons butter or margarine
½ cup milk
2 cups sifted confectioners sugar

Put the sugar, butter or margarine and milk into a saucepan over a moderate heat and stir until the sugar has dissolved. Allow to cool a little before stirring in the confectioners sugar. Stand the saucepan in a bowl filled with ice cubes and stir briskly until the frosting is cold and the consistency thick enough to coat the top and sides of a cake. If the consistency is still too soft when the frosting is quite cold, beat in more confectioners sugar.

Vanilla-flavored cream: Add ½ teaspoon vanilla extract with the butter.

Chocolate-flavored cream: Add 2-3 teaspoons cocoa powder to the butter, sugar and milk while the sugar is dissolving.

Coffee-flavored cream: Add 2-3 teaspoons of instant coffee powder to the butter, sugar and milk in the pan while the sugar is dissolving.

Peanut butter frosting

TOTAL CALORIES: 2225 (9300 kJ)
TOTAL PROTEIN CONTENT: 32 grams
PREPARATION TIME: 10 minutes

½ cup peanut butter
1 teaspoon lemon juice
3 cups sifted confectioners sugar
½ cup milk

Soften the peanut butter, if necessary, by standing the jar in a pan of warm water. Mix in the lemon juice and confectioners sugar, then add just enough milk to give a coating consistency. There will be enough frosting to cover the top and sides of an 8 inch diameter layer cake. Use Raspberry or Strawberry jam to sandwich the layers as a contrast.

Almond paste

TOTAL CALORIES: 3320 (13900 kJ)
TOTAL PROTEIN CONTENT: 61 grams
PREPARATION TIME: 10-20 minutes

2 cups sifted confectioners sugar
⅔ cup granulated sugar
2¾ cups ground almonds
1 whole egg and 1 egg yolk
1-2 teaspoons rose water (optional)
1 tablespoon lemon juice

Mix together 1¼ cups of the confectioners sugar, the granulated sugar and the almonds in a bowl. Beat the eggs with the rose water, if used, and lemon juice and pour into the dry ingredients. Mix thoroughly and turn out onto a board or work surface. Knead until smooth, adding more of the confectioners sugar if necessary to make a firm paste. Use as required.

Yogurt

Yogurt makes a pleasantly sour sauce for fresh or cooked fruit. Mixed with honey and served chilled it makes a refreshing dessert.

CALORIES PER PORTION: 165 (695 kJ)
PROTEIN CONTENT PER PORTION: 9 grams
PREPARATION TIME: 12 hours

1 quart milk
2 tablespoons fresh live yogurt or commercial yogurt culture (follow the manufacturer's instructions)

Make sure that the yogurt is genuine *natural* yogurt and that it contains live culture; it is important to make sure that all the utensils and equipment you use are spotlessly clean.

Bring the milk to boiling point and scald for 5 minutes. Allow to cool to just above body temperature. Meanwhile, thoroughly clean a large container. Pour in the warm milk, add the live yogurt and mix thoroughly. Cover the bowl and keep warm, at a temperature a little above blood heat, for 8-12 hours or until the yogurt has set. Allow to cool and then use as required. Retain a couple of tablespoons of this yogurt with which to start the next batch, but do not keep it longer than a couple of days. Store in the refrigerator, where it will keep fresh for 2-3 days.

When the yogurt begins to lose its strength, it will be necessary to start again with a fresh supply of live yogurt, or a dried culture.

Fat-free yogurt is made by using dried skimmed milk made up with sterile warm water that has been brought to a boil and allowed to cool.

Note: There are a number of very efficient commercial yogurt makers available and it may be worth investing in one of these.

Chhana

Makes 275 g (10 oz) cheese

CALORIES PER PORTION: 130 (545 kJ)
PROTEIN CONTENT PER PORTION: 12.5 grams
PREPARATION TIME: 12 hours

1 quart freshly made yogurt

Line a strainer or colander with a scrupulously clean piece of cheesecloth and put it over a bowl. Pour the yogurt into the lined strainer, cover it and leave it to drain overnight in a cool, insect-free, airy place. Turn the cheese out of the cloth, keep it in the refrigerator and use as required. It is slightly more acid than normal curd cheese, but is very good to eat with wholewheat bread or salads.

Use the whey as the cooking liquid in casseroles or for making stock; the slight acidity gives a pleasing piquancy to the finished food.

Panir

CALORIES PER PORTION: 130 (545 kJ)
PROTEIN CONTENT PER PORTION: 12.5 grams
PREPARATION TIME: 12¼ hours

Panir is a chhana which has been pressed; you can improvise a press quite easily if you have two cake pans of 6 inch diameter with removable bases. Use one outside pan and both bases.

Place a base inside the pan and line the bottom with 6 layers of paper towels, leaving a small space around the edge for the liquid to drain away during pressing. Line the inside of the pan with a layer of cheesecloth and on this spread the Chhana. Wrap the cheesecloth firmly around the chhana, or put another layer of cheesecloth over the top. Add 6 more layers of paper towels, then the second cake pan base and place a weight of approximately 4 lb on top. If the chhana begins to ooze out right away, try a slightly lighter weight. After about 4 hours the weight can be increased to about 6 lb, and, after 4 more hours, this weight can be doubled to about 12 lb. Leave for a further 4 hours, then carefully dismantle the press and remove the cheese. Strip off the cheesecloth and cut it into cubes.

To cook panir: Arrange the cubes in a well-buttered baking dish and brush the tops with melted butter. Bake in a 400°F oven for 30-40 minutes until they are golden brown but not dried out. Turn the pieces over about halfway through the cooking time.

Note: It is easier to bake homemade panir than to fry it, as it tends to disintegrate in the skillet. Add it to casseroles for extra protein, or eat with salads.

Garam masala

Indian cooking depends for its subtlety of flavor on the fact that Indian cooks mix their own spices for each dish. Commercially-made curry powder can be used instead, of course, but the difference in flavor if you blend your own cannot be compared.

The base
3 parts green cardamons
2 parts cinnamon
1-2 parts cumin seeds

For coriander-based
add 2 parts coriander seeds

For clove-based
add ¼-½ part cloves

For fennel-based
add ½ part of fennel seeds

Mix together all the ingredients and grind them to a fine powder either in a pestle and mortar or a small mill.

Sprouting beans and seeds

One of the great attractions of sprouting is that anyone with enough space to put a bottle or jar of ½-2 quarts can grow an appetizing and nutritious supplement to their diet. Many varieties of beans and seeds are now sold solely for sprouting and are readily available from healthfood stores.

There are various methods of sprouting seeds; if you keep the basic requirements of germination in mind, it is easy to find the simplest method. Seeds require moisture to germinate and, as they are being grown in greater concentration than in nature, certain waste products need to be dispersed.

There are commercially available sprouting trays with special draining systems and some people recommend ordinary kitchen strainers. I found that when I used a strainer, the roots grew straight through the holes in the mesh and were difficult to disentangle, and the commercially designed trays took up too much space — so I now use the simplest method, and in my opinion, the best.

Choose a wide necked bottle of about ½ quart capacity for smaller seeds and a 2 quart bottle for growing larger seeds and for production in quantity. You will also need a piece of nylon gauze or net of a mesh size smaller than any seed you intend sprouting and a piece of thin string or a rubber band to keep it in place over the top of the jar.

The seeds you intend to sprout must be of edible quality. That is why it is advisable to buy them from a healthfood store, particularly if you tell them what you are using them for, as some seeds will not sprout if they are too old and the store should know the state of their stock. Do not use horticultural seeds unless they are being sold for sprouting as they might otherwise be treated with insecticides, chemical retardants or fungicides.

Select good-quality, undamaged seeds and discard any that are split, chipped or blemished in any way as they will not germinate; worse, they might rot and taint the rest of your crop. Spread them out on a tray for inspection and pick out any bad ones. Most seeds expand to about eight times their original volume; 1 oz will give ½ lb of sprouts, enough for 2 servings. As a general rule, the smaller the seed the greater the increase in size.

Put them into a strainer and rinse them under cold running water. Then transfer them gently to the bottle, taking care not to damage them. Cover them with water, fasten the straining net securely over and leave them to soak overnight. The following morning, pour off the water, re-fill the bottle and immediately pour it off again so that the seeds have just the moisture which is clinging to them. Do not leave any excess water in the bottom of the jar. Put it in a cupboard or on a shelf at room temperature. In the evening, fill the jar with water again and drain it off, and repeat this routine again last thing at night. Continue this daily ritual until the shoots are the length you require, about 5-7 days, depending on the warmth of the atmosphere and the type of sprout. Never leave the seeds standing in water or they will rot, and take care to remove any seeds that have not sprouted within 36 hours of the first germination. Take out any that show signs of going mushy.

Soybeans, lentils, chick peas, wheat and many other seeds can be sprouted, so I suggest you find a specialist book on the subject (see Bibliography).

Alfalfa

Delicious in salads, the sprouts cook almost instantly. Use them on their own, or with a light salad dressing, or as a garnish to vegetable dishes.

Mung beans

These have a flavor similar to very young raw peas and will be recognized as an essential ingredient in many Chinese dishes. Use them when the root is 1½-2½ inches long. Stir fry them for 2-3 minutes.

Mustard and garden cress

This is grown in a totally different way, but is so easy that it has to be included. Put a layer of absorbent cotton in a shallow dish and moisten it lightly. Sprinkle the seeds sparsely over the surface and place the dish on a light windowsill but not in full sunlight. Keep the surface covered with a piece of card until the seeds germinate. If you want to harvest both mustard and cress at the same time, plant the mustard seed four days after the cress.

Preparation of accompanying vegetables

Vegetable	Quantity for 4	Preparation	Cooking instructions	Serving instructions
Roots				
Beets	1 lb	Do not peel and take care not to break the skin, otherwise the color will bleed. Trim off leaves 2 inches above the bulb.	Simmer 2-3 hours, depending on size. Best flavor and color is achieved by baking; wrap in foil and bake at 300°F for 2-3 hours.	Serve with butter and lemon juice; or Béchamel sauce and a little grated nutmeg.
Carrots	1 lb	Remove stem tops and scrape off skin if necessary. Scrub well and leave whole if very small, or split in half lengthwise. Slice or shred coarsely.	Simmer young small carrots for 10-15 minutes; whole large roots for 20-30 minutes. Stir-fry if shredded for 5 minutes. Try cooking young carrots in tonic water; or with a small piece of orange rind added.	Serve buttered, with chopped parsley or other herbs; mash or purée older carrots with cream or butter and parsley.
Celery root	1 lb	Trim off leaves and stem without peeling. Scrub well. Alternatively, peel and shred or peel and cut into 1 inch cubes. Put into acidulated water.	Simmer for 30-60 minutes if whole; 10-15 minutes if cubed. (It should still be slightly crisp.)	If cooked whole, peel and mash with butter or an equal quantity of potatoes. Add a little Dijon mustard and lemon juice. Serve cubes buttered.
Kohlrabi	1 lb	Cut the roots and leaves off very young ones, about 1-1½ inches diameter, and leave whole. Older ones need peeling, slice or dice.	Simmer for 20-30 minutes; braise older ones for 30-60 minutes in well-flavored stock.	Serve young ones with butter; or in Béchamel sauce. Mash old ones with plenty of butter, sour cream or plain yogurt.
Parsnips	1 lb	Cut off stem top and spindly root. Peel and dice, slice or cut into quarters or strips; remove fibrous core from old ones.	Simmer 10-15 minutes, depending on whether sliced or quartered; bake at 350°F for 30-45 minutes; or roast.	Serve parsnips buttered; or in Béchamel sauce. Mash them, dab the top with butter and brown under the broiler.
Radishes	½ lb	Cut off the tops and spindly roots. Leave whole, or slice.	Simmer 10-15 minutes; stir-fry slices for 3-5 minutes.	Add some melted butter or sprinkle over a little soy sauce.
Rutabaga	1 lb	Peel and remove any fibrous core. Rinse well, then slice, dice or cut into strips.	Simmer 15-30 minutes. Drain well and dry in warm oven.	Toss in butter or mash with cream or butter; or serve in Béchamel sauce.
Salsify or oyster plant	1 lb	Cut off tops and tapering root. Peel and immerse in acidulated water. Cut into 1-2 inch lengths.	Simmer for 15-20 minutes then finish in butter for 5 minutes over moderate heat.	Serve straight from the pan with the butter poured over; or with Hollandaise sauce.
Turnips	1 lb	Peel. If very young, leave whole; large ones can be sliced, cut in quarters or diced.	Simmer whole ones 10-30 minutes. Drain and dry in warm oven. Diced turnips need about 10 minutes.	Toss in butter with a little parsley; serve in a Béchamel sauce with a little lemon rind added.
Tubers				
Jerusalem artichokes	1 lb	Peel thinly, using a small knife to get between the knobs. Slice, leave whole or dice.	Simmer 15-20 minutes if whole; 10-15 minutes if sliced. Stir-fry thin slices for 5-10 minutes.	Serve with butter and a sprinkling of nutmeg; or masked in Béchamel sauce. Try stir-fried until still crisp; they taste like a strong water chestnut.
Potatoes	1-2 lb	Scrub well and remove any eyes or discolored patches. Leave skins on whenever possible, otherwise scrape off as thinly as possible. Leave whole, or cut in halves or quarters. New potatoes should only be scrubbed. **For French fries** Cut the potatoes into ½ inch slices and then cut the slices into strips of about the same thickness; leave in acidulated water until required. Dry them thoroughly before frying them. **For potato chips** Cut the potatoes into slices about $^1/_{10}$ inch thick.	Simmer new potatoes in their jackets for about 15-25 minutes; or cook in a covered casserole for 30-40 minutes at 400°F after brushing with oil or butter. Simmer whole maincrop potatoes 30-40 minutes; cut ones, 15 minutes. Brush the skin with oil or butter, sprinkle with salt, cut a small cross on top to allow the steam to escape and bake for 1-1½ hours at 350°F. Deep fry French fries at 350°F until golden brown and cooked through. Deep fry potato chips at 350°F keeping separate.	Serve boiled potatoes with melted butter and parsley or, after boiling, sauté in butter or oil until golden brown. It is essential to heat the milk to almost boiling point when mashing potatoes; ¾ cup of milk to 1 lb potatoes is about the correct proportion.
Sweet potatoes, Yams	1-2 lb	Scrub the skins. Peel after boiling or baking.	Simmer for 30-40 minutes; bake at 350°F for 45-60 minutes.	Serve peeled and mashed with butter and a dusting of cinnamon.

Preparation of accompanying vegetables—continued

Vegetable	Quantity for 4	Preparation	Cooking instructions	Serving instructions
Brassicas and leaves				
Broccoli	1 lb	Remove any large leaves and cut off any fibrous stem. Divide large heads into florets. Rinse well.	Simmer 10-15 minutes; steam 10-15 minutes.	Serve with a pat of butter and a dash of pepper; or with Hollandaise sauce; or sprinkle with grated cheese and finish under the broiler.
Brussels sprouts	1 lb	Remove outer leaves and ends of stems. Leave whole. If sprouts are large and stems are thick, cross-cut to ¼ way up.	Simmer 8-10 minutes; steam 10-20 minutes, depending on size.	Serve buttered with pepper; or buttered with lemon juice and chopped oregano; or browned in butter with chopped onion and boiled chestnuts.
Chinese cabbage	1 lb	Remove outer leaves. Tear the inner leaves into 2 inch squares and wash well.	Stir-fry 5-10 minutes.	Serve straight from the pan; or add a little shredded orange rind and juice.
Winter, summer or Savoy cabbage	1 lb	Remove bruised or damaged outer leaves and watch for caterpillars. Chop coarsely or shred finely after removing hard core.	Simmer 10-15 minutes.	Serve with a pat of butter and a dash of pepper.
Red cabbage	1 lb	As winter cabbage.	Braise with onions, garlic and/or apple, raisins, brown sugar, spices (shown right) and with vinegar. Cook in oven 2½ hours, on stove 1½.	Flavor with pickling spice, cloves or caraway seeds to taste.
White cabbage	1 lb	As winter cabbage.	Simmer 5-10 minutes; stir-fry 5-10 minutes; steam 5-10 minutes.	As winter cabbage; or try putting ½ teaspoon caraway seeds in to flavor the water, if boiling.
Cauliflower	1 medium head or 1 lb	Remove outer leaves and any discolored curd; leave whole or break into florets. Cut out part of the center core if leaving whole.	Simmer whole 20-30 minutes; simmer florets 5-10 minutes, depending on size.	Serve buttered; or with lemon and butter; or with a Béchamel or Cheese sauce.
Kale	1¼-2 lb	Discard all damaged or discolored leaves. Watch for insects. Rinse well.	Simmer in just enough water to cover; young leaves 5-15 minutes, older leaves 20-25 minutes. Steaming is not advisable.	Serve buttered and sprinkled with herbs; or with chopped onion; or with a chili sauce. Mask them in a rich Cream sauce or Cheese sauce, and finish under the broiler for a few moments.
Spinach	1¼-2 lb	Discard all damaged or discolored parts of leaves. Watch for insects. Wash leaf by leaf under cold running water. Remove all stems.	Cook in just the water clinging to the leaves. A little butter or oil on the bottom of the pan prevents them sticking; young leaves 5-10 minutes; older leaves 10-15 minutes. Steam for about 15 minutes; stir-fry 5-10 minutes.	Serve buttered; with chopped onion; in a Cream or Cheese sauce and browned under the broiler; or puréed and made into a soufflé.
Mild-flavored greens				
Beet tops, Chicory, Dandelion leaves, Lettuce, Spring cabbage, Watercress	1¼-2 lb	As spinach.	As spinach.	As spinach.
Strong-flavored greens				
Mustard greens		As kale.	As kale; or cook stems as a separate vegetable; simmer 20-25 minutes; steam 30 minutes.	As kale.
Swiss chard		As kale.	As mustard greens.	As kale.
Turnip tops		As kale.	As mustard greens.	As kale.

Other greens

Note: Cook all greens uncovered for the first 5 minutes to preserve their color. Keep any remaining liquid for use in stock. Keep some tender young leaves for use in salads.

Preparation of accompanying vegetables—continued

Vegetable	Quantity for 4	Preparation	Cooking instructions	Serving instructions
Stalks and shoots				
Asparagus	1-2 lb	Break off base of stalk as low down as possible – it should break cleanly; otherwise, cut off the lower woody part. Scrape off any remaining tough skin from the base of the stalk.	Cook vertically, tied in bunches, for 15-25 minutes, with only the lower part of the stalks in the water. The tips will cook in the steam.	Serve with melted butter or Hollandaise sauce.
Belgian endive	1 lb	Cut off root plate and remove any outer discolored leaves. Leave whole or chop.	Braise whole for 1¼ hours. Stir-fry chopped leaves 5-10 minutes.	Serve raw chopped leaves in orange Vinaigrette.
Cardoons	1 lb	Remove old or wilted stems. Break the rest into 3 inch pieces. Remove all strings. Trim heart and cut in half.	Simmer for 1-2 hours in vegetable stock with added lemon juice.	Serve with the reduced, thickened stock; or with Béchamel sauce.
Celery	1 lb	Cut off roots and leaves and remove all strings. Separate the stalks and break into 2-3 inch lengths. Rinse well.	Simmer 10 minutes; steam 12-15 minutes; stir-fry 10 minutes.	Serve buttered; or with a warm Vinaigrette sauce; or a Cheese sauce with a little cumin seed added.
Florence fennel	1 lb	Cut off root base and top leaves. If large, cut bulb into quarters; if small, cut in half.	Simmer 10-15 minutes or, cook separated "leaves" as celery.	Serve buttered, or with a mild Cheese sauce.
Globe artichokes	1 per person	Break off the stem as this pulls out more fibers than cutting will. Soak in salted water for 30 minutes to get rid of any insects. Trim off the points of the leaves.	Simmer in salted water coming half way up the artichoke, for 30-45 minutes; they are done when a leaf pulls out easily.	Serve hot with melted butter or Hollandaise sauce. Serve cold with Vinaigrette dressing or Mayonnaise.
Pods and seeds				
Green beans	1 lb	Remove tops and bottoms and any strings. Leave whole or cut diagonally into thin strips or straight across into 1 in lengths. Rinse well.	Simmer very young beans 5-10 minutes, older ones 15-20 minutes; steam 10-25 minutes; stir-fry young beans 5-10 minutes. Try flavoring the cooking water with a little savory.	Serve with butter, butter and lemon juice; or a herb butter.
Lima beans	3 lb unshelled	Remove beans from pods.	Simmer 10-30 minutes depending on age and size. The cooked beans should not be mushy.	Serve buttered, or with a herb sauce.
Corn	1 ear per person	Remove outer husk and silk. Either leave kernels on cob or strip them off.	On the cob, simmer in unsalted water for 10-20 minutes; off the cob, simmer 5-10 minutes. Or parboil for 5 minutes, brush with butter and broil for 10 minutes.	On the cob, buttered with salt and pepper. Off the cob, with butter or cream, salt and pepper.
Peas	3 lb unshelled	Shell immediately before cooking.	Simmer 10-15 minutes; add some of the pods for extra flavor. Stir-fry 10-15 minutes.	Serve buttered; or with butter and chopped herbs. Use mint very occasionally – it is monotonously associated with peas.
Snow or Sugar peas	1 lb	Remove tops and bottoms and any strings.	Steam 5-10 minutes; stir-fry 5 minutes.	Serve with the cooking juices; or with a little butter.
Okra	1 lb	Cut off stems and discard any discolored pods. Leave whole or cut into ½ inch lengths. Rinse well.	Simmer 10-15 minutes.	Serve with a little lemon juice; or in Tomato sauce.
Mushrooms				
Button mushrooms	1 lb	Wipe with a damp cloth; leave whole or cut in slices parallel to the stem.	Stir-fry in butter for 5-10 minutes. Add salt and pepper at half times.	Serve with the reduced juice.

Preparation of accompanying vegetables—continued

Vegetable	Quantity for 4	Preparation	Cooking instructions	Serving instructions
Large mushrooms (field or commercially-grown)	1-2 lb	Rinse gently, then peel and check for insects. Leave whole or cut into quarters, halves or slices parallel to the stem.	As button mushrooms; or broil for 5-10 minutes. Baste with oil or butter.	Serve as button mushrooms; or with finely-chopped fried onion. Add a little cream before serving and sprinkle with chopped parsley.
Truffles		Fresh truffles deteriorate so use as soon as possible. Peel thinly.	Shred over an omelet or a pasta dish. If you leave the unpeeled truffle in contact with eggs for some hours, the eggs will be flavored. You can then use the truffle in another way.	
Onions				
Pickling onions	1 lb	Blanch, cut off ends, then remove colored skins.	Simmer 15-20 minutes.	In a Béchamel sauce.
Maincrop or Globe, Bermuda, Spanish onions or Shallots		Remove tops and root plates, then peel. (Wearing glasses or peeling under running water helps prevent the tears.) Leave whole or slice into rings with a sharp knife.	Simmer small onions for 15-20 minutes; large ones 20-40 minutes. Bake large ones at 350°F for 45-60 minutes. Finish in butter so they are just colored. Stir-fry sliced onion for 10-15 minutes. Finish stir-frying in a little white wine for a treat. Dip separated rings in batter and deep fry.	Straight from the pan; or in a Béchamel sauce.
Scallions	1 lb (4 bunches)	Trim off the roots and any discolored outer leaves. Leave about 3 inches of green stem above the white part; total length should be about 8 inches.	Stir-fry for 5-10 minutes in butter or oil over gentle heat.	Straight from the pan.
Leeks	1 lb	Cut off roots. Discard discolored leaves and 3 inches of the tops above the white part. Cut in half lengthwise, taking care that the leaves do not come apart. Wash well under running water to get rid of all the grit trapped between the leaves. Leeks can also be cut across the stem and separated into 1 inch rings.	Simmer for 10-15 minutes; braise, covered, in well-flavored stock for 40-60 minutes. Stir-fry in oil for 10-15 minutes. The cross-cut strips will cook in 5-10 minutes if the leeks are young.	Serve with a pat of butter or mask with Béchamel or Mornay sauce.
Vegetable fruit				
Cucumber	1 lb	Peel (or not, as you wish). Cut lengthwise into halves or quarters, then into 2-3 inch chunks.	Blanch, refresh, then cook very gently in butter for 5-10 minutes.	Serve with a little parsley or fresh dill sprinkled over; or masked with Hollandaise sauce.
Eggplant	1½-2 lb	Cut off stem and flower ends; cut into slices about ¼-½ inch thick. Sprinkle with salt and leave to drain for 30-45 minutes. Rinse and pat dry before frying. Leave whole with both ends if baking.	Fry in a little olive oil for 5-10 minutes each side; fry in coating batter (page 194); bake 40-60 minutes at 350°F.	Straight from the pan; if baked, with a little fresh or sour cream poured on and well seasoned with salt and pepper.
Peppers (green & red)	1 lb	Remove stems, seeds and fibrous cores; leave whole for stuffing, or cut into ¼-½ inch slices, or dice.	Parboil whole peppers for 5 minutes; then stuff and bake for 25-30 minutes. Stir-fry sliced or diced peppers for 5-10 minutes.	Serve straight from the pan; or sprinkled with a little lemon juice or wine vinegar.
Pumpkin	1-1½ lb	Cut off required section and remove seeds and fibrous center. Peel and cut into chunks about 3 × 2 inches by the thickness of the pumpkin.	Simmer 25-30 minutes; or roast.	Mash with butter and season well with salt and pepper or cinnamon. Make into fritters by adding a well-beaten egg, seasoning and a little wholewheat flour; then fry in shallow oil on both sides.

Preparation of accompanying vegetables—continued

Vegetable	Quantity for 4	Preparation	Cooking instructions	Serving instructions
Large summer squash (yellow crookneck, straightneck)	1-1½ lb	Trim off stem and blossom ends; leave whole or cut in half, quarters or slices. Remove any large seeds and fibrous core.	Simmer for 10-30 minutes, depending on size. Stir-fry slices for 10-15 minutes. Bake round squash for 30-60 minutes; test with a skewer.	As small summer squash.
Winter squash (Banana, hubbard, butternut, acorn, des Moines, table queen).	1-1½ lb	Peel, if desired. Leave whole; or cut in half or slices, if large.	Simmer 20-30 minutes depending on size, or bake squash with appropriate stuffing (page 88). Bake halves of smaller squash on an oiled baking sheet, skin uppermost, at 350°F for 40-60 minutes; turn over at half time and put a pat of butter on top.	Serve buttered, or scoop out the insides and mash with cream and fresh herbs and fill the shells with the purée. Sprinkle grated cheese over mashed squash and brown under the broiler.
Tomatoes	1½-2 lb	Wipe skins; cut in half; brush with melted butter and sprinkle with salt and pepper, if broiling; dip into seasoned wholewheat flour, if frying.	Broil 10-15 minutes depending on size; fry 5 minutes cut side down, then turn and continue cooking until the juice starts boiling out.	Serve as they are cooked; vary by sprinkling with a little chopped basil or onion.
Zucchini	1-1½ lb	Trim off stem and blossom ends; leave whole, cut in half lengthwise, or slice. Sprinkle with salt and leave to drain for 30-45 minutes to remove bitter juices. Rinse and pat dry before cooking.	Simmer for 10-15 minutes. Stir-fry slices for 10 minutes with a little chopped onion, herbs, or garlic; or stir-fry with tomatoes and garlic.	If boiled, serve from the pan, or mashed with butter; if stir-fried, serve from the pan.

Freezing Fresh Vegetables

Vegetable	Preparation	Blanching time	Cooking time and method
Roots			
Beets	Choose young tender beets about the size of golf balls: if larger, cut into halves or quarters. Blanch, cool, peel and pack into freezer bags.	5-10 minutes	Cook from frozen in boiling salted water for 1¼ hour.
Carrots	Choose young tender roots; cut off tops and bottoms; if very young, leave the skins on, otherwise scrape them. Slice if very large. Blanch, cool and pack in freezer bags.	3-5 minutes	Cook from frozen in boiling salted water for 5-8 minutes; alternatively, sautée them in butter for 8-10 minutes.
Celery root or Celeriac	Wash, peel and cook; then purée. Pack in foil containers.		Reheat in the container or in a foil-covered baking dish, or in the top of a double boiler with a little cream or butter.
Jerusalem artichokes	Peel, cook with added lemon juice and purée them; pack in rigid containers.		Use for soups.
Kohlrabi	Choose small roots, a little larger than golf balls. Top, tail and peel. Blanch, strain, cool and pack in freezer bags.	2 minutes	Cook in boiling salted water for 10-15 minutes.
Parsnips	Peel and dice; drain and cool. Pack into freezer bags.	2 minutes	Cook from frozen in boiling salted water for 5-10 minutes.
Rutabaga and turnips	Peel and dice; blanch, cool and pack in freezer bags. Alternatively cook and purée.	2½ minutes	Cook from frozen in boiling salted water for 10 minutes. Reheat purée in the top of a double boiler with a little butter or cream.
Tubers and onions			
Onions	Peel and finely chop or thickly slice. Blanch, cool and pack in freezer bags or rigid containers. Put in a second bag for safety. Small onions can be peeled, then blanched whole.	chopped or sliced: 2 minutes small, whole: 4 minutes	Use as required in the recipe.
Potatoes and sweet potatoes	Cook and purée, then prepare as croquettes or duchesse potatoes and pack in rigid containers. Young, small, new potatoes can be frozen but lose flavor. Wipe, blanch, cool and pack in freezer bags.	3-5 minutes	Put croquettes or duchesse potatoes into a cold oven, set to 400°F and cook for 20-30 minutes. Cook new potatoes for 15 minutes in boiling salted water.

Freezing Fresh Vegetables—continued

Vegetable	Preparation	Blanching time	Cooking time and method
Vegetable fruits			
Eggplant	Wash and cut into ¾ inch thick slices. Blanch and cool on paper towels. Interleave with paper, in rigid containers.	4 minutes	Use from frozen in recipes as required, but take care as they are very soft and can easily disintegrate if overcooked.
Peppers	Wash, cut in half and remove core, seeds and pith. Blanch, drain, cool and pack separately. Or slice or dice, then blanch, cool, drain and bag.	halved: 3 minutes sliced or diced: 1½ minutes	Thaw halved ones and use as required in recipes. Dice or sliced ones can be used in casserole dishes.
Squash	Peel, cut into slices and remove the seeds. Blanch, drain, cool and pack.	2-3 minutes	Thaw and sauté in butter, or use in a casserole dish.
Tomatoes	Cook and purée; pack in convenient portions in foil or rigid containers.		Heat in the top of a double boiler. Add to sauces and casserole dishes.
Zucchini	Choose small ones. Wash, top and tail and cut into ¾ inch thick slices. Blanch, drain and cool; pack in bags interleaved with paper.	1 minute	Cook from frozen in a little boiling salted water for 3 minutes or thaw and sauté in butter.
Brassicas and leaves			
Broccoli	Choose young spears. Cut off any woody stem or tough outer leaves. Divide into sprigs and wash. Blanch, cool and drain. Pack in single layers or interleave with paper in rigid containers.	small sprigs: 3 minutes thick sprigs: 4 minutes	Cook from frozen in boiling salted water for 5-8 minutes.
Brussels sprouts	Choose small firm heads. Remove yellow and loose outer leaves; wash thoroughly. Blanch, cool, drain well and then pack in freezer bags.	2-3 minutes	Cook from frozen in boiling salted water for 6-8 minutes.
Cabbage, green or red	Discard outer leaves and cut out core; wash and shred finely. Blanch, cool, drain and bag.	1½ minutes	Cook from frozen in a little boiling salted water.
Cauliflower	Choose firm white heads. Cut off any tough stem; separate heads into small florets. Wash carefully and blanch in water with 2 teaspoons of lemon juice added to each 1 pint. Cool, drain and pack in layers, interleaved with non-stick paper in rigid containers.	3 minutes	Cook from frozen in boiling salted water for 5-8 minutes.
Spinach	Discard any bruised or blemished leaves; cut out any fibrous stems. Wash very carefully under cold running water. Blanch a little at a time and drain thoroughly. Pack in rigid containers.	2 minutes	Cook from frozen in a little butter and its own juice for 5 minutes. Take care that it does not stick and burn.
Stems and shoots			
Asparagus	Remove woody base of stalks; wash carefully, blanch and cool. Pack in layers interleaved with non-stick paper in rigid containers.	thin stems: 2 minutes thick stems: 3-4 minutes	Cook from frozen in boiling salted water for 5-8 minutes.
Celery	Wash carefully and remove any strings. Cut into ½ inch strips; blanch, cool and drain and pack into bags. (It will only be suitable for use in cooked dishes.)	3 minutes	Cook from frozen in boiling salted water for 10 minutes, or add to casserole dishes.
Fennel	Trim and cut the bulb in half, or separate the fronds. Blanch, cool and pack in freezer bags.	halved: 5 minutes leaves: 3 minutes	Cook from frozen in boiling salted water for 5-8 minutes.
Globe artichokes	Remove the stems; wash carefully. Trim off the sharp points of the leaves. Blanch in water with 2 teaspoons lemon juice added to each 1 pint. Cool rapidly, drain upside down; pack individually and freeze in freezer bags.	8-10 minutes depending on size	Cook from frozen in boiling salted water for about 8 minutes or until a leaf will pull out easily.
Pods and seeds			
Beans	Cut the tops and bottoms off green beans and trim off the sides if they are stringy. Slice green beans into 1½ inch pieces. Lima and other large beans should be shelled. Wash, blanch, cool, drain and pack in freezer bags.	2-3 minutes	Cook from frozen in boiling salted water; green beans for 5 minutes and broad beans and other large beans for 7-8 minutes.
Corn	Choose young cobs and remove husks, silk and stem. Blanch, cool, and wrap individually.	2-3 minutes	Cook from frozen in boiling salted water for 20-30 minutes.
Peas	Shell the peas, blanch, cool and pack in freezer bags.	1 minute; stir to make sure of even blanching	Cook in boiling salted water for 4-7 minutes.
Sugar or snowpeas	Cut off tops and bottoms; blanch and cool. Pack in freezer bags or rigid containers.	1 minute	Allow to thaw at room temperature. Cook in a little butter for 1-2 minutes.

Nutrition

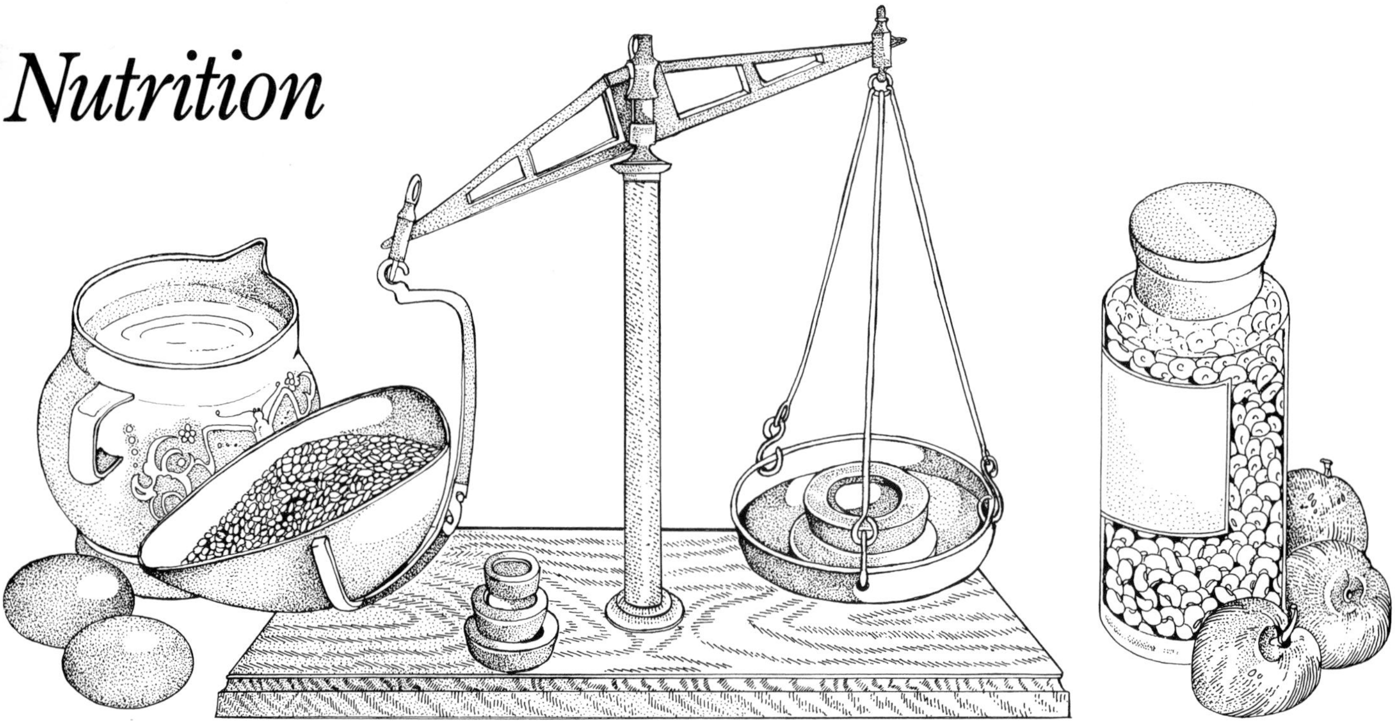

Good nutrition is a matter of eating adequate but not excessive amounts of all the nutrients necessary for maintaining the body in good health. These nutrients can be divided for convenience into five main groups — protein, carbohydrate, fat, minerals and vitamins — each of which has a different function in the body and in maintaining good health. Proteins are required for building and repairing the body's tissues, carbohydrate and fat are the major energy sources, and minerals and vitamins are needed for regulating the body's chemical or metabolic processes. Water and a certain amount of fiber are also essential for the body to function correctly — and produce a feeling of fitness. Most of the foods we eat are a mixture of these different nutrients, yet no one food is complete in itself. A balanced diet made up of a variety of foods is therefore necessary for us to obtain an adequate amount of all the nutrients. In a vegetarian diet, there are fewer foods to choose from, but the idea of eating mixtures of a variety of foods still applies. The strict vegetarian or 'Vegan' will eat no animal products whatsoever, and must obtain all his necessary nourishment from vegetables, fruits, nuts and cereals. Vegetarians who allow themselves to eat dairy products such as milk, yogurt, cheese, butter, eggs and cream in addition to the foods mentioned above are called Lacto-vegetarians, and for them the régime is not so strict. Many factors affect the choice of the foods we eat. They may be traditional, cultural or religious factors, prices, or such things as seasonal availability and our personal likes and dislikes. Everyone has his preferences for certain kinds of food and there is no need to eat foods which we find unpleasant — for reasons of taste or texture — simply because they are 'good for you'. On the whole, a balanced diet can be achieved by choosing foods which are varied, appetizing and satisfying without being excessive in quantity. It is unwise as well as wasteful to eat more food than you need.

TABLE 1
AVERAGE DAILY REQUIREMENTS OF PROTEIN AND ENERGY

	PROTEIN grams	ENERGY Mega Joules	Calories
Infants birth up to 1 year	20	3.3	800
Infants 1 up to 2 years	30	5.0	1200
Children 2 up to 5 years	35–40	5.9– 6.7	1400–1600
Children 5 up to 9 years	45–53	7.5– 8.8	1800–2100
Children 9 up to 12 years	58–63	9.6–10.5	2300–2500
Teenagers 12–18 years	58–75	9.6–12.6	2300–3000
Adult women	55–63	9.2–10.5	2200–2500
Adult men	68–90	11.3–15.1	2700–3600
Elderly people	48–59	8.0– 9.8	1900–2350

What are our needs?
One person's requirement for any nutrient can vary considerably from another's; even then, the needs of the individual will vary from day to day. Your age, level of activity, general state of health, sex and your own particular metabolism all have an effect on the body's needs. A young person who is still growing will need more nutrients than a less active, fully-grown adult. Similarly, a sick person needs more nutrients — to repair damaged tissues and fight infection — than a healthy person. For these reasons, then, it is not easy to lay down precise needs.

Table 1, which has been compiled from statistical information on a large number of people, gives *average* daily requirements for protein and energy, and this can be used as a guide. The Tables beginning on page 208 give the protein and energy content of most of the foods usually available for inclusion in a vegetarian diet. These, too, can be used as a guide when planning your meals and ensuring you have the correct balance of nutrients in your diet. The values for every single nutrient have not been included because, in general, when the body's requirements for protein and energy are satisfied, the other nutrients have also been taken.

ENERGY

Energy is what we need to keep us alive. Its gradual release in the body is controlled by special protein substances called enzymes. All the main nutrients such as carbohydrate, fat and protein can provide us with energy. Another source is the alcohol in alcoholic drinks; this however like sugar, has only energy and supplies no other nutrients. We need energy even when the body is at rest to maintain basic activities such as breathing and the maintenance of body temperature. Extra energy is required as soon as the body starts to move, and those indulging in strenuous activities such as sports or heavy manual work are obviously going to require a lot more energy for activity than someone who sits at a desk all day and gets very little exercise. Extra energy is also needed by growing children, mothers who are breast-feeding, and by invalids.

Unfortunately, your body never lets you know when it's time to stop eating. If you eat or drink foods which provide more energy than you need for simply keeping alive and for your daily activities, some of this will be converted into body fat and your body weight will increase as this fat is stored in the tissues. Continuous overindulgence will soon become apparent around the waistline; and in order to lose this fat, you must simply take in less energy than you are likely to use in a day. You can eat less (i.e. go on a low-calorie diet), or increase your level of physical activity — or combine both, after your doctor's advice has been sought. The amount of energy supplied by any item in the diet will be measured in units known as Kilojoules in the Metric system; this unit will replace the more familiar term of Calorie (1 Megajoule = 1000 Kilojoules = 240 Calories).

THE NUTRIENTS

Energy is vital to life, but we need more than just energy. We need nourishment from the foods we eat — and some foods are more nourishing than others. Some knowledge of the nutritional values of different foods and how to cook and process foods without destroying all the valuable nutrients they contain is useful, and will help you when working out a healthy eating pattern — whatever your diet. How do you select food for its nutritional value and not simply for its energy content? The following information will help and a summary of the main functions and main sources of each nutrients is given in Table 2.

Carbohydrates

Carbohydrates, usually present as starches and sugars, are our main sources of energy. *Starch* is found predominantly in the storage part of plants, for example in the tuber of the potato and the seeds of cereals — the grains. Thus we obtain starch from all cereals and their products, including flour, bread, pasta, cakes and cookies, as well as from vegetables. Naturally occurring *sugars* are found in milk (lactose), honey (fructose) and fruits

TABLE 2

Nutrients	Main Functions	Main Sources
PROTEIN	Provides materials for growth and repair of body tissue, and for the regulation of metabolic processes.	Eggs, cheese, milk, yogurt, cereals and cereal products, dried legumes, nuts and vegetables.
CARBOHYDRATE	Provides energy for bodily activities and for maintaining body temperature.	Cereals and cereal products such as bread, pasta, cookies and cakes; fruit, vegetables, sugar, candies, soft drinks.
FAT	Provides a concentrated source of energy. Contains fat soluble vitamins A, D, E and K.	Butter, margarine, vegetable oils, cream, cheese.
VITAMINS		
Vitamin A	For vision in dim light and the maintenance of healthy skin and body tissues.	Butter, margarine, green vegetables, carrots, milk.
Vitamin B complex B_1,B_2, biotin, nicotinic acid	For the gradual release and utilization of energy.	Fortified breakfast cereals, bread, flour, potatoes, eggs, milk.
B_6, B_{12}, folic acid	For protein metabolism and the formation of red blood cells.	Eggs; whole cereal and vegetables for B_6 and folic acid. **NB:** B_{12} is only found in dairy produce and this will be limiting in the Vegan diet.
Vitamin C	Maintains healthy tissues and aids healing of wounds. **NB:** The claims that large doses of vitamin C can prevent or cure colds are controversial. There is little scientific evidence to support them.	Citrus fruits, green vegetables, potatoes, rosehip and black currant fruits and syrups.
Vitamin E	As an antioxidant.	Cereals and cereal products, eggs, vegetable oils.
Vitamin K	For normal blood clotting.	Cereals and cereal products, vegetables. Also synthesized in the body itself.
Vitamin D	For calcium metabolism and bone development.	Milk, cheese, eggs, butter, margarine. Also synthesized in the skin by the action of sunlight.
MINERALS		
Calcium	For bone and tooth formation, blood clotting and muscle contraction.	Milk, cheese, white and brown bread and flours.
Phosphorus	For bone and tooth formation and the release and utilization of energy.	Present in nearly all foods.
Iron	For the formation of hemoglobin—the red blood pigment responsible for the transport of oxygen around the body.	White, brown and wholewheat bread and flour; potatoes, green vegetables, eggs.
Sodium & Chlorine	As sodium chloride (salt)—for maintaining water balance. Sodium maintains muscle and nerve activity.	Salt, bread and cereal products, vegetables, milk.
Potassium	For water balance in the body tissues.	Vegetables, fruit, milk.
Magnesium	For utilization of energy.	Widespread, especially in foods of vegetable origin.
Fluorine	Associated with the structure of bones and teeth and protects against tooth decay.	Tea, drinking water (fortified areas only).

(glucose). However, by far the largest part of the sugar we take in is in the form of sucrose, either on its own or as an ingredient in a wide variety of foods, including candy and soft drinks. Sucrose is a pure form of energy and contains no other nutrients. Furthermore, it is a direct cause of tooth decay. For these reasons, sugar-based foods are not a good choice for inclusion in the diet.

Fiber

This is another form of carbohydrate found in the diet and is commonly called roughage, but it produces a negligible amount of energy because we are unable to digest it. It is necessary, however, as it adds bulk and assists the passage of food through the digestive system. Fiber is found in whole cereals, bran, fruit and vegetables.

Fats

Fats and oils provide us with a concentrated source of energy in the diet, giving more than twice the amount of energy as that given by either proteins or carbohydrates. They also make an important contribution to the texture of foods, improving their flavor and making them more appetizing. Furthermore, because it is digested comparatively slowly, foods rich in fat have a high satiety value.

Fats are also a source of certain essential vitamins, and they provide a reserve store of energy in the insulating layer of fat under the skin. We can readily recognize a great deal of the fat we eat, for example, in butter, margarine and vegetable oils, but some of our fat intake is less obvious, such as that found in milk, cheese, nuts, chocolate, cakes, cookies and ice cream.

It is widely believed that a high fat intake has an undesirable effect on health over a number of years. The high energy value of fats and oils can easily cause weight gain if they are eaten in excess of the body's needs, and their role as a contributory factor in heart disease is a matter of considerable debate at the present time. Almost all the different fats found in foods contain substances called fatty acids. These are of two main types, saturated and polyunsaturated, which differ slightly in their chemical structure.

Fats containing saturated fatty acids generally come from animal sources and are contained in butter, cream, cheese, and of course, meat. Polyunsaturated fatty acids are contained in fats of vegetable origin, for example corn oil and sunflower seed oil. Cholesterol is another form of fat which is found in foods of animal origin; this and saturated fat have both been implicated in the causation of heart disease. There is some indication that polyunsaturated fats have a protective effect, although we usually recommend that fats in general should only be eaten in small quantities in any case. These small amounts are better obtained from vegetable sources where possible — polyunsaturated margarine and vegetable oils instead of butter.

Proteins

Proteins are an essential part of all living cells. The daily requirement for protein provides material for the growth and repair of body tissues. If you consume more than you need, any extra will be lost from the body, or used as an expensive source of energy — which may be stored as fat.

Proteins are made up of a complex combination of substances called *amino acids*. Some of these amino acids cannot be made in the body, but need to be provided in the diet. These are called the essential amino acids and they can be obtained from both animal and vegetable sources. The important protein-providing foods for a Lacto-vegetarian are cereals, nuts, dried legumes, eggs, milk and cheese. The Vegan, who eats no animal products, has to rely solely on the first three groups. As the body cannot store large quantities of amino acids, you should make sure that you eat high-protein foods at each meal, and since each foodstuff provides a different combination of amino acids — and may even be lacking in one or more of the essential ones — a good mixture of vegetable proteins is always necessary. A combination of cereals and dried legumes is particularly good (e.g. baked beans on toast, or lentil curry and rice).

During periods of growth, the body's protein requirements are increased. In childhood and adolescence, a child who is deprived of protein will not grow as well as he should; extra protein is also required during pregnancy and lactation. In illness — whether this is in the healing of a wound or the building up of muscles that have become weak due to infection — the protein intake should be stepped up to help repair the body tissues.

Vitamins and minerals

Vitamins and minerals are found in minute amounts in most foods. However, they are essential to the body for its growth, repair and general functioning of the metabolic processes. If you make sure you eat a good and varied diet, you will take in enough of these substances as a matter of course and it should not be necessary to resort to commercial vitamin tablets or supplements, except where these are prescribed during periods of growth, or for deficiency due to illness or exhaustion. Vitamins A, D, E and K are soluble in fat and can therefore be stored in the fatty tissues of the body. Vitamin C and those of the B group are water-soluble and cannot be stored in the tissues, so it is important that they are supplied daily.

Similarly all the necessary minerals are readily available in a sensible and appetizing mixed diet. They are needed to maintain body structure and for various metabolic processes. The main functions and sources of vitamins and minerals are summarized in Table 2. In addition to those listed, there are certain other substances that are required in very small amounts and these are known as *trace elements*. They include cobalt, copper, chromium, iodine, manganese and zinc. Dietary deficiencies of these are most unlikely to occur.

Deficiencies of vitamins or minerals only tend to happen in unusual circumstances, such as among those people who eat food from a single source, or a limited number of sources, or among alcoholics. The former group need not include Lacto-vegetarians or Vegans if they follow the golden rule of eating adequate amounts of a wide variety of different foods from within each of the food groups: cereals, nuts, dried legumes, fruits, vegetables and — for all except Vegans — dairy products.

Vitamin B_{12} is found only in animal foods, so that Vegans are at risk of developing some deficiency. Brewer's yeast is a good source of some of the B vitamins and also has a small but useful amount of B_{12}. It should be included daily in the Vegan diet. There are also certain groups of people who may be susceptible to vitamin or mineral deficiencies at certain times of life, because their needs are increased for various reasons. A woman needs more iron and folic acid during pregnancy — if these nutrients are not present in adequate amounts in the diet, she may develop anemia.

It is dangerous to take large doses of the fat-soluble vitamins over a long period of time as they can gradually accumulate in the body to a poisonous level. This would only occur in unusual circumstances — by taking commercial vitamin supplements to excess, or by drinking carrot juice every single day. This is quite the opposite of a sensible, balanced diet and should be avoided!

Water

Although water is not strictly a nutrient, it is essential for our survival. We obtain water not only from drinks but also from solid food. About two-thirds of the body's weight is comprised of water, and this is the medium in which most body processes take place.

Alcohol

Alcohol, like sugar, contains energy, but no useful nutrients. Alcoholic drinks such as beer contain a significant amount of the B vitamins — riboflavin and niacin — but spirits contain no vitamins. Varying amounts of carbohydrate may also be present in wines and beers, providing additional energy.

The effects of processing and cooking on nutritional value

The nutritional value of proteins, fats, carbohydrates and fat-soluble vitamins usually remains unaltered by normal cooking conditions. By contrast, though, the water-soluble B group vitamins, vitamin C and minerals largely provided by cereals, vegetables and fruits are very sensitive and easily lost in processing, preparation and cooking. After peeling or shredding vegetables, Vitamin C is rapidly destroyed. Its loss can be minimized by preparing vegetables just prior to use and by plunging them into boiling water to destroy the enzymes which cause this vitamin loss. Potatoes contain vitamin C just under the skin and there is less loss of vitamin C if they are not peeled, but cooked in their skins. During cooking, the vitamins and minerals from vegetables and fruits are either destroyed by heat or lost into the cooking water, so it makes sense to cook vegetables in the very minimum of water and to subsequently use this water for making stock. It is also a good idea not to allow your vegetables to overcook. Do not keep them waiting but serve them as soon as they are cooked, as keeping them hot for long periods will increase the loss of vitamin C. Green vegetables and fruits are especially valuable when eaten raw as they suffer no cooking losses. Dried fruits do not contain any vitamin C, as it is destroyed by the drying process.

The nutritional value of cereals depends on the extent of the processing before they reach the stores — whole grains and wholewheat products are obviously the wisest choice. The distribution of nutrients within the wheat grain is not uniform and the concentration of protein, minerals, and vitamins is higher in the germ and outer layers. These layers are lost during the milling of white and brown flours, or when polishing rice. The fiber content of cereals is also affected. After processing, the nutritional value of cereals is largely unchanged (except for some destruction of thiamin) by cooking.

ORGANIC AND HEALTH FOODS

Any food derived from plants or animals is organic, and all of these foods provide nourishment. Eaten as part of a balanced diet, they are conducive to good health. The term 'organic foods' tends to be associated with foods grown using organic fertilizers, without chemical pesticides and which are either processed or not, but *without the use of additives*. Their nutritional value is largely determined by the species of plant or animal from which they came.

A key to healthy eating

It is wise to have one main meal each day, one light meal — and breakfast. Each meal should include a number of protein sources such as cereals, nuts, dried legumes and for the non-Vegan, eggs, milk and cheese. Starchy foods — cereals, for example — will help satisfy hunger, but do not use too much fat. Aim to eat some fresh fruit or vegetables *at least once a day* and drink as much fluid (preferably unsweetened) as you like. Children and adults, too, should be discouraged from eating candy and chocolates between meals, as they will decrease the appetite for the next main meal. All man's nutritional requirements — with the exception of vitamin B_{12} — can be met by a diet composed entirely of plant foods, but to do so such a diet must be carefully planned and a wide variety of foods included. A mixture of plant proteins from cereals, dried legumes and nuts will provide sufficient protein of good quality. Lacto-vegetarians will also include milk, cheese and eggs as their protein sources. Vegans need to take special care to ensure that sufficient energy, calcium, iron, riboflavin, vitamin B_{12} and vitamin D are also included — refer, again, to Table 2. Vegetarians need to have an awareness of the nutritional value of the food they eat. A weekly review of your diet should give you some idea of what may be lacking, or taken in excess, but it is possible to eat healthily and well without being obsessive over every single meal.

It does no harm to have a fling occasionally if you are eating out or entertaining. Too much cream, butter or chocolates, for example, is definitely to be avoided, but their role in cooking, particularly for the gourmet, cannot be ignored when entertaining. Use them in judicious amounts and balance your diet by having simple meals on the days when you do not need to entertain — or be entertained. Eat slowly, enjoy your food and remember — there is nothing more tedious than a discussion of dietary habits and preferences to those who are not interested in the principles of good and healthy eating. A fit and healthy person is the very best of examples!

The tables on the following pages give counts for individual foods. Guide lines to the different types are given here.

DRIED LEGUMES

Dried legumes are rich in protein, and provide more energy and B vitamins than either green or root vegetables. Fresh peas and lima beans contain vitamin C, but this is lost when they are dried. Soaking dried peas and beans can result in some loss of the water-soluble vitamins and minerals into the soaking water.

NUTS

Nuts are rich in fat and protein and therefore a good and concentrated source of energy. They also contain B vitamins. They do not, however, contain any vitamin A or C.

FRUITS

Most fruits contain a little sugar and small amounts of minerals and B vitamins, but they are an important source of vitamin C. The vitamin content of fruit will vary with the type of fruit and will be lower in cooked fruit than in fresh fruit. Black currants, strawberries and soft fruits, oranges, grapefruit fruit drinks, nectars, and fruit juice cocktails are the richest fruit sources of vitamin C.

Dried fruits provide energy principally as sugar, but contain no vitamin C. Dried prunes and apricots are also sources of B-carotene.

CEREALS

Cereals contribute energy, protein, carbohydrate, iron, calcium, niacin and thiamin (vitamin B_1) to the diet. There is more protein, minerals and vitamins in the germ and outer layers of cereal grains, and these are lost when the grains are milled. White flours are therefore lower in nutritional value than brown flours, particularly wholewheat or graham. The latter will also contribute fiber to the diet if not sifted. As already mentioned, similar losses of nutrients will result from polishing rice. The cooking and processing of cereals may also destroy some of the thiamin content.

DAIRY PRODUCTS

Milk is high in nutritional value, being one of the most complete of all foods. It contains nearly all the constituents of nutritional importance to man and it is a particularly valuable source of good-quality protein, calcium and riboflavin (Vitamin B_2). It is comparatively deficient in iron and vitamins C and D, unless these vitamins have been added, but contains some carbohydrate in the form of milk sugar (lactose).

Milk should not be exposed to the sun for prolonged periods since a substantial amount of the riboflavin will be destroyed after one hour.

Dried milks contain all the nutrients of the original whole (or skimmed) milk apart from the B vitamins, which are destroyed by the drying process.

The nutritional value of *yogurt* will be similar to that of the milk upon which it is based — either skimmed or whole.

Vegetables:

Energy values of the following foods are given in calories and kilojoules, per 100 g and per oz. Protein values are given in grams, per 100 g and per oz.

Food	Description	per 100 g Energy units kcal	per 100 g Energy units kJ	per 100 g Protein (grams)	per oz Energy units kcal	per oz Energy units kJ	per oz Protein (grams)
Artichokes, Globe	Base of leaves and soft inside parts; cooked	15	62	1.1	4	2	0.3
Artichokes, Jerusalem	Flesh only; cooked	18	78	1.6	5	1	0.5
Asparagus	Soft tips only; cooked	18	75	3.4	5	1	1.0
Beans, green	Pods trimmed; raw	26	114	2.3	7	2	0.7
Beans, green	Pods trimmed; cooked	19	83	1.9	5	1	0.5
Bean sprouts	Canned; drained, heated	9	40	1.6	3	1	0.5
Beets	Flesh only; raw	28	118	1.3	8	2	0.4
Beets	Flesh only; cooked	44	189	1.8	12	3	0.5
Belgian endive	Stem and young leaves; raw	9	38	0.8	3	11	0.2
Broccoli	Tops; raw	23	96	3.3	7	2	0.9
Broccoli	Tops; cooked	18	78	3.1	5	1	0.9
Brussels sprouts	Inner leaves only; raw	26	111	4.0	7	2	1.1
Brussels sprouts	Inner leaves only; cooked	18	75	2.8	5	1	0.8
Cabbage, red	Inner leaves; raw	20	85	1.7	6	2	0.5
Cabbage, savoy	Inner leaves; raw	26	109	3.3	7	2	0.9
	Inner leaves; cooked	9	40	1.3	3	1	0.4
Cabbage, spring	Inner leaves; cooked	7	32	1.1	2	0.5	0.3
Cabbage, white	Whole cabbage; raw	22	93	1.9	6	2	0.5
Cabbage, winter	Inner leaves; raw	22	92	2.8	6	2	0.8

Food	Description	per 100 g Energy units kcal	per 100 g Energy units kJ	per 100 g Protein (grams)	per oz Energy units kcal	per oz Energy units kJ	per oz Protein (grams)
Cabbage, winter	Inner leaves; cooked	15	16	1.7	4	2	0.5
Carrots, old	Flesh only; raw	23	98	0.7	7	2	0.2
Carrots, old	Flesh only; cooked	19	79	0.6	5	1	0.2
Carrots, young	Flesh only; cooked	20	87	0.9	6	2	0.3
Carrots	Canned; drained, heated	19	82	0.7	5	1	0.2
Cauliflower	Flower and stalk; raw	13	56	1.9	4	1	0.5
Cauliflower	Flower and stalk; cooked	9	40	1.6	3	1	0.5
Celery	Stem only; raw	8	36	0.9	2	10	0.3
Celery	Stem only; cooked	5	21	0.6	1	6	0.2
Celery root	Flesh only; cooked	14	59	1.6	4	17	0.5
Chicory	Leaves only; raw	11	47	1.8	3	13	0.5
Corn	On-the-cob; kernels only; raw	127	538	4.1	36	152	1.1
Corn	On-the-cob; kernels only; cooked	123	520	4.1	35	141	1.1
Corn	Canned; kernels	76	325	2.9	22	92	0.8
Cucumber	Flesh only; raw	10	43	0.6	3	12	0.2
Eggplant	Flesh only; raw	14	62	0.7	4	1	0.2
Fennel	Leaves only; raw	28	117	2.8	8	33	0.8
Horseradish	Flesh of root; raw	59	253	4.5	16	72	1.3
Leeks	Bulb only; raw	31	128	1.9	8	36	0.5
Leeks	Bulb only; cooked	24	104	1.8	7	30	0.5
Lettuce	Inner leaves; raw	12	51	1.0	3	14	0.3
Mushrooms	Whole; raw	13	53	1.8	4	15	0.5
Mushrooms	Whole; fried	210	863	2.2	59	244	0.6

Cream is derived from fresh milk and is the separated-off fatty layer. The energy values of different types of cream vary with the fat content; half-and-half contains 12% by weight as milk fat, light cream contains 32% and heavy whipping cream 40%. Cream will contain the fat-soluble vitamins found in milk — particularly vitamin A and the remaining skimmed milk will contain most of the protein, calcium and B vitamins.

Butter is made by churning cream in order to separate fat globules from the liquid buttermilk. The butter must not by Federal law contain less than 80% milk fat. It contains the fat-soluble vitamins A and D — the exact amounts depending on the milk content.

Cheese is made by coagulating the milk proteins to form a curd which is then treated in a variety of ways to produce many different cheeses (see page 28). The curd contains most of the protein, fat and fat-soluble vitamins and most of the calcium from the milk. Lactose and the B vitamins are lost in the discarded whey. Cottage cheese is made from skimmed milk and therefore contains very little fat, whereas cream cheese has a particularly high fat content.

Eggs are useful sources of good-quality protein, vitamin D, vitamin A (retinol), riboflavin and iron. The amount of iron absorbed from eggs is dependent on other dietary factors; for example, a source of vitamin C such as fruit juice taken with eggs will aid absorption. The color of egg shells is not related to nutritional value, only to the breed of hen. Similarly, the differences in the color of the yolks are not important.

SUGARS AND PRESERVES

White sugar provides energy but no other nutrients. Similarly, brown sugars only contain insignificant quantities of minerals and vitamins in addition to energy. Some preserves contain vitamin C, and chocolate contains iron, but the primary function of these items in the diet is to improve palatability.

VEGETABLES

Vegetables contain 80-95% water but also provide valuable vitamins — particularly vitamin C minerals and small amounts of protein and energy. They are also a major source of dietary fiber. Green vegetables are good sources of vitamin C, B-carotene (which is converted to vitamin A in the body), folic acid, iron and other minerals.

Whenever possible, eat vegetables raw, wilted and cooked green vegetables contain less vitamin C than the raw vegetables. Cooking may also result in some loss of folic acid and minerals. Root vegetables are the storage parts of plants and contain more energy-providing starches and sugars than most green vegetables. Turnips, rutabagas, parsnips and potatoes are comparatively good sources of vitamin C, and carrots are particularly rich in B-carotene. The care needed in preparing and cooking vegetables in order to preserve their nutrient content has already been mentioned (page 106).

		per 100 g			per oz		
Food	**Description**	**Energy units**		**Protein**	**Energy units**		**Protein**
		kcal	**kJ**	**(grams)**	**kcal**	**kJ**	**(grams)**
Mustard & Garden Cress	Leaves and stems; raw	10	47	1.6	3	13	0.5
Okra	Whole; raw	17	71	2.0	5	20	0.6
Onions	Flesh only; raw	23	99	0.9	7	28	0.3
Onions	Flesh only; boiled	13	53	0.6	4	15	0.2
Onions	Flesh only; fried	345	1425	1.8	98	404	0.5
Parsley	Leaves; raw	21	88	5.2	6	25	1.4
Parsnips	Flesh only; raw	49	210	1.7	14	59	0.5
Parsnips	Flesh only; cooked	56	238	1.3	16	67	0.4
Peppers, red	Flesh only; raw	31	130	1.4	9	37	0.4
Peppers, red	Flesh only; cooked	26	109	1.2	7	31	0.3
Peppers, green	Flesh only; raw	15	65	0.9	4	18	0.3
Peppers, green	Flesh only; cooked	14	59	0.9	4	17	0.3
Plaintain, green	Flesh only; cooked	122	518	1.0	35	147	0.3
Plaintain, ripe	Flesh only; fried	267	1126	1.5	76	319	0.4
Potatoes, old	Flesh only; raw	87	372	2.1	25	105	0.6
Potatoes, old	Flesh only; boiled	80	343	1.4	23	97	0.4
Potatoes, old	Flesh only; baked in skins	105	448	2.6	30	127	0.7
Potatoes, old	Flesh only; shallow roasted	157	662	2.8	44	188	0.8
Potatoes, old	Flesh only; deep fried French fries	253	1065	3.8	72	302	1.1
Potatoes, new	Flesh only; boiled	76	324	1.6	22	92	0.5
Potatoes, new	Flesh only; canned, drained	53	226	1.2	15	64	0.3
Potatoes, instant	Powder; reconstituted	70	299	2.0	20	85	0.6

		per 100 g			per oz		
Food	**Description**	**Energy units**		**Protein**	**Energy units**		**Protein**
		kcal	**kJ**	**(grams)**	**kcal**	**kJ**	**(grams)**
Potatoes, chips	Plain and flavored	533	2224	6.3	151	630	1.8
Pumpkin	Flesh only; raw	15	65	0.6	4	18	0.2
Radishes	Flesh and skin; raw	15	62	1.0	4	18	0.3
Rutabaga	Flesh only; raw	21	88	1.1	6	25	0.3
Rutabaga	Flesh only; cooked	18	76	0.9	5	22	0.3
Scallions	Flesh of bulb; raw	35	151	0.9	10	43	0.3
Spinach	Leaves; cooked	30	128	5.1	8	36	1.4
Spring (collard) greens	Leaves; cooked	10	43	1.7	3	12	0.5
Squash	Flesh only; raw	16	69	0.6	5	20	0.2
Squash	Flesh only; cooked	7	29	0.4	2	8	0.1
Sweet potatoes	Flesh only; raw	91	387	1.2	26	110	0.3
Sweet potatoes	Flesh only; cooked	85	363	1.1	24	103	0.3
Tomatoes	Whole; raw	14	60	0.9	17	17	0.3
Tomatoes	Whole; shallow fried	69	288	1.0	20	82	0.3
Tomatoes	Whole; canned, drained	12	51	1.1	3	14	0.3
Turnips	Flesh only; raw	20	86	0.8	6	24	0.2
Turnips	Flesh only; cooked	14	60	0.7	4	17	0.2
Turnip tops	Leaves; cooked	11	48	2.7	3	14	0.8
Watercress	Leaves and stems, raw	14	61	2.9	4	17	0.8
Yam	Flesh only; raw	131	560	2.0	37	150	0.6
Yam	Flesh only; cooked	119	508	1.6	34	144	0.5
Zucchini	Flesh only; raw	16	69	0.6	5	20	0.2
Zucchini	Flesh only; cooked	7	29	0.4	2	8	0.1

Fruit

Food	Description	per 100 g Energy units kcal	per 100 g Energy units kJ	per 100 g Protein (grams)	per oz Energy units kcal	per oz Energy units kJ	per oz Protein (grams)
Apples, eating	Flesh only; raw	46	196	0.3	13	56	0.1
Apples, eating	Whole; raw	35	151	0.2	10	43	trace
Apples, cooking	Flesh only; raw	37	159	0.3	10	45	0.1
Apples, cooking	Flesh only; stewed; no sugar	32	136	0.3	9	39	0.1
Apricots	Fresh; pitted; raw	28	117	0.6	8	33	0.2
Apricots	Fresh; whole; raw	25	108	0.5	7	31	0.1
Apricots	Fresh; pitted; stewed; no sugar	23	98	0.4	7	28	0.1
Apricots	Dried; pitted; raw	182	776	4.8	52	220	1.4
Apricots	Dried; pitted; stewed; no sugar	66	288	1.8	19	65	0.5
Apricots	Canned; pitted fruit & syrup	106	452	0.5	30	128	0.1
Avocados	Flesh only; raw	223	922	4.2	63	261	1.2
Bananas	Flesh only; raw	79	337	1.1	22	96	0.3
Bananas	Whole fruit; raw	47	202	0.7	13	57	0.2
Blackberries	Whole fruit; raw	29	125	1.3	8	35	0.4
Blackberries	Whole fruit; stewed; no sugar	25	107	1.1	7	30	0.3
Cherries, eating	Pitted, raw	47	201	0.6	13	57	0.2
Cherries, eating	Whole; raw	41	175	0.5	12	50	0.1
Cherries, cooking	Pitted; raw	46	196	0.6	13	56	0.2
Cherries, cooking	Whole; raw	39	165	0.5	11	47	0.1
Cherries, cooking	Pitted; stewed; no sugar	39	165	0.5	11	47	0.1
Cherries candied		212	903	0.6	60	256	0.2
Cranberries	Whole fruit; raw	15	63	0.4	4	18	0.1
Currants, black	Whole fruit; raw	28	121	0.9	8	34	0.3
Currants, black	Whole fruit; stewed; no sugar	24	103	0.8	7	29	0.2
Currants, red	Whole fruit; raw	21	89	1.1	6	25	0.3
Currants, red	Whole fruit; stewed; no sugar	18	76	0.9	5	22	0.3
Currants, white	Whole fruit; raw	26	112	1.3	7	32	0.4
Currants, white	Whole fruit; stewed; no sugar	22	96	1.1	6.2	27	0.3
Currants, dried	Whole fruit	243	1039	1.7	69	294	0.5
Damsons	Pitted; raw	38	162	0.5	10	46	0.1
Damsons	Whole; raw	34	144	0.4	10	41	0.1
Damsons	Pitted; stewed	32	136	0.4	9	39	0.1
Dates	Dried; pitted	248	1056	2.0	70	299	0.6
Dates	Dried; whole	213	909	1.7	60	258	0.5
Figs	Green; whole fruit	41	174	1.3	12	49	0.4
Figs	Dried; whole fruit; raw	213	908	3.6	60	257	1.0
Figs	Dried; whole fruit; stewed; no sugar	118	504	2.0	33	143	0.6
Gooseberries	Fresh; ends cut off; raw	17	73	1.1	5	21	0.3
Gooseberries	Fresh; ends cut off; stewed; no sugar	14	62	0.9	4	18	0.3
Grapes, black	Flesh only; raw	61	258	0.6	17	73	0.2
Grapes, black	Whole fruit; raw	51	217	0.5	14	61	0.1
Grapes, green	Flesh only; raw	63	268	0.6	18	76	0.1
Grapes, green	Whole fruit; raw	60	255	0.6	17	72	0.1
Grapefruit	Flesh only; raw	22	95	0.6	6	27	0.1
Grapefruit	Canned; fruit & syrup	60	257	0.5	17	73	0.1
Grapefruit	Juice; canned; unsweetened	31	132	0.3	9	37	0.1
Lemons	Whole	15	65	0.8	4	18	0.2
Lemons	Fresh juice	7	31	0.3	2	9	0.1
Limes	Whole	28	117	0.7	8	33	0.2
Loganberries	Whole fruit; raw	17	73	1.1	5	21	0.3
Loganberries	Whole fruit; stewed; no sugar	16	67	1.0	5	21	0.3
Lychees	Flesh only; raw	64	271	0.9	18	77	0.3
Lychees	Canned; fruit & syrup	68	290	0.4	19	82	0.1
Mandarins	Canned; fruit & syrup	56	237	0.6	16	67	0.2
Mangoes	Flesh only; raw	59	253	0.5	17	72	0.1
Mangoes	Canned; fruit & syrup	77	330	0.3	22	93	0.1
Melons, Canteloupe	Flesh only; raw	24	102	1.0	7	29	0.3
Melons, Canteloupe	Whole; raw	15	63	0.6	4	18	0.2
Melons, Honeydew	Flesh only; raw	21	90	0.6	6	25	0.2
Melons, Honeydew	Whole; raw	13	56	0.4	4	16	0.1
Melons, water	Flesh only; raw	21	92	0.4	6	25	0.1
Melons, water	Whole; raw	11	47	0.2	3	13	0.1
Mulberries	Whole fruit; raw	36	152	1.3	10	43	0.4
Nectarines	Pitted; raw	50	214	0.9	14	61	0.3
Nectarines	Whole; raw	46	198	0.9	13	56	0.3
Olives, black	Whole; raw	129	540	1.1	37	153	0.3
Olives, green	Whole; raw	116	485	1.4	33	137	0.4
Oranges	Flesh only; raw	35	150	0.8	10	42	0.2
Orange juice	Fresh	38	161	0.6	11	46	0.2
Orange juice	Canned; unsweetened	33	143	0.4	9	41	0.1
Passion fruit	Skinned; raw	34	147	2.8	10	42	0.8
Paw paw	Canned; fruit & juice	65	275	0.2	18	78	0.1

Food	Description	per 100 g Energy units kcal	kJ	Protein (grams)	per oz Energy units kcal	kJ	Protein (grams)
Peaches	Fresh; pitted; raw	37	156	0.6	10	44	0.2
Peaches	Fresh; whole; raw	32	137	0.6	9	39	0.2
Peaches	Dried; pitted; raw	212	906	3.4	60	257	1.0
Peaches	Dried; pitted; stewed; no sugar	79	336	1.3	22	95	0.4
Peaches	Canned; fruit and syrup	87	373	0.4	25	106	0.1
Pears, eating	Flesh only; raw	41	175	0.3	12	50	0.1
Pears, eating	Whole; raw	29	125	0.2	8	35	0.1
Pears, cooking	Flesh only; raw	36	154	0.3	10	44	0.1
Pears, cooking	Flesh only; stewed; no sugar	30	130	0.2	8	37	0.1
Pears	Canned; fruit and syrup	77	327	0.4	22	93	0.1
Pineapple	Canned; fruit and syrup	76	325	0.3	22	93	0.1
Plums, eating	Pitted; raw	38	164	0.6	11	46	0.2
Plums, eating	Whole; raw	36	153	0.5	10	43	0.1
Plums, cooking	Pitted; raw	26	109	0.6	7	31	0.2
Plums, cooking	Pitted; stewed; no sugar	22	92	0.5	6	26	0.1
Pomegranate	Flesh only; raw	63	264	0.5	18	75	0.1
Prunes	Dried; pitted; raw	161	686	2.4	46	194	0.7
Prunes	Dried; whole; raw	134	570	2.0	38	161	0.6
Prunes	Dried; pitted; stewed; no sugar	82	349	1.3	23	99	0.4
Prunes	Dried; whole; stewed; no sugar	74	316	1.1	21	90	0.3
Quinces	Flesh only; raw	25	106	0.3	7	30	0.1
Raisins	Dried; seeded	246	1049	1.1	70	297	0.3
Raisins, seedless white	Dried; whole fruit	250	1066	1.8	71	302	0.5
Raspberries	Whole fruit; raw	25	105	0.9	7	30	0.3
Raspberries	Canned; fruit and syrup	87	370	0.6	25	105	0.2
Rhubarb	Stems only; raw	6	26	0.6	2	7	0.2
Rhubarb	Stems only; stewed; no sugar	6	25	0.6	2	7	0.2
Strawberries	Whole fruit; raw	26	109	0.6	7	31	0.2
Strawberries	Canned; fruit and syrup	81	344	0.4	23	97	0.1
Tangerines	Flesh only; raw	34	143	0.9	10	41	0.3

Legumes

Food	Description	per 100 g Energy units kcal	kJ	Protein (grams)	per oz Energy units kcal	kJ	Protein (grams)
Beans, baked	Canned in tomato sauce	64	270	5.1	18	76	1.4
Beans, butter	Dried; raw	273	1162	19.1	77	329	5.4
Beans, butter	Dried; cooked	95	405	7.1	27	115	2.0
Beans, lima	Fresh; beans only; cooked	48	206	4.1	14	58	1.2
Beans, lima	Dried; raw	338	1414	25.1	95	401	7.1
Beans, mixed	e.g. white, black eye, brown; raw	340	1423	22.3	96	403	6.3
Beans, mixed	as above; cooked	118	494	7.8	33	140	2.2
Beans, mung	Dried; raw	231	981	22.0	65	278	6.2
Beans, mung	Dried; cooked	106	447	6.4	30	127	1.8
Beans, navy	Dried; raw	271	1151	21.4	77	326	6.1
Beans, navy	Dried; cooked	93	396	6.6	26	112	1.9
Beans, red kidney	Dried; raw	272	1159	22.1	77	328	6.3
Beans, soy	Dried; raw	403	1686	34.1	114	478	9.7
Chick peas	Dried; raw	320	1362	20.2	91	386	5.7
Chick peas	Dried; cooked	144	610	8.0	41	173	2.3
Lentils	raw	304	1293	23.8	86	366	6.7
Lentils	cooked	99	420	7.6	28	119	2.2
Peas	Fresh; peas only; raw	67	283	5.8	19	80	1.6
Peas	Fresh; peas only; cooked	52	223	5.0	15	63	1.4
Peas	Frozen; peas only; raw	53	227	5.7	15	64	1.6
Peas	Frozen; peas only; cooked	41	175	5.4	12	50	1.5
Peas	Canned	47	201	4.6	13	57	1.3
Peas	Dried; raw	310	1318	21.6	88	373	6.1
Peas	Dried; cooked	118	503	6.9	33	142	2.0
Peas	Split; dried; raw	320	1362	22.1	91	386	6.3
Peas	Split; dried; cooked	144	610	8.3	41	173	2.4

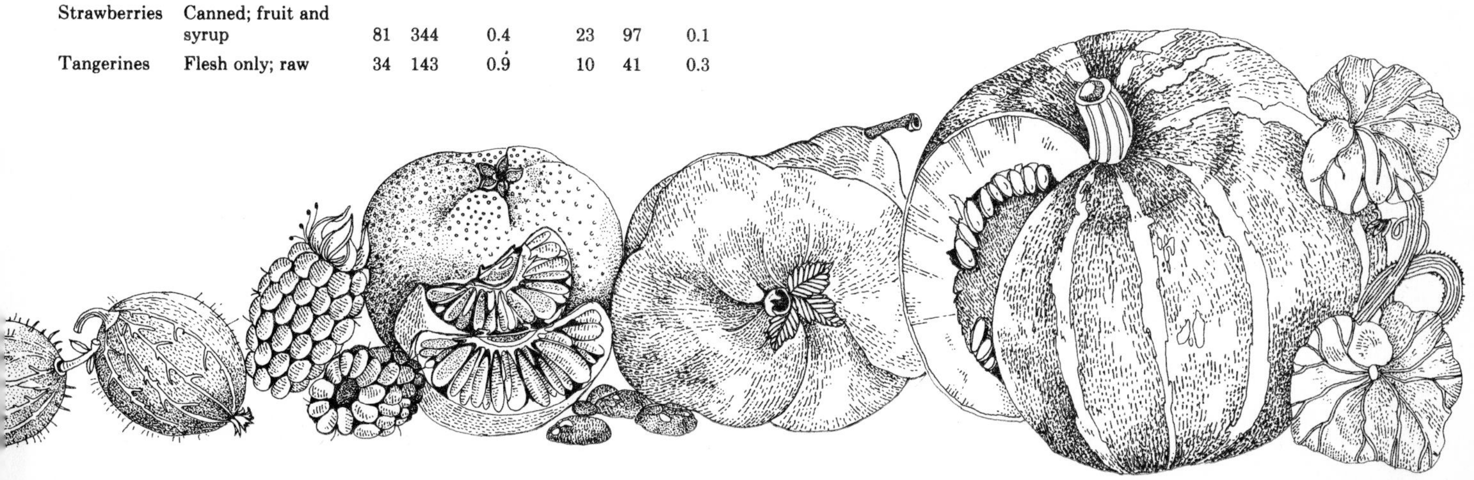

Dairy Produce

Food	Description	per 100 g Energy units kcal	kJ	Protein (grams)	per oz Energy units kcal	kJ	Protein (grams)
Butter	Unsalted or salted	740	3041	0.4	210	861	0.1
Cheese							
Camembert-type	e.g. Camembert, Brie	300	1246	22.8	85	353	6.5
Cheddar-type	e.g. Cheddar, Cheshire, Gruyère, Emmenthal	406	1682	26.0	115	476	7.4
Danish Blue-type	e.g. Danish Blue, Roquefort, Dolcelatte	355	1471	23.0	101	417	6.5
Edam-type	e.g. Edam, Gouda	304	1262	24.4	86	358	6.9
Parmesan		408	1696	35.1	116	480	9.9
Stilton		462	1915	25.6	131	542	7.3
Cottage cheese		96	402	13.6	27	114	3.9
Cream cheese		439	1807	3.1	124	512	0.9
Cream, sour		212	876	2.4	60	248	0.7
Cream, light		212	876	2.4	60	248	0.7
Cream, heavy		447	1841	1.5	127	522	0.4
Cream, whipping		332	1367	1.9	94	387	0.5
Eggs, hens'	Whole	147	612	12.3	42	173	3.5
Eggs, hens'	Yolk only	339	1402	16.1	96	397	4.6
Eggs, hens'	White only	36	153	9.0	10	43	2.5
Milk	Fresh; whole	65	272	3.3	18	77	0.9
Milk	Fresh; skimmed	33	142	3.4	9	40	1.0
Milk	Condensed; whole; sweetened	322	1362	8.3	91	386	2.4
Milk	Dried; whole	490	2051	26.3	139	581	7.5
Milk	Dried; skimmed	355	1512	36.4	101	428	10.3
Buttermilk	Fluid; cultured	36	151	3.6	10	43	1.0
Yogurt	Plain, low fat	52	216	5.0	15	61	1.4
Yogurt	Fruit-type, low fat	95	405	4.8	27	115	1.4

Cereal Products

Food	Description	per 100 g Energy units kcal	kJ	Protein (grams)	per oz Energy units kcal	kJ	Protein (grams)
Bread	Wholewheat	216	918	8.8	61	260	2.5
Bread	Brown	223	948	8.9	63	269	2.5
Bread	Buck wheat, dark	333	1393	11.7	94	395	3.3
Bread	White	233	991	7.8	66	281	2.2
Breakfast cereal	Cornflakes	368	1567	8.6	104	444	2.4
Breakfast cereal	Muesli	368	1556	12.9	104	441	3.7
Breakfast cereal	Puffed wheat	325	1386	14.2	92	393	4.0
Breakfast cereal	Rice Krispies	372	1584	5.9	105	449	1.7
Cookies	Chocolate-coated type	524	2197	5.7	148	622	1.6
Cookies	Plain sweet	471	1981	9.8	133	561	2.8
Cookies	Semi-sweet	457	1925	6.7	129	545	1.8
Crackers	Saltines	440	1857	9.5	125	526	2.7
Crackers	Crispbread	388	1642	45.3	110	465	12.8
Crackers	Crispbread; rye	321	1367	9.4	91	387	2.7
Crackers	Water biscuits	440	1859	10.8	125	524	3.1
Custard powder		354	1508	0.6	100	427	0.2
Oatmeal	Cooked in water	44	188	1.4	12	53	0.4
Pasta	Canneloni, lasagne, macaroni, ravioli squares (unfilled), spaghetti, stelletti, tagliatelle	378	1612	13.6	107	457	3.9

Cereals

Food	Description	per 100 g Energy units kcal	kJ	Protein (grams)	per oz Energy units kcal	kJ	Protein (grams)
Barley	Pearl; raw	360	1535	7.9	102	435	2.2
Barley	Pearl; boiled	120	510	2.7	34	144	0.8
Bran	Wheat	206	872	14.1	58	247	4.0
Cornstarch		354	1481	0.6	100	420	0.2
Cornmeal		355	1485	9.2	101	421	2.6
Flour, wholewheat	(100%)	318	1351	13.2	90	383	3.7
Flour, brown	(85%)	327	1392	12.8	93	394	3.6
Flour, white	All-purpose	350	1493	9.8	99	423	2.8
Flour, white	Self-rising	339	1443	9.3	96	409	2.6
Oatmeal		401	1698	12.4	114	481	3.5
Rice, white	Raw	361	1536	6.5	102	435	1.8
Rice, white	Boiled	123	522	2.2	35	148	0.6
Rice, brown	Raw	360	1506	7.5	102	427	2.1
Rice, brown	Boiled	119	498	2.5	34	141	0.7
Sago	Raw	355	1515	0.2	101	429	0.1
Semolina	Raw	350	1489	10.7	99	422	3.0
Wheat, grains	Raw; hard red winter	330	1381	12.3	93	391	3.5

Nuts and Seeds

Food	Description	per 100 g Energy units kcal	kJ	Protein (grams)	per oz Energy units kcal	kJ	Protein (grams)
Almonds	Shelled	565	2336	16.9	160	662	4.8
Almonds	Whole	210	865	6.3	59	245	1.8
Brazil nuts	Shelled	619	2545	12.0	176	721	3.4
Brazil nuts	Whole	277	1142	5.4	78	324	1.5
Cashew nuts	Shelled	561	2347	17.2	159	665	4.9
Chestnuts	Shelled	170	720	2.0	48	204	0.6
Chestnuts	Whole	140	595	1.6	40	169	0.5
Cob or hazel-nuts	Shelled	380	1570	7.6	108	445	2.2
Cob or hazel-nuts	Whole	137	567	2.8	39	161	0.8
Coconut	Fresh	351	1446	3.2	99	410	0.9
Coconut	Milk	21	91	0.3	6	26	0.1
Coconut	Shredded	604	2492	5.6	171	706	1.6
Peanuts	Fresh; shelled	570	2364	24.3	161	670	6.9
Peanuts	Fresh; whole	394	1631	16.8	112	462	4.8
Peanuts	Roasted; salted	570	2364	24.3	161	670	6.9
Peanut butter	Smooth	623	2581	22.6	176	731	6.4
Pecan/ walnuts	Shelled	525	2166	10.6	149	614	3.0
Pecan/ walnuts	Whole	336	1388	6.8	95	393	1.9
Pine nuts, pignolios		552	2310	31.1	156	654	8.8
Pine nuts, pinon		635	2657	13.0	180	753	3.6
Pistachio nuts	Shelled	594	2485	19.3	168	704	3.7
Sesame seeds	Dry; whole	563	2356	18.6	159	667	5.3
Sunflower seeds	Dry	560	2343	24.0	159	664	6.8
Water chestnuts	Chinese; raw	79	331	1.4	22	94	0.4

Sugar and Preserves

Food	Description	per 100 g Energy units kcal	kJ	Protein (grams)	per oz Energy units Kcal	kJ	Protein (grams)
Chocolate	Cooking	525	2197	4.7	149	622	1.3
Corn syrup	Light or dark	290	1213	0	82	344	0
Golden syrup		298	1269	0.3	84	359	0.1
Honey	Clear, thick, light or dark	288	1229	0.4	82	348	0.1
Jams and marmalade		261	1115	0.5	74	316	0.1
Maple syrup		252	1054	0	71	299	0
Molasses		257	1096	1.2	73	310	0.1
Sugar	Confectioners, raw brown, granulated	394	1681	trace	112	476	trace

Oils and Fats

Food	Description	per 100 g Energy units kcal	kJ	Protein (grams	per oz Energy units kcal	kJ	Protein (grams)
Butter	salted and unsalted	740	3041	0.4	210	861	0.1
Margarine	spreading and cooking	730	3000	0.1	207	850	trace
Vegetable oil	e.g. olive, sunflower, walnut, peanut etc	899	3696	trace	255	1047	trace

Beverages, Soft Drinks, Alcoholic Drinks

Food	Description	per 100 g Energy units kcal	kJ	Protein (grams)	per oz Energy units Kcal	kJ	Protein (grams)
Chocolate powder	sweetened	397	1683	5.5	113	479	1.6
Cocoa powder		312	1301	18.5	88	369	5.2
Coffee	Ground, roasted	287	1203	10.4	81	341	2.9
Coffee	Instant	100	424	14.6	28	120	4.1
Tea		0	0	0	0	0	0
Coca cola		39	168	trace	11	48	trace
Lemonade		21	90	trace	6	25	trace
Brewer's yeast		179	759	41.1	51	215	11.7
Wine	Red	68	284	0.2	19	80	trace
Wine	Rosé	71	294	0.1	20	83	trace
Wine	White-medium	75	275	0.1	21	78	trace
Champagne		76	315	0.3	22	89	0.1
Sherry	Medium	118	489	0.1	33	139	trace
Liqueurs	e.g. cherry brandy	255	1073	trace	72	304	trace
Spirits	70% proof e.g. gin, whisky	222	919	trace	63	260	trace

Index

D

T

U&V

Note: numbers in parentheses refer to a picture when this is not on the same page as the recipe.

BIBLIOGRAPHY

Janet BARKAS, *The Vegetable Passion*, Charles Scribner's Sons, 1975 (USA)
Howard E. BIGELOW, *Mushroom Pocket Field Guide*, Collier Books, A Division of Macmillan Publishing Co., 1974 (USA)
Elizabeth DAVID, *French Provincial Cooking*, Michael Joseph Ltd., 1960; Penguin Books Ltd., 1970 (USA)
Elizabeth DAVID, *Italian Food*, Macdonald, 1954; Penguin Books Ltd., 1970 (USA)
Auguste ESCOFFIER, *Guide Culinaire*, Crown Publishers, 1941 (USA)
Auguste ESCOFFIER, *Ma Cuisine*, A & W Publishers, 1978 (USA)
Ellen Buchman EWALD, *Recipes for a Small Planet*, Ballantine Books/Random House Inc., 1975 (USA)
Walter and Jenny FLEISS, *Modern Vegetarian Cookery*, Penguin Books Ltd., 1964 (UK)
Rosemary HEMPHILL, *The Penguin Book of Herbs and Spices*, Penguin Books Ltd., 1966 (UK)
Alan HOOKER, *Vegetarian Gourmet Cookery*, 101 Productions, 1971 (USA)
Dorothea van Gundy JONES, *The Soybean Cookbook*, Arco Publishing Company/The Devin Adair Company, 1963 (USA)
Frances Moore LAPPE, *Diet for a Small Planet*, Ballantine Books/Random House Inc., 1975 (USA)
Kenneth LO, *Chinese Vegetarian Cooking*, Pantheon Books, 1974 (USA)
Marie LOVEJOY, *International Vegetarian Cuisine*, Quest Books, 1978 (USA)
Orson K. MILLER, *Mushrooms of North America*, A Chanticleer Press Edition/E.P. Dutton, 1977 (USA)
Martha H. OLIVER, *Add a Few Sprouts*, Pivot Original Health Books/Keats Publishing Inc., 1975 (USA)
Claudia RODEN, *A Book of Middle Eastern Food*, Penguin Books Ltd., 1970 (UK); Alfred E. Knopf, 1972 (USA)
Jack SANTA MARIA, *Indian Vegetarian Cookery*, Samuel Weiser (USA)
George SEDDON and Helena RADECKA, *Your Kitchen Garden*, Simon and Schuster, 1978 (USA)
Anna THOMAS, *The Vegetarian Epicure*, Vintage Books, 1972 (USA)